THE SCHOLAR ADVENTURERS

ALSO BY RICHARD D. ALTICK

THE

Scholar Adventurers

RICHARD D. ALTICK

Ohio State University Press, *Columbus*

Library of Congress Cataloging-in-Publication Data
Altick, Richard Daniel, 1915 –
    The scholar adventurers.

    Reprint. Originally published: New York : Macmillan,
1950. With new pref.
    Bibliography: p.
    Includes index.
    1. English literature — Research.   2. Learning
    and scholarship — History.   3. Great Britain — Intellectual
life. I. Title.
P56.A7   1987   820′.72′0922   87–11064
ISBN 0–8142–0435–X

CONTENTS

PREFACE TO
THE OHIO STATE UNIVERSITY PRESS EDITION

FEW WRITERS are fortunate enough to see one of their books restored to print a full thirty-seven years after it first appeared. Its new publishers are pleased to call it a minor classic, and it unquestionably conforms to one definition of the genre, as a book of a certain age that has been read and remembered by many and bought (if one's old royalty statements are any indication) by remarkably few. Perhaps this reissue will redress the balance.

Across the years, a gratifying number of professional students of English and American literature have told me that reading *The Scholar Adventurers* for the first time was a memorable and even influential event in their education, revealing to them the pleasures and rewards, even the occasional thrills, that literary research involves. Nonacademic book lovers, people who simply like to read books about books and their fortunes in the world, have couched their appreciation somewhat differently. Both kinds of readers have now and then asked me when they might expect a sequel. But the fact is that in the intervening years not many stories of adventurous literary investigations or lucky finds have come to my attention. Several that I did happen to hear about, including the discovery of thirty-six sermons by the New England poet Edward Taylor in a Nebraska bookstore, the surfacing of the manuscripts of no fewer than seventeen Restoration plays in an English country house, and the use of modern scientific techniques to shed fresh light on the place of the Winchester manuscript in the textual tradition of Malory's *Morte d'Arthur,* are briefly told in the third edition of my *Art of Literary Research* (W. W. Norton, 1981). The "For Further Reading" list at the end of that volume, as well as certain of the practical exercises, supplement the bibliographical notes appended to the present one.

Still, somehow, finds continue to come to light. Ten or so years ago, a stamp dealer in Carlisle, England, sorting through a bundle of old letters he had bought for five pounds from someone he did

not publicly identify, found a large hoard of letters to and from
members of the Wordsworth family, the most precious of which
were thirty-one love letters exchanged between the poet and his
wife in 1810–12. No one knows how these were separated from
the main body of Wordsworth papers, or where they had been
all those years, or how they came finally to be sold as scrap. The
lot was bought by Cornell University to add to its rich Wordsworthian collection, but the British government withheld the
requisite export license and so the papers went instead to the
Wordsworth library at Grasmere.

Almost at the same moment (1976), a battered old traveling
trunk was opened in a private vault in an old London bank which
by that time had been acquired by Barclays. It had belonged to
Byron's rakish friend Scrope Davies, who left it there in 1820
when, pursued by importunate creditors, he fled to the continent,
never to return. The trunk proved to be laden with papers relating
to Byron and his circle — a mass of invitations, receipts, visiting
cards and other miscellaneous debris such as many people then
accumulated in the course of everyday life, and more important,
a fair copy of the original manuscript of *Childe Harold,* canto
three, early manuscripts of Shelley's "Hymn to Intellectual
Beauty" and "Mont Blanc," and a fine assortment of letters exchanged by Byron and a number of his friends. The full story of
the discovery and subsequent events, including the delivery of
the treasure to the British Library in a horse-drawn coach, has been
told by Bevis Hillier, who reported it for the London *Times,* in
the introduction to T. A. J. Burnett's *The Rise and Fall of a Regency Dandy: The Life and Times of Scrope Berdmore Davies*
(Little, Brown, 1981).

More recently, the international media headlined the discovery,
in the Bodleian Library at Oxford University, of a poem supposedly
by Shakespeare. Its presence in a manuscript anthology of poetry
dating from the 1630s, along with a note in an unknown hand

attributing it to Shakespeare, had been recorded in a printed catalogue almost a century ago, but nobody had previously taken the attribution seriously enough to look into the matter. Announcement of the find touched off a feverish debate among scholars, the progress of which can be conveniently traced through three issues of the *Shakespeare Newsletter* (Winter 1985–Summer 1986). To at least one disinterested observer, the quality of the lines Shakespeare allegedly wrote recalls Robert Browning's response, in a different context, "Did Shakespeare? If so, the less Shakespeare he!"

After this book was first published there were startling new developments in the long-running drama called here "The Case of the Curious Bibliographers," Thomas J. Wise's criminous bibliographical activities proving to have been considerably more complicated and ramified than his original accusers had known or even imagined. The whole story has recently been laid out with authority and in exhaustive detail — a masterpiece of forensic bibliographical analysis — in Nicolas Barker and John Collins's *A Sequel to "An Enquiry into the Nature of Certain XIXth Century Pamphlets" by John Carter and Graham Pollard: The Forgeries of H. Buxton Forman & T. J. Wise* (Scolar Press, 1983). The second edition of the 1934 *Enquiry,* which had long been out of print, was issued as a companion volume with an epilogue by Carter and Pollard themselves.

The first chapter in the present book, "The Secret of the Ebony Cabinet," also turned out to be only the prologue to a lengthy and equally absorbing course of events involving a series of further discoveries of Boswell papers and protracted behind-the-scenes wheeling and dealing on the part of sellers, buyers, libraries, and publishers. The complete inside story has now been told twice, from the quite different perspectives of a Scottish lawyer (David Buchanan's *The Treasure of Auchinleck,* McGraw-Hill, 1974) and the former head of Yale's "Boswell factory" (Frederick A. Pottle's *Pride and Negligence,* McGraw-Hill, 1984).

Finally, the long-desired full-dress life of the scholar-forger John Payne Collier was written by Dewey Ganzel under the title *Fortune and Men's Eyes* (Oxford University Press, 1982). It is evidently not everything that specialists would have wished it to be, but for the ordinary reader it is an adequate and lively narrative set in the Victorian book world, where enthusiasm and credulity were as yet uncurbed by the rigorous standards of modern bibliographical study.

I have allowed my introduction, "The Unsung Scholar," to stand as it was first printed. In a number of particulars it is obsolete or, to put the best face on it, has become a period piece. My remarks on the low pay scholars in the humanities received in 1950 are, happily, no longer applicable. If I were rewriting my paragraphs on the Modern Language Association meetings today, my comments would take a different tack and would perhaps be less amiable. But more than one comic novelist, bemused by the busy spectacle of thousands of professional literary and linguistic students gathered for their annual saturnalia, paper-readings, gossip fest, and employment market, has taken care of that topic for me.

Whatever promise these chapters implicitly contain of important discoveries still awaiting the doughty researcher must be modified in the light of new conditions. There is simply less material waiting to be found. The steady flow of manuscripts and printed rarities into the permanency of public-access collections during the past half century means that the reservoir of literary documents in private hands is, to that extent, diminished. And it is less likely nowadays that researchers will come upon valuable items that arrived at libraries long ago but somehow fell through the cracks during the cataloguing or shelving procedure.

The primary message of the introduction, however, remains unchanged. Since I wrote about other people's adventures in such places as English country houses, the Public Record Office, and the Folger Shakespeare Library I have had adventures of my own which fully validate my exposition of the pleasures of research.

None of my finds have been as dramatic or worth recording as those in this book (though I did contribute a piece called "An Uncommon Curiosity: In Search of the Shows of London" to the *Quarterly Journal of the Library of Congress* in 1981). Instead of seeking rare individual documents, my research has been concentrated on gathering together masses of hitherto discrete and scattered data and discovering the patterns into which they fall as significant literary or historical themes. Such inquiries have taken me into several relatively unexplored fields on the periphery of literary studies, especially certain aspects of the history of nineteenth-century English social life and popular culture. Accordingly, I have taken my rudimentary apparatus of notepads and ballpoint pens to institutions more or less off the strictly literary scholar's beat. Although none of these provides, perhaps, the special ambience that is associated with the Huntington Library at San Marino, California, where honey-dew and the milk of paradise are served every day at lunch, or the rather more austere amenities of the British Library and the old Public Record Office in Chancery Lane, each has yielded up ample quantities of its own kind of richness. Following endlessly winding paper trails in settings as different as those of the Yale Center for British Art, London's Guildhall Library, the library of the Victoria and Albert Museum, the British Library's newspaper library in a London suburb, and the John Johnson Collection of Printed Ephemera has always paid off in some fashion. Everywhere I have delved, I have found out many things I wanted to know and more things I didn't know I wanted to know but was glad to find out about just the same. And that, in the long run, is the present-day scholar adventurer's measure of success. I stand by every word I wrote in the last paragraph of my introduction.

R.D.A.

THE UNSUNG SCHOLAR

I

MANY of the men and women who teach English in our colleges and universities lead double lives. They earn their living in the classroom, doling out facts and opinions about English and American literary classics to students who are, to say the least, suspicious of art in any form. Despite the frustrations and disappointments which are the bitter but inevitable lot of their calling, they are not unhappy in their teaching. But their consuming passions lie elsewhere. For outside the classroom they are scholars: patient delvers into history and biography whose great design is to add to the world's store of literary knowledge, to provide the raw materials of fact by which they, and eventually the public, may clearly understand and evaluate a work of literary art. And in that scholarly role they have adventures which are as exciting as any that have ever been told of their better publicized colleagues, the research scientists.

The bacteriologists have had their Homer in Paul de Kruif, the chemists have had theirs in Bernard Jaffe, and, most recently, the nuclear physicists have heard their exploits sung by a whole chorus of celebrators (which, according to many theories, is what "Homer" really was). But the teacher whose *alter ego* is the literary scholar, whose excitements are found not among penicillin cultures and cyclotrons but in great research libraries and the mouse-chewed papers of an old family in a dormant English hamlet, has never been much written about. It is time, I think, for someone to atone for that neglect.

To some tastes, indeed, the literary researcher has the most colorful and dramatic of all the tasks of modern scholarship. He deals not with the inanimate or the subhuman phenomena of the world, but with human material; and he differs from the social scientist and the psychologist in that he is not primarily concerned with the mass behavior of men or the individual man as a scientific phenomenon, but with man as creator—the creator of one kind of art, the literary. Of course, his interest may nevertheless often overlap that of the social scientist and the psychologist. More and more, in recent years, the literary researcher has invaded the field of history itself in his desire to understand as fully as may be the various intellectual, social, and artistic milieus that furnished the raw materials of experience from which, by the mysterious catalysis we call the imagination, a work of literature was created. Similarly, the immense increase in psychological knowledge has afforded the literary scholar techniques hitherto unavailable to him for probing into the private temperament, the motivations, and the prejudices of a poet, no matter how long ago he may have lived. And so, borrowing knowledge and techniques on the one hand from the psychologist and on the other from the historian, the literary scholar goes forth to explore both the inner soul of a man and the outer envelope of contemporary circumstance which combined to make a poem or a drama what it is. He is, therefore, a historian of man in his imaginative-intellectual capacity.

But it is not this alone which lends literary scholarship its particular fascination. In addition, the literary researcher is confronted with a vast and tangled puzzle—the contradictions, the obscurities, the very silences which the passage of time leaves behind in the form of history. To repair the damage done by those who in past ages have falsified, distorted, or destroyed the written record, even in the dustiest corner of literary history or biography, requires detective talents—and staying power—of the highest order. The scholar's path may be barred at every turn by a result of one or another of the accidents of fate and human error. He must face the fact that a great deal more of the materials of literary history, including the very works of literature themselves, have been destroyed than have been preserved. He sustains the hope nevertheless that somehow the particular documents he needs have been spared from the bonfire of the moment and the damp of the centuries, and that somewhere, if only he can find where by the use of the Geiger counters of historical sleuthing, they are safe and await his coming. He must solve knotty mysteries by cryptography, scientific analysis of ink and paper, and the cunning use of, say, old railroad timetables and army muster rolls. He must acquaint himself with the methods and the motives of the forgers and liars who have contaminated historical records. In the hope of finding the solution to a literary mystery he may travel to Italy or the Dutch East Indies. At the end of his trail may lie the imposing criminal record of the man who wrote the *Morte Darthur,* the truth about the last days of Christopher Marlowe or of the wretched prostitute who had been Shelley's child-wife, the proof that certain "facts" about Shakespeare were the invention of a Victorian scholar's twisted mind, the forgotten diary of an American Pepys, or the revelation that the spiritual agony of a great romantic poet was due in part to his having begotten an illegitimate child.

Literary research is frequently dull and laborious beyond description, and even the most devoted scholar will admit as much. Much of it ends in despair, because history, however briskly prodded, simply refuses to talk. A great deal of it, furthermore, gives the world nothing but a heap of uninteresting and unusable facts dredged up from the silt where they might just as well have remained to the end of time; and here again those scholars who retain perspective along with their professional convictions would agree.* But that same research has nevertheless provided us with an understanding of the books we treasure which was impossible fifty or a hundred years ago. There is not a major author in English or American letters who has not emerged a clearer, more meaningful figure because of the work of the professional literary fact-finders, whether they have been breathing the choking dust of six hundred years in a grimy structure in London's

---

* In the last fifty years a great deal of ink has been spilt in the debate over the utility of literary research; but in this book I shall be happy to let the reader draw his own conclusions. It is worth remarking, though, that during the Second World War the highly refined techniques developed in such research were put to important use in fields remote from literature. Many peacetime literary scholars were quickly and profitably converted into intelligence officers, cryptographers, propagandists, historians, and so forth.

Chancery Lane, the air-conditioned immaculacy of the lovely Georgian building at Harvard where rest some of the finest of Keats's manuscripts, or the languorous breezes of Melville's South Pacific.

II

WHO, then, are these scholar adventurers?

Obviously there is no such person as a "typical" literary scholar, and there never has been. But it is remarkable that the greatest scholars two generations ago were, seemingly without exception, "characters": some in the mold of Sylvestre Bonnard, some a deal saltier. The pioneer medieval scholar and simplified spelling enthusiast F. J. Furnivall liked to scull on the Thames, while his long white whiskers streamed out behind him. The most famous of American scholars, George Lyman Kittredge, who was reputed to dip his beard in laundry bluing, strode across Harvard Square against the lights in defiance of trucks and streetcars ("Look out there, Santy Claus," cried the drivers and motormen), had a marvelous knack of timing his lecture and making his exit from the classroom so that his last word and his students' last glimpse of him chimed with the bell, held midnight conferences over cigars at his home which are fondly remembered by hundreds of his one-time graduate students, and had habits of leisure reading that resulted in the Harvard Library's acquiring over the years one of the world's finest collections of detective fiction. An Anglo-Saxon specialist almost killed the graduate study of English in one of our great universities because he insisted on teaching all the courses himself; and another great American medievalist lost his hat at a meeting of the Modern Language Association many years ago, when he was rosily under the influence, and thereby started a famous legend—

But the great "characters" belong now to history, and to the affections or at least the esteem of the men and women, now themselves in middle age, who sat at their feet. In their place has come a generation of comparatively conventional, unspectacular men in business suits who may have their individual eccentricities, but who in the mass look like a squadron of insurance salesmen. But even if these do **not** conform, externally at least, to the popular image of the unworldly academician, few of them, I suspect, are really at home with a group of prosperous businessmen. As John Livingston Lowes of Harvard, a prince among scholarly detectives, once observed, the college professor riding in a crowded Pullman smoking room at midnight tries his best to be unacademic, but the damnèd spot will not out.

It is my impression that in politics most scholars whose lives were at some point affected by the Great Depression—and that includes everyone who was struggling to make ends meet while in graduate school, or while holding his first job in a desperately impoverished college—are liberals of some sort, ranging from militant activity in the appropriate movements to a quiet attachment, sentimental or philosophical, to the principles of Franklin D. Roosevelt. Despite the wholly libelous legend that professional scholars take pride in having read nothing published since 1900, most of them, including some of the oldest, are deeply interested in contemporary literary trends, and can discuss Faulkner, Sartre, Kafka, Cyril Connolly, Ezra Pound, and all the splinter groups of poets and critics, with intelligence and heat of one sort or another. Most of them read the *New Yorker*, and not a few are Li'l Abner fans. Many of them collect records which they play, if they can afford to do so, on a custom-built phonograph with all the latest refinements of sound engineering. Their musical tastes are fairly sophisticated. I have a feeling that, if a poll were taken, the most favored of all composers would be Mozart; but Bach, Haydn, Beethoven, and Brahms are also strongly represented on the record shelves, and in many collections such moderns as Hindemith, Schönberg, Bartók, and Shostakovich find hospitality. Although a Johns Hopkins scholar, in an apologia for his colleagues written in 1938, maintained that most members of the profession have "a possessive attitude toward at least one Hollywood star," the times have changed, and today the profession as a whole seems to reserve its enthusiasm for such classics as *The Informer* and the vintage pleasantries of the Marx Brothers, and for the excellent foreign movies which have been increasingly popular in America since the war. It need hardly be added that a picture like Olivier's *Hamlet* is good for an hour's controversy any time two or more scholars get together.

A few scholars, like Wilmarth S. Lewis, the twentieth-century apostle of Horace Walpole, have comfortable private incomes, and the advantages inherent in their personal lives carry over into their scholarly pursuits. They may wear English tweeds, go abroad in state every summer, and mingle socially with rich book-collectors. Like Chauncey Brewster Tinker of Yale, they may build up their own personal collections of rare books and manuscripts, which they house in suitable comfort in a city apartment or a place in the country.

By no means all scholars are professional teachers. A great deal of valuable research, especially in the field of bibliography, has been accomplished by men and women attached to great libraries. Ever since the day of Sir Frederic Madden, a hundred years ago, the British Museum has had on its staff learned bookmen who have combined independent research with their official duties, to the great enrichment of scholarly knowledge. One of the best contemporary authorities on the older English printed books is William A. Jackson, of the Houghton Library at Harvard. Curt Bühler of the Pierpont Morgan Library in New York is another top expert in the field of early printing. Giles Dawson and E. E. Willoughby, Elizabethan bibliographical specialists, are on the staff of the Folger Library. Such men enjoy the advantage of the incomparable resources of their respective libraries almost within arm's reach, and in addition their daily business enables them constantly to profit from the knowledge of the specialists who work for the great rare-book dealers. The "curious bibliographers" who, as we shall soon discover, exposed the monumental fraud of Thomas J. Wise, were neither academic persons nor members of library staffs, but employees of rare-book firms.

Some distinguished scholars have done much of their work in what leisure they could find after completing their daily tasks in other professions. Two of the leading English experts on Elizabethan literature, Sir Edmund Chambers and John Dover Wilson, were for many years officials of the national Board of Education. Dr. Samuel A. Tannenbaum, whom we shall meet when we examine the case of John Payne Collier, was a Hungarian-born New Yorker who held an M.D. from the Columbia University medical school and had a busy practice in psychotherapy. Occasionally an important contribution to scholarly knowledge is made by a stranger to all the learned professions. Twenty years ago a New England textile manufacturer named Walter Oliver wandered into the office of the Modern Language Association to announce that he held the key to a riddle which had long baffled students of the medieval romance—the geography involved in the story of *King Horn*. Once he had identified the "Suddene" of the romance with Southdean, on the Borders of Scotland, where he had spent his boyhood, most of the other geographical details fell into place.

Nevertheless, most scholars earn their living in the classroom or the administrative offices of a university, even if they got there, so to speak, by the back door. A few dedicated spirits entered literary research only after having practiced and abandoned a career in some other field. John Livingston Lowes first was a professor of mathematics at Washington and Jefferson College. Carleton Brown of New York University was a railroader and a Unitarian minister before he began his great work as a specialist in the medieval lyric. A leading present-day Johnson expert holds a degree from the Massachusetts Institute of Technology. And a surprising number of our American scholars, if confronted with the record, would have to confess that they misspent their undergraduate years majoring in such subjects as business administration.

The sacrifices involved in deserting a prospective career as stockbroker or advertising executive for the life of scholarship are the more impressive when we consider what scholars were paid in the late 1940's, when academic salaries in the United States were the highest in history. An instructor, the occupant of the lowest rung on the ladder, whose professional training had been as long and as expensive as that of a surgeon, might receive up to $3,500 for a nine-month year. A man who had reached the dizzy eminence of a full professorship might receive $6,000 or even as much as $10,000. (Salaries were higher at a few institutions, such as Harvard, but to anyone not at Harvard the fact was only a curiosity to be noted wistfully in passing.) Such an income is not conducive to high living. It means limiting oneself to a Ford or a Plymouth, buying the bulk of one's groceries at the A. & P., serving an inexpensive brand of whisky at all parties except the ones celebrating a promotion or the publication of a book, and practicing all sorts of petty economies.

Among scholars there is a pleasant camaraderie which links a man at Columbia with one at the University of California and another at Oxford, in the same way in which, say, surgeons have almost a world-wide fraternity. Some friendships begin in graduate school, when the necessity of posing temporarily as a lover of the Anglo-Saxon tongue and of brazening through the grueling three-day qualifying examination for the Ph.D. makes all men brothers over the two A.M. coffee. They are augmented when the young scholar is striking out for the first time on his own, with a summer of research at the Harvard Library or the British Museum in London, and he meets other aspiring researchers in the reading rooms or at the inexpensive restaurants he patronizes. And they grow still more a little later, when, having published two or three articles, he becomes known as a budding specialist in the metaphysical poets or the Pre-Raphaelites or Jonathan Edwards, and workers in the same and adjoining vineyards begin to exchange information and discuss their problems with him.

The spirit of cooperation that exists in modern literary scholarship is unsurpassed, perhaps, in any of the other learned professions. I can speak with some authority on the subject, because in the course of gathering material for this book I have had occasion to ask the help of scores of busy scholars personally unknown to me, and seldom have I been turned away unsatisfied. That is not to say that relations among scholars are always sweetness and light. There are specialists who like to hold exclusive dominion over their particular area of research, and who go to unseemly lengths to try to keep out poachers. Some, having found valuable new documents, persuade the owners to forbid anyone else to use them. Often this exaggerated sense of possessiveness has its comic side. Forty years ago two indefatigable Shakespeare scholars, Professor Charles Wallace of the University of Nebraska and Mrs. Charlotte Stopes of Scotland, found themselves, to their mutual irritation, working side by side in the Public Record Office in London. Each knew that the other had the same design—to find hitherto undiscovered documents relating to Shakespeare. It is said that Mrs. Stopes was so much on Wallace's mind that, even when walking along the street with a companion, he would lower his voice and glance over his shoulder, fearful that she was trailing him in the hope of overhearing some valuable clue to the progress of his research. When he discovered a document, he would try (unsuccessfully) to have the Record Office authorities hide it away so that she would not know about it.

Once in a while, at the annual meeting of American literary scholars, two archrivals may be seen avoiding each other with desperate zeal. But the pervading atmosphere of these gatherings is decidedly fraternal. The Modern Language Association—"MLA" as it is always called by its members—is the professional organization for teachers and scholars in all the modern languages and literatures which are taught in American higher institutions. It is the counterpart, in the field of literary studies, of the American Association for the Advancement of Science, which regularly steals the headlines from it if their conventions happen to be held at the same time.

Every year for three days between Christmas and New Year's, the MLA holds a meeting in a hotel in one or another of the large eastern or midwestern cities. The lobbies and corridors are jammed by a polyglot mob, numbering as many as three thousand. In addition to scholars in English and American literature, the crowd includes bearded professors of French or Slavonic, smoking cigarettes down to the last half-inch; lonely graduate students who are there because they have already been told it is "the thing to do," and who gaze with awe—mingled with distaste—at the celebrities of scholarship whose books they have been required to read; and beaten-down middle-aged men and women hoping against hope to persuade somebody to rescue them from a living death, at $3,000 a year, at Dismal Seepage State Normal College.

The official reason for the MLA annual conclave is an elaborate system of small meetings in which some fifty groups of specialists in the various fields of research gather while three or four of their number read papers. To "read a paper at MLA," thereby getting one's name in the printed record, is one of the prescribed ways of advancing in the profession. It is generally agreed that nine-tenths of the papers read at these group meetings should have remained unread, if not actually unwritten; but since no one is obliged to listen to the papers and everybody in the room except the reader is spending his time looking for familiar faces or trying to catch the attention of his fellow Dryden expert from Michigan, no real harm is done. The formal purposes of the MLA convention, indeed, are held in humorous scorn by a substantial proportion of the membership. In reality most seasoned MLA-ers travel long distances each Christmas season for the sake of renewing old friendships, trading scholarly and academic gossip, and checking up on the progress of one another's research.

These vital functions are accomplished partly at bars in the hotel and the surrounding neighborhood, and in the hotel suites rented by textbook publishers, whose representatives play the genial host while inwardly worrying about what the front office will say when they turn in the liquor bill. But the most uninhibited and most valuable gatherings at MLA are those in the bedrooms of the members themselves. At two A.M., three ice pails and an empty soda bottle or two outside a door mark a smoke-choked room where a medieval scholar is playing host to a Whitman specialist, a Shakespearean, and a Miltonist (all sprawled on the single bed), a Meredithian (in the armchair), a Henry James specialist (in the other chair), a worker in eighteenth-century periodicals and a student of Franco-American literary relations (on the floor). In the morning it will be hard to get up in time for the nine o'clock section meetings, at which two or three of them are scheduled to read papers; but these bedroom convivialities have their place in the scholarly plan of things. In the course of the conversation, the Miltonist may accidentally suggest to the Whitman specialist some exciting ideas about the origins of Walt's metrical habits; and the Meredithian, listening to the worker in eighteenth-century periodicals discussing his present research, may suddenly remember that in his college library in the Midwest is a file of the obscure magazine for which his acquaintance has long been looking.

The *Publications of the Modern Language Association*, a thick quarterly periodical dressed in a bright blue cover, is, at least when measured by both bulk and total circulation, the leading American publication in the field of literary research. Besides *PMLA*, as it is always called (the scholarly profession was far in advance of the New

Deal in adopting time- and space-saving abbreviations), there are in America a handful of other quarterly and monthly publications, all circulating fewer than a thousand copies, in which the scholar publishes the results of his research with no other reward than a sheaf of off-prints to hand round to his colleagues and to people who may some day offer him a better academic post. Known to the learned by their initials rather than their formal titles—*MLN, ELH, PQ, SP, JEGP*, and so forth—these periodicals struggle along from year to year on the subsidies granted them by the universities where they are edited. The British have two comparable journals, the *Review of English Studies* at Oxford and the *Modern Language Review* at the University of London. In addition to these periodicals of general scholarly interest, there are also a number devoted to special slices of literature, ranging from *Speculum* (medieval studies) to the *Journal of Nineteenth Century Fiction.*

III

THE practice of literary scholarship, while it does not require expensive equipment such as is indispensable to scientific research, takes more money than the average professor can afford to spend. Scholars must own many expensive books important to their research; they need microfilms and photostats of their materials; they have to travel to the distant places where their quarry lies. The sums required are infinitesimal compared with those which are daily allotted to cancer researchers or to workers, for example, on Atomic Energy Commission projects; but they are much harder to get. Although some universities have relatively liberal provisions for aiding literary research—to the extent of a few hundred dollars per project—in others the scholar must pay his own way. He can escape doing so only by winning a grant or fellowship from one of the large libraries or foundations. A few of the great research libraries, such as the Folger, the Huntington, and the Newberry, award fellowships to scholars who have special programs of work they wish to pursue in those libraries. The Rockefeller Foundation has subsidized individual research in certain areas of American literature, as well as contributed heavily to projects, like the Union Catalog at the Library of Congress, which are of use to all scholars. Every year a fair number of Guggenheim Fellowships, which allow each winner $2,500 to $3,000 for a year's uninterrupted study, are allotted to literary investigators. The Fulbright Fellowships for foreign study, recently instituted by the United States Department of State, are a most welcome addition to this lamentably small list.

When the *magnum opus* is finished, the product of ten years of hard work and rigorous self-denial, the scholar need not dread having to fight off publishers frantic to have his manuscript. It never was too easy to find a publisher for a scholarly book, and in the past few years it has become much harder to do so, when production costs have virtually prohibited the publication of books with strictly limited appeal. The American scholar's only recourse is to one of the university presses, which fortunately are increasing both in number and in prestige. But even if his manuscript is accepted by one of these academic publishing houses, he may have to subsidize the venture himself to the extent of thousands of dollars, with little hope of getting any of the money back in profits.

Why, then, considering these handicaps—the constant uphill struggle to accomplish their research and then to publish its results—do so many scholars persist in their occupation? Early in these pages I suggested part of the answer; the rest will be clear when we reflect how literary scholars are made. For they *are* made—not born. No adolescent boy in history, unless there is a case somewhere in the clinical records, ever asserted that his passionate ambition was to be a literary researcher. It is normal to aspire to be a doctor or a lawyer or even a clergyman, and plenty of today's top scientists were busy with Chemcraft sets when they were eight; but any tender youth who expressed a desire to spend his life working in libraries and writing learned articles he could be sure that no more than a handful of people would ever read, could well be thought to be more than a trifle peculiar.

Most scholars are the product of that harsh but presumably necessary weeding-out process by which nature, or society, reduces the number of creative writers in every generation. The famous remark—

was it Sainte-Beuve's?—to the effect that every man over forty carries
a dead poet in his breast might have been made specifically of scholars.
When a boy who likes to read books is in high school and college, he
is going to be a writer—a journalist if he isn't aiming his sights too
high, otherwise a critic like Edmund Wilson, a poet like T. S. Eliot, or
a novelist like Thomas Wolfe. He probably gets some of his early
efforts into print, in his school magazines and even in commercial
publications. (An enterprising blackmailer, by the way, could do
worse than dig up the novels and books of verse which today's eminent
scholars published before they were thirty.) But somewhere along the
line the aspiring artist realizes that the belly's crass demands take
precedence over the fine frenzy of the spirit, and he must find some
way of making a steady living. The obvious answer, since he can't live
away from books, is to teach literature in what are somewhat dreamily
called institutions of higher learning. To do so with any prospect of
security and advancement he must have his Ph.D. So he goes to
graduate school; and there he hears about scholarship, rubs elbows
with practicing scholars, is even encouraged to take a trial flight himself. Despite the agonies he suffers when he is writing his doctoral
dissertation, scholarship gets into his blood. Slowly, and in most cases
painlessly (as the new fascination of historical inquiry fastens itself
upon him) the dream of becoming a littérateur fades away. What had
been, at least to this point, a third-rate writer dies, and what may possibly become a first-rate scholar is born. In very rare cases—two that
immediately come to mind are those of Douglas Bush and the late
John Livingston Lowes—the writer does not die, but is gloriously
assimilated in the scholar, the result being books of scholarly weight
and precision which are also joys to read. In some cases, the writer
lives on under an alias. It is a curious coincidence that both England
and America today have well known specialists in the Elizabethan
drama who turn out successful detective novels in their spare time.

A devotion to books, then, is the primary requisite of a scholar.
Such devotion extends not merely to their contents but to the sheer
physical sensations of handling them, taking pleasure in their binding
and typography and paper. There is a certain temperament, evident
to a degree, probably, in every reader of this book, to which the dry

odor of the stacks of a large library is heady perfume. A few years ago a humble employee of a federal mint grew tired of hauling new pennies around all day and got a job, at a much lower salary, as a page in a big university library—simply, as he expressed it, to be close to books. He had at least some of the makings of the genuine scholar.

But that is not enough. Although the attempts which were made a generation or two ago to place literary research on the same footing as the natural sciences were absurd, it is true that the literary scholar must have the scientist's deep concern for exactness, for objectivity, for thoroughness, for getting every detail just right. He will not be contented unless he feels the kind of satisfaction that comes from the mastery of specialized techniques, things which he realizes he can do well and few other people can do at all. He must have an extensive and precise knowledge of, among many other things, the ways to use the vast array of bibliographical tools which have been produced to guide him through the twenty or thirty million different books printed since Gutenberg. As his command of method increases, as he moves with more and more confidence through the complexities of libraries and archives and solves his problems with neatness and dispatch, his pleasure grows, just as does that of the scientist who solves a formidable problem by the sheer exercise of intricate technique. The more practice he has in the tricks of his trade, the more successfully can he urge the past to give up its secrets; and that is what he is a scholar for.

Put the two together—a lively imagination focused in the art of literature, and a scientific devotion to truth in its minutest detail—and you have the literary scholar. The demands which research makes upon both of these faculties are no less than those which the act of artistic creation makes upon the poet or the novelist, or the attempt to verify a hypothesis makes upon the experimental scientist. They are simply of another kind.

The scholar is confronted with a vast jigsaw puzzle made up of countless fragments of truth; but many pieces are missing, and others are fitted into the wrong places. His first task is to tidy up the tiny sector of the puzzle which he has chosen for his own province, finding some new pieces that fit neatly into place and properly rearranging some old ones. To do so, he must re-create in his imagination the circumstances under which the missing pieces were lost and the ill-fitting ones misplaced, and then, by a similar act of reconstruction, develop a plan for remedying the situation. This task calls for a high degree of ingenuity, patience, logic, and sheer imaginative talent. And in the process of assembling his materials, as well as in the synthesis that follows, the scholar must make even greater demands upon his imagination. To interpret the significance of this material in terms of literary art, he must re-create in his mind, in as minute and faithful detail as possible, the social, intellectual, and literary conditions of a past age, and make himself, as well, an intimate spectator of the inner life of a great artist. A Chaucerian must train himself to think according to medieval patterns of thought; a specialist in Hawthorne must recapture Hawthorne's special mood and outlook upon life. This is historical detective work, rooted in scientific command of numberless small facts but raised to the plane of the creative imagination, and it explains why literary scholarship has a peculiar fascination to perpetually inquisitive minds. In the chapters that follow, we shall get some idea of what a seventeenth-century Marquis of Halifax had in mind when he wrote of scholarly curiosity that it is "the direct incontinency of the Spirit," which "hath a pleasure in it like that of Wrestling with a fine Woman."

THE SECRET OF THE EBONY CABINET

I

WHAT James Boswell, Esq., of Auchinleck, Scotland, wanted most in life—apart from such immediate consolations as wine and complaisant ladies, both of which were always plentiful in his life—was fame. Probably his lifelong hunger for public notice was the result of a gnawing conviction of personal inadequacy and, as time went on, of failure. In any event, it led him (to mention only the most famous instances) to compete with Shakespeare for public attention during the Stratford Shakespeare jubilee of 1769, by parading the streets with a placard in his hat reading "Corsica Boswell"; to edify the audience at Drury Lane Theatre one night by giving spirited imitations of a cow's moo, followed by somewhat less successful imitations of other animals; to appear at a public execution atop a hearse; and to indulge a peculiar whim by returning to London, after a walk in the suburbs, perched conspicuously on a dung cart.

Such exhibitions as these earned Boswell, if not fame, at least notoriety; and notoriety, after all, was something; for the moment, at least, he was in the public eye. But Boswell still had his heart set on being remembered by uncounted ages to come. And that is one reason why he so industriously cultivated the company of Dr. Samuel Johnson. If Boswell were not to be remembered as a lawyer (he was an undistinguished one), or as an essayist and occasional poet (roles in which he displayed only the most mediocre gifts), perhaps he could cheat oblivion as the friend, and eventually the biographer, of Dr. Johnson.

And he did. His *Life of Johnson*, from the day it appeared, assured that the name of James Boswell would never be forgotten. But one can cheat oblivion in a number of ways, and the way in which Boswell did it was not the one that most of us would prefer. How much it cost him was summed up neatly, far too neatly, as we now realize, in Macaulay's famous paradox about the greatest English biographer being the greatest fool in history.

To any reader of the *Life of Johnson*, however, it is clear that Boswell yearned for a purer fame, a fame that comes not from making oneself appear a vain, stupid ass in order that the subject of one's biography should seem all the more imposing a figure, but from the sheer interest of one's own character. Boswell, above all, wanted to be remembered as James Boswell, Esq., a man worthy of permanent fame—not notoriety—for his own sake; who, even if every copy of the *Life of Johnson* were somehow wiped out, would still have an unchallenged place in the annals of eighteenth-century England.

Macaulay showed the world exactly how to view Boswell, and for nearly a century few readers doubted the justice of his estimate. But we can imagine the biographer shouting from his assigned seat in purgatory (where his sins of the flesh undoubtedly sent him), "The ebony cabinet! Look in the ebony cabinet!" For it was there that the real James Boswell, the Boswell who would count for something if anybody ever troubled to look him up, resided; at least, he had been placed there, lovingly and carefully, by the mortal James Boswell before he died.

In Boswell's will, when he died in 1795, was found a provision relating to a certain "ebony cabinet," a family heirloom which had come down to him from his great-grandmother, and which still remained in the ancestral home at Auchinleck, near Edinburgh. In his concern that the cabinet never leave the family, he provided in his will that any heir who "alienated" it was to forfeit a thousand pounds.

Why this anxiety for a piece of furniture? Partly, of course, because it *was* an heirloom, and the Boswells were very proud of their ancient line. But more importantly, because it contained the most valuable of

James Boswell's papers: the papers which, if the world ever saw them, would amply justify his faith that he would not be forgotten. For years Boswell had preserved the written records of his daily life with the assiduity of a Scottish magpie. The precise extent and nature of these records were known to no one but himself, but in the *Life of Johnson* he dropped teasing references to his "archives," which sounded pretentious enough. It was plain, at any rate, that those "archives" at Auchinleck contained many letters to and from Dr. Johnson, because they were often quoted in the *Life;* and was it not probable that they included also the great mass of notes from which Boswell had reconstructed the details of the Johnson story, of those wonderful days and nights of talk at Bolt Court and Streatham, and on the windswept highlands of Scotland?

His canny eye still fixed on posterity, Boswell in his will gave specific directions for the use to which the accumulated papers in the ebony cabinet were to be put. He directed that three of his friends—the Reverend William Johnson Temple, Sir William Forbes, and Edmond Malone—in their capacity as literary executors, should go through the archives and publish all such parts of it as they saw fit. What more could a man do to insure that he would be remembered after death?

But the public desire to read Boswell's personal papers, a desire which in any case Boswell certainly overestimated in respect to his own generation, was not gratified. As we now know, the appointed literary executors did go through the contents of the ebony cabinet very carefully; but then one of them died, and the two remaining executors decided to delay any further action in the matter until Boswell's second son, one of the younger children who Boswell had directed should share the proceeds of publication, was of age. No further attempt was made to edit or print the archives, and the only three men who knew what they contained died without revealing the secret.

And, as things were going, it was a secret which no one especially cared to disturb. For who, after all, was this strange being Boswell, who had written so inexhaustibly fascinating a book? Mr. Macaulay told the readers of the *Edinburgh Review,* and his words echoed down through the century: "He was . . . a man of the meanest and feeblest intellect . . . servile and impertinent, shallow and pedantic, a bigot and a sot, bloated with family pride, and eternally blustering about the dignity of a born gentleman, yet stooping to be a tale-bearer, an eaves-dropper, a common butt in the taverns of London." Thus, while the subjects of Queen Victoria were endlessly grateful to Boswell for having managed somehow, despite his intellectual vacuity and disgusting personality, to write a great book, they were not sorry to be deprived of any further knowledge of the author.

Only a few persistently curious bookmen, members of the clan who must know as much as can be found out about any literary figure, regardless of his manners or his morals, were bothered about Boswell. Agreed that he was all that he portrayed himself to be, with incredible ingenuousness, in the *Life of Johnson*—an impertinent, petty, vain, weak-willed, toadying, hypochondriac, superstitious, officious, inquisitive, shameless creature—was he nothing more? Did these self-revelations, seemingly so comprehensive, actually give us a complete picture of the man? Or might there not be another side to Boswell, a side which was revealed only in the private papers he had locked up for posterity in the ebony cabinet?

At the same time, of course, the riddle of the ebony cabinet was also on the minds of those who, much more in the tendency of their age, wished to know more about Dr. Johnson. But to all men, the cabinet at Auchinleck was adamantly denied by the Boswell family, which now consisted of ladies in the sternest Victorian mold who knew that the whole world shared Macaulay's opinion of their embarrassing ancestor. James Boswell, Esq., was a closed chapter in the family history, Dr. Johnson or no Dr. Johnson. And anyway, the cabinet was empty—for the Boswell ladies never contradicted the rumors which had spread through the literary world, early in the century, that Boswell's papers had been burned.

Apparently, then, Boswell's papers, whatever they contained, were gone. James Boswell would have to be content with being remembered as a conceited devotee of the fleshpots who had somehow blundered into writing a great book; the increasing fold of Johnsonians would have to remain deprived of the important knowledge of their idol which was contained in his biographer's files but not used in the *Life;* and the few Boswellians, a strange sect who could not help entertaining an inexplicable love for the man who could on occasion be so candid about his weaknesses, would know nothing more of him. And that was the situation in the middle of the nineteenth century.

But if ever coming events cast their shadows before, they did on a certain day in 1850 in the French town of Boulogne-sur-Mer, when one Major Stone of the East India Company, a gentleman otherwise unknown to history, happened into a little shop to make some casual purchases. When, upon his return to his lodgings, he unwrapped his parcel, he discovered that the wrapping paper was a fragment of an old letter—written in English. With idle curiosity he looked at the signature on the letter, and identified it immediately as that of a man known to every Englishman with a smattering of literary culture. It was "James Boswell"!

To the everlasting credit of the major, he immediately traced the source of the wrapping paper: an itinerant vender who was in the habit of passing through Boulogne once or twice a year, supplying the shops with their needs. And by good luck, the Boulogne shopkeeper had not yet used that portion of his newly purchased stock which contained the major's quarry. Money changed hands, and Major Stone found himself the owner of a large number of letters which Boswell had written to his most intimate friend, the Reverend William Johnson Temple.

How the Boswell-Temple letters got to the counter of a small shop in Boulogne can easily be explained. Temple's daughter Anne had married Charles Powlett, a clergyman who for some reason had moved from England, about 1825, to a little town only a few miles from Boulogne. So much is certain; for the rest, one need only postulate the death of the surviving member of the couple, or simply a general housecleaning, the two circumstances under which most masses of privately held documentary material emerge from hiding. The peddler happened by, bought masses of scrap paper, and began to resell it not long afterward in Boulogne.

The Boswell-Temple letters, published late in 1856, were the first important addition to public knowledge of Boswell since his death. Naturally there was some skepticism; forgers were at large in England,

and only four years earlier there had been the notorious case of twenty-five forged Shelley letters, for a proposed edition of which Browning had written an introduction. But all doubts of the authenticity of these Boswell letters were answered by their unquestionably genuine Boswellian flavor and the agreement of much internal evidence with the already established facts of his life. The contents of many of the letters, however, were not such as to invite public laments that the rest of his papers had perished. Even though they were severely expurgated before printing, they proved beyond question that Macaulay had been largely right in his condemnation of Boswell. In particular, Boswell's frequent confessions to Temple revealed him to be a rake of unusual persistence and not too fastidious tastes. He was not quite the man whom the Victorians wished to admit to their parlors. And so, after this brief flourish of interest, Boswell's fame remained just about what it had been before: highly dubious. The chief effect of the publication of the Temple letters was the still more resolute strengthening of the bars at Auchinleck against any impertinent inquirer. When, some twenty years later, George Birkbeck Hill, the editor of the great critical edition of the *Life of Johnson*, went in person to the Boswell seat, the door was virtually slammed in his face.

II

IN 1905 few people heard the news, and fewer gave any thought to it, that the last member of the family at Auchinleck had died, and that her estate had passed to the only remaining male descendant of James Boswell: his great-great-grandson, Lord Talbot de Malahide. In due time the Boswell heirlooms were transferred to the new owner's home at Malahide Castle, near Dublin. Presumably the ebony cabinet was among them. But it was a transaction of which the world of bookmen was told nothing.

Seventeen years later, an American scholar made the first great step toward rehabilitating Boswell as a man deserving of independent literary—and psychological—study. In his book *Young Boswell,* Professor Chauncey Brewster Tinker of Yale University, arguing that

Macaulay's influential verdict on Boswell's character was not necessarily the right one, approached Boswell with sympathy instead of disgust. And by concentrating attention on the younger Boswell, before his momentous friendship with Johnson really developed, Tinker demonstrated that Boswell was worth attention for reasons apart from his relationship with the more famous man.

The demonstration was continued, with greatly broadened scope, when, in 1924, Professor Tinker brought out his two-volume collection, the first ever made, of Boswell's private letters. Perhaps the most sensational aspect of this edition was the publication for the first time of those sections of Boswell's letters to Temple which had justly been thought unfit for Victorian eyes. But the Boswell letters had a deeper significance. It was not only that they displayed in more detail the impressive scale of Boswell's physical excesses. More relevantly, by the publication of a mass of Boswell's private letters to his friends, they threw light on facets of his personality which, for obvious reasons, are not prominent in the *Life of Johnson:* the often torturous self-reproaches and religious doubts, the frequent attacks of "the spleen," the honest resolves and high-minded aspirations which made Boswell's life a moral chiaroscuro. Now at long last it was plain that Boswell was infinitely more than Johnson's zany: he was a man who took himself with passionate seriousness, a man of almost pathologically introspective nature.

The evidence which Professor Tinker was able to set forth in the form of the then available letters of Boswell was sufficient to place the man in an entirely new light. But the real drama of Boswell and modern literary scholarship was only beginning. If so much of a hitherto unsuspected Boswell had been revealed by the careful collection and study of the letters known to be available, how much more could be learned if his extensive private archives were still in existence! If Boswell had displayed so much of himself in his private letters, what might he not have confessed in other, perhaps even more confidential, letters, or (was it not easily conceivable?) in diaries! The tradition persisted, of course, that the contents of the ebony cabinet had been destroyed. But while Professor Tinker was working in the manuscript collection of the Pierpont Morgan Library in New York, he came across a letter from Malone, one of Boswell's literary executors, to a daughter of Boswell, telling of the presence at Auchinleck *at that time* of a great mass of Boswell papers which he had gone through before the decision was reached to postpone the fulfilment of Boswell's will. This letter was dated 1809—and the rumor of the destruction of the papers had been abroad, and in print, at least two years earlier!

This at least was a clue: certainly not conclusive, but suggestive. At least, it proved that the now hoary rumor had not been correct during the first years of its circulation. But there was still the chance, a strong chance considering the way in which the Boswell descendants regarded their indiscreet forebear, that the papers had been destroyed at some subsequent time during the long century—perhaps after Macaulay's devastating attack, or after the publication of the letters to Temple. Anything to preserve what was left of the ancient Boswell family pride! In any event, there was the tradition—and nothing more. Could not the question whether the contents of the ebony cabinet still existed be settled, once for all?

By an incident proper to detective fiction, it was. During his systematic search for Boswell letters, Professor Tinker had advertised in Irish newspapers. Among the replies he had received had been a mysterious, unsigned note advising him to consider Malahide Castle. Tinker of course knew that the Boswell possessions had been transferred there in 1905; and so he wrote a letter of inquiry—a masterpiece of diplomacy, it must have been—to the present Lord Talbot. Lord Talbot replied in a brief and ambiguous note. And that was the end of that approach.

But for some time certain literary circles in England had been whispering that somebody—somebody—had actually gone to Malahide Castle and *seen* the precious contents of the ebony cabinet! One of these rumors eventually reached the ears of Wilmarth S. Lewis, now the editor of the great Yale edition of Horace Walpole's letters, who had been a student of Tinker's. Lewis passed the word to Tinker, and the latter decided that the only thing to do was to make a trip to Ireland.

In the summer of 1925, therefore, he presented himself at Malahide

Castle, one of the most ancient buildings in the British Isles still in-habited—a perfect setting for the romantic drama soon to be enacted there. He was admitted to the sacred precincts, and Lord Talbot readily admitted his possession of large quantities of Boswelliana. In fact, he showed Tinker the famed ebony cabinet itself, still full of papers. When Tinker asked about particular manuscripts which he knew had been in the Boswell archives, Talbot obligingly drew them forth and let him examine them.

Tinker, then, had discovered that the story of the destruction of Boswell's papers was false, that those papers were in existence, in obviously greater quantity than anyone had suspected. He suggested to Lord Talbot that some arrangement should be made for the scholarly study and arrangement of the hoard, but Talbot demurred. Tinker therefore returned to America for the academic year of 1925–26. He had had a dazzling glimpse of unimaginable riches, but his hands were empty.

And then, into the impasse, came a new figure, Lieutenant-Colonel Ralph Heyward Isham, a New York financier whose heart was firmly set in Johnsonian locales. Colonel Isham heard Tinker's story and made up his mind to lay siege to Malahide Castle. He had a powerful ally in the economic situation of the middle 1920's: the ancient British families were generally in a bad way because of the stiff income-tax rates, and at the same moment there were flush times in Wall Street. Doubly armed with Boswellian fervor and excellent financial cre-dentials, he visited Malahide in July, 1926, and left bearing in his hand as a souvenir an important letter from Goldsmith to Boswell and in his head the knowledge that Lord Talbot was open to persua-sion. The persuasion occupied a year and a half, at the end of which Colonel Isham returned to Malahide and brought away with him the greater part of the Boswell papers; the rest followed him to New York within the next eight months.

Colonel Isham had succeeded in buying from Lord Talbot over one million words of completely unexplored Boswelliana. Although, as I have said, Boswell had prided himself upon being an archivist, no one had ever suspected just how diligent a preserver of papers he really was. He had faithfully kept copies of a great many of his own letters. He had kept the letters sent him by the many notable figures of the time whom he "collected" in his own long career of tuft-hunting, as well as those he met in the Johnson circle. But most startling of all, it was now revealed that he had kept an intimate personal journal over a period of thirty-three years, a daily record filled not only with his reports of meetings with Johnson and other members of the famous company, but with ruthlessly frank accounts of his own complicated inner existence. Here was James Boswell, Esq., at length and in three dimensions.

But ironically enough, the opening of the cabinet, far from ending the long mystery, had simply substituted one riddle for another. The cabinet had proved to contain much that, in the light of previous knowledge of Boswell's archive-keeping habits, it had been expected to contain—and much, much more besides, such as the journal, an undreamed-of windfall. On the other hand, it did *not* contain a great mass of other material which should have been there. There were, for example, no letters from Dr. Johnson himself, and none from Wilkes or Garrick, two of the most important figures in the *Life of Johnson*. Why had they disappeared—and where were they now, if indeed they still existed?

And another precious relic of the Johnson-Boswell friendship was missing, although the reason for its absence seemed, unhappily, all too clear. One box, when it was opened, proved to contain little more than dust. The fragments of sixteen leaves, which were all that survived of the contents of the box, were identified as pages of the manuscript of the *Life of Johnson*. Evidently the large bundle of manuscript which had been shipped in this box from Auchinleck to Malahide had lain exposed to the damp for many decades and thus had become extremely fragile. At some point between Auchinleck and Malahide the box had received a jolt, and the paper had simply disintegrated into dust. If the surviving scraps were a sure indication of what the whole bundle had been composed of (and there was no reason to doubt it), the manuscript of the *Life of Johnson* was gone forever.

Severe though this loss was, the richness of Isham's treasure-trove made it seem, in comparison, almost trifling. He immediately arranged to have his acquisitions scrupulously edited and printed. They appeared in a sumptuous eighteen-volume limited edition, printed on antique paper with eighteenth-century type at the press of William Edwin Rudge in Mount Vernon, New York. In their bright red bindings, replete with inserted facsimiles of many of the most significant documents, they are an inexhaustible joy to the reader who has access to one of the 570 sets that were printed. One of the most interesting passages in the whole great work is a comment by Geoffrey Scott, the British scholar who saw the initial volumes through the press. Having enumerated the principal classes of missing documents, he wrote: "That the missing elements now exist is improbable. . . . Further discoveries . . . even in this realm of miracles, can hardly be looked for."

The words, written in 1928, represented the considered judgment of a hard-headed scholar not given to day-dreaming. What he failed to recognize was that this was no ordinary realm of miracles. For before the last volume of the edition came from the press in 1934, two more unanticipated events had occurred, each in its own way as dramatic as the revelation to the outside world 'of the contents of the ebony cabinet.

In April, 1930, members of the Talbot household happened to open a long disused croquet box stowed away in a closet. Instead of wickets and mallets, it proved to contain a whole new cache of Boswell papers, including the original manuscript of Boswell's second most famous work, the *Journal of a Tour to the Hebrides with Samuel Johnson, LL.D.!*

For the common reader the *Tour* is in many respects a better introduction than the *Life* to Johnson and Boswell. It is livelier, more continuously anecdotal; and it contains in essence all the qualities which make the *Life* so eminently readable, without the many slack passages of that work. The discovery of the manuscript of this book was a substantial consolation for the loss of the manuscript of the *Life*.

For the *Tour*, as published in 1785, was a decidedly indiscreet book. Boswell's "naïveté" never was more conspicuous than in his forthright comments on the decidedly rudimentary hospitality shown to Dr. Johnson and himself during their sightseeing jaunt in the Highlands in 1773. He was so forthright, indeed, that one offended Scottish laird challenged him to a duel, which was only narrowly averted. But the original manuscript from the croquet box proved to be infinitely more indiscreet than the published version. Boswell, under advice, had gone through it and done a wholesale job of cutting, paraphrasing, and otherwise censoring his own remarks. Some of his alterations were due to the presence in the England of his time of the first faint blushes of prudery; others obviously sprang from his anticipation, however incomplete, of the personal offense which many living persons would take, with justice, from his mention of them.

Colonel Isham acquired the contents of the croquet box, and the new purchase joined the other materials being edited by Professor Frederick A. Pottle of Yale as successor to Geoffrey Scott, who had died in 1929. Pottle and his assistants discovered that Boswell had been so eager to cancel certain passages in the manuscript that he had inked them out seemingly beyond possibility of recovery. Boswell, however, had not foreseen the tenacious devotion of twentieth-century scholars, who patiently read the deleted sentences, letter by letter, through the ink. The deletions were, one might add, well worth restoring, for they reveal Boswell at his most uninhibited and most entertaining.

III

AND so the neglected croquet box had provided a totally unsuspected treasure. What more was to be found? The longer Pottle and his associates worked among the papers from Malahide Castle, the more profoundly they realized their possession of a mass of manuscripts absolutely unique in its revelation of the life of a man. Yet they could not forget that the ebony cabinet had not yielded up all that had been expected, and Pottle wrote in the Preface to his catalogue of Isham's collection:

The Malahide Papers contain no letters of Johnson, no letters of Wilkes, no letters of Garrick. Documents which Boswell refers to in the *Life,* and copies which we know from the Journal he made of his own letters, are as often missing as not. The letters from more or less obscure correspondents, though large in number, can by no means include the entire contents of Boswell's files.*

The only portion of Boswell's papers in the Malahide purchases which Pottle regarded as virtually complete was the journals. Of these, only one section was missing; but it was one of the most serious gaps of all, because it covered the period of Boswell's first acquaintance with Johnson and thus probably contained his detailed account of his initial impressions of his idol.

Pottle wrote the passage I have quoted in 1930. So far as he knew, the materials whose absence he regretted were lost forever; in fact, he offered the theory that Boswell's younger son, James, might have removed from the cabinet "various dossiers of correspondence in which he was particularly interested," and that in the confusion following his death and that of Alexander, the eldest son, they might have been lost.

But here is the most astounding irony of all. Almost at the very moment when Professor Pottle was writing, a scholar three thousand miles away was bringing to light many of the very items which had disappeared "forever"!

In 1930, Claude Colleer Abbott, a lecturer in English literature at the University of Aberdeen, went seeking the papers of Sir William Forbes, Scottish banker and author of the official life of his friend, the eighteenth-century philosopher James Beattie. Another of Forbes's friends was Boswell, of whose literary estate he was an executor and of whose children he was the guardian. It was reasonable, Abbott thought, to expect that among Forbes's papers might be found some letters from Boswell. But his immediate interest was only in Forbes.

Forbes's papers were at Fettercairn House, the Scottish country place of Lord Clinton. With the permission of the owner, Abbott began to make a systematic search of the vast, rambling mansion.

---

* From Frederick A. and Marion S. Pottle, *The Private Papers of James Boswell from Malahide Castle* . . . New York: Oxford University Press, 1931.

Evidently Sir William and his son had been as conscientious archivists as Boswell himself. Abbott found himself waist-deep in eighteenth-century documents; there were papers everywhere—crammed into large wooden and metal boxes, piled on tables and floors. There was ample material on Beattie, and on Forbes's other acquaintances, many of them of some note in the latter part of the eighteenth century. But almost immediately Abbott realized that in this house of unsuspected treasures Beattie and Forbes were minor quarry indeed. At the bottom of one of the first piles he explored, he came upon a stout bundle of old manuscript which turned out to be, of all things, the missing section of Boswell's journal—the one for the first months of his acquaintance with Johnson! "At the moment," he writes, "my chief thought was: 'If this is here, well, anything not in the Ebony Cabinet may be here, too.' "

Perhaps it is just as well that few scholars ever find themselves in the situation in which Abbott was placed: the strain upon one's mind and will is so severe as to be almost unbearable. Surrounded by huge masses of entirely unsorted papers, knowing that at the top of the old mansion was a great attic crammed with the debris of generations, convinced now that unsuspected treasures lay everywhere around him—how was he to proceed? His own narrative of his successive short stays at Fettercairn House in the fall and winter of 1930–31 offers a vivid instance of how, on occasion, a researcher must draw upon every ounce of will-power in his constitution to keep from dashing off in all directions at once. He forced himself to proceed systematically, taking each bundle and box as it presented itself, moving from cupboard to cupboard—and trying not to think about the still unexplored attic. This stern self-control had its rewards; the discoveries were more evenly distributed through the whole term of his search.

In the bottom of a great wooden chest, mercifully in a corner which had not been attacked by the damp that had eaten away some of the other contents, Abbott discovered the letters written by Boswell to Forbes: a series as revealing in its own manner as that series to Temple which had been discovered so many years before in the little shop at Boulogne. And near by, wrapped in a tattered page of the London

Times for 1874, were wads of letters, over a hundred in all, from Dr. Johnson to various correspondents who appear prominently in the *Life*. Valuable though these were in themselves, they gave promise of still more precious revelations. Was it not within the realm of possibility that somewhere in this bewildering storehouse Abbott might find the lost letters of Johnson to Boswell himself?

Such ever present possibilities sustained Abbott's spirit as he worked through almost literally tons of material, much of it dealing with routine estate and business matters of the Forbes family, but interlarded time and again by papers directly concerned with Boswell and his circle: letters from Forbes to Boswell; a draft of a "Criminal Opera" by Boswell; miscellany relating to the *Life of Johnson*. And still the attic was to come!

At last, having surveyed the contents of every parcel and chest downstairs (more careful examination had, of course, to be postponed), Abbott was ready to invade the attic. That dark continent, as if to welcome him, yielded up one of its treasures almost immediately; for among the broken chairs, discarded ornaments, baskets, and other debris of an old family he found a large collection of letters to Boswell from other correspondents. Then his luck departed, and several days passed in hacking his way through the jungle, with dust in the lungs and aching muscles as his only tangible rewards. Large wooden boxes, pried with difficulty from the surrounding lumber, proved to hold only yellowed rolls of wallpaper. But, he writes,

when I removed the next up-sided table I saw, wedged in between other furniture, a small sack, rather like a small mail-bag, with rents here and there from which letters were ready to drop. Quickly I dragged it out. A loose letter fell. It was written to Boswell. Down the winding stairs I hurried the sack, wondering whether all the contents could possibly concern Boswell. Before emptying the papers I drew out another loose letter. The omen was favourable. Soon I knew the truth. The sack was stuffed tight with Boswell's papers, most of them arranged in stout wads, torn here and there, and dirty, but for the most part in excellent order. Neither damp nor worm nor mouse had gnawed at them. My luck held.*

* From Claude C. Abbott, *A Catalogue of Papers Relating to Boswell, Johnson, and Sir William Forbes Found at Fettercairn House, 1930–31*. Oxford: Clarendon Press, 1936. Quoted by permission of the publishers.

It was probably the richest find of all; for the bag, measuring twenty-five inches by nineteen and once used for seed beans, was crammed with such long-lost treasures as the correspondence between Boswell and the Corsican patriot General Paoli, letters from Wilkes and Burke to Boswell, and the letters of William Johnson Temple to Boswell which provided the other side of the correspondence found in Boulogne.

Abbott had not been disappointed, then: by a sure instinct, he had saved the icing of the cake until the last.

The discoveries at Fettercairn House accounted for much of the Boswell material which had been missing from Malahide Castle— except for items like the supremely desirable Johnson-Boswell correspondence, which Abbott was forced to report he could not find, and whose whereabouts remains a mystery today. How all these Boswelliana had found their way to Fettercairn was easily explained. Sir William Forbes, as one of Boswell's literary executors, had received the mass of documents for examination and ultimate editing and publication; but the death of Temple, another of the executors, had interrupted the project, as we have seen. Forbes never returned his share of the papers to the Boswell family; and upon his death, in 1806, all his effects, including the Boswell hoard, had been transferred to Fettercairn House, the seat of his son, who had married the only daughter of Fettercairn's owner, Sir John Stuart. And here they had remained, untouched except by damp and mice, until Professor Abbott, seeking information on Forbes, had stumbled upon them.

After the drama of Fettercairn House had been announced to the world, a nice question of ownership was raised and had to be settled before the papers themselves could be made available for scholarly research. Obviously the papers legally were the property of Boswell's heirs; but Colonel Isham had purchased from Lord Talbot the copyright of all of the Boswell papers in his possession. And was it not true that the newly found papers, though not physically in Talbot's possession, belonged to him—since he was the heir to the Auchinleck estate? Eventually litigation was instituted in the Scottish courts; and the resultant decision in 1939 involved as fine a Gordian knot as a Scottish judge ever contrived to tie. Lord Talbot, it was decreed, was entitled to a half-interest in the new treasure—which meant, actually, that Colonel Isham was entitled to it, as Talbot's assignee; but the other half-interest resided with the Cumberland Infirmary, the residuary legatee under the will of the last of the Auchinleck Boswells, who had died in 1905. Neither party, however, was prepared to buy out the other. And so matters stood when the war began. The Fettercairn papers were kept under lock and key, and the only information on their nature was that to be found in Abbott's printed catalogue, which listed over sixteen hundred items of choice Boswelliana in such economical terms as merely to intensify the impatience of scholars to see the documents themselves.

But even during the Second World War, indeed because of the war, the romance of Boswellian discovery went on. The scarcity of space for storing grain made it necessary that every disused building in Ireland be utilized for the purpose; and in 1940 the authorities requisitioned a ramshackle old cow barn on the estate at Malahide. Considering the record of that incredible estate, it would have been surprising indeed if something dramatic had not happened when the barn was examined. The barn was faithful to the tradition of its environment. In its loft was found one more cache of eighteenth-century papers—including some of the most valuable Boswell-Johnson treasures yet unearthed.

Lady Talbot notified Colonel Isham of the discovery, and after long negotiations Isham bought these newly found documents, which arrived in New York in the fall of 1946. Meanwhile he had also been negotiating for the purchase of the Fettercairn House papers, and at last these too fell into his possession. Thus he had made a clean sweep of the field. The original treasure from Malahide Castle, the windfall from the croquet box, the papers from Fettercairn House, the cache from the cow barn—all finally were brought together, after a century and a half of separation.

In November, 1948, Colonel Isham exhibited the newly arrived materials to some of America's leading eighteenth-century scholars. Despite the tense international situation, the aftermath of a memorable national election, and the supposed lack of popular interest in literary matters, Isham's formal unveiling of his treasures occasioned an extraordinary burst of journalistic discussion. The *New York*

Times devoted the better part of a page in its regular news section to excited articles on the dramatic episodes by which the papers had been discovered and on the superlative literary and biographical importance of the material. Newspapers all over America carried long press dispatches on their front pages, and popular columnists, in a totally unprecedented display of literary erudition, wrote dissertations on Boswell and Johnson.

Colonel Isham revealed that he was in possession of three times as many letters to and from Boswell as he had received in his original purchase: 2,200 letters to Boswell from such men as Edmond Malone, Sir Joshua Reynolds, and David Garrick, and 600 letters from him. There were 100 hitherto unknown letters from Dr. Johnson to correspondents other than Boswell; some equally unknown juvenile poems by Johnson, and copies of books by him of which no other copies are known to exist. There were important manuscripts by Reynolds, including a twenty-eight-page character sketch of Oliver Goldsmith whose existence had been unsuspected. And—possibly the most gratifying of all revelations—it was shown that the regret over the supposed disintegration of the manuscript of the *Life of Johnson* was premature. The manuscript had not, after all, been in the box which had proved to contain a heap of dust. Instead, here it was in Isham's possession: 1,300 pages of it, mainly pages torn from Boswell's ordinary journal, heavily edited by Boswell and then sent as copy to the printer.

One enthusiastic scholar said of Isham's incredible assemblage of documents that there was enough material to keep fifty scholars busy for fifty years. He was not exaggerating. Because Boswell knew so many of the leading literary and intellectual figures of his age, not only in Britain but on the Continent, and because he treasured up seemingly every scrap of information about them that he could obtain, the mass of papers originally housed in the ebony cabinet will throw new light on the personalities and careers of a score of men and women whose names are found in every history of English literature.

In the midst of the excitement over Isham's unveiling of his completed collection, a serious question haunted the scholars. It was known that he wished to sell the entire collection. The ideal place for it to go, of course, would be a large university library or other semipublic institution, where it could be efficiently classified and zealously preserved, and at the same time be available for scholarly examination. But the price of the collection, it was rumored, ran well into seven figures, seeming to bar that happy solution. The other alternative, of course, would be for the collection to be sold piecemeal—which would cancel out the fortunate developments of the past few years by scattering the various parcels again and, conceivably, making some of them as inaccessible as before. But scholars' fears have now been quieted. In 1949 a gift to Yale University from the Old Dominion Foundation, established by Paul Mellon, and a publishing arrangement with the McGraw-Hill Book Company, made it possible for the whole Isham collection to be acquired for the Yale University Library. Perhaps no more appropriate final disposition could have been made of the Boswell papers, because Isham once was a Yale student and two of the most prominent figures in the whole saga of the discoveries, Chauncey Brewster Tinker and Frederick A. Pottle, are members of the Yale faculty. The sheer bulk of the material to be studied, and the highly specialized scholarly knowledge necessary to interpret its full significance, have required the setting up of an elaborate system of advisers and editors, all distinguished specialists in eighteenth-century English literature, who will supervise the classifying, editing, and eventually the publishing of most of the papers.

No matter how radically the Malahide-Fettercairn documents may change our notions of Dr. Johnson or Goldsmith or Garrick or Reynolds, their deepest importance will reside in the amazingly detailed and vivid portrait they offer of James Boswell, Esq., whom, as Professor Pottle said some time before the new quota of discoveries was examined, "we are in a position to know more thoroughly than any other human being." The long journal now recovered from oblivion is, Pottle continued, "as frank as Pepys, and, like Pepys, is a trustworthy contemporary record, not remolded by the interests of a later stage of development. And it covers the whole of Boswell's adult life." Boswell seems to have had the instinctive conviction, not uncommon among neurotics, that a minute record of the ebb and flow of his daily sensibilities would be of general interest. The revelations of the journal do not essentially alter the impression he gives of himself in the *Life*, so far as superficial appearance is concerned; and, far from absolving him of any of Macaulay's specific charges, they provide extravagant documentation for virtually every one. But the journal does require a completely new interpretation of the facts. Macaulay viewed Boswell as a simple fool; and, as Professor Pottle pointed out, neither word applies. Actually, he was "one of the most complex literary characters on record, combining in uneasy equilibrium a host of contradictory traits." Far from being a fool, he could and did penetrate deep into men's souls, his own as well as others'. He had a special kind of sophistication, and was a man of keen intellectual and analytical powers.

It was such a man, then, and not an alternately exhibitionistic and maudlin buffoon, that wrote the *Life of Johnson*. And the newly discovered journal, together with the actual printer's copy for the *Life*, shows us exactly how he did it. The long entertained belief that Boswell scribbled down Johnson's words as they fell from his lips was mistaken. What he actually did was to jot down notes, in a chaotic sort of shorthand, as soon as possible after the event. From them he formed, days or months or years afterward, a smoothly written account, an imaginative re-creation. On the suggestions of these rough notes in his journal, supplemented by many materials he painstakingly collected, Boswell eventually based the *Life*. To trace the development of a famous Johnsonian scene from Boswell's first crude jottings to their final appearance in print is to realize, as one could never realize without the aid of the manuscript, how fine an artist, and how little a reporter, Boswell was.

And these, I am sure, are the things which Boswell must have intended us to learn when he gave such explicit directions for the editing and publication of his intimate papers. He knew all too well how he was regarded by many of his contemporaries, especially by those who envied him his closeness to Dr. Johnson. In a sense he spent his whole adult life preparing his vindication; for I do not think that it is oversentimentalizing Boswell to suggest that what he desired, most of all, was not simply fame but a *just* fame—understanding of the temperament which had been the subject of so many ribald jokes in eighteenth-century London. By an accident which he did not foresee, his vindication was withheld for a century and a half. But the ebony cabinet, the croquet box, and the cow barn at Malahide Castle, and the miscellaneous containers at Fettercairn House, preserved it well. Boswell, wherever he is, must be content at last; for now—as he so much desired—we can know him, not as the self-effacing artist of the *Life of Johnson,* nor as Macaulay saw fit to present him, but "in his habit as he lived."

THE CASE OF THE CURIOUS
BIBLIOGRAPHERS

I

TECHNICAL bibliography, as distinct from bibliography in its more familiar sense of the simple listing of books by or about a certain author, is a field of literary study which seldom touches the interests of the general reader, or, for that matter, those of many specialized literary researchers. Its concern is with the physical minutiae of books and their history in the printing house, and its most practical usefulness is found not in literary history but in the rare-book trade. If one is an American millionaire intent upon possessing every issue of every pamphlet or book bearing the name of Tennyson, the highly specialized knowledge and techniques of the bibliographer are indispensable; for he, and he alone, can detect tiny differences in typography and format and text. By reconstructing from these differences the exact order in which the various issues of a given work appeared, he can establish the priority, and thus in general the rarity, of each issue. It is a specialty that has its own peculiar charms and rewards, even for the amateur, but many would say that it lacks human interest. The protagonist in the drama of technical bibliography as a rule is nothing more lively than a certain kind of type face, a peculiarity of the title page, or a printer's error on page 19 which distinguishes the rare first issue from the entirely common second. Yet it was in this superficially unlikely environment that the most sensational literary scandal of our time was unfolded.

It all began in 1932, when two young men in the London rare-book trade, John Carter and Graham Pollard, exchanging notes on separate investigations they were conducting, suddenly realized that their researches were in fact intimately related and that, if they joined forces, they might come to some startling conclusions. I shall speak in a moment of what Carter had been up to; but let us begin with Pollard. In the course of preparing the section on Ruskin for the *Cambridge Bibliography of English Literature*, he had been having frequent occasion to consult the bibliographical notes in the massive Cook and Wedderburn edition of Ruskin. Among those notes, buried in small type, Pollard had recognized clues that might help explain a mystery then current in rare-book circles. Those clues had been in print for a generation, but seemingly no one before him had suspected their true significance.

The crucial small-type notes were assertions by one of the Ruskin editors that certain issues of obscure pamphlets by Ruskin were unquestionably forgeries. The reason for the accusation was simple. Although the pamphlets purported to be first issues, their text was that of a later, revised edition. If they had been genuine, their text would have resembled most closely that of the next earliest edition.

Now, as Pollard reminded Carter, those same Ruskin pamphlets, whose genuineness nobody but Ruskin's editors seemed to have doubted, had been commanding substantial prices in the collectors' market. And they recalled that, in the years since 1890, many other such booklets bearing the names of eminent Victorian authors—over fifty different titles in all—had been much sought after by collectors, who had been willing to pay prices running into hundreds of pounds for a single item when it came on the market. Only, curiously enough, these items seldom turned up singly; when they appeared they came, like King Claudius' sorrows, "not single spies, but in battalions!" This is a phenomenon unusual in the rare-book trade. On the infrequent occasions when well defined sets of rarities appear for sale without explanation, wise bookmen are prone to suspect a cache from which some mysterious collector or dealer is extracting hoarded wealth, perhaps to silence clamorous creditors.

With this information in hand, Carter and Pollard pondered

certain vague rumors which had lately been current—rumors that implied, though seemingly never on any solid basis of fact, that at least a few of these sought-after Victorian pamphlets were, in a favorite Victorian phrase, no better than they should be. It was known that certain reputable dealers were so suspicious that they refused to handle them. And why the periodic appearance of whole groups of the pamphlets in a single sale? Disliking this unsatisfactory state of knowledge, the young scholars consulted their files of sales catalogues, tracked down the sale records of as many actual copies of the pamphlets as they could, and emerged with several singular facts.

The pamphlets in question owed their rarity for the most part to the fact that they were said to have been printed in tiny editions, usually for the author—Browning, perhaps, or Tennyson or Swinburne or Ruskin or Kipling—to distribute to his friends in advance of publication, or, sometimes, to secure copyright. This was, and to some extent still is, a common practice. But for Carter and Pollard it was instructive to discover that none of the known copies of the fifty-odd pamphlets bore any inscription from the author, even though many were ostensibly printed as gift copies. Nor was any copy known which was in other than "mint" condition: none, that is, bore the signature of the owner or even any signs of normal wear. Nor had a single copy of any of the pamphlets appeared on the market before 1890. Nor was any pamphlet mentioned anywhere in the known letters, journals, or other papers of its author. Nor was there a single reference to the pamphlets in any bibliographies of their respective authors published before the 1890's, even though the oldest of the pamphlets had supposedly been printed in the 1840's. Nor was there any evidence—except that coming from one source, of which I shall speak in a moment—of the ownership of any of the pamphlets before the 1890's. In a word, Carter and Pollard were confronted with the strange circumstance that although on the title pages of the pamphlets were dates ranging up to half a century earlier, there was not a scrap of reliable evidence that they had actually existed before 1880! *

---

* In no case was there any question that the *contents* of the pamphlets were genuine; the text of each pamphlet is authenticated by its appearance in the authorized works of its writer.

This was a more serious matter than one might at first think. It was quite true that, if the pamphlets were not as represented, a considerable group of important collectors had been defrauded. But the case was even more disturbing from the point of view of literary history and biography. Following their appearance on the market the booklets had been included in the standard bibliographies, and biographers had taken due notice of them. The pamphlets had, indeed, become an accepted, almost totally unquestioned part of the literary histories of their respective authors.

Of those pamphlets, the one most prized by book collectors was "Sonnets by E.B.B."—later to be known as Mrs. Browning's *Sonnets from the Portuguese*—which bore on its title page the assurance that it had been printed at Reading in 1847, for private circulation only. Copies of this little item had brought as much as $1,250 on the open market, a figure which had caused raised eyebrows in the trade. Some experts had had a vague feeling that all was not right with that pamphlet, but they could find no tangible grounds for their suspicion. It was John Carter who had first subjected the item to critical scrutiny. What he had been able to tell Pollard as the result of his preliminary investigation was fully as instructive as what Pollard told him about the Ruskin pamphlets.

The high regard in which the "Reading 1847" sonnets was held was due at least in some measure to the romantic story behind it. In 1894 Edmund Gosse, one of the most popular and widely read critics of the time, had published an essay in which he told the story, thenceforth so beloved of Browning enthusiasts, of Mrs. Browning's shyly coming to her husband at breakfast during the first year of their marriage, thrusting a sheaf of manuscript into his pocket, and running back to her room. The manuscript was that of the sonnets, which Browning later declared to be the finest since Shakespeare's. Gosse said that Browning insisted that they be published. Mrs. Browning was loath to publish "what had been the very notes and chronicle of her betrothal" —they were too intimate, too sacred, to share with the world. But Browning's will prevailed, and his wife at length sent the manuscript to her friend Mary Russell Mitford, who had a few copies struck off by a small printing establishment in Reading and sent them to Italy for the Brownings to distribute among their close friends. It was these copies in beautiful mint condition, looking as if they had been untouched by human hands for seventy years, that were bringing up to $1,250 apiece in the 1920's.

Now $1,250 was not an excessive price to pay for such an item, provided the purchaser's zeal for an item associated with so touching an episode in the Brownings' idyll outweighed his regard for $1,250—and *provided*, above all, that the story of the origin of the pamphlet was true. There were, however, one or two irritating discrepancies in Gosse's account. He said that the breakfast-table scene occurred at Pisa early in 1847—some six months, perhaps, after the Brownings' elopement. But there also existed unimpeachable evidence, partly from Browning himself and partly from friends who had had the story from him, that the episode had happened not at Pisa but at Bagni di Lucca, and not in 1847 at all, but in 1849—two years after the private edition of the sonnets supposedly had been printed in Reading!

I should say at this point, to restore the serenity of such Browning lovers as read these pages, that the incident of the breakfast table did happen. The evidence we have, entirely apart from Gosse's account, makes so much clear. The only questionable element is the date, and incidentally the place, of the occurrence. Gosse put it, on what he said was Browning's evidence, in 1847; other writers—including Browning himself, in one of his letters—were equally sure that it was 1849. Who, then, was right: Browning or Gosse? And if Browning's date, 1849, was correct, how could one account for the 1847 pamphlet?

The obvious course for Carter and Pollard was to try to discover under what circumstances the pamphlet had first appeared on the market. The answer was not hard to find. Thomas J. Wise, the then undisputed monarch among early twentieth-century English bibliographers and collectors, had set it down partly in his exhaustive *Bibliography of the Writings in Prose and Verse of Elizabeth Barrett Browning* (1918) and more fully in *A Browning Library* (1929). After repeating Gosse's story of the breakfast table and of the subsequent printing of the sonnets at Reading, Wise told how Miss Mitford had given a number of copies of the pamphlet to a friend, Dr. W. C.

Bennett. "Somewhere about 1885," Wise recounted, he had become acquainted with Dr. Bennett, who had sold him a copy of the little book for £25 and later sold his remaining copies, ten or twelve in number, to other Browning enthusiasts, some of whom had later resold their copies. This was how they had come upon the market.

On its face, the whole Gosse-Wise story was plausible enough, and it gained added authority from Wise's immense prestige. But Carter and Pollard were satisfied with none of it. To begin with, Gosse, whom Wise quoted, had been vague about the source of some of his information. While the breakfast-table part of the story, wrong date and all, was assigned to Browning, the part relating to the Reading printing was said to have come to Gosse from an unidentified friend. Unidentified friends are the plague of conscientious scholars who require chapter and verse for every fact; but if their story is supported by independent evidence it may be tentatively accepted. In this case, there was no supporting evidence, and to make matters worse there were other inconvenient, and unanswered, problems. Why had Mrs. Browning sent the manuscript all the way back to England when she could have had it printed so much more easily in Italy? Why did Miss Mitford never refer in her published letters to her part in the printing? Why had she kept back ten or twelve copies instead of sending them all to Mrs. Browning? Why did she give them to Dr. Bennett? Why did the Brownings never mention this prepublication issue in their letters or conversations? Why was there no copy in Browning's library when it was sold in 1913? Why had no one ever seen a copy bearing any inscription from Mrs. Browning or, lacking that, some association with any of the intimate friends to whom she would have sent a copy? The reported history of the pamphlet went back to 1885 or thereabouts, and there, with the exception of Gosse's story, it stopped—obstinately and tantalizingly. Wise's story of the Bennett cache accounted for only a dozen copies; but at least seventeen others were known to exist in 1932, and their history before the 1890's was completely blank. Before the middle nineties, when copies of the 1847 printing first appeared in collections, bibliographers and biographers had agreed that the *Sonnets from the Portuguese* had first appeared in the 1850 trade edition of Mrs. Browning's collected poems.

There remained only one thing for Carter and Pollard to do: put the 1847 pamphlet to every possible test, in order to establish or definitely disprove its genuineness. In so doing, they developed new scientific techniques of bibliographical detection which now form an almost insuperable obstacle in the path of bookmen with intent to defraud.

For one thing, they found a new use for chemistry in bibliographical analysis. Long before the nineteenth-century pamphlets had come to the attention of investigators, it had been common practice to analyze the ink used in suspected documents in order to establish their approximate age. But Carter and Pollard now used chemistry to establish the age not of the ink but of the *paper* in the "Reading 1847" pamphlet. With the aid of expert technologists, they found that that paper was made of chemical wood pulp. This ingredient had been introduced in the paper-making industry only after the successful development of a method of sulphite bleaching in the early 1880's. Yet the Reading pamphlet of Mrs. Browning, made of such paper, was dated 1847!

The second test required a minute and complex inquiry into the type used in the pamphlet. One of the typographical peculiarities of the booklet was the use of a so-called "kernless" font—that is, a font in which no part of any letter, notably *f* and *j*, projects beyond the rectangular body of the type. Research in books on type founding revealed that kernless *f*'s and *j*'s had been introduced into the font from which the "1847" pamphlet was printed no earlier than 1880. Another peculiarity was the use of an unusual kind of question mark, narrower than the ordinary sort and with the dot set noticeably off center.

The earliest possible date of the so-called 1847 pamphlet was now ascertained beyond question, on the twin counts of anachronistic paper and anachronistic type. But now that Carter and Pollard had triumphed in their first inquiry they were faced with an even more challenging problem. If the "Reading 1847" pamphlet was a forgery, as it certainly was, who had printed it? It bore no printer's mark. Blessing the kind Fate which had restricted the number of type founders in nineteenth-century England, they gathered specimens of as many late nineteenth-century fonts as they could locate and examined them for the kernless *j* and *f*. They found that no fewer than twenty-seven kernless fonts had been produced before 1895. Carter and Pollard might at this point have begun to track down every firm known to have made such a font, found out the printers to whom each firm sold kernless fonts, and then combed the resultant list for possible suspects.

But—as if matters were not sufficiently complicated—none of the twenty-seven kernless fonts contained the eccentric question-mark. The only conclusion possible was that the printer of the forged pamphlet had used a hybrid font, part of which had been supplied by one type founder, the rest by another. But how could that printer be discovered? It meant putting virtually every printer, large or small, from Land's End to John o' Groat's, to the test. "Any comprehensive search of this kind," Carter and Pollard reluctantly decided, "was an obvious impossibility." And there the chase seemed to drag to a halt.

But luck intervened, as it has a pretty habit of doing when bibliographical detectives have labored faithfully and well. Carter and Pollard were examining—by no means accidentally, as we shall see—a copy of a type-facsimile reprint of Matthew Arnold's Rugby prize poem, *Alaric at Rome*. This was an item which Thomas J. Wise, whom we have already met, had had printed in London, for private circulation among collectors, in 1893. In it Carter and Pollard found exactly the same type font—kernless letters, unorthodox question mark, and all—which had been used in the printing of the spurious "Reading 1847" pamphlet. And at the end of the book, to their great joy, appeared what they had been seeking—a printer's mark. It was that of Richard Clay & Sons, an old-established, well known and completely respectable London firm.

The chase thus suddenly was renewed. Carter and Pollard made inquiries of the Clay firm, who replied that the hybrid font in question was first used in their printing work in the early 1880's; but their records for the period before 1911 had been destroyed, so that they could furnish no information as to the man or men responsible for printing the "Reading 1847" pamphlet.

And there the pursuit of tangible facts really did end, as far as the production of the pamphlet was concerned. Carter and Pollard had proved beyond question that the "Sonnets by E. B. B." purporting to have been issued at Reading in 1847 had actually been printed by Richard Clay & Sons in London, sometime between the early eighties and the middle nineties.

II

BUT this was merely a single exhibit in the amazing array of bibliographical inconsistencies that Carter and Pollard had discovered in the process. For the sake of simplicity I have followed their method as applied to one pamphlet alone, the most famous and most prized of the group of more than fifty rare items I mentioned at the beginning of this chapter. Actually, they had known from the beginning that whatever they found out about the "Reading 1847" booklet would probably affect the standing of many of the other items which had accompanied it, almost habitually, into the market. They had therefore subjected each of the suspected items to the exhaustive tests which had revealed such interesting things about the alleged first issue of Mrs. Browning's sonnets. The results amply repaid their pains. In the group were copies of no fewer than fifty-one different pamphlets. Of the twenty-seven issues which were printed on paper containing esparto, an ingredient derived from a long, coarse grass grown in Spain and northern Africa, ten bore imprint dates before 1861, the year in which esparto had begun to be used in papermaking, and thus were proved to be out-and-out forgeries, and some others were gravely suspect because they antedated the period when esparto came into general use. There were also thirteen cases in which the paper contained chemical wood pulp. All thirteen bore imprint dates before the year in which chemical pulp was used in papermaking.

Turning to the typographical test, Carter and Pollard found that sixteen of the pamphlets (including some which had already been condemned by the paper test) contained the telltale kernless letters, which meant that all sixteen had been printed from seven to thirty-eight years after their imprint date. The remaining pamphlets, however, provided something of a difficulty, because they were printed in a variety of types unlike the "kernless" font which had been already traced to Clay's. Even though most of the remaining pamphlets had already been exposed by the paper test, the possibility remained that, however fraudulent they were, they were not the work of the forger who had been using Clay's facilities. But this possibility vanished when Carter and Pollard delved further into the history of Clay's and found that the firm had used every one of the fonts represented in the pamphlets under scrutiny. Quite evidently, then, since it was unthinkable that two or more independent operators had had entrée to Clay's, they were dealing with the handiwork of a single forger or ring of forgers.

The tests completed—along with some new applications of the textual test used long ago by Ruskin's editors, which had proved that several "prepublication" pamphlets actually contained the text of a later edition—Carter and Pollard were able to sum up the strictly bibliographical part of their investigation. The record was impressive. Twenty-seven pamphlets had been proved, by one, two, or even three conclusive tests, to be forgeries. Some thirteen more were labelled as "highly suspicious," which meant merely that the cases against them were not quite as damning as those against the rest. There were also several unauthorized and unacknowledged facsimiles of existing rarities. In all, nearly half a hundred different "rare" items—"first editions" of poems and essays by such Victorian worthies as the Brownings, George Eliot, Ruskin, Tennyson, Matthew Arnold, Swinburne, and Thackeray—were unmasked. When you remember that scores of copies of each item were known to have gone through the market, and that in some cases a single copy brought more than £100, you see that the wholesale fraud which our curious bibliographers exposed was not of merely academic interest.

Who, then, was the forger?

Reviewing all the evidence they had gathered (and it was far more extensive and diversified than I have space to indicate), Carter and Pollard were able to construct a good hypothetical portrait of the criminal. His methods, his particular talents, his interests, even his very infrequent lapses of knowledge were faithfully mirrored in his work.

That he was a truly admirable bibliographical craftsman, there was no doubt. Taking a poem or an article from the collected works of Tennyson or Kipling or William Morris or from an old periodical, he would have it printed as a pamphlet, with the title page explaining the circumstances under which it was (allegedly) issued, always at a date prior to the generally accepted "first edition." These circumstances, the item's *raison d'être*, always fitted in beautifully with the known facts of its author's life and literary career. Each "first edition" thus manufactured came into the world, therefore, with every evidence of legitimacy. Again, the forger had shown his wiliness by almost never imitating a known edition. He thus eliminated the danger of a buyer's comparing his prize with another, authentic, copy. There were no authentic copies, because until he got to work there had never been such an edition! *

The man that Carter and Pollard were seeking was one extremely well versed in nineteenth-century bibliography. So much was argued by his genius for camouflaging his fake against a background of utterly truthful detail with which only a scholar could have been acquainted. He was equally well versed in the state of the rare-book market; he had a seventh sense that seemed always to tell him what sort of "first edition" would most appeal to the collectors of his day. Finally, he seemed to be in touch with current literary gossip. In selecting works by living authors for his attentions, he was careful to choose the works of those who, for one reason or another, would not be in a position to be asked, or would be temperamentally disinclined to answer, embarrassing questions about these putative first editions. His choice of Ruskin, for instance, seemed to have been dictated no more by the prevalent fashion for collecting Ruskiniana than by the fact that Ruskin, having lapsed permanently into insanity, was comfortably immune from the questions of inquisitive bibliographers.

Carter and Pollard then considered who might have perpetrated

* One danger, however, the forger had not eliminated—that of competition. After he had launched his fakes upon the book-collecting world, having taken care that they would be regarded as precious rarities, he had the chagrin of seeing *them* imitated in turn by some unknown forger eager for a share of the profits. I find something positively sublime in the idea of forgeries giving rise to forgeries of themselves. And what confusion in book-sale records the presence of these second generation forgeries has caused!

this wholesale deception. Years earlier, one or two similar pamphlets had been called into doubt, and suspicion had fallen upon Richard Herne Shepherd and John Camden Hotten, both late Victorian bookmen of qualified integrity. The suspicion rested, it is true, upon the word of only one man, but it was that of a man whose authority in such matters could scarcely be questioned. He was Thomas James Wise, sometime president of the Bibliographical Society, honorary Master of Arts of Oxford, member of the exclusive Roxburghe Club of book collectors, and one of the most learned bibliographers in England. Yet, after weighing the possibility that Shepherd or Hotten, or both, had been the culprits in these new cases, Carter and Pollard absolved them completely. Whatever his other sins, neither man, it was clear, had been mixed up in this particular business; for every bit of evidence Carter and Pollard had accumulated pointed obstinately in a different direction. At every turn in their inquiry, their clues led them back to the somewhat pontifical gentleman who was the avowed enemy of all sorts of chicanery in book-dealing and -collecting: Thomas James Wise himself.

For forty years—ever since he had made himself prominent in the affairs of the Shelley and Browning societies in the late 1880's—T. J. Wise had been the final court of appeal on matters bibliographical. Though by trade a member of a firm dealing in nothing more bookish than essential oils (used in the making of perfume and scented soap), he was by passionate avocation a rare-book man—one might almost say, a collectors' collector. He moved in the choicest circles of book dealers and bibliophiles; in his home he possessed the matchless "Ashley Library," the finest collection of rare modern books and manuscripts then in private hands in England; his word was law on anything concerning the priority of one Meredith issue over another, or the almost microscopic differences which made one Shelley pamphlet worth a thousand pounds and another, seemingly its twin, dear at five. As his friend Gosse is said to have remarked, "I am sure that on the Day of Judgment Wise will tell the good Lord that Genesis is not the true first edition." His library was a principal port of call for specialists in nineteenth-century literature. In hundreds of scholarly books, bibliographical and biographical alike, one finds warm mention of Wise's generosity in placing his wide technical knowledge, as well as the unmatched resources of his library, at the disposal of the writers. He was a virtually indispensable adjunct to literary learning; and not the least imposing part of his role as the Grand Mogul of book collecting was his frequently and vehemently expressed hatred of bibliographical carelessness and falsehood, such as attempts to sell or authenticate bogus copies of rare books.

Nevertheless, it was this man, rather than one of palpably unsavory character, that Carter and Pollard suspected. It took an effort of imagination for them even to conceive of Wise as being not above suspicion. They knew as well as any other rare-book specialist the almost completely unquestioned prestige which he had enjoyed for four decades.* But youth is traditionally irreverent, and our bibliographers were young. Furthermore, they were scholars, and with scholars the first article of faith is skepticism.

In retrospect, Wise's connection with the forged nineteenth-century pamphlets had been amazingly diverse—far more so than would have been the case had he had only a normal book collector's interest in them. We have already seen that he had given the only known explanation of how the "Reading 1847" pamphlets had first come on the market. His account took on added interest when Carter and Pollard realized that it represented one of the very few attempts ever made to explain the pedigrees of *any* of the fifty-odd spurious pamphlets. It became even more curious when they looked into the history of the Dr. Bennett who had received "ten or twelve" mint copies of the "Reading 1847" pamphlet from Miss Mitford. Wise had published his story in 1918; Dr. Bennett (LL.D., University of Tusculum, 1869!) had died twenty-three years before. Although Bennett undoubtedly had known Miss Mitford, it was highly unlikely that he knew her well enough for her to entrust him before her death in 1855 with a dozen copies of a pamphlet whose printing she had undertaken for Mrs. Browning

* In 1922, however, John W. Draper, an American scholar, had printed some caustic remarks about Wise's bibliographical carelessness in a long review of the catalogue of the Wrenn Library. Draper remarked that some of the many blunders in that catalogue, for which Wise said he was responsible, "suggest an intentional desire to mislead." When he hastily added that "to accuse Mr. Wise of such a thing is unthinkable" he was anticipating almost the very phraseology that Carter and Pollard were to use twelve years later; one wonders if his intention, like theirs, was ironical.

under conditions of sacred secrecy. And apart from Wise's own statement there was no proof that Wise had ever known him.

While Wise's story of his buying a "Reading 1847" copy from Bennett had its suspicious aspects, it was actually the least important of his associations with the history of the forgeries, for it connected him with but one of the spurious items. But Carter and Pollard's further evidence entangled him with the pamphlets *en masse*, and not once, but time after time over a period of at least forty years. Taking the chief strands one by one, they found:

(1) Since there was no evidence that the Clay officials knew to what nefarious use their type and their presses were being put, the forger must have been well known to them and trusted by them. For some years the Clay firm were the printers for the Browning and Shelley societies, both of which specialized in reprinting in facsimile, in very limited editions, rare issues of books by their patron poets. This involved, of course, expert imitation of typography and format, which is perfectly legitimate printing routine if the resulting facsimiles are clearly labeled as such. It was singular, however, that a number of Browning and Shelley Society facsimile reprints bore an obvious family resemblance to the forgeries; they had in fact been made from the same paper and type. And a leading figure in these printing societies, who was known to have seen some of the reprints through Clay's press, was Thomas J. Wise.

(2) In addition to being experienced in the fine art of imitation through his connection with the Browning and Shelley societies, Wise was himself an acknowledged manufacturer of bibliographical rarities. There is a class of book collectors who are willing to pay high prices for minutely accurate facsimile reprints of originals which are too rare or expensive for any but the wealthiest, or the luckiest, collector ever to hope to own. Wise catered to this demand by issuing such reprints as that of Arnold's *Alaric in Rome*, which gave Carter and Pollard the clue that sent them to Clay's. As the owner of the superb Ashley Library of rarities, reproductions of which were in great demand simply because they were so rare, Wise was in an extremely favorable position to turn an honest pound or two. Thus there could be no possible question of his lifelong devotion to the profitable hobby of facsimile reprinting; actu-

ally he issued more than several scores of printed works and of manuscripts in his possession, in extremely limited editions.

(3) Ever since copies of the fifty-odd spurious pamphlets had begun to wander into collectors' hands in the 1890's, Wise had distinguished himself by his readiness to put in a good word for them on every occasion—and occasions presented themselves with gratifying frequency when a man had as many bibliographical irons in the fire as he had. As a pioneer devotee of the then new sport of collecting first editions rather than Elzevirs, and trial issues rather than Caxtons, he was in an extraordinarily good position to influence the thinking of every man who followed him in the sport. In retrospect, it seemed to have been almost the invariable rule that when a new bibliography of a nineteenth-century author appeared, the compiler, gratefully acknowledging the unstinted help of Thomas J. Wise, included certain pamphlets which earlier bibliographers of the same author had somehow overlooked. But Wise's influence was even more powerful when it was exerted directly through his own publications. In 1895–96 he and William Robertson Nicoll, the editor of the London *Bookman,* had published two volumes called *Literary Anecdotes of the Nineteenth Century,* which contained bibliographical essays in which the forged pamphlets played prominent roles. And from then until his death Wise was the tireless compiler of author-bibliographies intended primarily for his fellow collectors, a series climaxed by the monumental catalogue of his own Ashley Library. Although these highly specialized bibliographies are still almost indispensable handbooks for the study of the authors with whom they deal, their reputation has been reduced considerably by Carter and Pollard's demonstration that many of them were used to insinuate the forged pamphlets into the respectable company of genuine items. Since the work of Carter and Pollard opened the sluice gates of suspicion, scholars have shown over and over again that Wise's statements in the bibliographies, even on matters far removed from the proved forgeries, cannot be trusted.

(4) But Wise's interest in the prosperity of this large group of forged rarities was by no means confined to his placing the full weight of his immense bibliographical prestige behind them in bibliographies and catalogues. Carter and Pollard found that, with the grand gesture

beloved in bibliophiles, he had given copies of many of the forgeries to the libraries of both the British Museum and Cambridge University, thus making them, so to speak, official. But Wise was not always so philanthropic when—according to his own story—he was so lucky as to come across an occasional duplicate of a pamphlet he already owned. Although the rare-book trade is notorious for its reticence, Carter and Pollard managed to find out that Wise had supplied several friends with copies as he "found" them and presumably had been well paid. Indeed, luck had been so constantly with him that over a period of years he had managed to find for the American millionaire, John Henry Wrenn, an absolutely complete set of the forgeries—the only complete one in the world except his own, unless somewhere there exists another whose possessor, a decade and a half after Carter and Pollard's disclosures, is still too embarrassed to confess.*

(5) All this evidence of Wise's deep, almost paternal concern for the pamphlets did not, of course, prove that he was responsible for the marketing of any but the few copies he was known to have sold as "duplicates" from his own collection. Carter and Pollard still were faced by the mystery of how so many recorded copies had come to sale. Indeed, one of the first peculiarities they had noticed as they combed the sales records at the beginning of their adventure was the fact that a remarkably large number of pamphlets had been offered for sale through the regular rare-book channels with no indication of their former owner; and, as we have already noticed, they had a peculiar habit of turning up in well defined clusters, as if someone were systematically feeding them to the market. It was not impossible to trace the source of supply. He was one Herbert Gorfin, since 1912 an antiquarian bookseller in the south of London. Carter and Pollard had to consider the possibility that Gorfin himself was the forger; but their suspicion veered away from him when they learned that in his youth Gorfin had been Wise's own office boy and had, in that capacity, occasionally sold on commission copies of the forged pamphlets which Wise had given him for the purpose! Whatever lingering doubt they

---

* The Huntington Library in California has a set complete but for one item. The lack of this single item is perhaps atoned for by the presence at the Huntington of two additional Wise forgeries which Carter and Pollard missed.

had of Gorfin's honesty was dispelled when they interviewed him. His shocked manner convinced them beyond question that they brought him the first intimation he had ever had of his role in a gigantic fraud. Immediately Gorfin put his business records at the disposal of the inquirers; and from those files he himself drew out papers showing that between 1909 and 1912 he had bought literally hundreds of copies of the forgeries—all from Thomas J. Wise. And thus the mystery of how the pamphlets had got into the market was solved. Gorfin had been judiciously sending them up for sale as conditions warranted, taking care to space the lots so far apart as to preserve the appearance of rarity. But the real importance of Carter and Pollard's visit to Gorfin was that it laid the guilt squarely at the doorstep of the celebrated owner of the Ashley Library.

In October of 1933 Pollard visited Wise, an ailing man of seventy-four, and quietly laid most of his cards on the table. Wise professed complete surprise; he had never imagined such a thing; there must be some terrible mistake. . . . What did Carter and Pollard plan to do with this amazing evidence? Publish it, Pollard said; but naturally they wanted Wise's side of the story. After all, he had been prominently identified with the pamphlets from the beginning. His explanation of how he had acquired his copies would surely be most valuable. . . . Wise promised to review his memory and such records as he possessed, and then to send Carter and Pollard an account of what he knew of the forgeries. But they heard nothing from him, and on July 2, 1934, their own report issued from the press, which was —of all possible presses—that of Richard Clay & Sons.

In exposing the fraud, Carter and Pollard had to choose one of two courses: they could tax Wise, on the basis of their mass of circumstantial evidence, with the actual forgery of some fifty rare nineteenth-century pamphlets; or they could profess complete ignorance of the forger's identity and at the same time pillory Wise, the titan of modern bibliography, as an incredibly gullible fool, the pliant victim—for more than forty years!—of an unidentified master criminal. They chose the second course because, while the circumstantial evidence they possessed was to them utterly convincing, they still lacked the absolutely airtight case which was necessary to protect them in the event of legal action.

Their book, called with deliberate modesty *An Enquiry into the Nature of Certain Nineteenth Century Pamphlets*, is now a classic, not only because of its exciting step-by-step exposure of the crime, but because of its superb use of unrelenting, icily polite irony. The consistent understatement of the case, even to the confession, so deceptive in its humility, that "we have no conclusive evidence of the forger's identity," enabled Carter and Pollard to indict Wise more effectively in the amazed eyes of the world than any forthright "J'accuse!" could have done.

Before the *Enquiry* was published Wise, forewarned by Pollard's visit to him six months earlier and by the dreadful rumors which had reached his ears, began desperately to manufacture an alibi. Not knowing that his former office boy and commission agent had told what he knew, he summoned Gorfin posthaste to his home and offered him £400 for his remaining stock of the pamphlets. The only condition he imposed was that Gorfin support the proposed explanation that Wise had received the pamphlets in quantity from the late Harry Buxton Forman, a distinguished bibliographer and collector of Wise's own generation. On Carter and Pollard's advice, Gorfin accepted the offer for the pamphlets but at the same time specifically repudiated the Forman myth. Wise paid the £400, and the pamphlets were burned in the presence of his lawyers.

When, on the publication of the book, the London papers sent reporters to interview Wise he defended himself in general terms but added nothing to the known facts in the case. His full defense, such as it was, was offered in two letters to the *Times Literary Supplement*. In them he committed the incredibly stupid blunder of attempting to pass off the Buxton Forman story which Gorfin had already repudiated in private. Although his story received a kind of support from Forman's son, himself a distinguished scholar, it called forth a biting public letter from Gorfin which flatly denied that Wise had ever mentioned the elder Forman's name in connection with the pamphlets until he tried to buy back the remaining copies late in 1933.

Behind the scenes, meanwhile, there was a lively exchange, through a third party, between Wise on the one hand and Carter and Pollard, whom Wise was calling "sewer rats" in his private correspondence, on the other. The bibliographers warned Wise that, unless he dropped his attempt to pin the guilt on Forman without substantiating his charges, they would be forced to play a few cards they retained in their hand, such as the story of Wise's foolish attempt to suborn the witness Gorfin. The intermediary, impressed by the cards they still held, refused to serve further as Wise's agent in an evidently hopeless case.

There the affair rested for the time. After the first flurry of headlines and interviews, the readers of the daily press soon forgot all about it; but the morocco-leather world of booksellers, collectors, and scholars never ceased talking. To hundreds of bookmen on both sides of the Atlantic, the Carter-Pollard revelations came as a stunning shock. Tom Wise unmasked as a master criminal! It was about as credible as a discovery, some fine morning, that the whistling milkman who had served your neighborhood for twenty years was in the habit of dosing every hundredth bottle of milk with strychnine. Some of his old friends and associates still went to see him; but Mrs. Wise or the younger Buxton Forman was always present to intervene in case the visitor or Wise himself happened to bring up the forgeries. After the pathetically ineffectual defense in his letters to the *Times Literary Supplement* and his interviews with the press during that fateful summer, Wise lapsed into silence. In 1937 he carried his secret into the grave.

III

IN 1918 the University of Texas had received for its library the rare-book collection of the late Chicago millionaire, Wrenn. Now this collection had been built largely with the assistance of Wise himself, who for many years had been Wrenn's London agent and adviser. When the scandal broke in 1934 people's thoughts turned at once to the Wrenn Library, because it contained not only a resplendently complete file of the forgeries but also Wise's letters to Wrenn over a long period of years. Knowing that the letters might conceivably throw valuable light on Wise's guilt, the Wrenn librarian, Fannie Ratchford, began to examine them. They proved so interesting that they were eventually published by Alfred A. Knopf, with a long introductory essay by Miss Ratchford.

The book provides a fascinating narrative of Wise's relations with one of his dupes. The letters Wise and Wrenn exchanged were full of cordiality, which steadily increased as the years went by. As Wrenn's trusted representative, Wise acted in his behalf at all the London book auctions and private sales that contained items in the scope of Wrenn's collecting interest.

But the appalling aspect of Wise's role in the building of his American friend's library is the manner in which he used his genuine services as a blind for the sale of the forged pamphlets. The Wise-Wrenn letters are as instructive a handbook for confidence men—and as useful a warning for prospective victims—as Greene's coney-catching tracts were for their Elizabethan ancestors. Wise's standard method, as revealed in Miss Ratchford's volume, was a masterpiece of calculated craft. He was in no hurry. In a business letter to Wrenn, complacently reporting that he had been able to buy certain desired books at much less than the expected price, he would allude casually to a copy of an exceedingly rare nineteenth-century pamphlet which he had just heard was in the possession of, say, an elderly descendant of a friend of the author. Knowing that Wrenn lacked the item, Wise would promise to keep an ear to the ground. For several months or even years thereafter his letters would contain no reference to the booklet. Then, again slipped into a letter on current dealings, would occur a brief announcement that the elderly gentleman had just died: Wise would make inquiries as to the disposition of his books. Several months would elapse, then more news: after some trouble Wise had been allowed to see the books of the deceased; the much desired pamphlet was there, in mint condition, a magnificent buy! He would keep Wrenn informed. And finally, after another plausible lapse of time, a triumphant cry from "the prince of bibliographers": he had won the treasure, and because he already possessed a copy, as Wrenn was aware, the new find was on its way to Chicago! Time after time the process was repeated, and the guileless American sent checks to Wise for pamphlets which, as we now know, were fresh from Wise's own hoard.

The Wise-Wrenn letters, then, admirably supplemented the case of

Carter and Pollard by illustrating the way in which Wise disposed of his pamphlets, piece by piece. The general pattern of his operations as manufacturer of rarities is now clear. Exploiting his close association with the firm of Richard Clay, he had, for a period of at least ten years before 1900, superintended the manufacture of a stock representing over fifty separate titles, each in a quantity far in excess of the ten or twenty copies to which the edition supposedly had been limited. He then began to plant allusions to the various items in the standard works of reference on their respective authors, in a few cases, such as that of the "Reading 1847" item, providing accounts of the circumstances under which they allegedly were issued. At the same time, capitalizing upon his unblemished reputation as a bibliographer and collector, he presented or sold copies to a few of his fellow collectors, thereby giving them a personal interest in expanding and substantiating the general reliance upon the booklets' authenticity. When the bibliographical reputation of each pamphlet was thus established beyond reasonable doubt, he began to filter copies upon the market, either through his own personal connections with collectors or through Gorfin. Although he disposed of quantities of the forgeries as "remainders" to Gorfin in 1912, he seems to have retained a sufficient stock for his own occasional use. After the Carter-Pollard sensation in 1934, one American bookseller recalled a visit he had paid to Wise's library some time before. Wise, wishing to find a certain volume which had come up in the course of their conversation, asked his visitor to open a drawer in a secretary. The American by mistake opened another drawer—and there, to his profound shock, he glimpsed a whole pile of unbound sheets of the "Reading 1847" forgery!

Wise's guilt today is proved seemingly beyond doubt. But one question—and an important one—remains unanswered. Are we to believe that he worked entirely singlehanded? Did none of the expert collectors with whom he was in constant personal association, and who prized copies of his various forgeries in their own rich libraries, ever suspect what he was up to? Was his maneuvering so clever, and his personal plausibility so hypnotizing, as to quiet any small stirring of doubt? Or, to take the other extreme possibility, is it conceivable that some of these gentlemen were in active connivance with him?

One or two passages in Carter and Pollard's book excited suspicions against two eminent contemporaries of Wise's: Sir Edmund Gosse and Harry Buxton Forman. The debate over their innocence or guilt, begun in 1934, was fanned to new flame by the publication of the Wise-Wrenn letters in 1944.

To take Sir Edmund first. We have already seen that he was the first to tell the story of the printing of the "Reading 1847" sonnets, which he said had been told him by an unnamed friend. The Carter-Pollard revelations point almost certainly to Wise as the friend. Wise's motive was, of course, to obtain printed authority for the genuineness of his forged Browning item at the time when he was beginning to circulate it. But was Gosse innocent of Wise's intent? If he was, why did he silently set the date of the famous breakfast table episode back the two years necessary to give credibility to the forged pamphlet?

Before Gosse's death in 1928, the discrepancy between his story of the breakfast table and that provided by other, unimpeachable, sources had been called to his attention. On that occasion he had reaffirmed that he had had the story, including the date and place, from Browning's own lips at a time when Browning knew that Gosse was taking notes. But, significantly, Gosse was vague about the exact year in which the conversation had occurred. I say "significantly" because the element in Gosse's make-up which has been fatal to his reputation as a scholar may be the salvation of his character as a man. He has long been known, on grounds far removed from the Wise affair, to have been not the most meticulous of scholars. His literary histories and biographies, with all their charm of manner and frequent flashes of critical acuteness, are thoroughly careless as to fact. If it were not for its fateful connection with Wise's most notorious forgery, his slip in the dating and placing of the breakfast table story would simply have taken its place among hundreds of similar inaccuracies in his books. It has been shown, furthermore, that this particular error was present in at least one book on the Brownings several years before Gosse recited it and before the forgery which it "authenticated" is thought to have been committed. There remains, then, the saving possibility that Gosse was simply repeating an older error, and that its connection with the "Reading 1847" pamphlet was entirely fortuitous—or that, as has recently been suggested, Wise seized upon his friend's innocent blunder as a gift from heaven, designed to serve his own rather uncelestial purpose.

Otherwise the case against Gosse, which has been prosecuted with tireless vigor by Miss Ratchford, rests on evidence offered by a written correction on a proof sheet of one of the forgeries, Mrs. Browning's *The Runaway Slave*, which Wise had "procured" for Wrenn. It is the single word "mangoes" written in the margin as a correction for a misprint. Miss Ratchford is convinced that the word is in Gosse's handwriting. In the hope of obtaining expert corroboration, she sent the proof sheet, along with authentic specimens of Gosse's handwriting, to the Identification Division of the Texas Department of Public Safety. These gentlemen, however, reported that the single word was insufficient evidence on which to base an opinion; a decision which reflects favorably upon the condition of justice in Texas. Few authorities, it may be said, share Miss Ratchford's certainty that Gosse figured in the Wise crime, unless as an innocent accessory.

Students of the Wise forgeries are more inclined to share Miss Ratchford's suspicions of Harry Buxton Forman. For one thing, it was noticed by Carter and Pollard that Forman, two years after Gosse had first put into print the story of the "Reading 1847" sonnets, delicately expressed his doubts of that story. "In three charming pages of picturesque writing," he wrote, "we get brought together the floating traditions of the episode, and over them is thrown the glamour of the personal acquaintance between Browning and his bright chronicler. Of course Mr. Gosse does not expect all this to be taken too seriously or literally." Forman, who must have selected the word "traditions" with malice aforethought, concluded by expressing the hope that Gosse would divulge the name of the "mysterious friend" to whom he said he owed the story of Miss Mitford and the Reading printer.

This is a puzzling passage. If Forman had his suspicions, why did he not pursue the truth of the matter? In his subsequent published writings there is no further reference to the "1847" sonnets. But he is known to have possessed not only a copy of this pamphlet but copies of over thirty of its sister forgeries. As we have seen, when in 1934 Wise found that Carter and Pollard had exploded his tale of Dr. Bennett's cache of the Browning sonnets, he hurriedly built a new story around Buxton Forman and feebly buttressed it by a statement supplied for the occasion by Forman's son. Why did Wise, in his frantic attempt to cover up, try to shift the blame to the elder Forman? Because Forman had died in 1917 and therefore could be depended upon not to reply? Or because he knew that Forman's hands were themselves not clean, and that he could therefore put pressure on his son? The peculiarly ironic, taunting tone of the passage in which Forman referred to the forged "1847" sonnets suggested that at least he knew much more about Wise's clandestine activities than Wise could have wished.

In their anxiety not to allow Wise to draw a red herring across their trail, Carter and Pollard probably underestimated the chances of Forman's involvement. At any rate, by a small and entirely forgivable mistake, they overlooked one avenue of investigation which paid off handsomely not long ago. In their *Enquiry* they referred to an article in Nicoll and Wise's *Literary Anecdotes of the Nineteenth Century* on "The Building of the *Idylls,*" some statements in which added credibility to several of the forged Tennyson items. Carter and Pollard assumed that the unsigned article was by Wise, who was one of the editors of the work, and thus provided one link between him and the forgeries which has not stood the test of later investigation.

In the wake of the great disclosure of 1934 came a brief pamphlet written by Dr. Gabriel Wells, the New York rare-book dealer, in a futile attempt to defend Wise. Wells pointed out that the article on Tennyson's *Idylls* had been written not by Wise but by Forman. He knew, because he had bought the manuscript, along with the proof and revises, at the sale of Forman's books in 1920.

At this point the clue was picked up by Carl H. Pforzheimer, one of the most celebrated of contemporary American book collectors. Mr. Pforzheimer recalled that the manuscript and proofs to which Wells referred were at that moment in his own library. After going through them, he showed them to Miss Ratchford and Mr. Carter, both of whom were duly impressed. Both of them, however, were committed to secrecy as to the actual contents of the packet. It took ten years for Miss Ratchford and other interested scholars to persuade

Mr. Pforzheimer to consent to the publication of his evidence. The result was the appearance, late in 1945, of a small volume entitled *Between the Lines*, published at the University of Texas under the editorship of Miss Ratchford. Now the cat *was* out of the bag, for this elegant little brochure contained proof that the eminent Harry Buxton Forman, collector, bibliographer, and editor, had at the very least been privy to Wise's adventure in crime.

When Forman's essay on "The Building of the *Idylls*" was being prepared for the press in 1896, the proof sheets passed back and forth between him and Wise. Both wrote frequent comments between the lines, on the margins, and even on separate slips of paper, so that in effect we have preserved for us in Mr. Pforzheimer's packet—and reproduced in facsimile in Miss Ratchford's book—a written dialogue, often ill humored, between Wise and Forman. The crowning interest of the Pforzheimer packet lies in a sentence occurring during a heated interlinear controversy between the two. The point at issue was the morality of Wise's studiedly ambiguous use of the term "a few copies" in connection with the issue of one of his artificial rarities—in this instance not a forgery, but a facsimile edition openly avowed by him. Forman, taking the side of the angels, protested against Wise's letting people think he had printed only, say, ten copies of the item when in actuality he had printed thirty. "Quite so," replied Wise. "And we print 'Last Tournament' * in 1896, and want 'some one to think' it was printed in 1871!"

There we have Wise's own confession of his guilt—the only scrap of direct evidence we possess, but a damning one. In two short sentences it gives away the secret which Carter and Pollard labored many months to uncover. More than that, it establishes that Buxton Forman knew what Wise was up to: not only issuing "rare" facsimiles in editions that were not so limited as he wished people to think, but above all, manufacturing outright forgeries. What the pronoun "we" implies— whether Forman was actually a coforger, whether his role was limited to that of an accessory after the fact, and whether the pronoun embraces other persons—is still undecided. Miss Ratchford, who has no confidence in anyone associated with the Wise circle, would, I think,

* One of Carter and Pollard's proved forgeries.

make Forman a defendant coequal with Wise, with all the honors and privileges thereunto appertaining.

That is the story of the Wise forgeries down to date. Sordid though it may sometimes appear, revealing an unexpectedly seamy side of a generally respectable science, it has certain features that would, I think, have delighted Aristotle if that gentleman had been of a bibliographical turn of mind. If the essence of tragedy consists in the fall of a hero from the heights of reputation to utter ruin, the saga of Thomas J. Wise is a tragedy. It would be possible to make an anthology of the praises that were sung of his name before the calamity of 1934. In his special field he reigned supreme; his word was law to all of his subjects, just as his library was the envy and despair of them all. But the day that Carter and Pollard revealed the fruits of their investigation, he shrank to the stature of a common.criminal.

What, we may well inquire, was the tragic flaw that brought about the catastrophe? Up to 1934, Wise's reputation had been virtually unblemished for the sufficient reason that there was nothing to be alleged against him. Although casual acquaintances found him blunt and somewhat magisterial, his scholarship, despite a tendency toward dogmatism, was generally regarded as sound, exact, and exhaustive; his business credit was unquestioned; and his personal life, while somewhat dull, was beyond reproach. The reasons why he embarked on his career of fraud, printing substantial stocks of fifty different forgeries within little more than a decade and then marketing them for three decades more, may always remain obscure. Perhaps the most acceptable explanation is that, as is attested by the numbers of otherwise virtuous men who have a persistent compulsion to steal books from libraries, the disease of bibliomania is sometimes attended by moral complications. In his youth, when the disease first struck, Wise was poor—a condition that is never comfortable at best, but that is a really intolerable nuisance when one is obsessed with the ambition to build up a library of rare books. So long as he had only his meager salary as clerk in an essential-oils house, Wise could not hope to buy the books he craved. But when he began to have a hand in the facsimile-printing activities of the Browning and Shelley societies, a new vista of possibility opened before him. Perhaps he began by selling copies of the legitimate facsimiles, which, when they were relieved of the title-pages proclaiming them to be facsimiles, he could easily pass off as original issues. His experiment meeting with success, he then struck out for himself, creating his own special brand of imitations which were actually fictitious first editions. With the pocket money thus acquired, he was able to build the foundations of the great Ashley Library.

Later, when he had succeeded in the essential-oils business, Wise had less need of this extra source of income. By shrewd dealing both in oils and in books—the classic example of his talents in the latter field being his cornering of Swinburne's library and papers before the poet was cold in the grave—he managed to put sufficient change in his purse to indulge his collector's mania. A less imaginative man might then have decided to let well enough alone: he had succeeded in foisting his fabrications upon the finest judges in the kingdom, and thereby obtained the money he needed—what more could he ask? But Wise by this time had become fascinated by his clandestine hobby. He had had an immense amount of sheer intellectual satisfaction in slipping his books into the market one by one, each scrupulously harmonized with the known facts of its author's life. The unquestioning acceptance of his authority by all the experts had been exquisitely sweet to a man of his vanity. And so, when the pamphlets had outlasted the need to which they owed their existence, Wise kept playing with them simply for the sardonic pleasure of gulling men who, in their absurd arrogance, prided themselves on knowing their way around the world of books.*

It may be that Thomas James Wise, the deposed prince of bibliographers, is now stewing in a region ruled by another fallen prince, who is also not unknown to the students of literature. If there is any justice at all in hell, his assigned place of abode is a luxuriously furnished alcove called, perhaps, the Ghastly Library. In it are a hundred thousand rare volumes, half of them genuine and half of them the most diabolically ingenious forgeries that the devil's bibliographical disciples could devise; and Wise's eternal task is to try to tell the true

---

* George Bernard Shaw recently expressed the opinion that Wise conducted the whole gigantic, forty-year fraud simply for the sake of hoaxing—as a genial practical joke. The view has been accepted no more seriously than Mr. Shaw perhaps meant it to be.

issues from the false. As he works at it day after day, his eyes often wander to an inscription carved for his encouragement above the asbestos-rock fireplace. It is a sentence he himself once wrote, when success had puffed him up and blinded him to its possible prophetic import. And what agony it had caused the author when it mocked him from the malicious motto-page of Carter and Pollard's book!

THE WHOLE THING PROVES ONCE MORE THAT, EASY AS IT APPEARS TO BE TO FABRICATE REPRINTS OF RARE BOOKS, IT IS IN ACTUAL PRACTICE ABSOLUTELY IMPOSSIBLE TO DO SO IN SUCH A MANNER THAT DETECTION CANNOT FOLLOW THE RESULT.

THREE

THE QUEST OF THE KNIGHT-PRISONER

IN the year 1485 there issued from the press of England's first printer, William Caxton, a volume he called the *Morte Darthur*. Although only one perfect copy of the original edition now exists, the influence of the work was destined to be tremendous. Henceforth the multifarious stories of King Arthur and his knights of the Round Table, which, in their long-winded French and Middle English texts, had been for centuries the favorite fireside reading of lords and ladies throughout western Europe, would be preserved in colloquial English. The work was, indeed, a late fifteenth-century Portable King Arthur, into which the English author had distilled the very essence of the wonderful Arthurian legend. A classic of literature in its own right, because of the author's narrative genius and his sense of racy, realistic prose, it is one of the few books (the Bible being, of course, another) which have had an almost continuous influence both on English literary style and on the subject matter of later literature.

In his notable Preface, Caxton said that he had printed the *Morte Darthur* "after a copye unto me delyverd, whyche copye syr Thomas Malorye dyd take oute of certeyn bookes of Frensshe and reduced it into Englysshe." And at the very end of the book, having seen Lancelot's body borne to the Joyous Gard for burial and having, Dickenslike, tied up numerous loose ends of narrative, the author himself wrote:

I praye you all Ientyl men and Ientyl wymmen that redeth this book of Arthur and hys knyghtes . . . praye for me whyle I am on lyue that god sende me good delyueraunce & whan I am deed I praye you all praye for my soule for this book was ended the ix yere of the reygne of kyng edward the fourth by syr Thomas Maleore knyght as Ihesu helpe hym for hys grete myght as he is the seruaunt of Ihesu bothe day and nyght.

This passage is largely conventional. Medieval writers almost automatically concluded their poem or prose piece with the same sort of explicit, or pious coda, saying in effect, whether it was strictly true or not, "I am a devoted servant of my God. And may all grateful readers of what I have here written pray for my well-being in life and my salvation after death." Since the phrase about good deliverance was a familiar formula, no one ever seems to have been struck by the possibility that it might have special significance in Malory's case. If anyone had had such an idea, and then tried to discover by research just what it was from which Malory so earnestly prayed good deliverance, the great mystery of his identity might have been solved earlier than it was.

For it *was* a mystery, which lasted more than four centuries. Despite the fame of his book, and the natural desire of many generations of readers and critics and historians to know something of the background and character of the man who was responsible for it, absolutely nothing was known of Sir Thomas Malory until the last sixty years. The restoration of the man as a figure in history has been one of the most exciting achievements of modern scholarship, the more exciting because the figure that has been rescued from the mists of oblivion is one that nobody bargained for.

Late in the nineteenth century several scholars made ineffectual attempts to identify Malory. Having found records of various families bearing the name, they assumed that Sir Thomas belonged to one or another of them, and let it go at that. But it was not until George Lyman Kittredge of Harvard, early in his illustrious career as scholar, attacked the problem systematically and with his usual amazing thoroughness that any progress was made. Whereas previous investigators had found but a few Malorys in history, Kittredge began by unearthing the names and habitations of hundreds of persons who lived in England before 1485 and were named Malory, Mallore, Maulore, Mallere, Malure, Mallery, Maleore, and so forth. Since medieval spelling was always flexible, especially in family names, these records were all possible clues at least to the writer's family. But to qualify as the author of the *Morte Darthur*, any Malory found in the historical records would, according to the evidence deduced from the book itself, have had not only to be named Thomas, but to be a knight, alive in the ninth year of Edward IV's reign (March 4, 1469, to March 3, 1470), and old enough at that time to write the book. Any Sir Thomas Malorys aged, say, eleven in 1470 need not apply.

From his large collection of Malorys, Kittredge isolated the sole figure who fitted all these requirements. He was the Sir Thomas Malory of Newbold Revel, Warwickshire, whose life (or the more seemly part of it, at any rate) had been outlined in print as long ago as 1656, in Sir William Dugdale's *Antiquities of Warwickshire*, one of the many great old-fashioned tomes of local history and genealogy that are the despair and sometimes the joy of modern researchers. Although Dugdale's work was standard for Warwickshire, and was in constant use by Shakespeare students, looking for ancestors or neighbors of the poet, nobody before Kittredge seems ever to have paused over the lines devoted to Sir Thomas Malory.

This Malory, Kittredge found in Dugdale, had been member of Parliament for his county in 1445 and had died on March 14, 1471. If he had a talent for English prose, he could have written the *Morte Darthur*. Whether he did or not, Kittredge had no way of knowing; but the possibility of his having done so, there being no other Malory in sight who suited the requirements, was enough to give interest to such meager further facts as Dugdale offered. Malory, Dugdale recorded, came of a family long settled in Warwickshire, and his father had held high local offices and had sat in Parliament. It was conceivable, then, that Sir Thomas had had a gentleman's education, the advantages of which were by no means universally enjoyed by men even of his superior station in the fifteenth century. But most suggestive of all was the fact that Malory early in life had been in the retinue of Richard de Beauchamp, Earl of Warwick, during the French wars. Beauchamp, as Kittredge pointed out, was recognized by all Europe "as embodying the knightly ideal of the age. The Emperor Sigismund . . . said to Henry V 'that no prince Christen for wisdom, norture, and manhode, hadde such another knyght as he had of therle [the Earl] Warrewyk; addyng therto that if al curtesye were lost, yet myght hit be founde ageyn in hym; and so ever after by the emperours auctorite he was called the Fadre of Curteisy.' " The very events of Warwick's life, indeed, were like pages out of the *Morte Darthur*. There could be no doubt, therefore, that even if this Malory had not written the *Morte Darthur*, his early association with a liege lord who behaved like a star member of the Round Table had admirably equipped him to do so.

Kittredge first printed his identification of Malory in an encyclopedia article published in 1894. Without having seen that article, an Englishman named Williams two years later announced his independent discovery of another record concerning a Sir Thomas Malory who could have been the author of the *Morte Darthur*. In an ancient manuscript at Wells Cathedral in England, Williams found that "Thomas Malorie, *miles*," along with several others, was specifically excluded from a general pardon issued by Edward IV in 1468. The record gave no hint as to why Malory was in need of a pardon, or why the King took pains to deny it to him. In any. case, Kittredge immediately assumed (rightly, as later discoveries were to prove) that this man and the one he had found mentioned in Dugdale were identical.

There the whole matter rested for twenty-five years, and in the interim the books that had occasion to speak of the *Morte Darthur* simply said that it might have been written by the gentleman from Newbold Revel who served with Richard de Beauchamp at Calais and died in 1471. This information was more than books published before Kittredge's announcement had contained; but it served only to sharpen the appetite for more relevant data.

In the early 1920's, several additional bits of data on a man (or separate men) named Thomas Malory were found. One was a brief mention, in a document from 1443, that one Thomas Smythe accused a man of that name of stealing goods and chattels. Another was an equally curt and tantalizing record that in 1451 Henry VI had had to intervene in some sort of dispute between a Malory and the Carthusian monks of the Priory of Axholme, Lincolnshire. A third document revealed that in the following year a warrant was out for Malory's arrest "to answer certain charges," unspecified. Finally, E. K. Chambers, who had discovered two of the preceding records, also found that Malory had been excluded from the terms of a second royal pardon in 1468, five months after the one earlier discovered by Williams. There was nothing specifically to connect the men named in these records with each other, or with the man discovered by Kittredge and Williams. There might, of course, have been more than one Sir Thomas Malory in the fifteenth century. But if there had been, it was remarkable that all of them seemed to share the same weakness for getting into trouble. However, the next discovery settled the question.

A device frequently used by historians to distinguish between two men of the same name who lived at the same time and in the same place is to assemble the available evidence into a presumptive pattern of conduct for at least one of them. If one John Smith can be proved to have been a rake and the other an ascetic, and if subsequently the record of a paternity suit is found naming an otherwise unidentified John Smith, the probability will be that the culprit was the former and not the latter. In the case of Malory, what clinched the matter was the neatness with which the evidence found by our next researcher fitted into the pattern already established.

This is what happened. In the mid-1920's, a former student of Kittredge's named Edward Hicks went to the Public Record Office in London determined to find, in that vast haystack of government documents, a needle or two pertaining to the career of the man who wrote the *Morte Darthur*. If anyone found anything he wanted in the first few weeks of his labors at the Public Record Office, his case would probably be seized upon by a society for psychical research. Hicks's experience followed the usual course. He looked through the obvious files, those of criminal cases tried in Warwickshire, without success. Like every worker in the P.R.O., he then had occasion to curse the disposition of arrangers of public records to relegate documents difficult to classify to the "Miscellaneous" file—thus saving themselves infinite labor and guaranteeing it to posterity. In this instance some old overworked clerk turned out to have lumped great masses of papers relating to fifteenth-century criminal cases under the capacious title "Divers Counties"—meaning, presumably, all the counties of England. Hicks took a long breath and plunged in. "After a prolonged turning over of parchment strips," he writes, "—some long, some short, and all more or less faded—and noting how in the fifteenth century the counties of 'Myddx' and Essex appeared to be responsible for most of the crime of England, the welcome words 'In Com. Warr.' attracted attention." Good: having gone through Middlesex and Essex, Hicks had come to a felony in the county of Warwick, and Malory was a Warwickshire man. He unrolled the parchment so labeled and found that it related to a stabbing affray in the streets of Warwick. Interesting enough, but no Malory was mentioned. More old parchments to turn over, no luck. Then another roll marked "In Com. Warr." Hicks opened it. "The document, of course, was in Latin, and a portion of the right-hand edge of it had been somewhat damaged; but, halfway down, the eye was caught and held by two words—'Thomas Malory'—written with almost copper-plate clearness. The hunt was over, the quarry secured!"

What Hicks held in his hands was the record of an inquisition (similar to a modern grand-jury hearing) held at Nuneaton, Warwickshire, on August 23, 1451. It recited an eight-count indictment drawn up against Sir Thomas Malory and presented to a commission composed of officials whose prominence in the county suggested that this was no ordinary occasion. Sir Thomas Malory, knight, was in trouble.

In fact, the future author of the *Morte Darthur* had been the ringleader in a Warwickshire crime wave. In chronological order (not the order given in the actual indictment) these had been his alleged offenses in the past year and a half:

January 4, 1450.* He and "26 other malefactors and breakers of the King's Peace, armed and arrayed in a warlike manner," had tried to ambush Humphrey, Duke of Buckingham. (They missed him, and Humphrey was now sitting, in defiance of what we would today consider the delicacies of legal procedure, on the bench at the hearing.)

May 23, 1450. Malory broke into the house of Hugh Smyth "and feloniously raped Joan, the wife of the said Hugh."

May 31, 1450. He extorted "by threats and oppression" from Mar-

* The authorities who have studied the records of Malory's career do not always agree on the exact dates of the various episodes. I have followed Vinaver's dating wherever a choice had to be made.

garet Kyng and William Hales, at Monks Kirby, his own parish, the sum of 100 shillings.

August 6, 1450. He made a return visit to Hugh Smyth's domicile, "feloniously raped Joan" (again!), and stole forty pounds' worth of Hugh's property.

August 31, 1450. He extorted twenty shillings from John Mylner, also of Monks Kirby.

June 4, 1451. Malory went across the border into Leicestershire and there took "seven cows, two calves, a cart worth £4, and 335 sheep worth £22," driving the whole lot back to his home at Newbold Revel.

(July 23, 1451. At this point the law caught up with Sir Thomas Malory. Astonishingly, the offense that finally delivered him into the King's custody was none of the foregoing but rather one which is not even mentioned in the Nuneaton indictment, although Hicks found it recorded in another document. That was the unpleasantness, not further specified, between Malory and the Carthusian monks at Axholme Priory, which, as Chambers had earlier discovered, had already forced the King to intervene in the interests of the peace. Malory might have gone on blithely committing his larcenies, rapes, and extortions, and the law might have gazed the other way—but this dispute with the monks evidently was too serious to be ignored. The result was, at long last, that he was clapped into Coventry jail.)

July 25, 1451. Stone walls do not a prison make, at least not one that could hold Sir Thomas. No sooner was he thrown into a cell than he broke jail, swam the deep, wide, sewage-filled moat, and escaped into the night.

July 28, 1451. Sir Thomas acted swiftly. He and several other men of various social stations were at the head of a large band of "malefactors and breakers of the King's peace in the manner of an insurrection" who assembled before the Cistercian Abbey of Blessed Mary at Coombe, near the knight's ancestral home of Newbold Revel, stove in its doors with great wooden battering rams, and ransacked the abbot's coffers over his vigorous protests and those of his monks and servants. When the invaders departed, they bore loot consisting of a substantial sum of money, together with jewels and ornaments belonging to the abbey church.

July 29, 1451. Incredible though it may seem, Malory allegedly led a return visit to the abbey the very next day, breaking down eighteen doors, insulting the abbot to his face, forcing open three iron chests, and escaping with more money and jewels and two bows and three sheaves of arrows.*

At that point Malory was rearrested, and Warwickshire and its surrounding counties breathed easier. In due time, the fifteen members of the grand jury, good and true, returned a true bill on all counts of the indictment.

It will now be convenient, as we proceed with our story, to merge the facts Hicks unearthed relating to Malory's subsequent career with the further ones discovered several years later by Professor Albert C. Baugh of the University of Pennsylvania. Baugh was working at the Public Record Office on a quest unrelated to Malory when he stumbled upon certain hitherto unknown fifteenth-century legal documents in which the errant knight's name figured. These provided him with clues which led him to a sheaf of about twenty additional documents, all of them helping to fill in the gaps in Malory's record. The following brief narrative is based on the combined data found by Hicks and Baugh, with the addition of one or two details found earlier and already mentioned in these pages.

Malory, then, stood indicted of the crimes alleged in the Nuneaton indictment. Within the next year all his accomplices had received sentences, most of them being outlawed. Malory, however, was taken before the King's court at Westminster and pleaded not guilty. Evidently he did not come to trial (indeed, there is no record of his ever having actually been tried by a jury, although he was on the verge of it several times), and within a year, or at the most two, he was again at liberty. From the contemporary records we may infer that it had been virtually a habit with the authorities to arrest Sir Thomas Malory

---

* Hicks suggests that this count of the indictment referred, like the preceding one, to the raid of July 28, and that there was in fact only one attack on the abbey. Although every student of the life of Malory since Hicks has assumed that there were two separate raids, the similarity of the charges contained in the two counts, especially the virtually duplicate estimates of the monetary value of the loot, gives credibility to his suggestion. The charges growing out of the July 28 affair may have been repeated simply to emphasize the heinousness of the crime.

every time he went free, whether lawfully or otherwise. So it was in 1453. Malory was brought to the Marshalsea Prison, and early in the next year, for reasons we may be allowed to guess, the government thought it advisable to issue a reminder to his custodian, the Knight Marshal, that he was to take care not to let Malory go free. No doubt the Marshal was relieved when Malory found bail a few months later (May, 1454) and could legally be released. This was the third time Malory had left prison, but it was not to be the last.

What did Malory do with his new-found freedom? What had he done a few years earlier, when he had emerged, dripping, on the far side of the moat outside Coventry jail? He had led the raid on Coombe Abbey. If it is permissible sometimes to reconstruct biography on the basis of the known proclivities of one's hero, one would surmise that on this new occasion he reverted to form. And so, apparently, he did. Baugh found that some time between 1452 and 1456—the record is not clear as to the precise date—Malory was accused by Katherine, wife of Sir William Peyto, of having stolen from her manor in Northamptonshire four oxen belonging to her bailiff, and driving them to his estate at Newbold Revel, which seems to have been a major depot for stolen goods. (Charmingly enough, Malory's memories of this incident were revived when Katherine's husband, Sir William, was sent up for assault and joined Malory in the Marshalsea Prison in 1456.) Was the ox-stealing episode the first fruit of Malory's liberation? We cannot be sure, but dating it at this time delights one's sense of fitness.

The terms under which he had been released in May, 1454, required that he appear before the court on the following October 29 for further action on his long pending case. But when that date rolled round, his sureties appeared in court without Malory. "Where is Sir Thomas?" inquired the court. "In jail," replied his bondsmen, bitterly.

Yes, he was in again. At least he was enjoying a measure of variety: he had never before had an opportunity to sample the food provided in the jail at Colchester, Essex, where he was detained "under suspicion of felony." This time it was the company he had been keeping. Although perhaps not a direct participant in John Aleyn's felonious enterprises, he was known to have given aid and comfort to that gentleman as he conducted a series of horse thefts in Essex villages during May and June. Furthermore, while enjoying Malory's hospitality and, no doubt, benefiting by his advice, Aleyn had plotted a housebreaking, which unfortunately had been interrupted at an awkward moment. It was as a result of these activities, which would sadden the heart of any parole officer, that Malory was now entered on the rolls of Colchester jail.

The court in London, upon hearing that Malory was detained in the provinces, immediately issued a writ to the Essex jailer, commanding him to send his prisoner to London. But the writ arrived too late: for the second time in his career, Malory, armed with daggers and swords, had broken jail. He had less than three weeks this time in which to carry out any plans, larcenous or otherwise, he may have had in mind, because the law caught up with him, and on November 18 he was delivered to the court in London, which forthwith ordered him back to his old domicile in the Marshalsea.

It was at this juncture that Malory became the hapless battledore in a game of shuttlecock played by the keepers of no fewer than four London jails. For reasons still unknown to us, the government kept transferring him from one prison to another. From the Marshalsea he was sent to the Tower. In February, 1456, he made a bid for freedom by flourishing in the faces of the court a pardon he had received from the Duke of York (the King being incapacitated at the time) for all felonies, transgressions, and so on committed before the preceding July. This was a potent argument for liberation; but bail was still required, and Malory could not raise it. For fairly obvious reasons, his former sureties had decided that they could put their money to better use than in guaranteeing the peaceable behavior of a man who might be depended upon to land back in jail within a few weeks. So Malory was sent, this time, to the Marshalsea. Within a year his place of residence became the Newgate, and in the course of nine months in 1457 his custody shifted from the Newgate to the Ludgate, to the Marshalsea, to the Sheriffs of London, and back to the Marshalsea. By this time he probably was dizzy, and welcomed the few months of liberty which were his at the end of the year, when he finally succeeded in raising bail. But before the year was out, he was back in the Marshalsea. It was now six years since his raid on Coombe

Abbey (which seems to have been his most serious offense in the eyes of the law); and, so far as we know, he had not yet come to trial.

But Malory still was not reconciled to the life of a chronic prisoner; his prayer, in the *Morte Darthur*, for "good deliverance" plainly came from the heart. Somehow in 1458 or 1459 he got out of the Marshalsea once more, because a document dated from the Easter season of 1459 records that he was at large in Warwickshire, and curtly directs the Knight Marshal to bring him back and keep him in jail. The order has a familiar ring.

The next year (1460) Malory was transferred once more, this time to Newgate, the prison which was fifteenth-century England's nearest approach to the Bastille—a place where dangerous or politically inconvenient characters could be detained indefinitely at the King's pleasure. But in 1462-63 he was free again; so much we know from records noting that he was with the Earl of Warwick on a military expedition. Five years later (1468), as we have seen, he was specifically excluded from the two general pardons issued to the Lancastrians by the Yorkist King, Edward IV. That fact, however, does not necessarily mean that he was in jail at the time. Apart from these meager data, Malory's whereabouts between 1460 and his death in March, 1471 is unknown, except for clues lately given us, as I shall show, in his own writings.

Although we know that Malory was out of jail for a period in 1462-63, it is tempting to assume that he was in Newgate at least most of the time between 1460 and 1471, simply because to hypothesize his presence there, rather than in another jail or even at liberty, provides a convenient explanation of how he obtained the books from which he made his own. For lawbreakers whose tastes were literary and whose suits were forlorn, the Newgate was most happily situated. Just across the road was the monastery of the order of the Gray Friars; and within the monastery was an excellent library, to the establishment of which no less a personage than the former Lord Mayor of London, the almost legendary Dick Whittington, had contributed a substantial sum. Perhaps Malory heard from the older inhabitants of the Newgate that a former illustrious captive, the bibliophile Charles, Duke of Orléans, had improved his years of captivity by borrowing manuscript books from across the way. However that may be, it seems fairly certain that it was from the Gray Friars Library that Malory, by buying such privileges from his keepers, got the "certain books of French" (and others in English which Caxton failed to mention) upon which he based his own English synthesis of the Arthurian legend.

If, that is, the Malory who seems to have been the very personification of the habitual criminal *was* the Malory who wrote the *Morte Darthur!* But so far we have not seen a shred of evidence, apart from the identity of the names, to connect the two. On the one side we have the numerous records, found in the past half-century or so, of a cattle-stealing, abbey-raiding, raping, extorting, jail-breaking Malory, and on the other the two pieces of evidence in the *Morte Darthur* itself that its author was named Sir Thomas Malory. Until only a few years ago, Malory was in precisely the state, historically speaking, in which Chaucer remains today. Diligent research has dug up a fairly large assortment of evidence relating to the official positions, the business and legal transactions, and the personal relationships of a fourteenth-century Geoffrey Chaucer; but there is still no positive proof that this man was the author of the *Canterbury Tales*, although no one today doubts that he was. In Malory's case the link *has* been found, through a dramatic discovery which has thrown a flood of light on the composition of the *Morte Darthur*. To show how that proof came into the open, we must take temporary leave of criminology and turn to the purer air of literature.

As was mentioned at the very opening of this chapter, only one perfect copy of Caxton's original edition of the *Morte Darthur* is known to exist. For it the late J. Pierpont Morgan paid in 1911 the then amazing price of $42,800, and it is now in the Morgan Library in New York. Only one other copy, lacking eleven leaves, exists; it is owned by the John Rylands Library in Manchester.

Early in the summer of 1934, W. F. Oakeshott, then the librarian of the Fellows' Library in Winchester College, the ancient English public school, was examining the contents of that collection in search of some item he needed. By accident he came upon a manuscript volume which had lost eight leaves at both the beginning and the end.

A cursory examination was enough to show that it was a manuscript of the *Morte Darthur*, dating from the time of Malory himself. Where it came from, no one knows; it had been in the Winchester library as early as 1839, but when it was catalogued in that year its identity was not discovered because it lacked beginning and end, and nobody had taken the trouble to look at it further.

At the time of its discovery, the greatest authority on Malory, Professor Eugène Vinaver of the University of Manchester, was about to complete a new edition of the *Morte Darthur*, based on the two extant printed copies. As soon as he examined the Winchester manuscript, he realized that a great deal of his text would have to be revised, because the manuscript evidently was closer to what Malory had actually written than that which Caxton had used for his printed book. By a technical process too complicated to explain here, but based on a close comparison of the printed and manuscript texts, he concluded that the Caxton and the Winchester versions each came from a separate older version, and that these older versions were both descended in turn from a single ancestor, which derived, finally, from Malory's own manuscript. The essential point is that the Winchester manuscript supplies what we might call a "control" text, relatively unaltered by an editor, while Caxton's printed volume, it is now clear, represented a great deal of blue-penciling and scissors-and-paste work on the part of Caxton himself.

The manuscript shows us what we could not have known before: that far from being an organic whole, unified in tone and structure, when it left its author's hands, the *Morte Darthur* was extremely uneven in workmanship. It grew and improved as Malory's command of his art grew and improved. Originally it was intended as a series of separate narratives, each dealing with some particular episode or set of episodes in Arthurian narrative. The first ones that Malory wrote are plainly trial runs; they are marked at every turn by inexpertness of style and narrative technique. But there is a steady improvement, until in the last books we find Malory's genius at its peak. Confronted with this unevenness of execution, Caxton, the first "creative publisher," rearranged the narratives as they had come from Malory's pen and rewrote them with sufficient cleverness to persuade most critics through the centuries that Malory had performed his whole task with a clear view of his whole design. The credit for much of Malory's grasp of structure, therefore, is rightly Caxton's.

It is not too much to say that the discovery of the Winchester manuscript, and the publication in 1947 of Vinaver's three-volume text based on both it and the printed edition, with his detailed comparison of the two, have revolutionized our view of Sir Thomas Malory, the first master of English prose narrative. Thanks to Oakeshott's lucky find at Winchester, we are admitted in effect to Malory's prison-house study, and can watch his art mature through the years. To only one other early English writer's development could we more eagerly desire such insight, and that is Chaucer's.

"Malory's prison-house study"? We return to our vital question: *was* there but one Sir Thomas Malory? To that riddle the Winchester manuscript gives us as nearly conclusive an answer as we shall ever have. Far from writing a long and unified book, Malory was simply writing short stories, one after another, to pass the time. This is proved by the fact that in the manuscript each separate narrative is concluded with an explicit. The explicit, a medieval literary convention, consists of variations of the same formula which, as we saw, served as a conclusion to the Caxton *Morte Darthur*. Two of these explicits in the manuscript, not adopted by Caxton in his revision, clinch the case. In one of them, at the end of the "Tale of Sir Gareth," Malory wrote: "And I pray you all that redyth this tale to pray for hym that this wrote, that God sende hym good delyveraunce sone and hastely. Amen." Which is to say: I am writing this in jail, and for heaven's sake, let me be set free. And at the end of another self-contained narrative he wrote: "And this book endyth whereas sir Launcelot and sir Trystrams com to courts. Who that woll make ony more lette hym seke other bookis of kynge Arthure or of sir Launcelot or sir Trystrams; for this was drawyn by a knyght presoner sir Thomas Malleorré, that God sende hym good recover. Amen . . ."

"For this was drawyn by a knyght presoner sir Thomas Malleorré": there it is. By almost incredibly good fortune, we have the proof that was needed. Whether or not Malory was in Newgate continuously from the date of his last recorded imprisonment, 1460, we cannot tell;

but we do know that he was in prison at the times he concluded two separate portions of his work, and that (from the evidence given at the very end of Caxton's book) he was there when the whole was finished. The Sir Thomas Malory of the criminal dossier and the Sir Thomas Malory of the *Morte Darthur*, dreaming perhaps hopelessly of release, were the same.

But now a final problem arises. Here we have the bare facts, wrung from old official documents. On the face of it, Malory was a remarkably persistent felon. May we then close our book and assume that a common criminal wrote the great English narrative of Arthur? It is not nearly so simple as that. For we have failed to consider the complex background of the times, the deeper implications of the charges made against Malory and of the way in which the government seemed dedicated to keeping him in its clutches. Just as today we are disinclined to dismiss a man with a protracted criminal record as being inherently and irreparably evil, and instead bring all our sociological and psychological knowledge to bear on the problem of why he behaves as he does, so it is necessary, in Malory's case, to try to reconstruct as best we can what his recorded career meant in fifteenth-century terms.

Thus the scholar must not merely be a discoverer of new facts; he must equip himself with an intimate knowledge of the historical background of those facts, which otherwise may be wholly misunderstood. Such knowledge is not easy to come by, especially for a period as remote and as chaotic as the fifteenth century. But by studying the histories of the men who appear with Malory in the records, either as his accusers or as his accomplices, by learning as much as possible of the position of the Church at the time and the swirling eddies of political struggle, and by shrewd application of facts learned from an analysis of parallel cases in Malory's age, it may be possible to understand, if not to palliate, his misdeeds.

The fifteenth century was a time of great confusion and insecurity throughout England. As one of the correspondents of the Paston family wrote without exaggeration, "the world is right wild." The Hundred Years' War drew to a weary end in 1453. The feudal order, which had kept society fairly well settled during the Middle Ages, was crumbling;

the supreme authority was passing, by no means painlessly, from the Church to the secular government, and from the feudal lords to the slowly emerging monarchy. During this long period of tortured transition, the forces of law and order had broken down, and men often felt that they had no alternative to asserting what they considered as their rights by direct and unlawful action.

Take, as an instance of how a wide historical knowledge may clarify the brief testimony of the records, the important matter of Malory's obvious antipathy toward the religious establishments. There was a rising tide of popular resentment in his time against the bloodsucking privileges of the religious houses, which had enjoyed for centuries the right to exact tithes and other payments from the laity. One manifestation of this antagonism—a noteworthy by-product of the shift from a corporate to an individualistic economy—was seen in the Lollard movement as early as Chaucer's time. What, then, caused the dispute between Malory and the Carthusians of Axholme, Lincolnshire? The answer may perhaps be conjectured from the fact that these monks owned *in absentia,* so to speak, the priory at Monks Kirby, only a mile or two from Malory's ancestral estate. Although the priory itself had declined into insignificance, the Carthusians still had the right to demand the traditional payments from landholders in its vicinity. Might not Malory then have taken some drastic steps to resist these levies or, having already paid them, to get them back?

Similarly, what of the raid on Coombe Abbey? Hicks was able to find in the early records several cases in which residents of the vicinity sought legal redress for the high-handed actions of the abbot, who had come to their properties and taken, "without reason or course of law," horses, cloth, and other chattels. He found, too, that in the very year before the Coombe Abbey affair, there had been a strikingly similar assault, by ninety men, on a Benedictine monastery in Huntingdonshire, and that that monastery had been pictured by a visiting bishop, a few years earlier, as everything that a religious house should not be:

The divine office, by night and likewise by day, is neglected; obedience is violated; the alms are wasted; hospitality is not kept. There is nothing else here but drunkenness and surfeit, disobedience and contempt, p[et]tie aggrandise[men]t & apostasy, drowsiness—we do not say incontinence—but sloth & every other thing which is on the downward path to evil & drags men to hell.

If it was true, as seems not unlikely, that the monks at Coombe Abbey had been similarly indifferent to the requirements of their calling, one can understand why their stubborn insistence on the payment of tithes was intolerable to men like Malory. The attack on the abbey therefore may have been simply one more event in the continuous struggle between the economically ambitious laity and a Church that had grown corrupt and indolent (except where the collection of tithes was concerned) from centuries of rich living at the expense of everyone else.

It is possible, likewise, that the several accusations that Malory "extorted" money, cattle, and other property from his neighbors, and was in league with other thieves, may be laid to the absence of efficient law enforcement and means for obtaining justice. Hugh Smyth, John Mylner, Margaret Peyto, and the other complainants, including the Duke and Duchess of Norfolk, who alleged that Malory had relieved their deer park of six does during his spree in that memorable summer of 1451, may have been his debtors, and he may have considered that what he took back with him to Newbold Revel was rightfully his property.

Such explanations are, of course, completely conjectural. They gain a certain plausibility from what we know of conditions in Malory's age, but there is no way of telling whether they really provide us with a justification of his high-handed actions. Malory students have not been immune to the quite human temptation to find extenuating circumstances for a man's sins, especially if he has attained some status in the history of literature. This is true especially of the most sensational charge made against him, that of twice raping Joan, the wife of Hugh Smyth. Here the apologist for Malory shows his true colors. Kittredge maintained that the charge of "raptus" was nothing but a legal formula. He wrote:

On May 23, 1450, Malory and his servants searched Smyth's house in vain. Smyth's wife, who objected to the search, may have been roughly treated; perhaps she was forcibly removed from the dwelling while it was ransacked. That would have been *raptus*. Then, on the first of August, the search was repeated with similar violence and with complete success, for goods and chattels valued (by Smyth!) at £40 were taken. On neither occasion is there any likelihood that Goodwife Smyth was actually ravished. The duplication of this particular charge is reason enough for rejecting such an idea; it is ridiculous to suppose that Malory actually ravished the woman twice. Anything, to be sure, is possible in what Sir Peter Teazle calls this "damned wicked world," but we are in pursuit of what is reasonable—and we are reading an indictment, not a verdict or the sentence of a judge.

Although one of the incidental purposes of this book is to suggest that literary scholars have a certain amount of worldly sophistication, Kittredge here, I am afraid, goes far to undermine my thesis. He was one of the greatest scholars of our time, but his refusal to believe that a man could rape the same woman twice reflects (to put it mildly!) a certain naïveté. The language of the indictment is so specific that the charge cannot possibly be dismissed as a mere legal formula. Malory, it was alleged, on the first occasion "Johannam uxorem dicti Hugonis ibidem adtunc felonice rapuit & cum ea carnaliter concubuit," and again, six weeks later, "Johannam . . . apud Coventre felonice rapuit & cum ea carnaliter concubuit." That seems plain enough. If only we knew what Humphrey, Duke of Buckingham, and his companions on the bench read into such language! Since we do not know, the most convenient verdict no doubt is that of "Not Proven"—to be handed down with the incredulous words of Sir Lancelot, in Malory's own version, haunting our ears: "What," said Sir Lancelot, "is he a thief and a knight *and* a ravyssher of women?"

Some apologists for Malory take the view that most, if not all, of the accusations against him were frame-ups, probably arising from the concern of his political enemies to keep him *hors de combat*. If this is true, it is a rare tribute to Malory's character as a dangerous opponent, because, despite his demonstrated slipperiness, for at least ten years his enemies found it worth their while to keep clapping him back into jail. But such a theory is only speculative, because we have no real evidence as to his political affiliations, which probably shifted with the extraordinary rapidity that was characteristic of the turbulent century in which he lived.

The most perplexing anomaly, however, appears only when we reflect on the incongruity between the book and the man. The *Morte Darthur* was sold to the public with the understanding that it was a work of uniformly edifying tendencies. According to his Preface, Caxton printed it

> to the entente that noble men may see and lerne the noble actes of chyvalrye, the jentyl and vertuous dedes that somme knyghtes used in tho[se] days, by whyche they came to honour, and how they that were vycious were punysshed and ofte put to shame and rebuke; humbly bysechyng al noble lordes and ladyes . . . that they take the good and honest actes in their remembraunce, and to folowe the same; . . . Doo after the good and leve the evyl, and it shal brynge you to good fame and renommee.

This pious assertion by a man anxious to sell his books stands in strange contrast to the judgment of Roger Ascham, less than a century later, that

> the whole pleasure of [this] book standeth in two special points, in open manslaughter and bold bawdry. In which book those be counted the noblest knights that do kill most men without any quarrel, and commit the foulest adulteries by subtlest shifts . . . This [he adds, ironically] is good stuff for wise men to laugh at, or honest men to take pleasure at.

Actually both Caxton and Ascham are right. The *Morte Darthur is* replete with "open manslaughter and bold bawdry," but there is no question that Malory was also sincerely concerned to exalt the virtues of the Christian chivalric code.

What manner of man was he, with his flamboyant criminal record, that he could write a book celebrating the many articles of knightly behavior which he himself had honored far more in the breach than in the observance? We cannot, at this distance of time, answer the question with assurance; but it seems unlikely that Malory was a hypocrite, and so it is possible to view the writing of his book not quite as an act of contrition, but as a slow awakening to the realization of what chivalry could mean. Through circumstances at which we can only guess, Malory's life at every point of which there is record found him betraying the ideals he had learned at the side of Beauchamp. When at last he began to write, a certain moral indifference was still in him. No modern reader of the opening stories of the *Morte Darthur* can help feeling that Malory's sole interest lay in telling the story and that he was quite unaware of—or uninterested in—the implications of the acts of even his heroes. "Open manslaughter and bold bawdry" are pale charges beside the actuality of deceit, rape, wanton cruelty, and even slaughter of the innocents that bloody these opening tales. The same reader, if he will follow the *Morte Darthur* to the end, will be deeply moved by the author's profound awareness of sin, of error, and of human responsibility—even more by Malory's compassion for the retribution which an errant humanity brings upon itself. The Malory who finally traced his tale through to its tragic end was not the Malory who started to while away boredom with the story of the begetting of Arthur or the taking of his kingdom.

How much time he had spent in prison reflecting on his own sins, we shall never know. Did he undertake deliberately to reaffirm the chivalry which he had been taught in his youth and from which he had departed so far? Perhaps. It would not have been the first time, nor the last, that a work of literature has sprung from a sensitive man's recognizing how tragically at variance his conduct had been from his ideals. But we can not doubt that under the spell of the books he read and the tales he found coming to life again under his hand he was deeply stirred by the meaning of the ideals he had violated. He was great enough to know them as impossible in a frail and tempting world, but he also knew—who better than the man who could not follow them?—how truly the fact that we cannot follow them is the stuff of human tragedy. Lancelot caught to the very end in his unhappy tangle of divided loves, Guenevere afraid to accept a final kiss, Bedivere fumbling between love for Arthur and greed for Excalibur—these are the final pictures of a man whose vision of reality simply transcended the vulgar counsel of Caxton. Thanks to our new understanding of the misspent life which preceded the writing of the *Morte Darthur*, we need no longer accept Caxton's explanation of the purposes that underlay its composition. Might not Malory, had he lived in another century, have wished instead to borrow for the epigraph to his book, the simple words of another repentant knight—Shakespeare's Prince Hal?

> For my part, I may speak it to my shame.
> I have a truant been to chivalry.

HUNTING FOR MANUSCRIPTS

I

THERE is not a single figure in the history of English or American literature whose biography may be sealed up and labeled "Completed." Year after year we learn more about the personal lives, the characters, and the literary careers of scores of great writers—and are forced to unlearn much that we had previously believed true. In the past thirty years thousands of letters written by Swift, Addison, Steele, Boswell, Johnson, Walpole, Scott, Lamb, Wordsworth, Coleridge, Byron, Shelley, the Brownings, Dickens, Emerson, and Thackeray have been published for the first time, with thousands more still to come. Our view of these men naturally must be revised in the light of the new information contained in their letters. Similarly, new scholarly editions of the works of the great English and American men of letters are revealing a great deal about the methods of composition and revision that lay behind the text of the earlier editions. Not until 1926, for instance, were we able to read Wordsworth's great philosophical poem, *The Prelude*, in the form in which the poet had first written it in 1805–06; until that time we knew the poem only in the much altered version which was published in 1850. A comparison of the original text with one that was the result of forty years of tinkering enables us to view with fresh insight the great changes Wordsworth's philosophical attitudes underwent as he grew older. In other cases a famous literary work was drastically expurgated when it was first published, and only now in these less squeamish times are we allowed to read what the author wrote. Boswell's *Tour to the*

Hebrides turns out to be even more entertaining in manuscript form than in its traditional printed version, and the full notes he made for his *Life of Johnson* may, when they are eventually printed, exceed our fondest expectations. The manuscripts of Nathaniel Hawthorne's *English* and *American Notebooks* tell us much more about England and America—and about Hawthorne—than his widow felt it proper to reveal in 1870. It is scarcely an exaggeration to say that our present methods of scholarship are turning up so much new material that if the present rate of discovery continues, every generation will find it necessary to rewrite the history of English literature and the biographies of many of its principal ornaments.

All sorts of specialized scholars have, of course, contributed to this steady increase of literary information. But no one has more adventures in the course of his work than the manuscript hunter, the man who tracks down the raw materials of literary biography. He may not always travel in distant countries, as hundreds of scholars have done in an attempt to overtake the ghost of a footloose author or his equally nomadic descendants. But he is guaranteed his moments of suspense and frustration and profound perplexity and occasional exultation. He meets all sorts of people; he finds himself in all sorts of interesting situations; and with all of them he must be equipped to deal.

The quarry is Literary Documents—a generic term which includes all kinds of written records that throw light on some aspect of a literary figure's life and work: the successive drafts and revisions of his writings; his diaries, letters, and autobiographical fragments; the letters and reminiscences of members of his family and his friends; legal records such as affidavits, deeds, and wills. The ultimate aim is twofold: first, to discover facts which previously have been unknown; second, to check the statements and quotations of earlier biographers and editors by going back to the original sources. This latter aim is more important than, on first thought, it might seem. There is no major literary figure whose biography has been innocent of falsehoods and half-truths, placed there by an early memoirist and then uncritically repeated from writer to writer—and usually embroidered in the transmission—until at last they are disproved by the researcher.

Every student who is seasoned in tracking down the myths that have been assimilated in biography admires canny old Dr. Johnson's statement of the case:

> Nothing but experience could evince the frequency of false information, or enable any man to conceive that so many groundless reports should be propagated, as every man of eminence may hear of himself. Some men relate what they think, as what they know; some men of confused memories and habitual inaccuracy, ascribe to one man what belongs to another; and some talk on, without thought or care. A few men are sufficient to broach falsehoods, which are afterwards innocently diffused by successive relaters.

As James R. Sutherland, a British scholar, remarked at the close of an instructive article in which he exposed "the progress of error" that attended the successive biographies of Mrs. Susanna Centlivre, the eighteenth-century dramatist: "The price of biographical truth appears, indeed, to be eternal vigilance, and eternal skepticism." And to the vigilant and skeptical scholar whom long and bitter experience has accustomed to doubting a great deal of what he finds in print, only original manuscripts are adequate to prove the truth or falsity of an alleged "fact."

If, that is, they can be found!

At the outset, the routine of the manuscript hunter is fairly well established. He goes to the most obvious places first. He consults a great array of scholarly reference books, such as the catalogues of manuscripts owned by the British Museum and the various libraries at Oxford and Cambridge. He writes to, or visits, all the large libraries that have manuscript collections. If he is lucky, he may discover that the papers of the author in whom he is interested have been preserved intact by his family and have eventually found their way to a library or a museum. The late Gordon Wordsworth, a direct descendant of the poet, some years ago gave his family archives to the Wordsworth Museum at Grasmere, in the Lake District. Scott's journal, a great mass of his correspondence, and many of his other papers are preserved at his famous home, Abbotsford. The main bulk of the papers of Longfellow is to be found at his old home, Craigie House, in Cambridge, Mass. The papers of Henry James and Emerson are now in the Harvard Library; those of Sherwood Anderson are in the Newberry Library, Chicago; and so on.

Or our scholar may find that though his author's papers once were widely scattered, some collector has devoted his life and fortune to reassembling them. This was the case with the Brontë material that was collected by a wealthy Philadelphian, Henry H. Bonnell, who generously returned it to the town of Haworth in Yorkshire; and with many of the papers of Leigh Hunt, which were amassed by Luther A. Brewer of Cedar Rapids, Iowa, and presented upon his death to the University of Iowa. Baylor University in Texas is world-famous for its rich Browning collection, the fruit of many years of devoted work by Professor A. J. Armstrong. One of the finest Keats collections in the world was amassed by the poet Amy Lowell, who bequeathed it to the Harvard University Library, where it was joined not long ago by the equally rich one of the Marquis of Crewe. The great manuscript collection of Dickens's friend and biographer John Forster, now in the Victoria and Albert Museum in London, is a starting-point for scholars wishing to do research on figures so diverse as Samuel Richardson and Dickens himself.

But there is no such thing as an even "reasonably" complete manuscript collection relating to a single author. A scholar working on Scott, for example, though he may find much to detain him at Abbotsford, must supplement what he learns there by examining the quantities of Scott manuscripts held by the British Museum, the University of Edinburgh, the National Library of Scotland, and a host of private collectors.

When, as happens more often than not, a scholar establishes with virtual certainty that there is no major concentration of the papers associated with his author, he must abandon his lazy man's dream of having his materials borne to him upon a silver platter, to the sound of trumpets, and get down to real work. He must comb every library, large and small, every archive, every institution where manuscripts may conceivably be kept; he must go through innumerable catalogues of book dealers and auctioneers to find out what manuscripts have turned up for sale in the last hundred years or so, and then try to trace them as they passed from collector to collector; he must try to communicate with every single person or institution that would have any reason for being interested in acquiring or preserving the manuscript relics of his author. It takes years of steady work to exhaust such possibilities. If you want an impressive illustration of the far-sweeping methods of the manuscript searcher, look at the long acknowledgment lists that preface such works as the monumental twelve-volume edition of Scott's letters collected by Sir Herbert Grierson and his associates, Ernest de Selincourt's six-volume edition of the Wordsworth correspondence, or R. L. Rusk's equally large edition of Emerson's letters.

As if it were not enough to have to write and visit hundreds of libraries and private collectors in quest of the elusive document, the lot of the manuscript hunter is made harder by a persistent suspicion that librarians and collectors, however systematic their cataloguing methods, often do not know what they actually possess. Such a suspicion arises less from an innate cynicism on the part of the scholar than from his own and his colleagues' actual experiences. One thinks, for instance, of the recent case of Dr. Campbell's diary. In the year 1854 there was published, in Sydney, Australia, a little book called *A Diary of a Visit to England in 1775, by an Irishman* (*The Reverend Doctor Thomas Campbell*). Its principal interest lay in its descriptions of meetings with Dr. Johnson, to whom Boswell introduced Campbell. The reviewers were skeptical about the book. For one thing, the history of the manuscript was disturbingly vague. The sponsor of the 1854 edition, an official of the Supreme Court of New South Wales, said that the manuscript had been found behind an old cupboard in one of the offices of his court. Without impugning the sincerity of the sponsor, it was pointed out that any common forgery could be "discovered" in the same way. Again, the diary, as published, contained little that was not already known about Johnson. But after considerable debate the English Johnsonians of mid-Victorian days decided, without having seen the manuscript, to accept the diary as genuine.

In the early 1930's, Professor James L. Clifford, who is now on the graduate faculty at Columbia University, decided to look into the question afresh. He faced difficulties at the very outset, for he could not find a copy of the 1854 volume anywhere in the United States; and only after extensive advertising in Australian papers was he able to locate a copy for sale. The next step was to try to discover the manuscript diary itself, in order to learn whether it contained material, omitted from the printed version, which would establish its authenticity beyond question. By diligent inquiry, Clifford found that the manuscript had long ago been given to the Mitchell Library in Sydney. But after making a thorough search the librarians reported that they could find no trace of it. Clifford then resigned himself to another advertising campagn in Australia; if the Mitchell Library did not have the diary, presumably someone did, and he was out to find who it was. But just as his campaign was getting under way he received an excited and somewhat apologetic letter from the officials of the Mitchell Library. The manuscript diary (genuine beyond doubt) had been discovered, quite by accident, in a long neglected drawer in the library!

Neglected drawers are, indeed, the despair of manuscript hunters— the more so because, as in Clifford's case, it is not easy to persuade one's correspondents, who may be halfway round the earth, that they have not looked everywhere that they should. Fortunate is the man who can examine drawers and closets and cupboards for himself. Mason Wade, when he was working on his biography of Francis Parkman, was puzzled to be unable to find any trace of the journals the historian wrote during his far-reaching travels in the great West. He knew that such journals had once existed, because two earlier writers on Parkman had drawn upon them. Parkman's historical papers had gone to the Massachusetts Historical Society, and his books to Harvard, while his descendants retained his personal papers; but none of the owners could locate the journals. Finally Wade, taking a long chance, went to the old house at 50 Chestnut Street, Boston, where Parkman had spent his later years. The attic study the historian had used, a romantic room decorated with Indian trophies and lined with books by Scott and Byron and Cooper, had not been disturbed since his death in 1893. In the center of the dusty, silent room stood Parkman's desk. Wade pulled out one row of drawers. All that they contained was the wire grid which the nearly blind Parkman had used to guide his handwriting. But when he pulled out the drawers on the other side of the desk the long-lost journals, together with a mass of other papers, lay revealed. Presumably Parkman's family, when they had gone through his effects to gather the material he had willed to the Historical Society and to Harvard, had overlooked those laden drawers.

But to return to the matter of hunting manuscripts in libraries. Americans especially, accustomed to the staggeringly efficient cataloguing systems of their great public and university libraries, find it hard to believe that hidden treasures still turn up in institutions specifically devoted to the care of books. Yet just at the moment that I am revising this chapter, the newspapers relate the story of a young library-school student who discovered a copy of the extremely rare first edition of Handel's *Messiah* blushing unseen on the shelves of the public library at Johnstown, Pennsylvania. An even greater find occurred recently at the public library in Sheffield, England. For centuries there had accumulated, in the muniment rooms of the mansion at Wentworth Woodhouse, papers of the utmost value to literary and political history; for the Straffords, Rockinghams, and Fitzwilliams, whose seat it has been, were prominent in public affairs from the time of the English Civil War. Some of the papers had been examined in the past by scholars working on particular phases of history; but they had never been generally available, let alone catalogued.

In the summer of 1949 the whole collection was transferred to the Sheffield library in three furniture vans, and scholars immediately flocked to the feast. Among them was Professor Thomas W. Copeland of the University of Chicago, who knew that it included many papers relating to Edmund Burke, whose patron, the second Marquis of Rockingham, had once owned Wentworth Woodhouse. While Copeland was at work on the Burke manuscripts that had already been sorted out, an assistant of his arrived from America. In order to familiarize him with the state of the papers, Professor Potter, a historian from the University of Sheffield who was supervising the opening of the collection, took him into the basement strong room where various boxes of materials were lying about. But let Copeland himself tell the story:

"This is the way these things looked when we first opened them up," Potter said, lighting on a box which had not yet been opened and was covered with a century's dust. "You see, the contents are tied up in dozens of little packets thrown in in no kind of order." He picked out a packet, wiped the dust off it, and undid the ribbon around it. By chance it was a packet of letters to Burke. He took out another packet— and then it turned out that the entire box was filled with packets just like it: about seven or eight hundred letters that had been overlooked in all previous hunts for Burke materials, some of them by Johnson, Boswell, Garrick, Reynolds, and other notables!

That story, of course, implies no reflection on the Sheffield cataloguing system, because it is a task of years to classify so enormous an aggregation of manuscripts, and rather than bar access to them until the job was finished (as some librarians would) the Sheffield authorities generously threw open the collection to impatient scholars who could therefore have their extra thrill of discovery. Even when manuscripts have been properly catalogued, however, it sometimes happens that scholars overlook them. Professor Leslie Marchand, during his "Byron pilgrimage" described elsewhere in this book, dropped into the library of Trinity College, Cambridge, where young Byron had lived the life of a lord from 1805 to 1808. He scarcely expected to find anything there, because he assumed that every Byron scholar would have examined the manuscripts as a matter of course. But when he took down the catalogue of the library's manuscript collection, he found that Trinity College owned half a dozen Byron letters of whose existence no previous student seemed ever to have been aware. And then there was the embarrassing experience of the scholars who produced the great edition of Milton published by Columbia University. During their comprehensive search for every bit of material Milton had ever written, they ran across a reference, in an old catalogue of a London bookseller, to a manuscript that contained some unprinted Milton writings. Try as they would, they could not learn where the manuscript had gone after it was sold. Finally they wrote the bookseller, begging him to reveal who had bought it from him. Dealers often decline to give out such information, for some collectors of rare literary material, partly to avoid being bothered by curious scholars, do not like to have news of their purchases get abroad. But in this case there was no difficulty; the bookseller, hard pressed to conceal his unholy glee, was happy to inform them that the Milton manuscript had been bought years ago by the Columbia University Library!

After ruefully telling me this story Professor Thomas O. Mabbott pointed the moral that they had learned the hard way: "If you are searching for something, the first place to look is where it should be." The Columbia University Library may not have been the most obvious place, but there is no denying that it was the nearest. He hastened to add: "If it isn't there, the next place to look is somewhere it *shouldn't* be. Guessing the 'shouldn't' of course is pure luck or something like telepathy."

But before telepathy or extrasensory perception is brought into play, there is one more course of action, intellectually the most challenging of all. The manuscript hunter who has failed to attain his goal through a systematic canvassing of libraries and private collections— the places where his quarry *should* be—does, in effect, what Sherlock Holmes was wont to do when he faced a blank wall. He may not recline the whole night long upon a pile of cushions, choking the room with clouds of strong tobacco smoke and sawing upon the fiddle that he has thrown across his knees; but his mental processes are the same. In a word, our scholar now employs the Science of Deduction.

II

HE may be looking for particular items, such as a journal or one side of an extended correspondence, or an unpublished essay, or an earlier version of a famous poem, which he knows once existed but has now dropped completely from view. Or he may not be looking for anything in particular; his search may be motivated simply by the circumstance that fewer papers of his author are known to exist than is quite reasonable, and that therefore more are awaiting rescue. In either case, once he is satisfied that whatever he is seeking is not to be found in any of the more or less logical places, he abandons the present and goes back to the past—to the time when his author died. What happened to the man's papers then? Who inherited them? What did he do with them? Or did the author somehow dispose of his manuscripts during his own lifetime? If so, where did they go?

The possibilities are as diverse as life itself. By the use of a great variety of tools—genealogical works, voluminous histories of small British and American localities, church records, post-office directories, alumni rolls of schools and universities, records of the probate courts, newspaper and magazine obituaries, the printed memoirs of everyone who had some association with the author or his family—the scholar begins the long, tortuous search for clues. If his author died, let us say, in 1750, he is sometimes obliged to completely reconstruct the history of the man's family, and often of the families of all his correspondents and publishers and biographers, for two centuries. In the history of the families involved he must take note of every occasion on which property may conceivably have changed hands—events such as marriages, removals, bankruptcies, financial settlements, and deaths. As he works out the early history of the family and its manuscript possessions, our scholar may be dismayed to see the original archives partitioned before his very eyes, one parcel of letters going to a biographer in 1840, a manuscript diary given to a souvenir collector in 1850, an unpublished autobiography disappearing during a family moving in 1860. . . . Having begun with one slender clue, he is likely to end up with fifty, each requiring a separate course of minute research. His problem is not unlike that of an observer who tries to follow the progress of fifty or a hundred selected ants through a swarming anthill. Here are only a few of the fates a certain lot of manuscripts may have met:

(1) The family which inherited them from the author preserved them, say through the next two generations. But then the family disappeared into the mists of time. Perhaps it died out. If so, did the last survivor still possess the manuscripts? Then what happened to them? The researcher must find his will, ascertain the testator's heirs, and begin to trace them and their heirs and assigns in turn. Or perhaps only the family name died out, through the childlessness of the sons and the marriage of the daughters. The daughters' families must be traced down through the years. Perhaps they in turn died out, and their

property went to a distant cousin. The cousin's family must be traced . . . and so on, almost *ad infinitum.*

(2) But suppose the author's immediate descendants had some reason, real or imaginary, to regret bearing his name—perhaps he had embraced an unpopular political cause, or had committed some moral indiscretions. They would not have been so careful to preserve his papers. Indeed, they might have chosen to destroy them—a deed which was long but unjustly imputed to Boswell's embarrassed Victorian descendants. Or at best they would have let the papers fall into dust, or casually given them away to anyone so eccentric as to want to possess the relics of a misspent life.

(3) Or perhaps the family needed money and was forced to sell its hero's papers. Who bought them? Heaven grant that they were sold *en bloc* rather than auctioned in parcels, like the papers of Garrick and Walpole! Even if they were bought as a whole, what happened to them on the death of the original purchaser?

(4) If some later generation left the family house, what happened to the papers? Scholars have found that it always pays to visit every house known to have been occupied by the family of a man of letters; there is always the chance that they left some papers behind that later occupants have never discovered or have failed to recognize at their true value.

(5) There is always the possibility that the appalled scholar will find that the family who owned the papers migrated to one of the outposts of the British Empire—taking the papers with them. Then what? The weary manuscript hunter faces some really first-class complications. Yet potentially there may be riches in store for him. It is an endlessly tantalizing thought that in obscure towns in Australia and Canada, even in the remote hills of India, today may rest documents of untold value for English literary history. Perhaps one of the most dramatic scholarly discoveries of the next few years will occur there—it is not at all impossible.

(6) The family may have held the papers until they were borrowed for use by an early biographer of the author. The biographer, in the easy-going way of Victorian gentlemen-scholars, may have failed to

return them. What became of them? Did they pass down through his own family?

(7) The author in question may have left his papers to a friend, perhaps his literary executor. Who were his friend's heirs? What did they do with the papers? (It was the strange failure of Boswell and Johnson scholars to ask this question that delayed until 1930 the discovery of the great cache of papers at Fettercairn House—the home of the son of one of Boswell's executors.)

This by no means exhausts the possibilities which the scholar must canvass for clues to the present location of his author's manuscripts. He must, indeed, follow the same process in the case of everyone who had some connection with the author. He must try to find the little notebook filled with personal reminiscences which was said to have been written late in life by the author's school friend. He must look up the family of every man with whom the author carried on a correspondence. He must try to discover whether the papers of our author's publishers are still extant; if so, they may contain not merely important letters but actual manuscripts and proof sheets. If the author contributed to periodicals, the scholar must explore the correspondence files of the publishers of the periodicals. But, as the leading authority on American author-publisher relations has discovered to his sorrow, nineteenth-century editors often regarded such correspondence as their personal property, and when they resigned their posts took along the files to add to their personal archives. Which means that the scholar must then proceed to trace down the editors' heirs.

Nor should lawyers' offices be neglected. Here is a good case in point. Everyone knows that in the eighteenth-century British theater Shakespeare's plays underwent all sorts of radical changes. None of these changes were for the better, and some of them were as dreadful as Nahum Tate's "improvement" of *King Lear,* which managed to provide a romantic love-affair between Edgar and Cordelia as well as a beatifically happy ending.

Now one of the most ruthless "improvers" of Shakespeare in the middle of the eighteenth century was the great actor David Garrick.

From his own time down to 1933, the list of Garrick's sins against the integrity of Shakespeare was headed by his revision of *Hamlet*. The actual text of that version was supposed to be destroyed, but all evidence pointed to its having been a perfectly dastardly offense, with the single aim of fattening still further the part of Hamlet, which was played by Garrick himself. Since Hamlet's role, as Shakespeare originally wrote it, is probably the fattest in dramatic literature, one may guess that Garrick was either a megalomaniac or a glutton for punishment. At any rate, the tradition of the outrageous liberties which Garrick had taken with *Hamlet* began with his first biographer and was repeated down through the whole of the nineteenth century and the first third of the twentieth.

Meanwhile the manuscript which would have proved the truth or error of the whole tradition was, unknown to everyone, still in existence. After Garrick's death in 1779 his rich dramatic library had passed down through his family until it was dispersed at public auction in 1823. In this sale, however, certain of the actor's manuscripts, among them that of his *Hamlet*, were not included, either through an oversight or because those in charge of the sale considered them too trivial to bother about. These neglected items were put into the hands of solicitors to be sold at some future date.

But the profession of law in England at this time was in the leisurely mood in which Dickens's *Bleak House* depicts it, and nothing was done. Instead, the manuscript was stored in a box along with the other unsold relics; and there it slumbered in perfect peace for seventy-five years, until, in 1900, the building which contained the firm's offices was marked for demolition. When, in the ensuing housecleaning, the box was examined, an alert partner recognized the value of its contents, which were sent to a dealer for rather belated auction. There H. C. Folger's agent bought the Garrick *Hamlet* manuscript, and it went across the sea to Brooklyn, where, evidently without having been even cursorily examined, it promptly went back to sleep in one of Folger's fabulous warehouses of literary treasure-trove. Only after his death, when the accumulations of his warehouses were taken to the new Folger Shakespeare Library at Washington and there revealed, did anyone have an opportunity to examine the manuscript. Professor

G. W. Stone of George Washington University promptly seized the opportunity, and discovered that tradition had been all wrong. Garrick's contemporaries, and following them his biographers, had done him an injustice. Compared with the other versions of *Hamlet* that were current in the eighteenth century, Garrick's is good Shakespeare.

Speaking of lawyers' offices and the unsuspected literary information they may contain, it is exciting to recall that a few years ago the office of a well known legal firm in New York turned out to hold what may be an essential clue to a famous real-life mystery which Edgar Allan Poe "solved" in one of his classic stories.

In 1841 a young tobacconist named John Anderson operated at 319 Broadway, New York City, one of the most prosperous cigar stores of the time. The merchandise it stocked no doubt was excellent, but. until the previous year, its success had been chiefly due to the presence behind the counter of an unusually beautiful girl. Her name was Mary Rogers.

On Sunday, July 25, 1841, Mary left her mother's house on what she said was a visit to her aunt. Not long afterward she was seen in the company of a tall, dark, well dressed young man aboard a ferry bound for Hoboken. Later in the same day the two stopped at a Hoboken tavern operated by one Mrs. Loss. Thereafter nothing was seen of Mary until the following Wednesday, when her body, bearing signs of violence, was found floating in the Hudson. Her clothing subsequently was discovered in a thicket near Mrs. Loss's tavern.

The mysterious death of Mary Rogers soon became one of the *causes célèbres* of the century. The New York newspapers rivaled one another in the fullness of their reports and the enterprise with which their reporters tried to dig up new information. The air was full of theories and rumors; but no positive solution was ever forthcoming. Some held to the belief that she had been raped and murdered by one or another of the gangs of ruffians who then frequented Hoboken. Others—probably the majority—maintained that she had died as the result of an abortion performed in the tavern. This latter view was based primarily upon a reported statement by Mrs. Loss as she lay dying not long afterward. It is doubtful that Mrs. Loss ever made any such statement, although the district attorney himself seems to have been partial to the abortion theory, perhaps on the basis of other, undisclosed evidence.

A year and a half later an American magazine, the *Ladies' Companion*, published "The Mystery of Marie Roget," by the young journalist Edgar Allan Poe. In this story, one of the first classics of detective literature, Poe set forth his solution of the mystery. Partly for prudential reasons, and partly because he had already created the character of Dupin, the sedentary French detective, he transferred the locale to Paris and made his characters French; but the disguise was purely perfunctory. Everyone knew he was really telling the story of Mary Rogers—and it is even clearer now that diligent investigators have read the files of all the New York papers of the time and shown that the lengthy excerpts from the "Paris" papers from which Dupin derived his facts were almost completely based upon the actual journalistic reports of the Rogers case. Poe himself was no mean researcher.

Poe's own solution, reached after a brilliant but not always cogent exercise of what he loved to call "ratiocination," was that Mary Rogers died during or after an abortion performed at Mrs. Loss's tavern. The man on the ferry he identified as the mysterious young naval man who had figured conspicuously in the newspaper speculations at the time. Such a man was known to have been an admirer of Mary's, and the heaviest suspicion had fallen upon him, although no prosecution was ever brought against him or anyone else.

Among those who were *not* suspected, at least so far as the newspapers knew, was Mary's former employer, John Anderson. Even though deprived of her glamour behind the counter, his business continued to flourish. His tobacco was sold in enormous quantities to the soldiers in the Mexican War, and later he branched out with equal success into real estate speculation, eventually becoming a millionaire. After his death in Paris in 1881, his heirs began a long drawn-out litigation over his will. During the various trials it was revealed (and reported in the newspapers) that Anderson often recalled that in the years immediately following Mary's death he "had had many, *very* many unhappy days and nights in regard to her," and had been in frequent communication with her spirit.

In December of 1891, the litigation entered the phase known to the legal records as Laura V. Appleton *v.* The New York Life Insurance Company and Frederick A. Hammond. In this action, brought before the Supreme Court of New York County, Anderson's daughter sought to break her father's will on the ground that when he had signed it he was mentally incompetent.

Now students who were intrigued by the mystery of Mary Rogers knew of this case, and suspected that in the course of the trial further evidence might have been heard relating to Anderson's preoccupation with the fate of his unfortunate shopgirl. No actual record of the testimony, however, was known to exist, because the case had been settled out of court and the official record ordered destroyed. But Samuel Copp Worthen, a lawyer closely associated with Mrs. Appleton, had been a student of one of the first reliable biographers of Poe, George Edward Woodberry of Columbia University, and had never lost his interest in literature, and specifically in Poe. He knew that in the testimony during the trial in 1891 there had been important revelations—and he also knew that his firm had retained in its files a copy of that testimony. Worthen kept his secret for almost fifty years; but in 1948 he decided that the time had come to reveal it, and he wrote an article for the scholarly periodical *American Literature.* This is what he reported.

Mrs. Appleton's lawyers had gone to much trouble to bring before the court and jury testimony that would tend to prove Anderson's mental incompetence. Perhaps that part which related to Anderson's communion with Mary Rogers's ghost did have such a tendency. But why had Anderson been so disturbed over her death if he had merely been her employer? The answer was provided in the testimony of acquaintances to whom he had talked about his connection with the case. To them he revealed that after Mary's body was found he had been arrested and examined, but released for want of evidence. This, apparently, had never got into the papers; but the fact of his arrest became known to several persons, including James Gordon Bennett, the famous editor of the *New York Herald,* and the resultant damage to his reputation preyed on his mind. Years later, after Anderson became prominent, the reigning Tammany boss, Fernando Wood, asked him to be a candidate for mayor of New York; but, fearing what might be said during the campaign about his connection with the Rogers case, he refused to run.

And then the testimony in 1891 brought out the most startling fact of all—one that previously had been completely unknown. Anderson, it was deposed, had confessed to his friends that before Mary's death he had paid for an abortion she had had, and that he had got "in some trouble over it." But apart from that earlier episode, he had continued, he had not had "anything, *directly, himself*," to do with Mary Rogers's difficulties. Note the significant qualifications.

Whether Anderson was reporting the actual truth in these statements is, of course, open to question. If his mental balance was sufficiently precarious to substantiate a lengthy attempt to break his will, his credibility must not be accepted without reservation. Yet Worthen, a man of long legal experience, felt that he was speaking the truth. His reconstruction of Anderson's part in the Mary Rogers mystery was this. Anderson, according to his own statement, had already financed one abortion for Mary. (Whether or not he was responsible for her pregnancy on that occasion or the subsequent one is a matter upon which scholarship feels itself incompetent to pronounce.)

When in 1841, after she had left his employ, she again found herself in what would then have been called "an interesting condition," she appealed to him for help; and, if only for the reason that the prosperity of his cigar store owed a great deal to her bewitching presence, he again came to the rescue. The tall, dark man on the ferryboat therefore would have been the abortionist. After Mary's death in Mrs. Loss's tavern he, or Mrs. Loss's sons, disposed of her body in the river and arranged her clothing in the thicket so as to give rise to the theory that a felonious gang had done her to death.

If Worthen's theory based on this newly revealed evidence is correct, then Poe hit upon the right solution in his story. His chief error was in eliminating Anderson from suspicion of complicity; but it was an error common to all who followed the case while it was unfolding in the newspapers. Neither he nor anyone else, with the possible exception of the authorities who arrested Anderson for questioning, knew that the young tobacconist had abetted the earlier abortion.

But we have spent enough time in lawyers' offices, which are, after all, only one of the many places where documents of importance to literary history lie.

There remain, for example, the unknown potentialities of official archives—not only the best known ones like the vast collection at the Public Record Office in London, but the multitude of local record collections in England and America and every other country where English-speaking men of letters have been. If our author was once a soldier or a sailor, there are undoubtedly some records of him and, if he had a responsible position, even detailed files of his reports in the War and Admiralty offices in London and the corresponding departments in Washington. The records of the American Adjutant General, for example, have yielded information on Poe's brief and unhappy career as a soldier; and in the archives of the Ministère de la Marine in Paris Professor Charles R. Anderson found the logbook of the French frigate whose cutter had quelled the South Sea island brawl Melville describes in *Omoo,* and in whose brig Melville and his companions were allowed to cool off. If the author worked for a governmental or quasi-governmental agency—like Anthony Trollope as an inspector for the British Post Office, or Charles Lamb as a clerk in the East India Office, or Walt Whitman as an employee of the United States Department of the Interior—the thorough scholar must not neglect the chance that in those voluminous archives are hidden papers which may by no means be restricted in their interest to the narrowly workaday side of the author's life. If he was an American diplomat, like Washington Irving or Nathaniel Hawthorne or James Russell Lowell or Bret Harte, the records of the State Department must be searched. And even if he was a more or less common citizen, he may have had financial dealings or legal complications whose trail can be followed with profit by a diligent inquirer. A few years ago Professor Dixon Wecter threw valuable new light on Edmund Burke by pursuing such a superficially unpromising lead.

Even more recently, the late Professor Newman Ivey White made one of the most provocative finds in the history of Shelley scholarship by a search of public records. Among the perplexing mysteries of Shelley's life has always been the identity of the "Neapolitan ward" who is mentioned briefly and evasively in one or two of his letters in 1820. The child remained a vague wraith until White in 1936, through the American consul-general at Naples, engaged an Italian professor, Alberto Tortaglione, to search the records in Naples for documentary evidence of the child's birth and its parentage. Tortaglione discovered a document certifying that on December 27, 1818, a daughter, Elena Adelaide, was born to Shelley and "Maria Padurin, his legitimate wife," as well as a death certificate for the child, dated some fifteen months later and repeating the same information except that the Italian version of Mary Godwin's name had become "Maria Gebuin." Since it is plain from Mrs. Shelley's journal and other evidence that she did not bear a child in December, 1818, Shelley obviously perpetrated a fraud upon the authorities.

Who was Elena Adelaide? Shelley's daughter by someone else? The illegitimate child of a maidservant in Shelley's household? And why did Shelley perjure himself in order to adopt her? In 1820, the Shelley-Byron circle was thrown into an uproar by the maidservant's story that the baby was Shelley's child by Jane Clairmont, who earlier had been Byron's mistress. Since one of the meager clues we possess in the case is a statement in Mary Shelley's journal that Jane was ill on the day on which Elena is supposed to have been born, Professor White examined Jane Clairmont's unpublished diary, then in the library of Thomas J. Wise. In the pages referring to the period when the maidservant was accusing Jane of being Elena's mother, White found several passages carefully crossed out. Hoping for some clue in the deletions, he placed the pages under the infrared lamp; but he found no allusion to the "Neapolitan affair." His discovery of the birth and death records, far from solving the mystery, has served only to muddy the swirling waters of controversy over Elena's identity. Shelley scholars still may be conveniently divided into those who think that Shelley was the child's father, and those who think he was not; and those who think that Jane Clairmont was her mother, and those who think not.

From what has been said thus far, it should be fairly obvious that hunting for manuscripts is not a profession for a lazy man. The search

for clues and the subsequent weary following down of each one—
the great majority of which are doomed to lead nowhere—occupy
countless hours of routine work punctuated only on rare occasions by
the thrill of discovery. Yet, as a wise amateur scholar once remarked,
"the test of a vocation is a love of the drudgery it involves." At the
end of the trail, if one is lucky, may lie that precious new fragment
of information one has sought so long—some new sidelight on a great
author, or even an unknown example of his work; and if so much is
found there is always the possibility that unsuspected riches may be
somewhere in the immediate neighborhood.

It is this ever present chance that urges the scholar to keep working
away, despite constant disappointments. So long as he believes in what
Horace Walpole called "serendipity"—"the faculty of making happy
and unexpected discoveries by accident"—he does not worry unduly,
even when months and years have gone by without result. Some years
ago Professor Anna Kitchel went to London to gather material for a
life of George Eliot and her extra-legal husband, G. H. Lewes. Despite
all her efforts, she was unable to find much hitherto unknown material.
Near the end of her stay in London, Miss Kitchel, riding on a London bus, remarked to her companion how disappointing her expedition
had been. The woman in the seat ahead turned and quietly asked,
"Would you care to see George Lewes's diaries?" Through this *dea ex
machina* she received an introduction to Lewes's granddaughters, Mrs.
Hopwood and Mrs. Ouvry. Mrs. Ouvry invited her to the villa in
Kent which had once been the home of Lewes's son, shared all her
reminiscences of George Lewes and his friends, and sent the American
scholar back to her hotel with a large bag full of Lewes's diaries and
letters addressed to him.

Although I hesitate to mention it, for fear of putting dangerous
ideas into the heads of novices, the fact is that once in a while sheer
ignorance pays off handsomely. Professor Mabbott, who has long been
interested in recovering the fugitive writings of Poe, likes to tell this
story against himself. Students of Poe long had known that in 1844
he had contributed a series of New York news-letters to the *Spy*, a
paper published in Columbia, Pennsylvania; but no file of the *Spy*

was known to exist. Twenty or more years ago Mabbott was in correspondence on other matters with J. E. Spannuth, a book dealer in Pottsville, Pennsylvania. Thinking that Columbia and Pottsville were virtually adjacent, Mabbott asked him if he knew of any file of the *Spy* in his vicinity. Spannuth replied that for years he had been trying to find such a file, but without any success. However, he said he would make one more attempt. Within a few weeks, he reported back to Mabbott that he had located and bought the editor's own file of the *Spy!* Spurred on by Mabbott's inquiry, he had found that the *Spy's* editor, when he retired from his post, had moved to Pottsville, taking the file with him. Now despite Mabbott's notion, Columbia and Pottsville are not adjacent; they are seventy or eighty miles apart. "Had I known how far apart they were," says Mabbott, "I don't think I'd have written Spannuth on the subject at all." Thanks to his blithe ignorance of Pennsylvania geography, and to a startling coincidence, he had the pleasure of unearthing some new examples of Poe's prose.

The story of the discovery of several other Poe items may handily be used to introduce the second major phase of the manuscript hunter's routine, even though the quarry in this case also happened not to be documents in the strict sense, but the long lost file of a periodical. In the winter of 1917–18, Professor John C. French was talking to a class in American literature at Johns Hopkins University. "If you ever come upon a small pamphlet entitled '*Tamerlane* by a Bostonian,'" he urged his students, "don't toss it away. You could trade it for a Pierce-Arrow car.* And if you find an old file of the *Baltimore Saturday Visiter* for 1833 you will have something that students of Poe have not been able to examine." He went on to explain that Poe's biographers had long known that his famous "MS. Found in a Bottle" had won the fifty-dollar first prize in a contest conducted by that periodical, which subsequently printed the story for the first time. No

* The first edition of *Tamerlane* is among the rarest of Poe's books. In 1925 Vincent Starrett published in the *Saturday Evening Post* an article called "Have You a *Tamerlane* in Your Attic?" in which he described the riches awaiting the householder who happened to find this or other rare literary items among his discarded family effects. A woman in Worcester, Mass., read the article and wondered if she had a *Tamerlane* in her attic. She went upstairs—and she did. She sold the copy for $17,500, enough to buy several Pierce-Arrows.

Poe scholar, however, as French said, had ever seen the *Visiter* itself. After class one of the students, a teacher in the Baltimore public schools, came up to French's desk and startled him by saying, "I know where there is a file of the *Saturday Visiter*." She knew two ladies who were granddaughters of one of the original editors of the paper, and was sure that they would be happy to let him see the file. But at the next meeting of the class she had to report, in some embarrassment, that when she called upon the ladies and told them of her teacher's interest in the file, they had been curiously evasive about it. However, she gave him the name and address of the elder of the two ladies.

French now faced the problem familiar to so many scholars. He knew where this long-lost material was. But how was he to persuade the owners to let him see it? He recalls:

I wrote to this lady, explaining the great interest the *Visiter* had for all students of Poe and begging for a chance to see it. I received no reply. It seemed like a case in which good manners might yield to literary interest; and on a chilly Sunday afternoon I went out into the suburbs and rang the doorbell at her home. As I had hoped, her native politeness was such that she could not turn me away, and I was permitted to see the bound volume of the *Visiter* for 1833. I worked in an unheated room and on a winter's afternoon with the light soon beginning to fade; but I never read a more interesting newspaper. Examination of it showed at once that the reminiscences of Latrobe and Hewitt * were surprisingly inaccurate. After looking over the announcement of the contest and the later printing of Poe's story, I turned other pages and found a short poem signed "Tamerlane" and then one entitled "Serenade" by E. A. Poe, and yet another very like Poe's style.

All three were poems hitherto unknown! After French had proved to the lady that he was not exaggerating when he said that her volume was important to Poe study, she permitted other students to examine it.

And so, while luck does have a pleasant habit of rewarding the diligent and ingenious searcher after new literary items, one other talent, besides detective skill and industry, is required of the investigator: the power to make friends. As we shall now see illustrated from the annals of modern scholarship.

* Two contemporaries of Poe who are the chief sources of information about his winning the prize contest.

III

THE Sherlock Holmesian part of research is virtually ended when the literary detective, closing his last book, or reading the last answer to his letters of inquiry (or receiving a clue from a breathless student!), points to an obscure village on a map of England or America, or to a name in *Who's Who*, and exclaims, "There lies the treasure!" Any sense of elation at this juncture, however, would not only be distinctly premature; it would sorely tempt the Fates which are specially delegated to punish the proud. Up to now, the scholar has been in command of the situation. By a cunning series of investigations he has wrested his secret from the shadows of history; unless his calculations have been very, very wrong, he now knows where the papers are, or at least where they should be. But how can he manage to see them? Now begins the second phase of his routine—the point at which Henry James's *Aspern Papers*, the classic fictional treatment of the search for literary manuscripts, begins.

Lest a totally unfair generalization be made from some of the tales I propose to tell, I hasten to recall the old saying that the more attractive side of human nature seldom makes front-page news. The same remark is certainly applicable to scholarly gossip. It is true that many of the favorite stories that have grown up around the sport of manuscript hunting throw no very favorable light upon the character of that natural prey of the scholar, the manuscript owner. But the real fact is that in most cases contemporary scholars meet with courtesy, hospitality, and unreserved generosity when they approach the owners of manuscripts they desire to study. The prefaces to the great majority of scholarly biographies and editions of letters published nowadays refer with unfeigned warmth to the cooperation of such persons; indeed, what begins as a purely formal relationship may blossom in time into a genuine personal friendship. Out of countless instances one might select the cordiality that has existed for so long between Earl Leslie Griggs, the distinguished Coleridge scholar, and the present representatives of the Coleridge family; or the friendship between

Horace Eaton of Syracuse University and the two Misses Bairdsmith, the granddaughters of Thomas DeQuincey, who aided him immeasurably in his writing of the standard life of the opium-eater.

If you were to take at its face value the gossip you sometimes hear when manuscript hunters get together, you would think that God had created a special race of men and women especially to plague them— the men and women to whom He has given possession of precious literary materials. In the heat of their passion for the almighty document, they sometimes forget that intelligent human beings may quite legitimately value their family pride or their personal privacy more highly than the increase of literary knowledge. Too, some scholars have invited defeat by their signally undiplomatic methods of dealing with those who were in a position to help them. And so their execrations often are unjust. Nevertheless, to anyone who sympathizes with the scholars' ambition to bring new manuscripts to light, some of their stories of encounters with the owners of such papers are, to say the very least, depressing.

One hears, for instance, of the fictitious but not necessarily untypical nobleman whose ancestral estate somewhere in the country contains a magnificent library, complete with librarian; in that library is a great and largely unexplored set of family archives dating from the time when the head of the family was as complete a courtier as Sidney and almost as complete a poet as Spenser. Scholars working on editions or biographies of Queen Elizabeth's Lord X have tried for generations to insinuate themselves into that rich hoard of manuscript. But the present Lord X comes down from London only for the hunting season; he never bothers to answer the letters he gets from scholars; his librarian has strict instructions to allow no one inside the library; in a word, Lord X is entirely indifferent to the progress of learning. Why, he wonders, should anyone want to get dirty poking about among old parchments written in crabbed hands that no one can read?

Although a number of Lord X's are still extant in Britain—and certainly in America there are just as many rich collectors who refuse access to their treasures—the brand of indifference usually manifested by manuscript owners, especially by those on a slightly less exalted social plane, is more annoying than formidable. In both England and

America are many families in whom no trace survives of the literary tastes that characterized their celebrated ancestor. Their philistinism does not necessarily mean that they will bar the way to the inquiring scholar. "Herman Melville?" they will say. "Oh, yes, he wrote a book about a whale. We once heard that our great-aunt Thelma had some papers of his. They can't be of much value, though; mostly just personal letters. We never saw the papers. They must be in an old trunk down at the storage warehouse. It would be pretty hard to get at them . . ." But if the scholar persists, in a tactful way, a member of the family may eventually agree to drive down to the warehouse with him.

Logan Pearsall Smith, the American-born essayist and amateur scholar who spent his whole adult life in England, once was working on a biography of the early seventeenth-century poet-diplomat Sir Henry Wotton. In one of the many volumes of *Reports of the Royal Historical Manuscripts Commission,* an indispensable aid to manuscript searchers, he found that a generation earlier, in 1878, a manuscript volume said to contain "copies of letters seemingly by and to Sir Henry Wotton" was in the library at a great country mansion. After some inquiry, Smith managed to find someone who gave him an introduction to the elderly retired colonel who was then occupying the house. The colonel wrote back a polite note, saying that he knew nothing about such a volume, but that Mr. Smith was welcome to come and look around if it would make him feel any better. Smith went, and found the house to be one of the largest in England, a perfectly immense structure with (according to his own account) a twenty-acre courtyard and everything else on a similar scale. The colonel, who bore a curious resemblance to the Duke of Wellington, greeted him at the door with what Smith took to be "a somewhat malicious chuckle" and ushered him into the vast library. Obviously it had not been used for many years. Its farthest horizontal reaches were laden with miscellaneous junk, while vertically the bookshelves seemed to lose themselves in the clouds. He was appalled at the prospect of trying to find his little riches in this infinite room, especially as it was a bleak November day and there was no vestige of a fire. But he set to work, and miraculously, within half an hour, he had in his hands the book he wanted. A quick glance through it revealed that it was far more important than the hurried cataloguer in 1878 had suspected; for in addition to copies of many of Wotton's unpublished letters, it contained a large collection of "table talk" compiled by someone in Wotton's household while he was ambassador to Venice and including many anecdotes of Queen Elizabeth, James I, Bacon, Lord Essex, and other celebrities of the age—to say nothing of a number of manuscript poems and hitherto unknown letters from John Donne.

Clutching his treasure in his hands, Smith hurried from the dank precincts of the library to his host's living quarters, where a brisk fire was burning. As he tremblingly turned over the leaves of this book, he was conscious of the colonel staring at him curiously over the top of that morning's *Times*. What in the world would any sane man want with such an old book filled with indecipherable writing? But the colonel was willing enough to let Smith take the book to Oxford to have it carefully transcribed. He probably would have cared not a whit if Smith had succumbed to the dreadful temptation he says he felt to insert into the "table talk" section of the manuscript a sly reference or two to Francis Bacon's abilities as a playwright. In any event, it was fortunate that he allowed Smith to have the book copied, because soon after it was returned from Oxford it was lost in a fire that destroyed the whole immense mansion.

It may be that the colonel was all the more skeptical because Smith was a native of America. If so, he was merely sharing a prejudice which remained common until quite recently among English possessors of manuscripts. When American scholars first began to ransack the English libraries and archives for literary materials, their dreadful efficiency and thoroughness puzzled those who were accustomed to the relatively easy-going research methods of British biographers. It is said that the authorities at the Public Record Office took many years to recover from their shock at the desperate zeal exhibited there by Professor Charles W. Wallace of the University of Nebraska, who was determined to dig up documents concerning Shakespeare—and did. Again, when the great millionaire collectors like Folger and Huntington spirited untold numbers of rare books and manuscripts from their ancient resting places to America, national pride, understandably enough, was hurt, and the resentment was transferred, logically or not, to American scholars who merely wished to use, but obviously could not dream of buying, the treasures that remained in Britain. For such reasons as these, some British possessors of literary material still cherish an animus against American scholars. Their number, happily, grows smaller year by year.

But I doubt that the manuscript hunter's lot is any happier in America. In Britain it is usually accounted an honor and a privilege for a family to be asked to help a member of one of the universities in his research; in the United States, on the other hand, there are plenty of families who would be offended if "some college professor" asked to be allowed to examine the papers in their old trunks. There may even be an element of completely irrelevant bigotry involved; during the Presidency of Franklin D. Roosevelt the owners of an unpublished notebook of Thoreau refused to let a Columbia University professor study it on the ground that Columbia was a nest of New Dealers.

Probably the strongest motive behind a family's hostility to scholarly inquiry is a desire to keep absolute control over what the world shall and shall not know about its forebear. Sometimes, indeed usually, the family is motivated by shame: Great-Uncle Alfred, they reason, did get into the most awful messes over women, and even though he undoubtedly was a great novelist we still bear his name . . . Today some families refuse access to their papers, not because there is anything shameful to conceal, but simply because they feel that the intimate life of their celebrated ancestor was his own affair, and not the world's. Who can say they are wrong?

Everyone knows the sorry story of the feud in Emily Dickinson's family which has kept at least some of the truth about her from being known—the result being the growth of a whole series of romantic myths about the recluse-poet and her alleged love affair.* It is not a

---

* Just as this book was going to the printers, it was announced that the papers of Emily Dickinson, including the manuscripts of her poems, had been purchased by Harvard University. They will be edited by Thomas H. Johnson and published by the Harvard University Press. "Now at last, three quarters of a century after Emily Dickinson's death," says Johnson, "scholars will be able to determine with some accuracy the rank she may take among world poets."

unique instance by any means. There are scholars today who are stale-mated by family squabbles reaching back a century or more. Some-times, however, a family's reluctance to deal with manuscript seekers has a more reasonable basis. Nineteenth-century literary biographers and editors had no such code of professional ethics as governs most of their descendants. The Victorian descendants of a departed author, happy to find that at last a biographer planned to bring him back into the public eye, would lend some of their papers to the applicant for the term of his study; and that would be the last they would see of their precious manuscripts. Naturally, they did not welcome the next applicant with a brass band. Professor Tremaine McDowell of the University of Minnesota traced some fifty diaries of William Cullen Bryant's mother to members of the family living in the Midwest. When his letters elicited decidedly frigid replies, he made a special trip to their home. They then told him a story calculated to make any scholar's blood run cold. Some years earlier another college professor had appeared on their doorstep on the same errand. They had will-ingly displayed the diaries to him; but since the manuscripts were extensive and required leisurely study, he asked permission to take forty of them with him to his hotel. The family cheerfully agreed—and that was the last they saw of the diaries, or of the professor. Later they consulted a fortune teller, whose crystal ball revealed a clear view of the missing diaries. They had landed in a museum, whose name, un-fortunately, was too faint to be deciphered. And to this day those diaries of Bryant's mother remain lost.

Then there are those humble citizens who, like an occasional library or a millionaire collector, simply do not know what riches they pos-sess. One writes to them, citing good and sufficient reasons why he suspects they may have such-and-such a series of letters; and they promptly reply that they are quite sure they have no papers of any literary interest whatsoever. This is a knotty problem for the scholar to solve, because the statutes of most states make no provision for the use of a search-warrant in an attempt to extend the boundaries of knowledge, and burglary is not one of the arts normally taught in our graduate schools. His only recourse is to try by every means at his command to persuade his correspondents to search their possessions, or better still, since he would be certain to make a more thorough job of it, to let him look about on his own. There are a number of homes in the United States and Great Britain where important literary documents are thought to be hidden, but no investigator has yet devised a way of persuading the owners to hunt for them.

Indifference, hostility, ignorance, and finally avarice: the least pleasant of all the human frailties the manuscript hunter must contend with, but unfortunately not the least prevalent. In the past few years the scholar searching for manuscripts in America has encountered stiffening resistance among those who read in the newspapers how much his university is spending every year for scientific research. If there is so much money around, he is asked, why can't some of it be spent for my grandfather's cousin's papers? And then (this is almost inevitable): Didn't I read somewhere that a New York dealer paid $50,000 for the manuscript of *Alice in Wonderland?*

IV

UNFORTUNATELY many owners of valuable manuscripts cannot be approached directly: their life has no room for people who have not been properly introduced. The scholar's first problem in such cases is to search for someone who knows someone else who can perhaps put in a good word for him. Today's scholar never knows when a casual acquaintance may become the crucial link between him and the crusty old Duke of Omnium, a neighbor of the aforementioned Lord X, whose great Tudor place at Fourteen Oaks harbors hundreds of letters, full of gossip about Restoration London, which Pepys and Evelyn and Dryden and the Earl of Rochester addressed to an earlier noble tenant. Scholars, British and American alike, have been trying for thirty years to get inside the library at Fourteen Oaks. One man, however, is a shade more resourceful than his predecessors. His tennis partner on summer afternoons (a man who teaches biochemistry in the university) has a favorite aunt in New York whose husband is an importer. The importer's correspondent in London, the head of a great exporting firm, is a veteran of the Boer War, in which he served with distinction alongside the youth who was later to become seventeenth Duke of Omnium. And since wide cracks appear in the Duke's habitual armor when he is reminded of happy days in the Regiment . . . The word passes along the chain—from the professor of biochemistry to the New York importer to the London exporter; the Londoner encounters the Duke of Omnium at the annual regimental dinner and begins to talk about the fine young American scholar who is so deeply interested in Pepys and Evelyn. His Grace is in one of his rare complaisant moods; of course, he says, the boy is welcome to see the library at Fourteen Oaks. The word passes back along the chain. The next summer, our scholar is in London. He writes to the Duke, mentioning the name of his fellow officer on the veldt. The Duke has completely forgotten the conversation that occurred last winter over the regimental wine, but he cannot welsh on what evidently was a kind of promise; so he sends a polite little note to the American. . . . The walls of the citadel, at long last, are breached—and our store of literary knowledge is enriched.

This hypothetical example is possibly a bit overcomplicated, but stratagems similar to it actually are used. When Professor Gordon S. Haight was collecting manuscript letters of George Eliot in preparation for the Yale edition, he discovered that a large group of them were in the hands of two old ladies in England who were distant relatives of George Eliot's family.

"I got into communication," he tells me, "with a niece of theirs who tried in vain to persuade them to let me have the letters copied. After I had long given up hope of securing access to the material, I met an English friend in this country who was about to return home. He asked if there was anything he could do to help in my work. I said that there was one group of letters I wanted very much to see, but that I thought it was hopeless to try to get at them.

" 'Where are they?' he asked.

" 'In ——,' I replied, mentioning the name of the town.

" 'Why, I was born in ——,' he said. 'What is their family name?'

"I mentioned the name.

" 'Why,' he said, 'I went to school with Gwen.'

"Within a few weeks," Haight concludes, "I was put in touch with the immediate family of the old ladies, who were persuaded to allow me to use the letters."

When we remember the bus-top experience of Anna Kitchel, related earlier in this chapter, it seems likely that a special providence attends the labors of George Eliot scholars.

Luckily, such circuitous methods do not have to be called into play very often. But practically every scholar at some time or other has found himself in a situation in which the owner of the papers he wants to see is not hostile but simply hesitant about opening them to his gaze. That is when the art of unobtrusive flattery comes in handy. The scholar writes a masterly letter, glowing with enthusiasm about the author in whom he is interested (a figure of first importance, really, although the textbooks inexplicably dismiss him with a paragraph or two), and reciting a few obscure but respectable facts about the man which the family is not likely to know. Only a man or woman devoid of the least tincture of common humanity can withstand that sort of approach. If, they reflect, this professor knows so much already about Great-great-uncle John, surely there will be no harm in letting him see those old papers. And we hadn't realized before that Uncle John was so imposing a figure in literature. Perhaps it really is time that a full-length biography of him be written from the original records!

But the two most requisite "personality traits" in a manuscript hunter remain to be mentioned. One is the simple quality of patience once the quarry seems to be in sight—patience that will prevent an impetuous move that may undo in a minute the careful work of years, patience that will maintain the outward composure when one is ready to scream, patience that will help one to accept with equanimity the prospect of waiting years to examine a treasure located after much hard work.

The other most requisite trait, not specified thus far, has been implied in all I have said. It can be described only by that highly unsatisfactory and sadly abused word "charm." Unless the inquiring scholar can be urbane and reasonably sophisticated when he is dealing with urbane and sophisticated owners of manuscripts, and simple and respectful when he is dealing with old ladies; unless he can work up an instant enthusiasm about a retired colonel's experiences at Gallipoli, or a middle-aged businessman's hatred of bureaucratic government, he is lost. He must be all things to all kinds of people—and he never knows what kind he will have to deal with next.

Some scholars, who are frustrated actors at heart, like to play the role they feel is required by the circumstances. For example, they will cram on an esoteric subject which they know is their quarry's hobby, so as to approach him from his weak side; and, after he has been softened up, they will hasten to the kill. They sometimes succeed, if their victim is not very penetrating, and then they have a wonderful story to tell at the next meeting of the Modern Language Association. But oftener the best, and certainly the least cynical, policy is to be one's self.

One of the most spectacular success stories in recent literary scholarship involves no pose, no great luck, and no detective work at all. After Thackeray's death in 1863, his family—as represented by his two daughters and then by their children—sedulously observed his command that no biography be written of him. They relaxed the observance sufficiently to permit publication of some of his letters, under their immediate supervision. But they would not allow scholars access to their family archives, and more than once, when they received word of the impending publication of letters which had fallen into other hands, they took legal action against the publishers. Down to 1939, therefore, the Thackeray papers (like those of a few other great Victorian men of letters) were *terra incognita* to scholars.

In the summer of that year Gordon N. Ray, then a graduate student at Harvard, went to England to gather materials for his doctoral dissertation on Thackeray. Through the American Universities Union he obtained an introduction to Thackeray's grandson, who invited him to his home in the country. As a result of that visit, Ray was introduced to the novelist's granddaughter, Hester Thackeray Fuller, at whose London home the Thackeray papers were stored. Although he did not know it then, his meeting with Mrs. Fuller was perfectly timed. The family had decided that any further withholding of Thackeray's papers would merely assist the growth of unjust legends about him. They had not, however, chosen a scholar to superintend the publication of the rich mass of material, which was so important and extensive that it seemed to call for the attention of a scholar of long experience; and plenty of seasoned scholars, both British and American, would have given their right arms for the privilege of editing it. Ray, still a novice in scholarship, was only in his middle twenties. But Mrs. Fuller discerned in this tall, husky American the editor she felt her grandfather's letters and private papers deserved; and so, before the outbreak of the war forced him to leave England, he was appointed the official editor of the Thackeray letters. With the microfilms arranged for during his visit, he devoted the time remaining before he entered the United States Navy to preparing a four-volume edition of the letters. After the war * he returned to Mrs. Fuller's house in London and occupied a suite of rooms set aside for his use while he made a complete examination of the other Thackeray papers, which had been impossible in 1939. At the same time he scoured English collections for additional letters. During this leisurely and systematic research he collected material enough for at least one supplementary volume of letters, which he plans to follow with the first biography of Thackeray to be authorized by the family.

The peroration of this chapter may well be devoted to a single anecdote of research which sums up more of the points made here than any other I know. It comes to me from Professor Clifford, whom we have already met. When he was a graduate student at Columbia University he selected as his dissertation topic the life of Mrs. Hester Lynch Salusbury Thrale Piozzi, the bluestocking who figures so prominently in the biography of Dr. Johnson. In 1935 he went to England on a traveling fellowship, hired a bicycle, and pedaled through the mountains of Wales in search of manuscripts. His startling adventures on this expedition are worth an essay in themselves, and he assures me that he will write it when the time is ripe. Suffice it to say here that he found much more than he dreamed he would, under the most peculiar circumstances.

During the Welsh tour Clifford met a Miss Mainwaring, an old lady

---

* The captain of the aircraft carrier *Belleau Wood* was not impressed when he was told that Lieutenant Ray's specialty in civilian life was Thackeray. "How does that help us?" he demanded. But later, after the ship and her men had been proved in battle, he confided to his junior officer, "You know, Mr. Ray, it's the drunks and the intellects that are winning the war."

who owned Mrs. Piozzi's furniture and plate. In the course of conversation she told him that her half-sister, Mrs. A. M. Knollys, might
be able to help him, since she was a granddaughter of Sir John Salusbury, Mrs. Piozzi's adopted son. The following autumn, when he returned to London, he looked up Mrs. Knollys, but learned from her
daughter that she had had a stroke and was in a nursing home in South
Kensington. The daughter told her of Clifford's interest in Mrs. Piozzi,
however, and the old lady, then over eighty, insisted that he be asked
to visit her in the nursing home.

"You can imagine my fears and trepidations," Clifford says. "The
poor old lady couldn't speak, and if excited might have another stroke.
But the daughter insisted that her mother was determined to tell me
something. A beautiful white-haired lady, who had been presented to
Queen Victoria and was something of a person, she really was delightful to see.

"The daughter," he continues, "had worked out a means of communication with her mother, by signs and nods, and by long questioning and nodding was able to get out of her that she had many years
before seen a letter of proposal from Thrale [Mrs. Piozzi's first hus-
band] to Hester Lynch Salusbury—a very ardent letter. The whole
tale didn't sound credible to me for many reasons. An important letter
of this kind would certainly have been known by the scholars, and I
had never heard about it before. Also, Thrale's known stolid temperament made the ardent part very dubious. But the possibility that the
letter existed was exciting. After another half-hour of questionings
and noddings the daughter was able to ascertain that Mrs. Knollys
had seen the letter many years before, at which time it had been in
the possession of a friend now dead. However, her daughter knew the
son of the friend and promised to find out from him whether there was
anything at all in the story. And so ended this bizarre interview.

"A few weeks later I had a note from a Major John Delmar Morgan
asking me to come to tea with him and his wife in Chelsea the next
Sunday. It turned out that Mrs. Morgan had known Tennyson intimately. She insisted on talking about Tennyson all afternoon, while
I kept trying to get in a word about the Thrale letter. They remembered
that they had owned some Thrale manuscripts but were vague about

what they were. Also, they couldn't remember when they had had them—but they were certain that they had sold them long ago at Sotheby's, the famous London book auctioneers. After long probing, I finally ascertained that because they had kept the manuscripts in a particular closet in a house they had lived in directly after the First World War, they probably had sold the papers about then. That was the best I could do.

"The next step was to go the next day to Sotheby's and ask them to check whether they had ever sold anything for Major Delmar Morgan. They looked in their ledgers and found that on February 3, 1919, they had sold a lot of letters for him. At the British Museum I was able to find a marked copy of the catalogue of the sale for that day, and there, listed as lot 382, was a so-called letter of proposal from Thrale to Mrs. and Miss Salusbury, dated June 28, 1763. The letter was listed as having been purchased by Brown and Stevens, London dealers.

"At Brown and Stevens I was able to find little to help me. They insisted that they kept no records of the sale of individual manuscripts. They bought them and sold them as soon as they could. I was up against a stone wall. After long questioning as to who might in 1919 have been buying such manuscripts, they indicated that almost everything was going to America. I knew, of course, that in that case the most likely purchaser would have been R. B. Adam of Buffalo, New York, who was then building his great collection of materials relating to Dr. Johnson and his circle. But I also knew that in 1929 Adam had published his sumptuous three-volume catalogue of his complete collection, and no such letter was listed. It certainly seemed as if I was beaten.

"But the next year, when I was back in the United States, just on a chance, I wrote to Adam telling him of my long search for the Thrale letter and asking if he knew anything at all about it. He replied promptly that he owned the letter—had had it since 1919—and couldn't for the life of him explain why it had been left out of his catalogue. If I would stop by Buffalo sometime, I could see it. So finally, in 1937, I believe, almost two years after I had first heard of the letter, I saw it and secured a copy for my book."

Well, you ask, was the letter, when Clifford finally caught up with it, worth the search? Remember that Mrs. Knollys, lying in her bed in the South Kensington nursing home, had been interrogated by her daughter: "Was it a love letter from Thrale?" A nod. "Was it a letter of proposal?" A nod. "What was it like—was it very ardent?" An emphatic nod of assent. But Clifford had been incredulous. Could Henry Thrale, a phlegmatic, prosaic London brewer, ever have composed an *ardent* letter? Throughout his long search, Clifford had been doubtful. But this is what Thrale had written, and you can judge for yourself whether the old lady was right:

Mr. Thrale presents His most respectfull compliments to Mrs. & Miss Salusbury & wishes to God He could have communicated His Sentiments to them last night, which is absolutely impossible for Him to do to any other Person breathing; He therefore most ardently begs to see Them at any Hour this afternoon, & He will at all Events immediately enter upon this very interesting Subject, & when once begun, there is no Danger of His wandering upon any other: in short, see them, He must, for He assures them, with the greatest Truth & Sincerity, that They have murder'd Peace & Happiness at Home.

As Clifford says, the morals attached to his story are numerous and obvious; and I shall not spell them out here. But it illustrates, perhaps more comprehensively than any other narrative in this chapter, the truth that the quest of literary manuscripts, full of drudgery and disappointments as it is, has—shall we say?—its moments!

EXIT A LADY, ENTER
ANOTHER

I

OF all the elements in the lives of literary people which have complicated the tasks of their biographers and critics, the most troublesome are loosely comprehended under the capacious heading of Sex. The modern scholar has only scorn for the practice, fashionable among best-selling biographers in the past thirty years, of emphasizing the sexual interest in an author's life above all else. Nevertheless, if we are to have as broad and deep an understanding of a man of letters as possible, we must candidly place the fact that he sowed his youthful wild oats rather lavishly, or was impotent, or had a mistress in addition to a wife, alongside everything else we can learn of him. One aspect of an author's life may illuminate many others, and knowledge of his sexual transgressions or peculiarities may be absolutely essential to a full grasp of his temperament, and through his temperament, of the meanings in his work. It is impossible to understand Ruskin, for example, without a dispassionate recognition of his tragic psychic abnormalities—the subject of renewed controversy since the publication of his wife's letters to her family. No biographer of Hazlitt may overlook the unpleasant episode of his infatuation with Sarah Walker which he recorded in that strange confession, *Liber Amoris*. Walt Whitman's boasts about the number of illegitimate children he had sired in his youth are highly suggestive, simply because dogged research has failed to reveal any evidence to support his grandiose statistics.

122

But the job of discovering the truth about matters which are among a man's most private concerns is formidable. There is a very sound historical reason for this. Perhaps nothing in the cultural and social climate of a given age is more sensitive to the shifting currents of moral, religious, and philosophical opinion than its attitudes toward sexual behavior. And these attitudes, tolerant in one period and inflexibly strait-laced in another, seriously prejudice the sources of our information.

If our author lived in the free-and-easy Restoration, for example, his sexual habits would be the subject of much matter-of-fact gossip in contemporary letters or in Pepys's diary and, no doubt, of some extremely ribald versified squibs. But precisely because such matters were so freely discussed, the factor of exaggeration must be taken into account. Recent scholarly studies of the lives of the Restoration wits, without appreciably changing the traditional belief that the period was one of almost unparalleled moral relaxation, have shown in many cases that the contemporary accounts were gaudier, at least in details, than the facts warranted.

If, on the other hand, our subject was a Victorian, one would be hard pressed to find, at least in print, any contemporary reference to such aspects of his life; and whatever private letters bearing on the subject have escaped destruction by the man himself or his family may be closely guarded by his descendants. There is at least one well known English author of the nineteenth century in whose immediate family is said to have occurred a series of lurid events worthy of treatment by a Shirley or a Ford—but the rumor has, I think, never appeared in print. Furthermore, during such an age as the Victorian, the records of the sexual proclivities of earlier figures are likely to be seriously distorted in transmission, because any mention of them will be colored by the special moral prejudices of the time; and so what may have been in the beginning a rather routine or even innocent episode takes on, thanks to the indignation or deprecation of the biographer, gratuitous overtones which it is the duty of the later researcher to detect and disentangle once more.

Despite these formidable barriers—the necessity for discovering authentic records in the first place, and then for peeling off the successive layers of embroidery with which later generations have adorned them—the scholar persists in trying to find out the truth. From the time that Chaucer, according to a contemporary legal document, was accused "de raptu meo" by a lady with the enchanting name of Cecily de Chaumpaigne, literary biography has been thickly sprinkled with ladies whose relationships with men of letters require exegesis. "Cherchez la femme" is a motto of the literary detective as much as it is of the fictional criminologist; and scholars would not be human if they did not betray a certain zest in running down the often delectable details. But they must draw a careful line between the episode which, however sensational it may have been, lacks real relevance to the literary production of an author, and that which can be an important clue to his personality or a profound influence on his later life and his work. In the following pages we shall see an example of each type.

II

AMONG the other errors for which the Puritans of the late sixteenth and the seventeenth century have to answer is serious pollution of the stream of literary historical evidence. For three hundred years we were told that the outdoor playhouses in which the dramas of Shakespeare and his fellows were performed were sinks of iniquity, haunted by all the riffraff of London, to which no decent citizen would think of taking his family. Probably the Globe drew no more than the normal number of pickpockets and prostitutes; if contemporary accounts were true, and the audience had been composed almost *entirely* of such professionals, the law of diminishing returns, as a learned student of the English drama once remarked, would have set in very quickly. The reason why we read so much in the older books (Robert Bridges' essay on Shakespeare's audience is possibly the latest example) about the dubious moral tendencies of Shakespeare's audience is that virtually all the contemporary information we have on the subject was written by Puritan pamphleteers who waged a bitter and unceasing war against the stage, its audiences, its playwrights, and its actors,

from the 1580's onward. To the Puritans, in their passionate concern
for salvation, the theater was a place of veritably Babylonian de-
bauchery; and in this conviction they painted a vivid and detailed
picture of the evils surrounding the playhouse which has served until
recently, *faute de mieux*, as "historical evidence." Of course it is nothing of the sort. It is grossly, fantastically distorted propaganda for a
cause.

It is to the Puritans, likewise, that until almost yesterday we owed
virtually all our knowledge of the misspent life of the playwright
Christopher Marlowe. According to the standard narrative, which
is to be found in even the most reputable reference works published
before 1925, Marlowe lived a life that could not end otherwise than
in the sort of death he died. And it was upon the nature of his passing
that the early narratives concentrated with pious relish.

The first man to tell the story at length was Thomas Beard, a
fanatical Puritan who in 1597, four years after Marlowe's death, published *The Theatre of Gods Judgements*, a marvelous farrago of hundreds of tales of God's wrath upon Papists, non-Puritans of all sorts,
and above all, as the very title of his work suggests, the blasphemous
people of the stage. Beard was an indefatigable collector of all scraps
of fact or legend which could be made to prove that an angry God
could be trusted to lay His heavy hand upon transgressors. At the
very time that he was writing his book, there came to his attention an
example seemingly sent from heaven for his purposes. After describing
in colorful generalizations the life of crime and blatant atheism that
Marlowe had led, he wrote:

It so fell out, that in London streets as he purposed to stab one whome
hee [owed] a grudge vnto with his dagger, the other party perceiuing
so auoided the stroke, that withall catching hold of his wrest, he stabbed
his owne dagger into his owne head, in such sort, that notwithstanding
all the meanes of surgerie that could be wrought, hee shortly after died
thereof. The manner of his death being so terrible (for hee euen cursed
and blasphemed to his last gaspe, and togither with his breath an oth
flew out of his mouth) that it was not only a manifest signe of Gods
iudgement, but also an horrible and fearefull terrour to all that beheld
him. But herein did the iustice of God most notably appeare, in that

hee compelled his owne hand which had written those blasphemies to be the instrument to punish him, and that in his braine, which had deuised the same.

And so forth; the nice irony of Marlowe's reported manner of death spurred Beard's pen to an ecstasy of edifying reflections.

Now in the Puritan age, as in all others, writers copied one another; once a good thing was in print, it was a shame not to use it again. Thus when Edmund Rudierd wrote a similar collection of sensational tales with righteous point called *The Thunderbolt of Gods Wrath against Hard-Hearted and stiffe-necked Sinners* (1618) he condensed Beard's story and added a few touches of his own; for example: "So blaspheming and cursing, he yeelded vp his stinking breath: marke this yee Players, that liue by making fooles laugh at sinne and wickednesse." Some twenty years later, although in the interim the Puritans had locked up the playhouses, the actors and playwrights were still fair game for propagandistic assaults on the secular way of life; and once again Beard's version of Marlowe's death appeared in print, in Samuel Clark's *Mirrour, or Looking-Glass both for Saints and Sinners* (1645/6). Meanwhile other allusions to the dreadful circumstances of Marlowe's passing, not demonstrably borrowed from Beard, had appeared in print, so that by the middle of the seventeenth century this had become the accepted account; and it continued to be accepted in its essentials down to our own time.

None of these accounts named the murderer, and Beard's "in London streets" was not very specific as to the scene of the assault. But another atheist-hater, William Vaughan, in his *Golden Grove* (1600), wrote:

It so hapned, that at Detford, a litle village about three miles distant from London, as he meant to stab with his ponyard one named Ingram, that had inuited him thither to a feast, and was then playing at tables, he quickly perceyuing it, so auoyded the thrust, that withall drawing out his dagger for his defence, hee stabd this Marlow into the eye, in such sort, that his braines comming out at the daggers point, hee shortlie after dyed.

There we have the assailant, "one named Ingram," and the place, Deptford—more particularly, a place where low fellows like atheists dined and gamed, *videlicet* a tavern or, as it soon became in the pages of the commentators, a brothel.

But from these narratives one vital detail is inexplicably absent— that of the Light Woman who figured in an independent account of Marlowe's murder that appeared only a year after Beard's. One wonders why the divines didn't snap her up at once, for her presence would have added even more impressiveness to their account. Since Marlowe already stood convicted of horrible atheism, blasphemy, playwriting, gluttony, and gaming, why not add lechery to the abominations of which he was guilty? In 1598 the Reverend Francis Meres published his *Palladis Tamia, or Wit's Treasury*, an anthology of choice passages from great authors which is most famous because of its numerous flattering allusions to Shakespeare. Meres was no Puritan, but his allusion to Marlowe's demise had a moral just the same. He wrote:

As Iodelle, a French tragical poet, beeing an epicure and an atheist, made a pitifull end: so our tragicall poet Marlow for his Epicurism and Atheisme had a tragical death. . . . As the poet Lycophron was shot to death by a certain riual of his: so Christopher Marlow was stabd to death by a bawdy Servingman, a riual of his in his lewde loue.

In this way the indispensable sex interest entered Marlowe biography, or pseudobiography, providing the immediate *casus belli* which Beard (to whom Meres referred his readers for further information) had not defined. A century later the gossipy *Athenae Oxonienses*, a biographical encyclopedia of the worthies associated with Oxford University, after reproducing Beard's account seized upon Meres's special angle and enlarged upon it:

For so it fell out, that he being deeply in love with a certain Woman, had for his rival a bawdy serving man, one rather fit to be a Pimp, than an ingenious *Amoretto* as *Marlo* conceived himself to be. Whereupon *Marlo* taking it to be a high affront, rush'd in upon, to stab, him, with his dagger.

With each retelling after this initial coalescence of the Beard and the Meres versions, the story grew, to include proportionately more of the "certain Woman" and less (as the fashion declined) of the appalling blasphemies of the dying Marlowe. A notable advance in circumstantial detail was provided by William Rufus Chetwood, in his *British Theatre* (1750):

> Having an intrigue with a loose woman, he came unexpectedly into her Chamber, and caught her in the Embraces of another Gallant. This so much enraged him, that he drew his Dagger and attempted to Stab him; but in the Struggle, the Paramour seized Marlow, turnd the Point into his Head, and killed him on the spot in 1592.

One suspects that Chetwood, perhaps unconsciously, was confusing the Marlowe episode with a similar one reported (entirely without confirmation) of Shakespeare. Shakespeare, having overheard his fellow actor Richard Burbage make an assignation with a lady of pleasure, reached the appointed place first and gleefully cried out, when Burbage entered and ventured to object, "William the Conqueror came before Richard!" No blood was shed, although Burbage would seem to have had ample provocation. In any case, Chetwood was the first writer to report the presence of the mysterious woman at the fatal brawl.

As interest in the history of the English theater and its playwrights grew, more and more people wrote about Marlowe's sorry though not undramatic end—all of them, of course, borrowing from the preceding accounts. Nobody was obliged to reproduce the words of his source, and so each new writer played interesting variations on the facts as they were originally set down. The meager and oblique hint by Meres as to the character of the lady in question—"his lewde loue"—resulted in her appearance in the 1797 edition of the *Encyclopædia Britannica* as a "low girl," in the pages of Hippolyte Taine (1863, translated 1872) as "a drab," and in a German work on English customs (1912) as "a camp-follower." The occupation of Marlowe's assailant was variously reported as that of a lackey, a valet, a footman, and a scullion. Eventually the novelists and dramatists got wind of this historic episode, and in at least a dozen novels and plays, the best known of which is Miss Clemence Dane's *Will Shakespeare* (1922), new extravagant embroidery was added to the bare thread of reported fact with which the story had begun.

But in the early nineteenth century the antiquarians, the lineal ancestors of modern researchers, busied themselves with the Marlowe

problem, and uncovered the first really authentic data on his life, referring chiefly to his university career. The search for enlightenment
on the facts of his death, however, was destined to lead up a blind alley.
In 1820 James Broughton asked the vicar of St. Nicholas', Deptford,
to examine the register of burials in his church for possible mention
of Marlowe's burial. The parson found the entry: "1st June, 1593.
Christopher Marlowe, slain by Francis Archer." At last, a clue! But
the discovery served only to muddy the waters, because the vicar, who
was inexperienced in reading Elizabethan handwriting, misread the
entry, and what he took to be "Francis Archer" was not that at all.
For decades, scholars searched in vain for records of the mythical
Archer. Then others looked at the record and found that it really read
"Francis Frezer" or "Frizer." This sent them off on a new trail. They
had no way of knowing that even though they had read the name
aright, the record itself was wrong so far as the slayer's Christian name
was concerned. But the family name was correct, and an American
investigator's remembrance of it enabled him finally to reveal the
true circumstances of Marlowe's murder.

In 1924 John Leslie Hotson, freshly endowed with the Ph.D. of
Harvard University, found himself in the gloomy precincts of the
Public Record Office in Chancery Lane, London. It houses an immense
and still largely unexplored collection of the governmental and legal
records of England, dating from the Middle Ages to the nineteenth
century. Such indexes and catalogues as exist to this incredible monument to six centuries of official paperwork are incomplete and sometimes baffling in their own right. To work in the P.R.O. with even a
faint chance of finding what one wishes to find depends upon two
things: a specialized knowledge of the complicated and ever shifting
relationships and functions of English governmental offices and courts
—without which one cannot hope to light upon even the right category
of documents—and infinite patience. The only additional factor that
improves one's chances is luck, and as a matter of fact the most important literary discoveries that have occurred in Chancery Lane have
been due more to luck than to good management.

Hotson had gone to the Public Record Office on a mission quite unrelated to Marlowe. But as he was inspecting the Calendar of Close

Rolls (an index to the P.R.O.'s huge accumulation of a certain class of Tudor documents) he happened to note an entry referring to "Ingram Frizer." Immediately he recalled the occurrence of those two names in the Marlowe mystery, though it had been assumed that they were borne by two different men. He called for the document referred to, but to his disappointment it dealt merely with the transfer of a small piece of property. Still, he had established that there had been, in Marlowe's time, a man named Ingram Frizer. It was perhaps more than a coincidence that the man bore both of the names connected by tradition with the murder. So he turned to the bulky P.R.O. calendars, many of them in the handwriting of three hundred years earlier, which are an index of sorts to the proceedings of the Elizabethan courts.

Hotson searched for days. The Inquisitions Post Mortem for the period, hundreds of pages of indexed names, contained no Ingram Frizer. The criminal records of the Court of the Queen's Bench furnished "an arduous and eye-wearying hunt," as Hotson says, but still no Frizer. Nor had he any better luck on his third try, the Rolls of the Assizes on the South-Eastern Circuit. These, presumably, were the only places where one could find documents relating to a murder in 1593. But suddenly he recalled that the old accounts mentioned specifically that Marlowe had been the aggressor. If that were true, then certainly the murderer would have pleaded for a pardon on the ground of self-defense. Hotson therefore turned to one more manuscript index, that of the pardons in the Patent Rolls of the Chancery. Feverishly his eyes ran down one page of legal Latin, then the next and the next, until, among the entries for the summer of 1593, they lighted upon lines which he translated as: "The Queen 28th day of June granted pardon to Ingram Frisar [for homicide] in self-defense."

There was the entry; now for the record itself. The appeal for pardon must have been accompanied by a circumstantial narrative of the homicide, perhaps the statements of witnesses—perhaps even one by the certain Woman. Hotson filled out a form requesting the document.

But it was 4:25 P.M. and at that moment the Public Record Office closed for the day.

Hotson spent a sleepless night, one of the longest, it is said, in the history of literary research. He was on the steps of the archive building before it opened the next morning, and no doubt he was the first reader to hand in a call slip to the attendant. In due time the Patent Roll was brought to his desk. His were the first eyes to examine it since it had been filed away among thousands of similar rolled-up documents, heavy with seals and ribbons, in the time of Queen Elizabeth.

And there it was: the exact terms of the Queen's pardon to Ingram Frizer for the murder of Christopher Marlowe, together with a summary of the evidence given at the inquest over the dead man's body. Hotson read the document carefully. It threw a flood of light on the events in the tavern the night Marlowe was killed. But it was only a summary, and somewhere there should be the official report. Probably it was in the miscellaneous series of Chancery Papers, to which all such documents at that time were consigned. But that immense gathering of papers, the detritus of the exceedingly diversified operations of Chancery from the time of Edward I to that of Charles I, was indexed not by year but only by county. Indomitably Hotson plowed through the thousands and thousands of manuscript entries relating to virtually every occurrence that had ever come to official notice of the County of Kent, where Deptford is located. At long last he came upon the entry he was seeking. He filled out another form; the document appeared, containing the full text of the coroner's inquiry—and the quest was at an end.

What, then, had really happened? In the first place, one must observe that a useful axiom, when scholars are dealing with biographical statements almost contemporary with the author's life, is that where there's smoke, there's fire. No matter how untrustworthy a piece of old evidence obviously may be, the odds are strongly in favor of its having begun with a germ of truth. The details may be contradictory or palpably impossible; nevertheless, they demand close analysis, because by trying to find out *how* they came to be wrong, one may find the way to truth. For example, Beard's statement that the brawl occurred "in London streets" has been shown not to be too wrong after all: there was a "London Street" in Deptford, very near where the murder occurred. In other respects, the contemporary writers were not far off: there *was* a brawl, of course, and it ended fatally; Marlowe *was* the aggressor; his assailant *was* named Ingram, though this was his first name and not his last, a circumstance that students, forgetting the common Elizabethan habit of referring to a man by his given name, had failed to consider; the assault *had* followed supper and a game of backgammon (the "tables" of Vaughan's account). Whether the scene, described before the coroner as the house of a widow named Eleanor Bull, was a tavern or a private home is not decided.

In that locale, at ten o'clock in the morning of May 30, 1593, Marlowe began a long and very private conference with three other men, Ingram Frizer, Nicholas Skeres, and Robert Poley. At the time of Hotson's discovery the names meant nothing, although they provided the essential clues by which scholars subsequently discovered much that had preceded, and perhaps motivated, the slaying. The four were there all day. After supper Marlowe, no doubt somewhat affected by the wine consumed during the lengthy meeting, lay down on a bed, and the other three men sat on a bench at a table before him. Somehow a dispute began; according to the testimony before the coroner, Frizer and Marlowe "were in speech & uttered one to the other divers malicious words for the reason that they could not be at one nor agree about the payment of the sum of pence, that is, *le reckinynge* there." The dagger at Frizer's belt, as common an item of Elizabethan accouterment as a wrist watch is today, hung within reach of Marlowe, who was now supposedly on his feet. He grabbed it and hit Frizer on the head with it, inflicting two wounds.

Frizer, at a disadvantage because his legs were under the table, wrested the dagger from Marlowe, and "gave the said Christopher then & there a mortal wound over his right eye of the depth of two inches & of the width of one inch; of which mortal wound the aforesaid Christopher Marlowe then & there instantly died." The last two words, it will be noted, scarcely accord with the Puritan divines' horrified report of Marlowe's well chosen blasphemous remarks as he lay dying. And indeed there is reason to doubt the accuracy of the coroner's statement. Medical men maintain that a wound of this description would have caused a coma, but not instant death.

But what of the "certain Woman" who has vanished from our most recent pages? Alas, she has vanished just as completely from the pages of scholarly Marlowe biography, though her wraith persists, as it probably always will, in the popularized accounts of the murder. It is doubtless a sorry anticlimax to discover that the most romantic figure in the history of Elizabethan drama met his death not in a fight for the charms of a lady, but because (it was alleged) he had been negligent in reaching for the check. But sober history is no respecter of tastes, and the fact is that, while Marlowe may have had numerous "lewde loues" during his lurid life, none of them figured in his murder.

How, then, can we account for Meres's statement, made only a few years after the murder, that there *was* a woman in the case? Here is an instance where the smoke that may mean fire in reality is an optical illusion. The mischievous statement, which endowed the story of Marlowe's murder with a "romantic" angle it never really possessed, came not from any circumstantial fact but from Meres's need of a completing term in his rhetorical equation. If you will turn back to his actual words, you will note that he was writing in the starchily formal style popularized by Lyly in his *Euphues.* B had to balance A, C had to be followed by D. In this passage, Meres was intent upon drawing a neat euphuistic parallel between classical legend and contemporary fact. As our French "tragical poet" made a pitiful end, so did Marlowe, being also an epicure, an atheist, and a tragical poet; as Lycophron, on the authority of Ovid, was killed by a rival lover while acting on the stage . . . How to complete the parallel? Obviously, by having Marlowe killed also *by a rival lover,* and let the drab facts go hang.

And so the venerable ghost of Marlowe's female nemesis was laid. But as a matter of fact Hotson's discovery raised more questions than it solved. Who were the three companions with whom he was engaged in secret parley the whole long day and into the evening? Were they really so drunk that they drew daggers over the reckoning, or was that merely a convenient tale to cloak the real subject of their quarrels? When Hotson made his discovery it was already known, on the evidence of a document in the records of the County of Middlesex, that Marlowe had been released from Newgate prison on bond in 1589. What had been his offense? From hints gleaned here and there it seemed probable that writing for the stage was definitely a side line with this young firebrand lately come from the university. What, then, in short, was Marlowe's game?

While we do not yet know all the answers, patient inquirers following in Hotson's footsteps have learned a great deal in recent years, and it is quite plain that Marlowe led a secret life whose melodramatic qualities and connections with murky governmental intrigue compare very favorably with anything yet divulged of the operations of modern secret agents. But that is another story.

Having disposed of the imaginary Light Lady, let us proceed to an indubitably real lady who was of far greater literary importance than the other, for she was the cause of a severe mental crisis in the life of one of our most famous poets.

III

WILLIAM WORDSWORTH, having made his permanent place among the poets by the writings of scarcely more than a single decade of his youth, lapsed into stuffiness and complacency for the remaining forty years of his life. At his home at Rydal Mount, he watched the world slowly come round to agreeing with his own favorable opinion of his poetry, turned out reams of dull verse, received pilgrims to the shrine, and inveighed against the railroads, the Reform Bill, and everything else in the new age that offended his Tory convictions. In his last years he was Poet Laureate. Nobody could have filled the role more agreeably (except perhaps his successor, Tennyson), because to the early Victorians poetry was above all an instrument for the moral improvement of the individual and of society, and poets could not be *great* poets unless their personal lives were exemplary and pure. Wordsworth not only wrote poems about morality; he *was* morality. Not a breath of scandal hovered about the aging Laureate; one could easily forgive his youthful sympathies with French radicalism, since he had recanted so handsomely and copiously, and as for the rest—well, Wordsworth was, and always had been, completely respectable. He was, long before Walt Whitman became identified with the description, the Good Gray Poet.

And so he remained into the twentieth century, while his simple lyrics were memorized by schoolchildren and book after book of explanation and praise came from the critics and biographers. Here and there a perceptive reader became uncomfortable as he realized that Wordsworth seemed at one time to have been extraordinarily preoccupied with the theme of the betrayed maid and the deserted mother, which he treated with great pathos in such poems as "Vaudracour and Julia," "The Thorn," "The Ruined Cottage," and "Her eyes are wild." But no one dreamed of seeking an autobiographical explanation of the poet's fondness for little stories of seduction and desertion.

In 1896 Professor Émile Legouis, a student of Wordsworth and one of the best foreign interpreters of English literature, published *La Jeunesse de William Wordsworth* (translated into English the following year), in which he traced for the first time in detail the formative years of the poet, the development of his nature-philosophy, and the impact upon him of French revolutionary thought. Some time after the book appeared, Legouis met in London his friend Thomas Hutchinson, a man of letters who later was to publish editions of Wordsworth, Shelley, and Lamb. Hutchinson asked if he had ever heard the story, passed down through the Coleridge family, that "Wordsworth, during his stay in France, had of a young French lady a son, who afterwards visited him at Rydal Mount." This was news to Legouis; he was aware only of what the whole world knew, that Wordsworth had married in 1802 Miss Mary Hutchinson (no relation to Thomas) and that the union had been blessed with a number of children. He was interested, naturally, but he made no attempt to verify the tradition and turned to other scholarly matters.

More than fifteen years later Professor George McLean Harper of Princeton University was busy on his projected life of Wordsworth, which was destined to become the standard work on the subject. Knowing of Legouis's deep interest in Wordsworth, he communicated with him and learned the still entirely unsubstantiated story of the French son. Shortly afterwards, in the winter of 1914–15, Harper went to England to continue his researches. In the British Museum he found a collection of letters from Wordsworth's sister Dorothy to her friend Mrs. Thomas Clarkson that referred frequently to her brother's daughter Caroline, whose mother was French. Among other things, the letters spoke of the approaching marriage of Caroline to

Jean Baptiste Martin Baudoin. A little later, in Dr. Williams's Library in London, Harper examined the voluminous diary of Henry Crabb Robinson, a London lawyer who had known virtually everyone worth knowing in the world of polite learning in the first half of the nineteenth century. In that manuscript diary—only an eighth of it had been published in 1915, and a great deal of it remains unpublished today—Harper found, under the year 1820, an account of a tour of the Continent with the Wordsworths. In October, Robinson recorded, they visited Paris and spent some time with Caroline and Jean Baudoin and with Caroline's mother, "Mme. Vallon."

By these discoveries, Harper surprised the great secret of Wordsworth's life. From what he had learned thus far, it appeared that the poet had met Marie-Anne ("Annette") Vallon, presumably during his stay in France in 1792; they had had a daughter, Caroline (*not* a son—the Coleridge family tradition was wrong); for some reason he had not married Annette; but there was obviously no attempt to disclaim or conceal Caroline's paternity. Wordsworth's friends knew of the relationship, and in 1820 his sister and his wife, together with several of their friends, enjoyed a visit with the mistress of his youth and their illegitimate daughter.

"The discovery," Harper wrote later, "did not surprise me. I had long been convinced, more by omissions than by positive traces in his poems and letters, that his nature had received, while he was in France, a blow from which he never wholly recovered and whose causes had not been made known to the world." Wordsworth, a sensitive idealist, had had what may well have been an idyllic liaison with the Frenchwoman; and his separation from her and their baby daughter because of the war between France and England, together with his failure to legitimatize Caroline, shook his whole being. Once the key was provided, as Harper provided it in his biography published in 1916, it was possible to read Wordsworth's poems for the years following the liaison with new insight. It was clear, for instance, why he had removed "Vaudracour and Julia," his longest narrative on the seduction-and-desertion theme, from *The Prelude*, his great autobiographical poem, and published it separately: he was afraid that if it were included in a context of avowed autobiography, its personal application might be suspected. Late in life, when he was annotating his poems, he said that he had heard it "from the mouth of a French lady, who had been an eye-and-ear-witness of all that was done and said"—a somewhat extravagant claim, since the poem narrates the intimate history of a strictly clandestine love affair. On the other hand, his further statement, that "the facts are true; no invention as to these has been exercised, as none was needed," had unexpected significance to those who read it following Harper's announcement.

But now that the main fact of Wordsworth's youthful indiscretion had been revealed, the details remained to be discovered. Who was Annette Vallon? Under what circumstances did Wordsworth meet her? When and where was Caroline born? What stood in the way of the marriage of her parents? Such questions had to be answered if the full nature and extent of Wordsworth's spiritual crisis in the middle 1790's was to be known.

In 1917 Harper went to France to help in the American Hospital at Neuilly. In his spare time he continued his inquiry into the dark chapter of Wordsworth's life. A search of the archives of the Department of Loiret, at Orléans, produced the crucial birth certificate: "On the fifteenth day of December, of the year one thousand seven hundred and ninety-two, the first of the Republic . . . a girl, born . . . to Williams Wordswodsth, an Englishman, and Marie-Anne Vallon, her father and mother . . ." Wordsworth (whose name offered an insuperable difficulty to the local official—"Wordsodsth" and "Wordworsth" are other versions appearing in the same document) was present only by proxy. In the archives of the Prefecture of the Seine at Paris, during the same summer, Harper found the certificate of marriage between Caroline, who used the name of Wordsworth rather than that of Vallon, and Jean Baptiste Baudoin. And, perhaps most important of all for the new leads it produced, he made the discovery that Annette was the sister-in-law of a Mme. Vallon whose personal memoirs of the period from 1791 to the end of the Reign of Terror had been printed as recently as 1913.

From this last source it was evident that Annette had been a member of a Royalist and Catholic family deeply embroiled in the tumultuous political upheavals of the 1790's, to which, it had always been known, Wordsworth had been for a brief period an intensely interested witness. Learning more of the Vallon family and its political activities and connections might mean learning more also of the precise influences which had shaped Wordsworth's own political ideas.

Harper, however, had to return to Princeton, and he asked his friend Legouis to continue his work. In the years just after the war Legouis received information which resulted at length in his locating the direct descendants of Caroline and Jean Baudoin, and therefore of Wordsworth himself—a numerous and prosperous clan. From the eldest great-grandchild of Caroline, Legouis obtained a portrait of Caroline in her old age, and other memorabilia; and through this branch of the family he was enabled to get in touch with the descendants of Annette's brother, Paul Vallon, who proved to have even more valuable family papers, many of them dating from the time of the Revolution.

Legouis's collection of data mounted by the month. A whole panorama of political intrigue, underground activity, hairbreadth escapes from the police and probably the guillotine opened before him. In it Wordsworth appeared only by inference. But because of his deep personal concern for Annette and Caroline, and his positive knowledge that the Vallons were deep in conspiracy against the revolutionary government, it became plain how desperate he was for news of the family after he was forced to return to England at the very time of his child's birth. That he was deprived of news of Annette's welfare which he might otherwise have had was proved when the archivist at Blois, who had published Mme. Vallon's memoirs in 1913, discovered a pair of long letters Annette wrote in 1793 to Wordsworth and his sister. Because of the state of war between the two countries, the French police had confiscated them; and instead of traveling to England they had found their way into the official records of the province. In such letters as did somehow pass the blockade, we know from Dorothy Wordsworth's journal and letters, Annette mentioned having written many others that never arrived. There is some evidence to suggest that Wordsworth, risking his life, went to France in 1793 in a futile attempt to see Annette and Caroline.

In addition to his personal anxiety for Annette and Caroline, Wordsworth must have been torn by two other emotions. While he was in France in 1792, at the very time that he was learning the language from Annette Vallon, he had acquired from Michel Beaupuy, a young officer in the revolutionary army, a deep loyalty to the revolutionary cause. This he brought back to England with him; but when France declared war on his own country, and the Terror broke out, the young poet's political notions were thrown into turmoil; what had been passionate convictions a few months earlier began to crumble into doubt and finally into denial. Yet he could not accept the reactionary stand so fervently adopted by the family of the mother of his child. It is little wonder, then, that some of his utterances in the middle of the 1790's were little less than frantic. But until the discoveries of Harper and Legouis no one knew that his emotional state was due as much to causes related to his personal life as to his crushing loss of faith in the revolutionary experiment.

It was not until after the treaty of Amiens in 1802 suspended the war for a time that Dorothy and William Wordsworth could go to France and see Annette. They met her and her daughter at Calais. Annette Vallon learned that Wordsworth was to marry Mary Hutchinson in a few months; but she cherished no hard feelings. The tranquillity induced by their meeting after ten years is mirrored in Wordsworth's lovely sonnet, "It is a beauteous evening, calm and free." For lack of any better explanation, the "dear child" whom Wordsworth addresses in it was long thought to be Dorothy, although the terms in which he speaks of her contradict everything we know about her, including the fact that she was not a child. Now, of course, it is certain that the child was Caroline.

So the Wordsworths returned to England. William knew, if he had not known it before, that his passion for Annette was spent. In the years since the liaison at Blois, he had matured. In the company of Coleridge and of his sister he had found adequate intellectual stimulation; in Mary Hutchinson he had found a satisfactory English mate; his poetry was beginning to win attention; his political questionings had been resolved. Annette, he found, shared none of his interests. Like all her family she was wrapped up in the never-ending royalist intrigues; and she herself was enrolled on the police lists as a "Widow Williams" who should be watched closely because of her known part in harboring émigrés and the clergy. As the records of the government's detective force were to reveal to Legouis, her brother Paul, at the very time of the Calais meeting, was in the midst of a series of mysterious Bourbonist intrigues involving a glamorous but slightly shopworn adventuress named De Bonneuil. The Vallon family as a whole was too busy fighting Napoleon to care about impulses from a vernal wood.

The French episode, then, apart from the duty of making honorable amends whenever he could, was a closed book to Wordsworth. But what of the "son" who was alleged to have visited him at Rydal Mount? Once the connection of Caroline with the Baudoin family became clear, the "son's" identity was no longer a mystery. He was in reality Eustace Baudoin, a French officer captured by the British, who made the Wordsworths' acquaintance while interned and perhaps carried back to France a message for Annette. He was instrumental in introducing his brother Jean Baptiste to Annette's daughter, who, as we have seen, later married him. Dorothy Wordsworth planned to attend the wedding, as Harper had read in her letters to Mrs. Clarkson, but was prevented by the return of Napoleon from Elba and the ensuing turmoil of the Hundred Days. Only in 1820 did the Wordsworths return to France, and then Mrs. Wordsworth met her husband's grandchild, for the Baudoins by that time had become parents.

In 1843, two years after Annette died, Caroline and her family wanted Wordsworth to recognize their relationship. Nothing came of the plan, possibly because the aged Wordsworth, who had just become Poet Laureate, had no desire to rake the ashes of his distant past. After he died his widow, his nephew Christopher (later Bishop) Wordsworth, and Crabb Robinson almost decided to make some public statement concerning his relations with Annette; but again nothing was done. At that time there existed in the family papers considerable documentary evidence of the liaison; but when Christopher Wordsworth wrote the life of his uncle—the first use made of the papers—he destroyed all of it. The fact that he did so perfectly illustrates one of those shifts in moral climate which are the despair of the later biographer. In the early part of the century, the Annette affair was known to the intimates of the Wordsworth group and accepted by them; the existence of a natural child, according to the mores of the time, might be embarrassing to a man, but it was certainly not something to be concealed at all costs. By 1850, however, when Christopher Wordsworth went through the family papers, illegitimacy was not spoken of in polite circles, least of all in connection with a Poet Laureate.

And so a Harper who would uncover Dorothy Wordsworth's neglected letters in the British Museum, and a Legouis who would comb the French archives, were required before the secret of a great poet's youthful love affair could be revealed to the world. The revelation brought a sudden revival of interest in Wordsworth, now as a subject for psychoanalytical interpretation. Critics and biographers, who in the cynical fashion of the postwar years had disposed of him as personally pompous and philosophically infantile, now gleefully proceeded to explain everything in terms of Annette Vallon. She was, it seems, writ large in his work from 1792 on, and the failure of his muse was attributable to his lifelong gnawing remorse for his failure to make Annette an honest woman; the poet of "Peter Bell" was in reality a sadly frustrated voluptuary.

This extreme view died of its own absurdity, and the Vallon story has now been assimilated into the rest of Wordsworthian biography. While there can be no question that it left its mark upon the Wordsworth of the 1790's, the wounds healed at least as soon as the poet was comfortably settled with his wedded wife. But the discoveries of Legouis and Harper have guaranteed that he will never be regarded as he was before 1916; the story they uncovered has added to our picture of the poet a sorely needed touch of common humanity. As Professor Douglas Bush has observed, "The Victorians, beset by science and skepticism, and groping for an undogmatic faith, reverenced the poet who gave them a natural religion. We, who have got far beyond such naïve gropings, and recoil from a plaster embodiment of virtue and nobility, have acquired a new respect for the poet who gave to society a natural daughter."

A GALLERY OF INVENTORS

NOT many people know that the New York Public Library, that wonderful institution behind the lions at Fifth Avenue and Forty-first Street which is so rich in the things of the spirit and chronically so poor in this world's goods, takes a special pride in its collection of literary forgeries. Most libraries, with understandable fastidiousness, decline to buy what is guaranteed to be fraudulent; and if some prying scholar proves to a library that a manuscript about whose possession it has boasted is a demonstrable fake, the embarrassment of the staff is painful to behold. But not so at the New York Public Library. It is a joy, as Chaucer would say, to see the gusto with which, now and then, the library's monthly *Bulletin* announces that the institution has just come into the possession of some "splendid forgeries." No doubt part of that exaltation springs from the humane delight in the criminological which inspired De Quincey's dissertation on the fine art of murder; but there is also a more practical reason. Time after time scholars are confronted with the problem of determining the authenticity of the documents with which they are working, and nothing helps so much in solving it as material that can be used for comparison. If one suspects the hand of a forger in some literary correspondence one is examining, the best way to settle the doubt is to compare the peculiarities of the questioned documents—the handwriting, the characteristics of the paper, the habitual turns of expression in the writing itself—with authenticated examples of the forger's work. And so the "New York Public" has for a number of years welcomed and cherished all the fraudulent documents that have been offered to it, and placed them in an isolation ward. In this laudable scheme the library enjoys the enthusiastic cooperation of

142

dealers and collectors, who are only too glad to have the perilous stuff quarantined once for all.

The art of literary forgery is an ancient one. Scarcely an age or a nation has been without its misguided literati who have foisted off their own productions as the work of greater men. Probably the best remembered of all forgers, at least in modern times, was the Frenchman Vrain Lucas, who in the middle of the nineteenth century manufactured more than 27,000 pieces of manuscript which he sold to an open-pursed mathematician, a compatriot of his, whose gullibility remains one of the wonders of history. The collection included fascinating letters by Alcibiades, Pontius Pilate, Cleopatra, Ovid, Aeschylus, Alexander the Great, Cervantes, Pascal, Shakespeare, Mary Magdalene, Judas Iscariot, Boccaccio, Luther, and Dante—all written in modern French. But England has had its own eminent fabricators.

The latter half of the eighteenth century saw three celebrated British forgers at work. One was Thomas Chatterton, "the marvellous boy," who won fleeting acclaim and lasting notoriety as the "discoverer," actually the inventor, of the poems of a medieval monk named Rowley, and who had for his nemesis the cynical Horace Walpole. Another was James Macpherson, who forged Gaelic epics allegedly written by one Ossian, a northern Homer, and who was rash enough to insist upon his integrity in the face of Dr. Johnson's disbelief. Johnson wrote:

I thought your book an imposture; I think it an imposture still. For this opinion I have given my reasons to the publick, which I here dare you to refute. Your rage I defy. Your abilities . . . are not so formidable; and what I hear of your morals, inclines me to pay regard not to what you shall say, but what you shall prove. You may print this if you will.

The last of the three great Georgian fabricators, young William Ireland, dazzled England in the 1790's by his "discovery" of new manuscript plays by William Shakespeare, and was ardently admired by James Boswell, who seems not to have profited by his mentor's demolition of Macpherson.

These famous cases, however, are closed. All the forgeries perpetrated by the curious eighteenth-century trio presumably were exposed in their own time, and if by an improbable chance one of their heretofore undetected productions should now turn up, it would trick nobody. So crude was the work of Chatterton and Ireland in particular that an effort of the imagination is needed for us to conceive how anyone, even Boswell, ever took it seriously. But in spite of that the sinister shadow of the forger falls over many scholarly problems of today, and researchers often have to cope with forgeries that are far more clever than any known before the last century. One reason is the fact that the motivation of the forger has changed. By a pleasant coincidence, Chatterton and his ilk were hungry for fame at the same time that antiquarians and other bookmen were hungry for literary documents of a departed age, and so they traded, neither being too concerned about getting the genuine article. After their time, however, the collecting of literary documents and rare books became the sport of millionaires; the materials for literary study came into the marketplace, not as records of a culture but as chattels to be bought and sold. Under such circumstances, it was natural that a few clever men in each generation should see the rewards awaiting them in the manufacture of literary items for the rich collector. Spurred by a motive even more powerful than the desire for celebrity, and at the same time put on their mettle by the steady growth of skepticism among scholars, dealers, and even millionaires, these men fabricated what were in many instances extraordinarily cunning imitations of letters and manuscripts of men like Dickens and Thackeray, whose memorabilia were currently in demand on the collectors' market. In the last decade or two, the forgeries have become increasingly available to scholars, especially as the private collections have found their way into university or public libraries. But they are always, of course, mingled with genuine material. The job of separating the goats from the sheep is the modern scholar's headache.

I

THE man who accomplished the most impressive job of deception in the nineteenth century, however, belonged to the older school. So far as we know, the forgeries of John Payne Collier were actuated not by greed but by a curious perversion of temperament which forbade his ever being content with such fame as might accompany the scholar's function of discovering and interpreting true information. His is the classic case of the man with genuine talents for scholarship who went wrong.

Collier lived at a time when most of the original documents relating to Shakespeare and the theater of his age were still buried in the chaotic libraries of private institutions and old families, and in the even more chaotic archives of the government. Only one man before him, a tireless burrower into the past named Edmond Malone, had brought to light a substantial amount of material. Collier devoted his long life to adding to what Malone had discovered; and, because he was gifted with patience and enthusiasm, he succeeded in discovering more new data, perhaps, than any other worker in his field. But Collier's tragedy was that he was never satisfied. He was so eager to solve mysteries, such as the date of the first performance of a Shakespearean play, or the authorship of an anonymous play of the 1590's, or the relationship of one playwright to a certain repertory company, that when his documents did not supply the answer he supplied it himself. He had a fatal urge to put words into Clio's mouth.

By vocation a journalist, Collier first became a familiar and highly respected figure in London literary and antiquarian circles during the Regency. His *History of English Dramatic Poetry and Annals of the Stage* (1831), an erudite summing-up of the state of knowledge to that time, together with a few early examples of his own inimitable improvements upon history, won him the admiration of all serious students of the Tudor and Stuart stage. More than this, it obtained for him entrée to two of the greatest private collections then in existence of rare books and manuscripts relating to the period, the Duke of Devonshire's and the Bridgewater House library of Lord Egerton (later Earl of Ellesmere).

Now a scholar of our own day who might have the sensational luck to receive the free run of two such libraries, neither of which had ever been well explored, would count his fortune made. All he would have to do would be to transcribe faithfully, annotate, and publish the materials he discovered; the world would beat a path to his door. But Collier was not content. The documents before him told much that had never been known about the conditions under which Shakespeare and his fellows wrote and performed, about the chronology of plays, the personnel and histories of the performing troupes, the meaning of obscure allusions in the plays. But on some particular points on which Collier fervently desired information, principally to support his preconceived theories, they were stubbornly silent. And so he proceeded to invent documents that gave the answers he desired, slipped them into the genuine papers at Bridgewater House, and then published them as having been "found" there. In such a manner he shed light (or darkness visible!) on Shakespeare's connection with the Blackfriars playhouse, a pet hobby of Collier's. In a similar way, by endowing his own personal collection with the studiously contrived products of his pen, he was able to give the world such items of interest as a ballad called "The Inchanted Island" whose plot seemed to have suggested that of *The Tempest,* and supposed contemporary evidence of hitherto unrecorded performances of *Othello.*

When he published his discoveries, real and imaginary, in several brochures, few if any of his fellow Shakespeareans suspected that they were of somewhat uneven authenticity. Collier, like his spiritual descendant Thomas J. Wise, was so learned in his field that he could fit his forgeries into the known historical background with almost perfect plausibility. In many small details, as our subsequent increase in knowledge allows us to realize, he went wrong; but at the time other scholars could only envy him his brilliant luck. Encouraged by the steadily growing plaudits of his colleagues in the newly formed Shakespeare Society of London, Collier found fresh fields to conquer and, incidentally, to ravage.

Shortly before Shakespeare died Edward Alleyn, the first star actor in English theatrical history, used his comfortable fortune to found the College of God's Gift at Dulwich. To the college he also gave his personal papers and, even more important, those of his father-in-law, Philip Henslowe, who had been the leading impresario in the Elizabethan theater. Henslowe's "diary," or account book, was and is by all odds the most valuable source of information on the day-by-day operations of the stage that Shakespeare knew. It lists the performances of companies in which Henslowe was financially interested, box-office receipts, the expenses to which he was put for costumes and stage accessories, his payments to his stable of playwrights for new or revamped plays, and a host of other details. Although Malone had already examined the Henslowe-Alleyn papers and published a few extracts from them, Collier was the first to print them *in extenso*. He borrowed the manuscript volumes from the library at Dulwich College—they have not been circulated since, for a reason that can be anticipated even at this point—and made a transcript of them. Between 1841 and 1845, under the auspices of the Shakespeare Society, Collier presented to a grateful world the fruits of his labors. Once again, few Shakespeareans were disposed to be finicky about his accuracy. One or two voices were raised to point out contradictions between the facts newly discovered in Henslowe and those already known from other sources; but to the innocent bystander such cavils seemed to spring from professional jealousy. Shakespeare study always has been something of a cockpit where short-tempered and dogmatic scholars settle their differences with beak and spur, and it was especially so in the middle of the nineteenth century, when rivalry among editors and commentators was keen. It is understandable, therefore, that a few of Collier's fellow bardolators were less than magnanimous in their reception of his discoveries.

Untroubled by an occasional snort from the skeptics, Collier prospered mightily in these middle years. Thanks to his discoveries, the outlook for Shakespeare study was highly favorable: if so much had been unearthed in one or two decades by the exertions of one man, might not much more reasonably be expected in the future? Collier seems, not unnaturally, to have shared the general exuberance. Confident of his own powers and assured of the world's eager attention, he took the step that led to his downfall.

In January of 1852 he announced in the *Athenæum*, the leading Victorian literary weekly, the greatest of all his discoveries. Some years earlier, he wrote, he had picked up in the shop of a London bookseller, now dead, a copy of the 1632 folio edition of Shakespeare's plays. He had paid only thirty shillings for it, because the volume was in bad shape; but he needed it only to supply some leaves missing from another copy of the same edition that he already owned. For various reasons, however, he had failed to examine his new acquisition carefully; and only recently had he discovered that what he had bought was actually the Shakespearean find of the century. On almost every page of this dilapidated book were annotations in the hand of a seventeenth-century writer—corrected punctuation, substituted words and lines, new stage directions, even additions of whole passages to Shakespeare's text!

As everyone knows, the text of Shakespeare's plays is full of perplexities. Largely because of the careless copying of the manuscript that went to the printer, and the equally careless typesetting of the first editions, there are thousands of lines which have had to be corrected, in one way or another, by every editor. What Collier had miraculously found was a volume bearing the signature of Thomas Perkins on one of the covers: a man otherwise unknown to history who somehow had had access to a much more faithful text than any found in the printed editions, perhaps even to Shakespeare's own manuscripts. Perkins had gone through the whole folio and corrected the corrupt text in the light of his unique information. His marginal notes, therefore, provided readers with answers to the swarming riddles of Shakespeare's actual text.

Unfortunately for Collier, some Shakespeare scholars who, like himself, had spent years puzzling over the text in preparation for new editions of the plays, failed to share his enthusiasm for the thirty thousand improvements inscribed in his copy, half of which he published some months after his *Athenæum* announcement; and they complained that many, if not most, of the new readings were no better than the old, merely substituting one difficulty for another. Others made obscure what had previously been plain. If the mysterious Thomas Perkins had indeed had some text of Shakespeare which came closer to what the dramatist had written than any of the printed versions, it was curious, to say the least, that some of his corrections succeeded in making so little sense even to those steeped in Shakespeare's idiom. Finally, it was pointed out that many of the corrections had already been proposed by various Shakespeare editors in the past century and a half—and that they seemed particularly to lend authority to the readings incorporated into the edition published ten years earlier by John Payne Collier, Esquire. On the evidence supplied by the Perkins Folio, Collier had been a strikingly accurate diviner of Shakespeare's real intentions.

Collier went through the motions of allowing his fellow Shakespeareans to examine the wonderful folio, but he never permitted anyone to have more than a superficial look at it. If the claims made for the book were to be attacked, then, they would have to be on the ground of internal evidence alone; that is, whether or not the corrections seemed "right" in their context, whether they reflected Shakespeare's usage elsewhere, and so on. One of Collier's rival editors, Samuel Weller Singer, touched off the fireworks in 1853 with a pamphlet called *The Text of Shakespeare Vindicated*. It was followed by a whole series of tracts pro and con, until the precincts of Victorian Shakespearean study resembled a waterfront saloon on Saturday night.

The quarrel generated far more heat than light. The proposition first publicly advanced by Singer, that the annotations in the Perkins folio were a forgery, could not be proved or disproved without a thorough examination of the book itself; and Collier forestalled that for the time being by presenting the book to his patron the sixth Duke of Devonshire, who died in 1858. At Devonshire House it remained secure against inquisitive Collier-baiters, for the ducal librarian guarded his employer's books with the diligence with which, in older times, noblemen's chaplains were supposed to provide for the salvation of their masters' souls.

But by 1859 so much pressure had been put upon Sir Frederic Madden, the Keeper of Manuscripts at the British Museum, to have the Perkins Folio lent to that institution for inspection, that he wrote to the new Duke begging that favor. His Grace acceded to the request, and in late May of that year the controversial book was in Madden's office. At long last, by Madden's invitation, the scholars could gaze at Perkins's thirty thousand annotations to their hearts' content.

It is not a professional Shakespearean but N. E. S. A. Hamilton, a member of the British Museum staff, who deserves the chief credit for exposing the fraudulence of the Perkins Folio. Within two or three weeks after the volume reached the British Museum, he detected what became the most damaging evidence against its authenticity: the presence on the margins, at places where the "old corrector" had written his inked annotations, of innumerable pencil marks. An attempt had been made to erase most of these marks; but many were still faintly visible to the naked eye, and many more under the microscope. In nearly every case the pencilings coincided in meaning with the ink corrections; but instead of being written, as the ink corrections were, in what passed for a seventeenth-century hand, they were in a "bold, clear handwriting of the present day."

Hamilton called Madden's attention to the pencilings, and together they recruited the help of another member of the museum staff, the mineralogist Professor M. H. N. Maskelyne. This is one of the first cases of suspected forgery in which expert scientific testimony was employed. Maskelyne made a series of tests, chemical and other, which confirmed Hamilton's impression that the pencil marks lay under, rather than over, the ink in every case. The conclusion, therefore, was inescapable. Someone, and no one connected with the inquiry seemed to have any doubt as to who it was, had gone through the folio and painstakingly marked out, in pencil, thousands upon thousands of corrections to the printed text. He had later thought better of many of these corrections and had erased them with his dampened finger, a penknife or a chemical, or even with hot ashes. (Collier had noted that many pages of his prize had suffered in the past from tobacco ashes or wine dropped on them.) The rest of the pencil marks served as guides for his pen work; but instead of simply tracing over the pencilings he had sedulously tried to imitate a seventeenth-century hand—too sedulously, because to Hamilton's practiced eye many of the markings exaggerated the characteristics of such handwriting, or showed signs of being carefully touched up.

These discoveries, and the conclusion drawn from them, formed the substance of two letters which Hamilton wrote to the *Times* in July, 1859. Their publication was the deathblow to Collier's pretenses. Although he defended himself in a pamphlet saturated with personal acrimony and insinuations of persecution by the British Museum staff, and although he still had some fervent partisans, he was never able to refute Hamilton's evidence. For a time he depended strongly on the fortuitous support of one Francis C. Parry, who in 1853, when the original controversy was at its height, had volunteered the information that he had once owned, and subsequently lost, the Perkins Folio, and that the debated annotations had been in it then. Collier cultivated him in the intervening years for all he was worth; but the value of Parry's testimony shrank when it was shown that he had made his statement without seeing that folio, and on the innocent assumption that there could be only one annotated copy of a Shakespearean folio in the world; and its value vanished completely when he examined the book in Madden's office and flatly denied that it was the one he had once possessed. Even today, so far as I am aware, nobody knows the previous history of the Perkins Folio, although there is little reason to doubt Collier's story that he bought it at Rodd's bookshop in Newport Street—without the annotations, of course. This copy of the 1632 folio, though a ragged orphan of uncertain ancestry whose only claim to celebrity is the mistreatment it received from a nineteenth-century forger, is much prized by its present owner, the Huntington Library in California.

After Collier had been branded a forger on the strength of Hamilton's disclosures, no new revelation of his activities could cause much surprise. Within two years it was shown that a handful of the documents at Dulwich College which he had published were forged; and twenty years later an expert engaged in making a complete index to the Dulwich papers revealed that, in addition, a number of undoubtedly genuine Alleyn and Henslowe papers had been altered or even mutilated by scissors. No suspicion attached to Malone, and the only other person besides Collier to have borrowed the manuscripts had been the Archbishop of Canterbury in 1819, so that the inference was plain enough. When the still unconfessed Collier died in 1883 at the age of ninety-four, the inference became a certainty, for in his papers was found the transcript he had made of Alleyn's diary. It contained the same interlineations, some of them referring to Shakespeare, as the original manuscript at Dulwich. The give-away was that the interlineations had been written into the transcript some time after the transcript itself was finished. Evidently, then, Collier had first made a true copy of the document as it had come down from Alleyn, and then at his leisure had devised suitable additions, which he inserted first into his transcript, and then, to give them a spurious authenticity, into the original manuscript. The eventual result of this blithe doctoring of primary source material, so far as scholarship was concerned, was that an honest Elizabethan specialist, Dr. W. W. Greg, had to edit the Henslowe-Alleyn papers all over again, always with a keen eye for Collier's alterations. He found sixteen instances of such tampering in Henslowe's diary alone. Later scholars have run across additional traces of Collier at Dulwich. Not content to limit his attentions to the manuscripts, he seems to have planted evidence in books·as well. For example, a certain Elizabethan tract had long been attributed to Stephen Gosson solely on the strength of Collier's assertion that an inscription in a copy of the book at Dulwich named him as author. Only a few years ago Professor William Ringler of Princeton discovered that the inscription in the volume bore the classic marks of a Collier fabrication.

One of Collier's main interests, apart from the history of the drama, was the old ballads that were printed on broadsheets and hawked in the streets of London in the sixteenth and seventeenth centuries. Because they often refer to persons or events that figure in the drama and elsewhere in literature, they are valuable explanatory material. As we have seen, Collier once printed, from a manuscript in his possession, a ballad called "The Inchanted Island" which had a plot suggestive of that of *The Tempest*. Later in life, he had occasion to print other ballads from the same manuscript. After his death it was found that the manuscript was his own creation. The majority of the ballads it contained were genuine enough, having been taken from old books. But a few, some of a decidedly ribald nature, were his own brainchildren, with allusions designed, like so many of his other forgeries, to support favorite theories.

This penchant for fabricating ballads seems to have originated partly in a need to satisfy a sneaking, un-Victorian taste for obscenity. More than twenty years ago Professor Hazelton Spencer reported on a Collier item in the Harvard University Library which bears out this suspicion. The item is a 470-page manuscript history of the

London stage from 1660 to 1723. About 100 pages are fair copy; the rest is a rough early draft, with many revisions and pasted-in addenda. In the latter are found many ballads which Collier planned to quote in order to illustrate various points in the history of the Restoration theater. The evidence contained in them was flatly contradicted by other credible sources, and Spencer concluded that Collier had forged them. Perhaps the most interesting of the ballads is one on Nell Gwyn which appears in the manuscript in two separate drafts, the "later" one being much altered for the sake of additional bawdiness. Spencer theorized that Collier had contrived the ballad for scholarly purposes, and then added the obscenity simply for his personal gratification.

One of the most recent Collier ballad-books to fall under suspicion is now in the Folger Library. It is the commonplace book of one Joseph Hall, written about 1630 and containing copious excerpts from the theological and poetical books of the day. There is no question that these excerpts were written by Hall. But as he continued his commonplace book, he seems to have had the habit of leaving as many as ten or fifteen blank pages between entries. When the book came into Collier's possession, some time before 1848, those pages must have delighted him. Indeed, it might almost be said that the existence of white space in the manuscripts and books he handled was Collier's lifelong nemesis. Once more, in the case of Hall's commonplace book, he used it to write what had failed to be written two hundred years before. In editing extracts from the Register of the Stationers' Company, the sixteenth-century analogue of our modern copyright record, he found many references to the "entry" (or copyright) of ballads not known to survive. Rather than note after such titles that the ballads themselves were lost, he composed ballads to suit the titles, entered them, in appropriate handwriting, in Hall's blank pages, and then quoted extracts from them in his edition, noting once more that his material was "taken from a manuscript in my possession." But he overlooked one detail. The ballad texts were supposed to fit titles entered in the Stationers' Register between 1557 and 1587; yet he had allegedly found them in a manuscript dating from the 1630's! Since street ballads were the most ephemeral sort of literature, it is highly improbable that Joseph Hall knew as many as eighty-nine examples printed from fifty to eighty years before he compiled his book of extracts, and even less likely that anyone would have copied them into the commonplace book at a later time. On this reasonable hypothesis, supported by the fact that the handwriting is a little too regular and careful, "too nearly like what might be called standard or normal," Dr. Giles E. Dawson of the Folger Library staff some years ago branded the ballad additions in the Hall manuscript a probable Collier forgery.

Yet, as Dawson himself admitted when he announced his suspicions, there is an ever present danger of blaming Collier for more crimes than he committed. At the very time that the Perkins Folio question was being debated, Collier was accused of having forged some short-hand notes of Coleridge's lectures on Shakespeare and Milton which he published in 1856. Today, however, it is universally agreed that Collier, a shorthand-writing journalist, actually had made those notes as Coleridge spoke. While it is true that he fabricated manuscripts with a lavish hand, it is not true (as a critic once remarked of Wordsworth's liaison with Annette Vallon) that he was *always* doing it. Apart from his record of convictions, one of the main reasons why Collier is constantly open to fresh suspicion is that in his pioneering volumes he had the habit of referring to books or documents which he presumably was the first to report on. Some modern investigators take this as *a priori* evidence of forgery. In the light of Collier's known habits, any item to which he refers is automatically suspect if its history cannot be traced before him—and even if, like Hall's manuscript, it is proved to have existed before he saw it, there is always the question of how it read before it came within range of his improving pen. But it is too often forgotten that, because he was tireless in his pursuit of the lost fact, in hundreds of cases Collier really *was* the first to report on genuine books and documents which had lain undisturbed for centuries, and of which no previous record existed simply because nobody had been sufficiently interested to make one. Ironically, by his wanton forgeries he destroyed the luster of his own achievement. Instead of honoring him for his indisputably valuable discoveries, we almost instinctively suspect everything that he claimed to have discovered.

The way in which his known proclivities tempt scholars to charge Collier with deeds of which he may well have been innocent is illustrated by the case of the manuscript "Book of Plaies" by Dr. Simon Forman. Forman, a contemporary of Shakespeare, was a colorful astrologer and quack whose final graceful act was to die on the very day for which he had predicted his demise. He left behind him a manuscript miscellany, on certain pages of which occur memoranda concerning four plays he had attended at the Globe playhouse: a non-Shakespearean *Richard II,* and Shakespeare's *Winter's Tale, Cymbeline,* and *Macbeth:*

. . . The[re] stode befor them 3 women feiries or Numphes, And Saluted Mackbeth, sayinge, 3 tyms vnto him, haille Mackbeth, king of Codon; for thou shalt be a kinge, but shalt beget No kinges, &c. Then said Bancko, What all to Mackbeth And nothing to me. Yes, said the nimphes, haille to thee Bancko, thou shalt beget kinges, yet be no kinge. . . .

The manuscript containing these pages came to Oxford in the great collection of Elias Ashmole in 1682. Although the volume was studied rather intensively by various antiquarians between that date and the advent of Collier, none of them, strangely enough, recorded the presence of these first-hand accounts of early Shakespearean productions. The first intimation of their existence came with their first appearance in print, in Collier's *New Particulars Regarding the Works of Shakespeare* (1836). Immediately the Forman notes were accepted as genuine, and even during the unmasking of Collier's deceptions no one questioned their authenticity. It was only in the twentieth century that scholars called attention to certain peculiarities in the notes. One was that Forman, although as an astrologer he might be presumed to have a special concern for chronological accuracy, made a mistake in dating his notes on *Macbeth;* either he wrote "Saturday" instead of "Friday," or the year itself was wrong. Another difficulty was that the *Macbeth* notes, though they bore the earliest date, stood last in the series of the four plays. A third was that (as Joseph Quincy Adams pointed out in 1931) those same notes were strongly reminiscent of certain phrases in Holinshed's *Chronicle,* Shakespeare's source for *Macbeth,* and less so of the play itself.

In 1933 an elaborate case against the genuineness of the Forman notes was published by Samuel A. Tannenbaum, a New York physician who was a passionate student of Elizabethan handwriting and bibliography and a stormy petrel in scholarly circles. He pointed out that none of the students who had examined the manuscript before Collier had observed these notes. He called attention to Collier's vagueness as to how he had got hold of the Forman notes: he had recounted how, when he was working at Oxford about 1829, he had heard of the existence of the manuscript, but after a prolonged search had been unable to find it in the Bodleian Library; but several years later "a gentleman . . . was employed to make a catalogue of the Ashmolean MSS. only, and he, very unexpectedly, found among them the notes I had anxiously sought in a different direction. He instantly forwarded a copy of them to me." Tannenbaum discovered in this story all the earmarks of a Collier myth. No names were given, either of those who had reported the existence of the manuscript to him, or of the gentleman who eventually found it and gave him a transcript—by which means Collier had taken care that there could be no checking on his story. Such vagueness Tannenbaum found most suspicious. Finally, he brought his imposing technical equipment to bear upon the handwriting of the notes, concluding that the penmanship was not Forman's at all, but Collier's brand of imitation.

Now an early examiner of the manuscript, long before Collier, had recorded the existence of pages headed "A Book of Places" at the location in the volume where the "Book of Plaies" is now found. Failing to consider the possibility that this man had misread "Plaies" as "Places," Tannenbaum assumed that originally Forman had written some notes on places he had visited in England. Collier then, in looking through the manuscript, noticed how easily "Places" could be read "Plaies," and saw his chance to settle the bothersome problem of when *Cymbeline* and *The Winter's Tale* had their early performances. He therefore removed the seven sheets of "Places" from the binding (supervision was not very strict in the Oxford libraries at the time) and either substituted for them an equal number of sheets of his own, on which he had forged the play notes, or eradicated Forman's writing with chemicals and wrote his newly invented notes on the original sheets.

Thus ran Tannenbaum's theory, announced in his essay of 1933. Superficially, it was rather persuasive. But it ran into opposition from the beginning. One reader of the essay examined the manuscript at the Bodleian under the ultraviolet light and found no sign of the erasure of previous writing; nor did he, or any later scholar, discover any indication that the crucial sheets had been removed from the binding. The odd, unchronological sequence of the notes on the four plays had been accounted for, even before Tannenbaum wrote, on the supposition that the sheets simply had been bound up in the wrong order. But the *coup de grâce* to his hypothesis was not administered until 1945. In that year Professor J. Dover Wilson, a Shakespeare scholar who has been editing the plays according to the new methods of textual analysis developed in the past forty years, decided that it was high time to settle the question. He had earlier announced his belief that the Forman notes were a Collier forgery; but now he was working on a new edition of *Macbeth*, and the riddle had crucial importance for him. He consulted Dr. Greg, the expert in Elizabethan bibliography and paleographer who, as we have seen, edited Henslowe's diary. Greg, though he had not examined the Forman manuscript, had read Tannenbaum's article; and "his remarks upon that," Wilson afterward reported with delicate circumspection, "were sufficiently cogent to convince me that I might go forward with every confidence in the authenticity of the document."

A few months later Wilson was in Oxford and had a look at the Forman manuscript, verifying the observations of previous scholars that there was no sign whatsoever that anyone had ever tampered with it. The Keeper of the Western Manuscripts at the Bodleian Library, Dr. R. W. Hunt, hearing of his visit, examined the manuscript from the point of view of the trained paleographer. He found no evidence that the handwriting was other than Forman's; the burden of Tannenbaum's case against its genuineness rested on the sample of Forman's genuine writing he had taken from a note written ten years after the "Book of Plaies." It is axiomatic in handwriting analysis that a scientific comparison of handwriting must use as "control" a genuine specimen written at the same time as the suspected document. Furthermore, Hunt pointed out that Tannenbaum had worked with photostats only;

and, immeasurably valuable though all kinds of photo-reproduction
have been to scholarship, the originals must be examined in the minute
study required by handwriting analysis.*

But the climax came when Hunt checked the records of the Bodleian Library on Collier's suspicious account of his futile search for
the Forman notes themselves and his eventual acquisition of a transcript. Collier had said that rumor located the manuscript in the
Bodleian, and that he had looked for it there; but rumor had been
wrong. At that date the Ashmolean Collection, in which the manuscript rested, was not housed in the Bodleian, but in a separate building. Collier or his informant simply had committed the understandable error of assuming that an item said to be "at Oxford" was therefore in the Bodleian. Hence there is no reason at all to doubt that he
actually searched in the Bodleian, as he said he did, and every reason
in the world why he was doomed to be unsuccessful in the quest. But
what about the mysterious "gentleman" who, he said, gave him the
transcript several years later? Hunt cleared that up once for all. The
gentleman was W. H. Black, who at that time *was* making a catalogue
of the Ashmolean Collection. In an interleaved copy of the proofs of
his catalogue, now in the library archives at the Bodleian, he wrote
opposite the entry for the "Book of Plaies": "I made a transcript of
this curious article, in 1832, for my friend J. P. Collier, which he
designed to print. He did so, but without the old orthography, in . . ."
Failing to recall the year, Black left the date blank.

Unless, as is not probable, somebody comes forward to maintain that
Collier forged that entry in Black's handwriting to perfect his alibi, it
seems that he has been entirely exonerated from the charge of fab-

---

* The same is true of detailed analysis of printing. The Droeshout portrait of
Shakespeare which was used as frontispiece in the first folio (1623) has been the
subject of intensive study because it is found in several "states." Twenty-five or
more years ago, a leading authority on the portrait saw a photograph of the one
in the Halliwell copy of the first folio. Noting that a colon occurred in the legend
below the portrait, whereas all other known copies had a period, he jumped to the
conclusion that here was a hitherto unrecorded "state" of the engraving. If he
had been able to examine the book itself instead of a reproduction, he would have
noticed that the upper dot of the colon had been supplied not by a printer but
by a fly.

ricating the Forman notes. Far from tampering with them, it is plain that he never even saw them, but relied, as he said he did, on a transcript.

Although not every scholar who sallies out after Collier is able to bring back a piece of his scalp, our roster of his misdoings is still incomplete. Consider these depressing circumstances: (a) Apart from his manifold activities as a historian of the Elizabethan and Jacobean stage, he printed the texts of scores of rare pieces of nondramatic literature in tiny editions for various Victorian bibliophile clubs. No scholar may ever rely on those printed texts; he must find the manuscript or printed volume from which Collier worked. When he finds that source, he must be perpetually considering the possibility of forgery. (b) In his time Collier worked through tons of manuscripts and annotated old books in the private libraries of his blue-blooded patrons, in Dulwich College, in government archives, and in the large collection which he himself amassed in the course of a long and acquisitive career at a time when rarities could be had for a few shillings in the London bookshops. No single page of this material can be free from suspicion. Even if Collier did not quote from it in his printed works, he may have tampered with it simply out of his queer urge to amplify history for his private delectation. (c) He did not leave dependable accounts of where and how he had acquired his materials. Sometimes his failure to mention names and dates leaves him open to suspicions that prove to be unfounded. The only error he can be charged with in such instances is that of following what was too often the easy-going practice of perfectly reputable Victorian scholars. Today, of course, the scholar is required by the rules of his craft to record precisely the whereabouts of all the material he uses, as well as the names of those who have helped him locate and examine it. But on too many other occasions either that same vagueness, or a plausible circumstantial account that may have holes in it, has been shown to be a deliberate attempt to cover up the forger's tracks. Remembering the way in which Collier defended the authenticity of the Perkins Folio corrections by rehearsing the story of Rodd's bookshop and Mr. Parry's lost folio, we cannot afford to take on faith any of his accounts of provenance.

Therefore, whether one works with Collier's printed volumes or with original materials he is known to have had the chance to befoul, one must always be on guard. To add the final complication, it is not easy even today, with our highly sophisticated methods of testing the genuineness of documents, to pin down a Collier fabrication. In his prime, Collier was a pretty competent imitator of old handwritings, probably as clever as some modern experts who essay to unmask him. He was careful to concoct appropriate ink, and, in the case of whole new inventions, to use paper of the correct age. Possibly the weakest part of his equipment was his knowledge of old spelling and word-usage. But because Shakespeare's contemporaries were gloriously individualistic in their orthography, and because even the *Oxford English Dictionary* (published since Collier's time) does not give us the final answer on the meanings and usages of words in the sixteenth and seventeenth centuries, it is not easy to surprise Collier, learned as he was, in indisputable error. For building a case against him today a whole cluster of newly developed techniques must be used, minutely to reconstruct the writer's every move as he composed the document in question. Often such techniques reveal that the document contains telltale bits of evidence which point to a forger. And although recent paleographical detective-work has sometimes failed to convict Collier, in the future it may well reveal instances of his activity even now unsuspected.

In one sense, modern scholars have reason to be grateful: Collier's aberrations have supplied extra zest to research. But scholarship centering in the history of English drama especially has never needed meretricious enlivening. There was no need at all for Collier to interpolate his own extra dash of criminality. The available sources of sixteenth- and seventeenth-century literary history were complicated enough, even in his own time, without his gratuitous introduction of fresh confusions. Once the first charm of dealing with the great forger has worn off, scholars come to develop a justifiable animus against him. They look upon his strenuous efforts to improve upon history not as a grand-scale episode of literary imposture but merely as an unmitigated nuisance.

II

IT was in the pages of the *Athenæum*, you remember, that Collier first proclaimed the existence of the Perkins Folio. A few weeks later, on March 6, 1852, the *Athenæum* reported that "a great variety of communications" had come into the office since Collier's two exciting articles and that they all treated the event as "one of the most important and interesting that has for a long time arisen in the history of Shakespeare comment." Yet in that same issue appeared the statement that a newly published volume of letters by the poet Shelley (which, incidentally, the *Athenæum* had praised the week before) had been withdrawn from sale because they had been proved to be forgeries. Later in the year, when the full story came out, the self-righteous weekly leveled its heavy guns against those who had been duped by or perhaps abetted *that* forgery. But it continued to applaud Collier, and when Hamilton of the British Museum exposed the fraud it devoted many columns to attacks on him and his colleagues and attempts to riddle their evidence. If the bound volumes of periodicals could blush, explorers in the dim stacks of libraries today could be guided to the whole *Athenæum* file for the 1850's by a rosy glow.

The gentleman at whose dubious operations the *Athenæum* gagged, at the same time that it was swallowing the Collier enormity whole, was George Gordon Byron, Esq., the second most mischievous Victorian literary forger. The name of Byron really did not belong to him, any more than the title of major which he prefixed to it a few years later. To the Society of Guardians for the Protection of Trade, a sort of Better Business Bureau, he was known as "de Gibler," which may or may not have been his real name. In any event, he first turned up in history in 1843, when he wrote from Wilkes-Barre, Pennsylvania, to the third John Murray, son of Byron's publisher. He explained that he was an illegitimate son of the poet by a Spanish noblewoman, born in Spain in 1810, and asked Murray for a set of Byron's works and a Byron autograph. In the four years following, a number of persons reputed to have collections of Byroniana, among them surviving friends of the poet, received similar letters from the gentleman, who now resided near London, requesting that they trace out copies of their manuscripts for him, or otherwise provide him with unpublished material for a proposed life of his illustrious father. As the campaign progressed, he included in his letters an invitation to subscribe to the projected volume.

Some of his letters seem to have had results, because by the spring of 1848 he was able to announce the impending publication of his work in monthly parts: *Lord Byron's Inedited Works, Now First Published from His Letters, Journals, and Other Manuscripts, in the Possession of His Son, George Gordon Byron, Esq.* Rashly, he let it be known that he had received some of his new material from his putative father's half-sister, Mrs. Leigh. Within a week Mrs. Leigh's lawyers announced in the press that this new Byron had received no papers from the family with whom he claimed connection, that the claim of relationship itself was entirely false, and that a letter was en route to him "stating rather disagreeable views of theirs [the family's] on the subject."

That effectively ended the publishing project, at least within the jurisdiction of the British courts. But the self-styled natural son of Childe Harold was gifted with the sanguine, enterprising temperament of Shakespeare's classic bastard Edmund. He had other strings to his bow.

In 1845, three years before the disclaimer by the poet's family, the pretender had made contact, through an intermediary, with Mary Wollstonecraft Shelley, to whom he offered to sell certain letters of her husband which he had acquired. Mrs. Shelley, though convinced from the first that she was dealing with "a rogue," "a low fellow," "a rascal," and "a swindler," and that the letters he possessed actually had been stolen from her many years ago, was desperately eager to recover them; but she held off, principally because she was reluctant to pay the prices Byron asked. It was only after she had been thoroughly frightened by his "blackguard and threatening" letters (she was referring no doubt to implications by Byron about the contents of some of the poet's missives) that she capitulated. How many pieces of Shelley manuscript she bought in, we do not know. But the fact that

Mary Shelley, at this time and again a few years later, added to her family papers manuscripts from George Gordon Byron has been responsible for scholarly perplexity ever since.

Byron's next client, so far as is known, was a Pall Mall bookseller named William White. Soon after Mrs. Leigh and her solicitors took their stand against his plans for a volume of the poet's "inedited works," there appeared in Mr. White's shop a young lady who inquired, with suitable timidity, whether he would be interested in buying two letters written by Lord Byron. White bought them, and a few days later she was back with two more. It was, he thought, time for an explanation; and the lady readily obliged. She said she was the daughter of a recently deceased autograph-collecting surgeon, who had attended Byron's faithful valet, Fletcher, in his last illness, and to whom Fletcher had given these letters and some of Byron's own books as a token of gratitude. This explanation seemed to White adequate enough to account for the parcels the lady then brought to him, in visit after visit. After he had bought some forty-seven Byron letters from her, for variety's sake she changed over to Shelley items, of which her father seemed to have had an equally copious supply. White appears to have been completely incurious as to the details of her father's collecting activities. But when he mentioned his acquisitions to friends in the book trade two of them independently remarked that a certain Mr. Byron had had some connection with the recent history of some of the items being peddled by the mysterious stranger. Only then did White question her more particularly. After some pressing, she freely admitted that the story of the deceased surgeon was false, and that she was really the wife of Mr. Byron; they had had misfortunes, she said, and were forced to adopt this means of finding ready cash. Later her husband himself came by invitation to the shop and explained, again to White's complete satisfaction, that the manuscripts his wife had been selling had been collected legitimately in the course of his wide travels through the regions visited by his father the poet, or else acquired in auctions. Shelley's letters, or some of them at least, had come from a box left behind at Marlow in 1818. He supplied White with his certificate of the genuineness of everything White had purchased.

With his mind thus set at rest, White sold the Byron papers to John Murray, and tried to interest Mrs. Shelley in the letters from her husband. That lady, however, refused to buy them, and White sent them up for auction in 1851. Eleven of them were bought by the poet's son and twenty-three others were acquired by Edward Moxon. Moxon added two more letters to his parcel and in February, 1852, published the whole group of twenty-five in a slender volume to which Robert Browning supplied a long introduction, which until the recent discovery of his "Essay on Chatterton" was thought to be the only longish piece of prose he had ever printed. (Browning, it should be added, never saw the original Shelley letters; he was in Paris at the time, and Moxon provided him only with a transcript of their texts.)

By a peculiar combination of circumstances, the fact that Moxon had unwittingly published a set of forgeries was discovered almost before copies landed on the bookstalls. He had sent a copy of his volume to the new poet laureate, Alfred Tennyson. Staying at Tennyson's home at the time the book arrived was his friend Francis Turner Palgrave, the future editor of the *Golden Treasury*. Palgrave idly picked up the book, and his eyes lighted on a passage, supposedly written by Shelley, which he at once recognized as having been written by his own father, Sir Francis, and published in the *Quarterly Review* in 1840! The elder Palgrave wrote at once to Moxon, who then went to John Murray for advice. Murray got out from his great store of genuine Byron letters specimens which Byron had written and mailed at the same place and time as those in Moxon's Shelley collection. Moxon was crushed when he discovered that the postmarks did not agree. Those on the Shelley letters obviously had been forged. His only course was to withdraw the volume from sale—an incident which, as we have seen, the *Athenæum* reported on the page on which it described Mr. Payne Collier's present immense renown in the world of Shakespeare lovers.

At that time, the plagiarism from Palgrave and the testimony of the postmarks were the only definite evidence of forgery in the case of most of the Moxon letters. Later researchers, however, have traced the text of the majority of the letters. The forger had copied out whole paragraphs from Shelley letters and essays that were already in print;

in other letters he had lifted whole passages from articles, printed in English magazines, which had nothing to do with Shelley. In some instances he composed a letter partly with genuine Shelley passages, partly with passages from other sources; and in all cases he gave the letter a place and date, and incidental circumstantial details, which would fit in with the known movements, residences, and activities of the poet.

After the unmasking of the forgery, Murray and Moxon returned their spurious treasures to White, who refunded their money and presented both lots to the British Museum. They were thus permanently removed from circulation. But Mary Shelley and her son Sir Percy retained the unknown number they had bought.

Meanwhile Major Byron, as he now styled himself, prudently had not lingered on the English scene. Soon after his profitable dealings with White he and his wife returned to America, where, safe from the wrath of Mrs. Leigh, he revived his project of publishing the *Inedited Works of Lord Byron*. Two monthly numbers actually were issued in New York in 1849–50; but only two, and from that point onward the major's career can be traced only dimly. He is said to have been an officer (demoted somehow to a captaincy) under General Frémont in the American Civil War, and later to have figured in the New York scene as journalist, diplomat, spy, broker, British army officer, British naval officer, mining prospector, bookseller, Oriental traveler, commission agent, patent agent, and/or aristocratic exile—depending, evidently, on what struck his fancy on a particular day. His wife meanwhile worked as housekeeper at the Hoffman House. The last recorded word of him is his presence in New York, nominally as a merchant, in 1885. Who he really was, nobody knows.

It is often forgotten in the case of Major Byron, as it is of many successful forgers, that his spurious documents were often mixed with absolutely authentic ones. During years of begging autographs from friends of the poet Byron and collectors of his manuscripts, the major had, it seems, accumulated a respectable store of genuine items. This may have been true also of the papers which he sold to Shelley's widow and son; for the Shelleys *had* left papers behind at Marlow, and Byron could conceivably have stumbled on them. Because the Shelleys immediately mixed Major Byron's parcels with their other papers, the great riddle that he bequeathed to contemporary scholars is how to detect his manuscripts in the first place and, having done that, how to distinguish between the genuine letters he simply transmitted from an earlier owner and the letters he forged. This problem has presented itself repeatedly as fresh portions of the Shelley family papers have become available for study.

One of the most crucial issues in Shelley biography is the character of the poet's first wife, Harriet Westbrook, and the circumstances of her death. The story is familiar enough. Shelley left Harriet to live with Mary Godwin; Harriet drowned herself in the Serpentine. The precise circumstances surrounding this tragic episode are almost a touchstone to the biographical interpretation of Shelley. But the facts are meager and much disputed. Our only relatively immediate source of information is a letter Shelley wrote to Mary on December 16, 1816, six days after Harriet's body was found, reporting that "Harriet descended the steps of prostitution until she lived with a groom of the name of Smith." Almost the only other data we have are such items as a brief newspaper notice of the recovery of Harriet's body, stating that she was in "an advanced state of pregnancy." To some biographers, the manner of her death has seemed one of the gravest charges against Shelley; his infidelity drove her to prostitution—an allegation found only in his letter, as the evidence of her pregnancy rests only on the newspaper item and her landlady's casual impression. Shelley's apologists, on the other hand, maintaining that her (reputed) career after he left her is a true indication of her character, completely relieved him of responsibility for her end.

The rub is that there is not one copy of Shelley's letter of December 16, but *four*—all with essentially the same text and, to the layman's eye at least, the same handwriting. Obviously three of the four must be forgeries, for Shelley was no more addicted than other English men of letters to writing personal letters in quadruplicate. But which three of the four are forgeries? The question, which has occupied Shelley scholars for many years, is a tangled one, because all four copies were at some time in the possession of the Shelley family. We know that at least two were bought from Major Byron, but we do not know which two. Furthermore, one of the four has a mysterious history. Somehow, having (supposedly!) passed through the mails in 1816, it got back into them a second time in 1859 and, failing to find Mary this time—she had died eight years earlier—landed in the Dead Letter Office. There it was discovered by a sharp-eyed official, who restored it in 1867 to a member of the Shelley family. Eventually it was bought by Thomas J. Wise, whom not even the Shelley scholars most obsessed by the prevalence of forgers suspect in this case; and it went with the rest of his collection to the British Museum. It is this letter which most experts have accepted, after a prolonged controversy in the 1930's, as the one which Shelley really wrote. But who owned it in 1859, when it was accidentally slipped into the post? And if it was then in the possession of the family, might it not, far from being the original, be one of the forged copies that they had bought some years before?

The idea occurred to Robert M. Smith, a professor at Lehigh University, some years ago. Smith set out to prove that the Wise copy, like the other three, is a Major Byron forgery. It might, he admitted, be based on a (now lost) original letter from Shelley, and its account of Harriet's degradation may have represented Shelley's own views at that time under the influence of Godwin. But until the original letter was forthcoming, there was, Smith said, no way of discovering how much of it may have been the ingenious mosaic work of the forger. To what extent, in this letter, did he follow his usual practice of inserting material that would appeal to the widowed Mary Shelley's ambition to build up an idealized picture of her husband—a picture that would suit the prevalent Victorian sentiments?

But if this crucial letter was a forgery, and the information it contained was untrue, what of the subsequent letters between Shelley and Mary which referred to it? Professor Smith sought the advice of Louis A. Waters of Syracuse, New York, a professional analyst of questioned documents. After comparing photostats of the Wise copy and of the other related letters with genuine examples of Shelley's writing and with proved specimens of Major Byron's fabrications, the expert reported that the Wise copy and at least two of the letters of later date were forgeries. The conclusion Professor Smith reached, on the basis of this evidence, was that the whole account of Harriet's immoral conduct prior to her suicide was deliberately concocted to absolve Shelley from the blame that had for so long been his.

If true, this disclosure could shatter one of the foundation stones of the accepted edifice of Shelley biography. In 1945 Professor Smith and three co-workers published *The Shelley Legend,* in which an elaborate attempt was made to show that a great deal of our knowledge of Shelley was based on the testimony of documents forged by Major Byron—perhaps, it was implied, with the encouragement of the Shelley family.

The Shelley Legend called forth three devastating replies from leading American Shelley specialists, requiring seventy-four closely printed pages in the scholarly journals. Perhaps no other scholarly book in recent times has been more savagely handled. Brushing aside the testimony of the handwriting expert, who based his opinion on photostats alone, the expert reviewers maintained that the Wise copy of the December 16 letter was not a forgery, and that, even if it were assumed to be one, its text would still have had to be copied from a genuine letter. For none of them doubted that Shelley wrote such a letter, since the existence of later letters alluding to it would prove that much. Smith's claim that those later letters were forged in order to substantiate the first was, of course, rejected. Furthermore, the specialists pointed out that unquestionable, though admittedly meager, contemporary evidence from other sources supports the narrative of Harriet's downfall contained in the Shelley correspondence.

The fact seems to be that, despite the sensational alarms raised by Professor Smith, Major Byron's forgeries have not seriously contaminated our store of information about Shelley, although their existence is always a potential trap for the unwary. It is true beyond doubt that some of the letters Mary and her son bought from him were forged. But these seem to have been pretty definitely identified; the standard catalogue of Shelley letters, compiled by Seymour de Ricci, isolated some fifty forgeries out of a total of eight hundred extant letters bearing Shelley's signature.

However, the whole story—I have grossly simplified one of the most complicated puzzles in recent scholarship, as anyone who refers to *The Shelley Legend* and the reviews of it will discover—illustrates the way in which forgery somewhere in the past can desperately becloud an issue in literary biography.*

III

COMPARED with the giants of forgery whom we have just been discussing, Mr. Alexander Howland ("Antique") Smith was a small operator; which is to say that, although his accomplishments have been a constant nuisance, they have occasioned no great controversies in the scholarly world. He was endowed neither with Collier's large literary erudition nor with Major Byron's romantic aura; but he was scarcely less prolific than they, and Heaven only knows how many of his productions are still at large and undetected. While they remain so, specialists in Burns and Scott must regard with cool skepticism any letter purportedly written by those authors, or any book bearing what is alleged to be their markings.

During the later 1880's a number of booksellers and collectors, principally in Scotland, noticed that the market was being flooded with letters and old books relating to Burns and Scott as well as such other celebrities as Mary Stuart, Bothwell, James I, and John Knox. Any sudden increase in the normal market supply of literary items of a certain sort arouses comment, and in this case the comment was spiced with reports of several instances in which Burns and Scott items had caused a bit of unpleasantness. In 1886, for example, a gentleman browsing through the bookshop of Andrew Brown in Edinburgh turned up an album of letters from literary celebrities, including Scott and Thackeray, and asked the price. Brown set it at a pound and remarked, as the customer opened his pocketbook, that he had purchased the album only a short while earlier from a man who, he indicated with a nod of his head, was still there in the shop. The buyer of the album departed without taking any particular note of the man.

* It may be added that in September, 1949, Dr. Theodore G. Ehrsam, one of the collaborators in *The Shelley Legend*, who made a special study of Major Byron following the publication of that book, reversed his earlier judgment and announced his conviction that the Wise copy of the controversial letter is genuine after all.

Later he returned and was shown some other documents. Brown said he had obtained these from the same person but, when pressed for an explanation of how the unnamed seller of the documents had acquired them in the first place, told a story which failed to satisfy the gentleman, who left without buying anything more. The album he got on his first visit was to have unexpected interest six years later, and he was to regret not having taken closer notice of the man in the shop.

In 1889 another Edinburgh bookseller, an irascible old man named James Stillie, sold some letters of Burns and Scott which were promptly returned to him on the ground that they were forgeries. He refused to refund the purchase price, saying in effect that he was second to none in his knowledge of Burns; as for Scott, he had known him for more than fifty years and could be depended upon to be a better judge of the novelist's handwriting than any upstart of an expert. The buyer thus done out of his money went away muttering, in the words of a later chronicler, that "to have enjoyed the friendship of Scott for so long a period the veteran must have known him since he was ten or eleven years old, and must himself be at that time upwards of 107."

A year or two later Stillie became involved in a transatlantic lawsuit. A New York banker, John Stewart Kennedy, had bought from him for £750, and then presented to the Lenox Library (afterwards to form a part of the New York Public Library), a collection of two hundred manuscripts relating to Burns, 155 of which were said to be in Burns's hand. The Lenox librarian, after looking the gift horse in the mouth, decided that it would not be amiss to have the experts at the British Museum take a look too. They did, and reported that the gift was chiefly valuable as an assortment of forgeries. Whereupon the infuriated Kennedy sued Stillie. Stillie snarled back that he had not represented the documents to be genuine—hence there was no question of false pretense—and that, on the other hand, he himself had no doubt that they *were* genuine—so that there was at the same time no question of his judgment. Eventually, upon being told of Stillie's advanced years and bad health, Kennedy dropped the suit and charged the £750 to experience.

In the same year that the Kennedy collection went to the Lenox Library, still another Edinburgh bookseller, attending a public auction, purchased a parcel of old books bearing inscriptions and annotations by Scottish heroes, including Burns, which had been sent in by a pawnbroker as an unredeemed pledge. Many of the volumes bore the bookplate of a great collector of Caledoniana, Whitefoord Mackenzie, whose library had been sold off years earlier, and an accompanying list asserted that these had been bought at that sale. But the bookseller, upon referring to the printed catalogue of the Mackenzie sale, found that none of the books bearing this bookplate had been in Mackenzie's library. The obvious inference was that somebody had bought some very cheap items at the Mackenzie sale, soaked off the bookplates, and pasted them in the present volumes to give them and their patently forged inscriptions and annotations the aegis of a great collector's authority.

In a Scottish country paper, in August, 1891, one James Mackenzie, a chemist and Burns enthusiast—no relative, apparently, of Whitefoord—printed a letter from his collection which Burns wrote to a certain "John Hill, weaver," who presumably was an old friend living at Cumnock at the time of the poet's marriage. Immediately several other Burns enthusiasts rose up to challenge the authenticity of the letter. Mackenzie, however, indignantly turned down their proposal that it be lent to the British Museum for examination. After all, he had been a Burns collector for a quarter of a century, and his fellow collector, Stillie, agreed with him that the letter was genuine. By way of voting confidence in himself he proceeded to print some of Burns's poems from manuscripts in his possession. But the inconvenient fact remained that John Hill was otherwise unknown even to the best students of Burns, who had made minute inquiries into all members of his circle; and when it was shown that one of the poems Mackenzie published had come from the pen of a future provost of Eton and had been printed in the *London Magazine* in 1766, when Burns was just seven years old, it seemed that the evidence against Mackenzie's prizes was overwhelming. As William Roughead, the great Edinburgh connoisseur of human error, once remarked: "After making every allowance for the earliest possible development of his genius, it was difficult to believe that the bard, however precocious, wrote in his seventh year the line 'No lawless passion swelled my even breast,' while a reference to his

prattling children playing round his knees seemed equally premature."
But Mackenzie declined to be convinced, and he clung to his story of
having found the manuscripts many years before, in that faithful
stand-by of the cornered collector, the secret drawer of an old cabinet
he had picked up for a song.

But all these separate developments, while they clearly suggested
that somebody was making fools of respected Burns students, gave no
clue to the culprit's identity. His eventual unmasking resulted from a
smart piece of Edinburgh journalism. In November, 1892, the *Evening
Dispatch* began a series of articles summing up the gossip in local
collectors' circles and asking in effect, "Who has been forging our
Burns?" No sooner was the series under way than the readers of the
paper began to remember things. A bookseller on George IV Bridge
recalled that he had had many visits from an odd-looking customer
who was always wanting old folio books with "fair and ample fly-
leaves" and books bound in vellum. Could this be our man, looking for
raw materials upon which to forge his letters? The bookseller had no
notion who the man was, because his purchases had always been cash-
and-carry; he left no name behind.

Another reader was the gentleman who had bought the autograph
album from Andrew Brown in 1886. He took the album down from
his shelves and ruefully observed, as no doubt he had done many
times since his ill advised purchase, the remarkable resemblance
which the penciled notes by the man who had collected the manuscript
scraps bore to the writing of the scraps themselves; the collector and
the collected even seemed to share the same misapprehensions on the
score of spelling, for both of them wrote "philosophcal." And elsewhere
in Edinburgh other frequenters of the shop of Andrew Brown brought
forth for more careful scrutiny manuscripts and annotated books they
had understood him to say came from the same mysterious source.

But the most interested reader of all was a lawyer who looked upon
the *Dispatch*'s facsimiles of some of the fake manuscripts and recognized the handwriting as that of a copying clerk he had once employed
in his own office—Alexander Howland Smith, known familiarly as
"Antique" because he seemed always to be peddling old documents or
other curiosities as a sideline. The lawyer took his information to the

delighted *Dispatch*, the Edinburgh police were sent into action, and within a matter of days "Antique" Smith was in jail.

Alexander Howland Smith is said to have been at the time about thirty years old, with sallow complexion, dark mustache, small side whiskers, and a "plausible and insinuating" manner: the perfect model for one of Sherlock Holmes's more contemptible adversaries, such as James Windibanks, whom Dr. Watson had described in almost identical terms in the year before Smith came into the clutches of the law. Evidently he bore no grudge against the *Dispatch*, for in his cell he talked freely to its star reporter. His story was that he had once worked for a law firm which was an agent for several old families in Scotland. During a housecleaning on the premises, he was told to dispose of a large quantity of documents which had accumulated in the course of generations. With a frugality which did more honor to his nationality than his subsequent cashing-in on the passion of his compatriots to own mementoes of their heroes, he took them out and sold them on the secondhand booksellers' market. Evidently the law firm had no objections to his getting rid of their waste paper in this way; but a short time later he was dismissed for making off with two other interesting documents, a pair of negotiable checks. Out of work, impressed by the price old papers with some historical or literary significance commanded, and at a loss for a means of obtaining such papers readymade, he turned to the next best thing—wholesale manufacture of them. He asserted to the *Dispatch* reporter that he had enjoyed a fairly constant demand for his work, Andrew Brown, James Mackenzie, and James Stillie having been among his most faithful customers. When these gentlemen were temporarily sated, he would send off a parcel of forged documents and annotated books to a public auction, or sacrifice them to a pawnbroker for what would turn out to be a permanent loan.

In its forgivable enthusiasm for playing up Smith as a forger infinitely more talented than Chatterton or Ireland, the *Evening Dispatch* was unjust to all parties concerned. Chatterton and Ireland, while they hoodwinked some of the best people of their time, actually were bungling amateurs when judged by modern standards; and, to speak the bitter truth, "Antique" Smith was even less gifted than they. The jury required only half an hour to convict him on all counts, and the judge who sentenced him to twelve months in jail seems to have shared its opinion and that of the expert witnesses when he remarked that those whom Smith had gulled were almost as culpable as he. The carelessness of his work could have deceived only those who went out of their way to be deceived. Either the credulous French mathematician who bought Vrain Lucas's absurd fabrications by the thousands had Scottish cousins in the book trade—or Stillie, Mackenzie, Brown, *et al.* were engaged in a profitable racket. Opinion in Edinburgh at the time seems to have inclined toward the latter view.

Unlike the products of Collier and Major Byron, Smith's wares are seldom or never the occasion of a quarrel among the experts. He never stopped to study the writing habits of the men whose letters he forged. He uniformly imitated the chirography of the mature Burns, no matter what the date of the letter was. He wrote slowly and laboriously, with a steel pen, whereas genuine Burns letters were written swiftly, with a quill. Burns, though he used plenty of capital letters, always did so with a clear reason; Smith, observing only that Burns had sprinkled capitals about with a lavish hand, never bothered to be consistent. These and other equally plain differences are almost infallible means of distinguishing between an authentic piece of Burns's writing and one of Smith's imitations.

The 170 examples of Smith's handiwork exhibited at his trial are thought to have been only a tiny portion of his total production. At one time or another he seems to have copied into "Burns manuscripts" most of the poems in the collected editions; he gathered from eighteenth-century magazines "unpublished" verses that had nothing to do with Burns; and he composed uncounted "new" letters and duplicates of known ones. Crude though his fabrications are, the unwary are still taken in by them, and every time a new batch of Burns material comes upon the market from private hands it must be carefully combed for Smith forgeries. Once in a while a forgery passes muster and appears in the sale catalogue of a highly reputable dealer. Even Professor DeLancey Ferguson, the editor of the standard edition of Burns's letters, was temporarily deceived when he accepted as genuine a letter he found from Burns to his younger brother warning against the perils of whoring. Later, in the Burns Birthplace Museum at Alloway, he discovered a duplicate of the letter which turned out to be the genuine original from which Smith had made a copy.

It is no wonder, then, that the name of "Antique" Smith is a bugaboo to everyone determined to find out the truth about Burns; and that scholars call a librarian blessed when he detects a Smith forgery and permanently and irrevocably labels it as such. The New York Public Library, over forty years after its predecessor received Kennedy's dubious gift, was once more in receipt of a questionable Burns item—a copy of the valuable first London edition of the *Poems* (1787) in which the proper names, omitted by the printer, had been filled in, apparently by the poet himself. If the volume had been what it purported to be, a printer's copy prepared by Burns for a new edition, it would have been a most useful aid to scholarship, and a bibliophile's prize in addition. But, alas, it was just one more example of Smith's art. "Although it is bound in sheep, we recognize the wolf beneath," wisecracked a member of the library staff—and the volume joined hundreds of others in the rogues' gallery of the forgery collection.

THE SCHOLAR AND THE SCIENTIST

I

AMONG your memories of what some people have called the first great English novel, Chaucer's *Troilus and Criseyde,* you doubtless treasure the climactic scene in the third book. Shrewd, genial Pandarus, whose name is so unjustly preserved in an unpleasant English verb, has finally succeeded in bringing together under the same roof the valiant warrior, Troilus, and the lady for whose love he has been languishing, the lovely young widow Criseyde. Having hidden Troilus in a closet, Pandarus entertains the unsuspecting Criseyde at supper, and afterwards, "with hertes fresshe and glade," Pandarus sings to Criseyde and tells her a story about a famous hero named Wade. "But at the laste," Chaucer records, "as every thyng hath ende, She took hire leve, and nedes wolde wende."

But Pandarus looks out the window, and "al was on a flod."

> The bente moone with hire hornes pale,
> Saturne, and Jove, in Cancro joyned were,
> That swych a reyn from heven gan avale,
> That every maner womman that was there
> Hadde of that smoky reyn a verray feere;
> At which Pandare tho lough, and seyde thenne,
> "Now were it tyme a lady to go henne!"
>
> "But goode nece, if I myghte evere plese
> Yow any thyng, than prey ich yow," quod he,

"To don myn herte as now so gret an ese
As for to dwelle here al this nyght with me,
For-whi this is youre owen hous, parde.
For, by my trouthe, I sey it nought a-game,
To wende as now, it were to me a shame."

Criseyde, being a sensible as well as a superlatively attractive lady, agrees—it would be folly indeed to venture out on such a night. So Pandarus escorts her to his best guest room, where, he says, "ye neither shullen, dar I seye, Heren noyse of reynes nor of thonder." Having made sure that she lacks no comfort, he says good night to her and bustles down to the closet where Troilus has been secreted these many weary hours. And that night (to make a long story short, and thus avoid what Chaucer calls "diffusioun of speche") Pandarus escorts Troilus to Criseyde's bed, where she

Made hym swich feste, it joye was to seene,
Whan she his trouthe and clene entente wiste;
And as aboute a tree, with many a twiste,
Bytrent and writh the swote wodebynde,
Gan ech of hem in armes other wynde.

Our scene shifts to the campus of Princeton University, three or four thousand years after the above episode supposedly took place, and almost five and a half centuries after Chaucer wrote his masterly account of it. It was a fine morning in 1923, and Professor Robert K. Root, a distinguished Chaucer specialist, was in his office, poring over the text of *Troilus and Criseyde*, of which he was preparing a scholarly edition. When he reached the description of the rainy evening in Book III, he stopped and pondered.

Because Chaucer's poetry is full of allusions to Ptolemaic astronomy and the closely related medieval astrology, Root had had to make a special study of those sciences. It was customary in Chaucer's day, of course, to reckon the progress of the seasons in astrological terms; one recalls the familiar passage early in the General Prologue to the *Canterbury Tales*, "the yonge sonne Hath in the Ram his halve cours yronne"—that is, the sun is on the way out of the first sign of the zodiac, which means that when Chaucer's variegated company of pilgrims were gathering at Harry Bailey's snug inn in Southwark, the season was the middle of April. Similarly, Root recognized that the season of Pandarus' dinner party was indicated by the fact that the crescent moon was in the sign of Cancer, which would mean in turn that the sun either was approaching or had already entered the sign of Gemini; in modern reckoning, therefore, it was the middle of May.

So much, Root reflected that morning in 1923, was obvious and indisputable. But there were other astrological references in this passage. Chaucer had said that not only the moon was in Cancer, but also two other planets, Saturn and Jupiter. The presence of three planets within a single segment of the heavens surely was unusual; perhaps impossible. Why, then, had Chaucer placed them there? Might it have been because the three actually *were* there at the time he wrote? Although the story of *Troilus and Criseyde* supposedly occurred in the ancient Troy of Homeric legend, Chaucer always had mixed up the ancient and the contemporary, and the surroundings and the habits of Troilus, Criseyde, and Pandarus were far more those of fourteenth-century Englishmen than they were those of the Trojans. Like all medieval artists, Chaucer had had little sense of historical perspective; he had drawn his circumstantial details from life as it was lived in the days of Richard II, regardless of the putative date of the events described. If this was so, might not the unusual conjunction of the planets in Book III be a reflection of some contemporary event? And if it were—might not one thus have the solution to one of the most puzzling conundrums of Chaucer scholarship? For down to this time, despite the immense amount of research that had been done on Chaucer and his poetry, the date of the writing of *Troilus and Criseyde*, which is second only to the *Canterbury Tales* among his masterpieces, had been a mystery. Scholars were able to agree only that it had been written some time between 1373 and 1386. But, as is the case with every great artist, the accurate dating of Chaucer's works is essential to an understanding of the way his genius developed. Hence the importance that Chaucer students attached to the precise date of the *Troilus.*

That afternoon there was a Princeton faculty meeting, one of those presumably necessary distractions in academic life during which scholars preoccupied with their current problems of research hear the voice of the dean only distantly as he sets forth petty questions of policy for the solemn consideration of his colleagues. When the meeting was breaking up, Root happened to encounter Professor Henry N. Russell, of the department of astronomy, and briefly outlined his problem.

'Could this configuration of the three planets in a single sign of the zodiac actually have happened?" he asked.

"Perfectly possible," Russell said, "but extremely infrequent. I could find out for you whether it ever occurred during Chaucer's lifetime."

Root begged him to do so, and they went home to their respective dinners.

A week or two later, Russell came to Root's office with some sheets of paper covered with mathematical data. He had gone to Newcomb's Planetary Tables, a standard reference work, and with its aid had worked out some complicated calculations—"computations," Root modestly recalls, "that would have been far beyond my own astronomical competence." And there the answer was.

Just as Russell had said, the occurrence of the moon in Cancer was an entirely ordinary phenomenon, but the conjunction of the other two planets was decidedly uncommon. The arrangement and functioning of the heavenly bodies are such that there are periods of about two hundred years in which Saturn and Jupiter meet in the sign of Cancer every sixty years. But these alternate with periods of over six hundred years in which the two planets *never* meet in Cancer. The calculations based on Newcomb showed that Chaucer's early life coincided with the end of a six-hundred-year period in which Cancer never had had the pleasure of entertaining Saturn and Jupiter simultaneously. The last time they had met there was A.D. 769. Then, six centuries of absence. And then one of the two-hundred-year periods began, with the result that in the year 1385—on the thirteenth day of April, to be exact—Saturn and Jupiter were once again in conjunction. This conjunction, as a matter of fact, began near the end of the sign of Gemini; within a few days the reunited planets moved into Cancer, where they remained until the end of June. The moon joined them there, as a pale crescent, in the middle of May.

Chaucer, like every other cultivated man of his time, was thoroughly conversant with what went on in the heavens, especially because it was believed that the goings-on among the planets had a direct and often baleful influence on the affairs of men. Unusual celestial phenomena, such as meteors or unheard-of conjunctions of the planets in a single sign of the zodiac, foretold "some strange eruption to our state"—civil commotions, natural calamities, dreadful upheavals of all sorts. And so, as now became plain to Root, Chaucer had witnessed this striking sight in the evening sky over London, which was far more remarkable than the appearance of Halley's comet; and because it was much on his mind, he wrote it into the poem he was working on. He may well have felt it to be a fittingly spectacular, even symbolic, accompaniment to the scene in which the star-crossed love of Troilus and Criseyde is consummated.

The long-sought date of *Troilus and Criseyde*, therefore (or at least of the writing of the rainy-night scene in Book III), could not be earlier than the middle of May, 1385. Having settled so much, Root thanked his colleague from the observatory, who, he says, was "very much thrilled to find that he had contributed something of importance to literary history," and proceeded on his own. Now that he was assured of the year and the season in which Chaucer conceived his storm scene, he went to the voluminous chronicle of the medieval historian Thomas Walsingham and looked up the year 1385; and there he found a reference to the celestial display and to the awe and foreboding that it aroused in the breasts of those who watched. The citizens of England waited two months before the sequel to the ominous planetary conjunction was unfolded. Then, as Walsingham recounts, at three o'clock in the afternoon of July 14, 1385, a terrific thunderstorm broke over England, the like of which had not been seen by mortal men. There, embedded in sober historical narrative, was the very storm which shook Pandarus' stout mansion and alarmed the gentle Criseyde! Chaucer, with shrewd artistic economy, had combined the two separate events—the unusual planetary conjunction and the great storm—into one.

Yes, stargazers have their uses in literary scholarship. Many scientists do, as a matter of fact. In the pages that follow, we shall discover a few of the ways in which the two great branches of learning, natural science (especially its offspring, the applied sciences) and the so-called "humanities," join hands. More and more, in recent years, the literary scholar has had occasion to visit the laboratory, and often with surprising results; but, before we leave astronomy, let me cite another instance of the usefulness of the stargazer to the student of letters.

In February of 1813, an eccentric youth by the name of Percy Bysshe Shelley was living with his even younger wife, Harriet Westbrook, in the Welsh town of Tanyrallt. Although he had arrived only a short time before, he had already become the object of local attention, on account of his uncommon appearance and habits and the rumors of his unorthodox political and religious opinions. On a certain night late in that month, a night reportedly as tempestuous as the one in 1385, Shelley for some reason expected trouble, and sat in the dark armed with two pistols. About eleven o'clock he found a man leaving the cottage through a window. The man fired at Shelley, whose own pistol missed fire. A scuffle ensued, during which Shelley was knocked to the floor but managed to fire his second pistol and (he later claimed) wounded his assailant. After uttering a terrible curse in the manner of early nineteenth-century melodrama, the intruder disappeared into the storm.

The household, aroused by the mêlée, assembled in the parlor and kept vigil, again in the dark, for two hours. When they returned to bed, Shelley remained on guard, this time armed with a pistol and a sword. At about four o'clock a man fired from a window, the bullet piercing the curtain and Shelley's dressing gown. Shelley's pistol again failed him, but he went at the marauder with his sword. Just then his manservant entered the room and the assailant fled.

This was the account given by Harriet two weeks later. But the next morning Shelley's story was strikingly different. He had, he said, seen a face at the window and fired at it. Rushing onto the lawn, he had seen the devil himself leaning against a tree. And to illustrate what he had seen, he made a pen-and-ink sketch of the apparition on a wooden screen, which he then tried to destroy.

An examination of the grounds by the townspeople revealed signs of a struggle; but there was only one set of footprints and only one bullet mark, which seemed to have been made by a pistol fired from within the house. They looked upon the whole episode as one more proof that the pale young man was quite mad, and even his friends were inclined to agree that he had imagined it all. Nevertheless the events of the night were vivid enough in Shelley's own mind to prostrate him for several days, and to lead to the immediate removal of the household from the haunted vicinity.

Now superficially this may seem like just one more of those fantastic episodes which decorate literary biography and are responsible for the common superstition that most, if not all, great poets are insane. One of the most praiseworthy effects of modern scholarship has been to prove that many such stories owe their mischievous existence to the desire of earlier biographers to add romantic interest to their narratives. In case after case it has been shown that such yarns, if not outright creations of someone's imagination, had their ultimate source in some fragment of badly reported or grossly misinterpreted fact. With Shelley, however, it is quite different. There is no question that he suffered from hallucinations. On one memorable occasion he writhed on the floor, exclaiming that he was stricken with elephantiasis; and on another he screamed that he saw eyes staring at him from the breasts of his second wife, Mary Godwin. Such stories are too numerous, and too well authenticated by his most intimate friends, to be written off as romantic inventions. And they have a genuine importance in Shelley biography, in that they give us significant clues to the unquestionably abnormal personality that produced some magnificent poetry.

Until 1905 most biographers, reviewing the conflicting stories of that night in Wales and the absence of any tangible evidence to the contrary, agreed that Shelley's assailant had never existed outside the poet's own frantic imagination. But in that year two sisters who had lived in Tanyrallt in their childhood reported that in 1862, almost fifty years after the event, one Robert Williams, the son of the local postmaster, had told them that he had fired the shots. Shelley, it seemed (and this is thoroughly in accord with all that we know of his somewhat quixotic idealism), had been in the habit of roaming the fields and mercifully shooting sick sheep to put them out of their misery. The farmers had taken offense at this humanitarian interference with their property, and Williams, along with several of his neighbors, had formed an expedition whose avowed purpose was to frighten the Shelley household from the neighborhood. In 1905, when this story was published in an American magazine, it was accompanied by a photograph of a sketch copied from the one which Shelley allegedly had made of the devil leaning against a tree.

Although the ladies who reported Williams's story were themselves skeptical of its truth, it was adopted without question by Shelley's biographers. It was concluded that, on one occasion at least, Shelley had not been seeing things—even though possibly it was not really the devil that had leaned against the tree.

But a generation later a new Shelley scholar entered the field, Professor Newman Ivey White of Duke University, whose two-volume biography of the poet is one of the great monuments of Shelley scholarship. White was frankly dubious of the story. He found that in the 1860's Williams had been the owner of a farm perched on a plateau beyond the village, access to which could be had only by climbing a high, almost perpendicular cliff. What sort of man, White asked, could have given the lithe twenty-year-old Shelley a tussle for his money in 1813 and yet remained athletic enough to regularly scale and descend a cliff fifty years later? Interviewing one of the now aged sisters, he found her as dubious as he was; but she insisted that Williams had really told the story around town. He therefore went to the public records and found Williams's death certificate. It was just as he had thought. When Williams had died in 1878, he was sixty-eight—which made him precisely three years old at the time of his alleged foray into the Shelley parlor!

Having thus disposed of Williams's story, White found himself allied with the earlier investigators who had written off the whole episode as a Shelleyan delusion. There was, however, one more clue to follow. Shelley himself had said that he "saw" his attacker, even though the night allegedly was wild and stormy. If the storm was added to the tale to enhance its melodramatic flavor, and the night actually was clear, would there have been light enough for him to see his tormentor, whether man or devil?

Perhaps recalling the celebrated forensic coup of Abraham Lincoln on a faintly similar occasion, White consulted the astronomers. He found that in 1918 a Cambridge astronomer, in answering the same question, had calculated that on February 26, 1813, in that part of Wales the moon had risen about 3:45 A.M. To check this conclusion, White went to an official of the Hayden Planetarium in New York, who came up with the figure of 5:50 and, when the two-hour discrepancy was pointed out to him, blushed and said that the moon wouldn't have risen before five o'clock at the earliest. However, the difference of an hour or two either way was immaterial. What mattered was that there was no moon in the sky during the first of the two attacks, and that when the second attack occurred, at four o'clock, the moon would have been just on the point of rising; and in any event, visible or not, the moon would have been nearly through its last quarter. Therefore, even without a storm there would have been no moonlight, and Shelley could not possibly have seen anyone, the devil included. That he had had a hallucination seems fairly plain.

II

BUT let us turn from astronomy to some of the other sciences that have come to the aid of literary scholarship.

In the last few years the newspapers and magazines have published articles on the use of microphotography in preserving files of newspapers and of governmental and business records. Little, however, has been said of the usefulness of the new process to literary scholars. It is no exaggeration to say that microfilms are revolutionizing the methods of scholarly research.

Until about a dozen years ago, scholars who had to work with rare books and manuscripts had only two choices open to them. They could, of course, consult the books and manuscripts in the libraries owning them. But since English literary material is concentrated in the British Isles, in a few eastern cities of the United States, and at some points reaching across the American continent, scholars who lived elsewhere had to find money for trips to these citadels of research during summer vacations and sabbatical years. Most of them could not afford such expensive pleasures; and even those who could were handicapped by having to make their own notes and transcripts —a maddeningly slow process when materials are abundant and time is short—for use when they got back to their homes in Iowa or Oregon. The other alternative was to order photostats of the rare material. Although less costly than a round trip across the Atlantic and a summer's stay in London, photostats always have been expensive; and on many problems of research thousands may be required.

But in the 1930's manufacturers of photographic equipment came to the rescue with a camera which could quickly record books and documents on ordinary motion-picture film, at a cost of only a cent or two an exposure. At the same time, projectors were developed which threw enlargements of these microfilm pictures on a ground-glass screen. It is now possible, therefore, for a scholar teaching in a remote college to order microfilms of whatever material he needs, from the great Vatican Library in Rome, or the Bibliothèque Nationale in Paris, or the British Museum, or the Library of Congress. In due time he receives a roll of film in a small cardboard box. He takes the film to the projector in his college library, and there, ready for his leisurely study, are exact copies of all the manuscripts or rare books he wishes to examine. His bill comes only to a few dollars.

With the cooperation of large libraries and research foundations, great collections of microfilms of literary and historical material are being built up both in England and in America. During the Second World War, under an emergency grant of $130,000 from the Rockefeller Foundation, over 6,000,000 pages of irreplaceable manuscripts in the public and private collections of besieged England were filmed and the reels were sent by diplomatic pouch to the Library of Congress. There they are now freely available to scholars, who, if they wish, may order prints of the material which they need to study. A project that has been going on for a dozen years is the systematic filming of all books printed in England, or in the English language, before 1600. Under this arrangement, American libraries which subscribe to the service receive every year some 100,000 filmed pages of rare printed material. Similarly, the files of all American periodicals published before 1825, and of 125 English periodicals of the eighteenth and nineteenth centuries, are being made available on microfilm. In addition to adding undreamed-of convenience to literary study, and drastically reducing the expense, this large-scale photographing of precious and often fragile books and manuscripts saves wear and tear on the originals. Once the films are made, there is seldom any need for the scholar to go back to the books and documents themselves. Thus, by an application of science to humanistic research—greatly facilitated by the widespread use of microfilm during the war for V-mail and for the quick transmission of vital scientific information published in foreign journals—scholarly routine is being made infinitely more efficient.

The now ubiquitous microfilm had an important part in the development of the most ingenious gadget yet devised for the aid of literary scholarship. Collation (the minute comparison of two different printed versions of the same text) is one of the most laborious and time-consuming jobs in research. Yet it has to be done; its role has become more and more important in the past half-century, since scholars have discovered that in the sixteenth and seventeenth centuries it was the practice in printing shops to make corrections at any time while the successive sheets of a book were being printed off. Thus there may be almost innumerable "states" of a single edition, each state being distinguished from the rest by certain differences in the text, such as a substituted word, a corrected spelling, or an added bit of punctuation. In order to reconstruct the story of the way a book passed through the press, which may reveal valuable points about the original text as it came from the author and other data of literary significance, it is necessary to compare copies of all known states, line by line, comma by comma, through hundreds of pages. The result to the painstaking collator, it need scarcely be said, is exceeding weariness of the flesh and dizziness of the brain.

Charlton Hinman, a Johns Hopkins scholar whose specialty was this sort of bibliographical examination, wondered if—in the midst of the most highly developed technological civilization the world had ever known, where motorists no longer had to crank their cars and housewives no longer had to wash their dishes—it were really necessary for scholars to put two old books before them and wear out their eyes shifting them from one page to the other, back and forth, in search of the telltale variant. During the Second World War Hinman went into the Navy and spent four years in the Pacific, and in the quiet of the tropical night he continued to brood over his problem.

When he came back to the United States, he was determined to find an answer. Fortunately, the war had played into his hands. In 1939–45 a question far more urgent than that of taking the labor out of bibliographical collation had been that of finding out what damage had been done to an enemy installation or an industrial city by an aerial bombing. Reconnaissance planes went out over a prospective target and took pictures. After a bombing they went out again, and from exactly the same height and angle, so far as these could be attained, they took other pictures. Intelligence officers at the base then had the job of finding differences between the two sets of pictures, which would presumably reveal what damage had been done. But the photographs covered so wide a territory and were taken from such great heights that it was necessary to go over them with infinite care in order to detect any differences at all. The process, of course, was time-consuming and inefficient. Therefore somebody got the idea, suggested, certainly, by the basic principle of the motion picture, of inserting one "before" and one "after" picture of the same area in separate projectors, and flashing them on a screen in split-second alternation. If there were no changes in the area shown, the eye would not detect this alternation; there would be the effect simply of one photograph. But if there *were* changes—a bomb-ravaged factory, for example, or a ruined railway yard—these would show up as a flicker or a wobble on the screen when the two pictures were quickly alternated, and would direct attention to the part of the pictures which deserved minute examination. So, at least, ran the theory; in practice it seems not to have worked, principally because the two pictures, in order to register perfectly, would have had to be taken from precisely identical positions and cover identical areas, and this ideal, obviously, could seldom if ever be achieved.

But the theory interested and inspired Hinman. If one could take microfilms of the pages of two copies of a book to be collated and flash them in rapid alternation on a screen, page against page, the same thing would happen. If the two pages were absolutely identical, the image on the screen would remain steady; but if there was any variation at all, a substituted word, for example, it would show up as a telltale wobble. One could then record it without the trouble of scanning all the rest of the page.

With the aid of the Veterans' Administration, the Bureau of Standards, and other government agencies, Hinman set to work at the Folger Library in Washington, where, because of its rich collection of the various issues of sixteenth- and seventeenth-century books, collation is a daily occupation of scholars. From the Folger bindery he got some pieces of heavy cardboard; from an alley he salvaged a wooden apple crate; and from the son of a friend he hijacked parts of a rusty Erector set. The eventual result was a strange contraption which looked like a product of the inventive brain of Rube Goldberg; but it worked even in its crude state, collating the pages of rare books more swiftly than this had ever been done before.

The obstacle that had confronted the reconnaissance officers in the war remained. Although it is easier for a stationary camera to photograph the pages of an open book than for a camera in a speeding plane to take pictures of enemy targets, still it is hard to make microfilms so precise that the images of the same page in a number of different volumes will always be in register when they are flashed, two by two, on a screen. Rather than wait for optical technicians to devise a means of providing this perfect register, Hinman abandoned his first gadget and turned to the construction of a second machine which would work with the original volumes rather than with microfilm reproductions. In July, 1949, he took this second instrument for its trial runs in the Folger Library. The results, he tells me, were excellent. He was able to collate the text of *Othello* in the eighty Folger copies of the First Folio—a matter of three thousand pages—in six weeks, instead of the two or three years that a non-mechanized collation would have required. When the machine has been perfected, Hinman feels, scholars will be able for the first time to arrive at the long dreamed-of definitive text of the First Folio which takes into account all the changes which were made during its printing, and thus restores the text of the manuscript from which the printers worked.

Those who watched Hinman's experiments with his first machine were irresistibly reminded of the first great occasion on which photography was used to solve a mystery surrounding the publication of Shakespeare's plays. That earlier episode remains one of the classic stories of literary scholarship.

Seventeen of Shakespeare's plays were first printed in what are called quartos—thin volumes, really no more than pamphlets, measuring about nine by twelve inches, a play to a volume. These quartos were sold unbound, and because relatively few purchasers ever bothered to have them put into a permanent binding, they are today extremely scarce. Enthusiasts for the drama who did want to preserve their copies usually waited until they had enough to make a substantial volume, and then had them bound. Many other collections of quartos in modern libraries were not bound together until the eighteenth or nineteenth century. In any case, each volume was bound up independently, so that the contents of a given volume, say eight or ten quarto plays, are entirely unpredictable. There is no pattern to them at all.

That is why, when A. W. Pollard, a bibliographer on the staff of the British Museum, came across several volumes of Shakespearean quartos that did have a common pattern, he was mystified. On separate occasions at the beginning of the present century, there came to his notice no fewer than three bound collections of quartos which contained copies of the same nine Shakespearean, or pseudo-Shakespearean, plays.* One of the plays was in a binding which obviously

* After Pollard had published his first article on the subject, he learned that a fourth volume, containing the same nine plays, had been owned by the University of Virginia, but had perished in a fire at the university library in 1895. In the spring of 1946 an agent of a London auctioneer, acting on a report of a very rare book contained in the library of an old manor house in Lincolnshire, made a trip to that house. The book was not what he had hoped; but he looked at the other books in the house, just in case—and happened upon a small volume

had been made in the early seventeenth century. It was clear, therefore, that these quartos had existed, as a well defined group, almost in
Shakespeare's own time. Why, Pollard wondered, had they clung together? No other group of quartos had done so, and among these nine
plays there was no apparent bond of affinity. The most reasonable
explanation was that they had been published within a short span of
time, and thus would have been naturally associated in the collections
of contemporary play buyers.

But to this theory there seemed to be a fatal objection, for the
nine plays bore widely different dates. Three of them (*A Midsummer-
Night's Dream, The Merchant of Venice,* and *Sir John Oldcastle,* a
non-Shakespearean play about the historical figure whom Shakespeare
turned into Falstaff) were, according to their title pages, printed in
1600; two (*King Lear* and *Henry V*) were printed in 1608; three
(*A Yorkshire Tragedy,* which was also non-Shakespearean, *Pericles,*
and *The Merry Wives of Windsor*) were dated 1619; and one (*The
Whole Contention Between the Two Famous Houses, Lancaster and
York*—a mangled version of the second and third parts of *Henry VI*)
bore no date at all. All of these editions had long been known to
Shakespeare students, and the veracity of their dates had seldom, if
ever, been questioned.

And so Pollard returned to his riddle. Why, if these plays had been
printed over a period of nineteen years, did they turn up in clusters
three centuries later? It was a similar question, you remember,
which later put John Carter and another Pollard on the trail of
Thomas J. Wise. Pollard, clinging to the supposition that the nine
quartos must have come upon the market almost simultaneously, decided that here we had a memento of an early seventeenth-century
bargain sale. A bookseller, most probably the Thomas Pavier whose
initials appeared on the three 1619 quartos, had somehow come into
possession of the remaining stocks of the 1600 and 1608 plays, all but
one of which had come from other booksellers, and had got rid of
them in a sort of tie-in arrangement with the three newest plays.
That, Pollard suggested, was how they had become associated.

---

whose binding was lettered "Shakes. Plays." He found that he was holding in
his hand one more collection of the nine quartos.

He announced his theory in 1906. Two years later another eminent student of Shakespearean bibliography, W. W. Greg, published two articles in which he entered strong objections to Pollard's stand. In the first place, he said, the type on *all* the title pages, regardless of the date, was the same. Was it very likely, in view of normal practices in the printing houses of the time, that the same type had been used in 1600 *and* 1619, without any signs of wear? Again, certain large numerals in the imprints were open to suspicion, because they were not known to appear in any other books printed before 1610. How then did they come to be in quartos dated 1600 and 1608? Similarly, the ornamental printer's devices on the title pages were not known in any other books printed between 1596 and 1610. As a final telling bit of evidence, he pointed out that all nine quartos, regardless of their announced date, were printed on the same mixed stock of paper! To Greg there was only one conclusion: the "1600" and "1608" quartos could not possibly have been printed in those years, and must be of the same vintage as the 1619 ones.

Immediately the conservative wing of Shakespeare scholarship, outraged by Greg's suggestion that the earlier quartos were evidence of some sort of fraud on the part of the printers, tried to shake his argument. Pollard, however, was so deeply impressed that he cheerfully abandoned his own theory and took position alongside Greg, even providing some additional bits of evidence to support his erstwhile adversary. Yet the case was not proved. Nor *could* it be proved by any method then known to bibliographical scholarship.

On the other side of the Atlantic a young teacher at the University of Wisconsin followed with intense interest the debate in the leading British literary journals. A few years earlier William J. Neidig, then a graduate student at the University of Chicago, recognizing how inadequate were the existing techniques of bibliographical detection, had wished to do something about the situation. The detailed comparison of editions and issues was then limited to examining, with the aid of a magnifying glass, differences in ornaments, type faces, and other such evidence. But such a method inevitably was fallible; and Neidig, as he later wrote, "proposed to supplement this impressionistic judgment by the testimony of physical science. To speak by analogy,

I proposed to apply to the study of the printed page a system of exact measurements not unlike the modern Bertillon system of measuring criminals." But there was no good problem upon which to try it out, and Neidig, after devising his system of measurements, filed the idea away for future reference.

Then came the controversy touched off by Pollard and Greg, which seemed made to order for Neidig. He had the title pages of the nine quartos accurately photographed from the copies in the Boston Public Library. Then he got to work with rulers, blocking off and measuring every segment of type which had been used in each title-page—in other words, reconstructing the exact layout of the type as it had appeared in the printer's chase. And then, to make his demonstration complete, he had a photographer in Madison make a series of composite photographs, superimposing one title-page upon another. Probably the most amazing of the photographs thus produced was one in which the title page of the 1600 *Merchant of Venice* was superimposed on that of the 1619 *Pericles*. The upper halves of the two pages, of course, were different, because each bore the name of a different play. But the lower halves registered perfectly, down to the tiny nicks in the worn type and the details of the woodcut ornament. Even the first two numerals of the date, "16", appeared in the composite photograph as if they were from a single title page. (The last two numerals, naturally, were different—"00" in the one and "19" in the other.) Both the "1600" and the "1619" printings, then, had been done from the same basic standing of type!

It was unthinkable that a printer, with his severely limited supply of types, would have kept the "1600" title page intact for nineteen years; and it was equally impossible that such a coincidence could be the result of accident or of a deliberate intention to copy the earlier title pages. As Neidig wrote: "Even were there a conceivable reason why the compositor of the 1619 *Pericles* title-page should have copied the typography of the lower part of the 1600 *Merchant of Venice* title-page—and there is none—it is not possible for him to have succeeded in duplicating in every detail so complex a system of composition as this. As any printer knows, no compositor even today could achieve such a feat except by putting an unreasonable amount of care and time on the work—and even then he would not succeed upon his first trial, nor his second. Every individual measurement would have to be made separately and duplicated separately." The only conceivable answer to the problem was that the nine quartos were set up and printed in the shop of William Jaggard, Pavier's printer, in 1619—the dates on their title pages notwithstanding.

By his Bertillon-like measurements and his composite photographs, Neidig was able to reconstruct the exact order in which the title pages of these quartos had been set up within a span of a few days; indeed, he followed the typesetter's every move. First came the undated *Whole Contention;* then *A Yorkshire Tragedy;* then *Pericles,* whose imprint line was carried over unchanged from the preceding play; then *The Merchant of Venice,* for which the compositor had made a "pick-up" of the entire bottom portion of the *Pericles* page, changing only the last two numerals of the date; then *The Merry Wives, Lear, Henry V,* and *Sir John Oldcastle.* The last quarto in the series, that of the "1600" *Midsummer-Night's Dream,* for some reason had had the honor of receiving a freshly made title page. The compositor, it was evident, would have been a joy to any modern industrial efficiency expert. As Neidig observed, he was either exceptionally lazy or in a great hurry, for he had a genius for salvaging every possible bit of the layout for one title page as he prepared his type for the next.

Neidig thus proved beyond doubt that five venerable Shakespearean quartos bore the wrong dates, which meant that some kind of skulduggery had been afoot in the Jacobean printing trade. What was it? Nobody yet knows for sure. But the hypothesis that is most widely accepted is that of Greg, whose suspicions Neidig had so brilliantly confirmed. In the year 1616 Shakespeare died; and in the same year Ben Jonson's collected works were published. The coincidence, Greg argued, set people to thinking: If Ben Jonson deserved a collected edition, why didn't Shakespeare? Apart from the sentiment involved, a "complete Shakespeare" might be a profitable publishing enterprise. So thought Thomas Pavier, the bookseller, who already held the publishing rights to four of the master's plays. He got busy, and within the next two or three years obtained five more plays, his legal rights to several of which were highly dubious. Thus he had nine plays, enough to make a stout quarto; and then, if his luck held, he might be able to round up an equal number for a second volume. Thereupon he called upon his friend Isaac Jaggard, who was working in the printing house of his father, William Jaggard, and outlined his proposal. Young Jaggard was enthusiastic, and forthwith began setting type for *The Whole Contention,* the two parts of which were to be the opening plays of the series.

But at this point (so Greg's theory runs) the King's Men got wind of the project, perhaps through an incautious word dropped by the elder Jaggard. Now the players, Shakespeare's own company, owned some of the actual manuscripts of his plays; and they had been planning to issue an authorized edition, based not upon the often corrupt and unauthorized printed texts to which Pavier had got access, but upon the playhouse scripts. The success of their more ambitious project, to issue a collection of Shakespeare's works which would equal in dignity that of Jonson's, would be seriously endangered by Pavier's petty scheme. They may have told Jaggard that if he would make Pavier abandon his idea, he, Jaggard, would receive the honor of printing the official collection, as he subsequently did. It is a fact that in May, 1619, William Herbert, the Earl of Pembroke, as Lord Chamberlain on an appeal from the King's Men ordered the Stationers' Company to forbid the printing of any of Shakespeare's plays without the players' consent. Pavier's reaction to this move may be imagined; he had probably spent much money having the texts of the plays printed off, and therefore faced a serious financial loss. He decided to get around the Stationers' Company's injunction by issuing the quartos with deceptive title pages, so as to make them appear to be remainders rather than newly printed volumes. (Although he probably did not foresee the development of twentieth-century bibliography, Pavier's ghost must have derived considerable satisfaction from watching Pollard fall into the trap, three centuries later!) But once or twice Pavier slipped up. Instead of giving his new edition of *The Merry Wives of Windsor* the date of the earlier edition, 1602, he thoughtlessly dated it 1619, and when he adapted the title page of the "1608" *Lear* for the next play he set up, *Henry V,* he retained the date 1608 instead of substituting 1602, as he should have done to be consistent.

In such a fashion, then, Pavier, no doubt with Jaggard's connivance, salvaged his scheme for a collected Shakespeare. He did not dare sell a stout omnibus quarto in the face of the King's Men's disapproval, but he could at least sell the separate plays, if they masqueraded as old editions. And so, in July, 1619, he vended his nine plays; the bogus 1600 and 1608 quartos thus got into circulation, and for three hundred years Shakespeare students were none the wiser.

III

NEIDIG'S dramatic discovery underscored the need for a more minute examination of books and documents than is possible with the unaided eye. Science came to the rescue, and in American libraries like the Folger and the Huntington which own large collections of rare literary material, whole laboratories, replete with formidable-looking instruments, have been established to pierce beneath the outward appearance of rare books and manuscripts.

There are, for one thing, whole arrays of delicate magnifiers and microscopes. Even among the hand magnifiers the most humble is a precision-made optical instrument—not the kind which one picks up in a five-and-ten-cent store. Then there are compound binocular microscopes (the most generally useful instrument for examining manuscripts); ultraopaque microscopes whose special function is to examine the composition of the paper and the minute characteristics of pen strokes; and comparison microscopes, which bring two separate specimens of handwriting or of printing together in one field of vision and thus enable the researcher to compare them for tiny variations. There are Lovibond tintometer glasses—small glass slides, delicately graduated in shades of red, yellow, and blue. When they are fitted into the comparison microscope they can be used to examine the ink of an old manuscript for the detection of words and sentences inserted after the body of the writing was completed. Thus a scholar, by noting variations in the color of the ink which are otherwise invisible, can distinguish the text as written by the original author or copyist from the alterations and interpolations made by some later copyist or editor.

But this is only one of the uses of magnifying equipment. In addition, these expensive and complicated instruments can tell the story of pencil marks, including their approximate age and even in some cases the make of pencil used; they can give more detailed information on watermarks and on the other distinguishing features of paper, so that the date of a manuscript can be more definitely fixed; they can rescue details of half-obliterated postmarks; they can even help the investigator find out what substance was responsible for the stain on a page of medieval vellum manuscript.

And when the magnifiers and microscopes fail, there are ultraviolet, infrared, and fluorescent lamps, aided by special cameras fitted with sensitive filters. A passage may have been carefully erased by chemicals; but when the page is photographed under ultraviolet light the deletion is restored. Or a penciled comment may have been erased; but even though no trace of the graphite remains the minute depressions left by the pencil point can be restored. If a manuscript has been badly charred, as the unique manuscript of *Beowulf* was, the writing on the burned part can be restored by the use of infrared rays. If the writing has been obliterated by stains, made by anything from human blood to the damp of English centuries, it can be brought back by ultraviolet rays. There are still unsolved problems, however—such as how to restore portions of a manuscript which have been chewed away by rats.

With the obvious exception of the Carter and Pollard exposé and the restoration of many deleted passages in famous literary documents like the Boswell papers and Hawthorne's journals, modern scientific techniques have not yet produced sensational results so far as the literary interests of the general reader are concerned. But they have been instrumental time after time in clearing up small bibliographical problems which absorb the attention of many scholars. And ten years ago they helped catapult an old book from the discard pile to an honored place on the shelves of the Folger Library.

In 1938 the Folger authorities bought for a pound in an English auction a parcel of books which included a dilapidated copy of William Lambarde's APXAIONOMIA, a paraphrase of Anglo-Saxon laws printed in 1568. The lot was purchased for the sake of another title it contained; and the Lambarde work—which not only duplicated a fine copy the library already had but was badly damaged by water, the paper being fragile and the title page wrinkled—was slated for discard. When it was examined, however, the inside front cover proved to contain some eighteenth-century handwriting: "Mr Wm Shakespeare lived at No 1 Little Crown Street Westminster. NB near Dorset steps St James Park." The men at the Folger were immediately interested, because this was the first intimation known to scholars that Shakespeare had ever lived in Westminster, where his friend Ben Jonson definitely did reside. Therefore, even though the authority for the statement was remote, dating only from the eighteenth century and being in addition entirely anonymous, this derelict volume provided a fresh piece of evidence linking the two great playwrights.

The Folger officials were at a loss to explain why this note on Shakespeare should occur in a volume which had no other apparent association with the poet. While they pondered the question, they sent the book to the bindery to have the wrinkled title page ironed out. Before long the bindery manager came hurrying into the library offices with a startling story. His workman in smoothing the title page had revealed a signature in Elizabethan handwriting hitherto hidden in one of the tight wrinkles: "Wm Shakespeare"!

The library staff got busy with magnifying glass and ultraviolet and infrared lamps. They were not excessively excited, because no realm of literary scholarship has been more plagued with forgeries than Shakespearean study, and the Folger Library, with more Shakespearean material than any other single collection, has had long and instructive experience with frauds. They first considered the possibility of a recent forgery; but this was ruled out because the wrinkles certainly had been made a long time ago, and the signature had been written in the volume before the wrinkling occurred. The second possibility was that the signature was an eighteenth-century forgery; but this too was ruled out, because eighteenth-century forgers of Shakespeare, although numerous, were contemptibly poor craftsmen according to modern standards, and this signature was amazingly like the ones which were known to be genuine. The third possibility was that it was an even earlier forgery, done in the seventeenth century.

Further analysis therefore was in order, and the ΑΡΧΑΙΟΝΟΜΙΑ, so dramatically reprieved from the rubbish heap, was sent to the laboratories of the National Archives, where it was put through a series of delicate tests, photographic, chemical, and microscopic. The results established conclusively that the ink was genuinely Elizabethan, not a cunningly contrived imitation, and that the signature had been written on the leaf in Elizabethan times. There remains the slight chance that the signature is that of another William Shakespeare. But if it is really that of the dramatist, the Folger Library now possesses one of the two or three books which are known to have passed through Shakespeare's hands.

In another curious episode, at the Huntington Library, scientific examination of a document was responsible for expunging a word from the English language. In the unique manuscript of the Towneley cycle of mystery plays a passage alludes to the medieval women's fashion of wearing a headdress in the form of cow's horns. When the manuscript was examined seventy-five years ago by scholars gleaning words for the monumental *Oxford English Dictionary*, the word "cuker," evidently referring to this headdress, was found and duly entered in the dictionary. No other occurrence was known. But when, a few years ago, the Towneley manuscript was examined for the first time under the ultraviolet light the word turned out to be "culer," so that when the dictionary is revised "cuker" must be deleted and "culer" substituted.

The odds are a million to one that the reader of these pages has never included "cuker" in his active vocabulary, and certainly the news that there is no such word will not cause any radical revision of his *Weltanschauung* or even of his daily habits of life. Admittedly such discoveries as this are of significance only to a few lexicographers or specialized scholars. But the new methods of laboratory inspection of documents are still in their infancy, and the possibilities inherent in those methods are unlimited. We are coming increasingly to understand that with the aid of microscopes, special lighting, and exact camera work, a book or manuscript may tell us much more of its origin and its provenance than has hitherto been suspected. What can the scientist do for the literary scholar? Since neither breed is lacking in imagination or ingenuity, we may confidently look forward to a collaboration which will be more and more fruitful.

SECRETS IN CIPHER

IT is agreeable to be able to report that literary scholars are some-times in a position to repay their scientist-colleagues for the aid they receive from the observatories and the laboratories. The case of John Matthews Manly and the Voynich manuscript is possibly the most spectacular instance.

Manly was a distinguished Chaucer scholar. His greatest achieve-ment no doubt was the compilation of the great eight-volume work, *The Text of the Canterbury Tales,* in which he and his collaborator, Edith Rickert, compared the readings of all the available manuscript texts—over eighty in all—of Chaucer's masterpiece. Glancing through the pages of one of these blue-bound volumes, the lay reader inevitably is mystified: what does all this recondite apparatus, this swarming of technical symbols at the bottom of every page, mean? It means, simply, that Manly and Rickert are showing, line by line and word for word, the variant readings of every one of the manuscripts they studied. So intricate is the apparatus that to have set up the eight volumes in type would have been prohibitively expensive; instead, they were printed by an offset process from pages laboriously type-written and meticulously proofread.

Few scholars could have produced such a work. For note what Manly and Miss Rickert had to do. They were confronted with more than eighty different manuscripts of portions of the *Canterbury Tales,* none of which came directly from the pen of Geoffrey Chaucer. Their task—its scholarly name is "textual criticism"—was to deter-mine, from the evidence of these manuscripts, what Chaucer really wrote.

Every one of the manuscripts contains readings at variance with those found in the others. The variant readings were produced by a number of causes. The scribe who copied an older manuscript may have failed to understand a word or two, and have written what he *thought* the words were; or he may have undertaken to improve the phrasing; or he may have been interrupted at his work, and have missed the place when he resumed copying; or he may have inadvertently repeated a word or two. Thus, the completed copy would leave his hands with a number of errors not in the older manuscript. And when in turn *his* manuscript served some years later as a model for a new copy the new scribe not only faithfully repeated most of the errors but added some fresh ones of his own. In such a fashion the errors were compounded from copy to copy.

What the student of a medieval text must do, therefore—and what Manly and Rickert did in the case of the *Canterbury Tales*—is to study every known manuscript of the work and compare its set of variants with that found in every other one. By laboriously classifying the manuscripts according to the position, number, and nature of the variants, he can in time erect a *Stammbaum*—a family tree of manuscripts, which shows how Manuscript Z was derived from Manuscript Y, which in turn was copied from Manuscript X; and Manuscript X may have been a fourth-generation descendant of Manuscript Q, from which, by an independent line of descent, Manuscripts R, S, and T, which have a quite different set of variants, were successively copied. The eventual result of all this work is the pushing of the text back through the centuries to the manuscript that seems to have been the ultimate ancestor of all the different branches of the family, as is shown by the fact that it has fewer of the errors that characterize the rest as a result of successive recopying. This version, the Cain of the line if not the Adam, is called the (relatively) "pure text." While it may not represent exactly what the author himself wrote, it is the closest the scholar can come to it in lack of the author's own manuscript.

Such a task, possibly the most complicated that literary scholarship offers, requires above all a mind that can assemble and sort out innumerable tiny details, that can organize these details into some sort of rational pattern and eventually work out complex relationships.

Some might call it a mathematical mind; and it is not surprising to know that J. M. Manly early in life was a professor of mathematics.

Or some might call it a cipher mind. The organizers of the first cryptographic bureau ever established in the American Army, in fact, recognized it as such. For in 1917, when the bureau was set up, Manly was called from his post as chairman of the Department of English at the University of Chicago to become one of the chief Army cryptographers. It was undoubtedly the memory of his brilliant success in his wartime role that led the armed forces during the Second World War to draw some of their cipher experts from the ranks of literary scholars. The full story of the cunning and complex battle of the ciphers during the recent war has not yet been told. Among the men who know some of the secrets (and are telling none of them) are half a hundred members of the Modern Language Association, most of whom may now be found again peacefully teaching *Piers Plowman,* Spenser, and Emerson in the classrooms of American universities.

Several years before Professor Manly left his post at the University of Chicago to become a captain and then a major, a rare-book dealer named Wilfred M. Voynich had brought to the United States what Manly was later to call, without exaggeration, "the most mysterious manuscript in the world." He had found it in 1912 in the treasure chest of an Italian castle. With it was a letter showing that in the seventeenth century it had been the property successively of two continental savants, and asserting, without substantiation, that it was the work of Roger Bacon.

Roger Bacon is, of course, one of the most fascinating figures in the history of western thought. A thirteenth-century English philosopher, alchemist, and (as some alleged) necromancer, in some respects he was startlingly in advance of his time. With amazing prescience he foretold the telescope and the microscope—inventions which were destined not to occur until centuries after his death.

The Voynich manuscript, then, was supposed, on the authority of the letter accompanying it, to be from the pen of Roger Bacon. But what did it contain? The most learned experts in the reading of medieval manuscripts pored through its 116 folio pages and were completely mystified. On many pages were drawings accompanied by inscriptions in a strange sort of writing which had no counterpart in the known manuscripts of any age. The drawings themselves, many of them, seemed to represent whole plants, or roots and leaves; others were clearly astronomical diagrams, with strong indications of occultism; still others appeared to represent cell structures, ova, spermatozoa, and other biological phenomena. But the legends and the running text were absolutely indecipherable, so that no one could be sure. As a whole, the manuscript appeared to be a treatise on medical science, in which, during the Middle Ages, the properties of herbal and medicinal plants, as well as the pseudoscience of astrology, played conspicuous parts.

Although many cryptographers and specialists in the history of science examined the Voynich manuscript, and attempted to break its cipher, only one was able to announce success. In 1921, before a widely publicized meeting of the American Philosophical Society in Philadelphia, a great specialist in medieval history and philosophy, W. Romaine Newbold of the University of Pennsylvania, revealed that he had been able to read some portions of the document. Although few who listened to his explanation professed to understand the methods he had used, it was generally agreed that he had pierced the mystery of one of the most important documents in the history of scientific thought. His conclusion was that the manuscript was indeed what it had been believed to be, the work of Roger Bacon; and in it (to use the words of Professor Manly, reviewing the announcement ten years later) "the thirteenth-century friar, to avoid the dangers then awaiting the unconventional thinker, had secretly recorded discoveries made with a compound microscope—constructed centuries before its known invention—discoveries in which this unparalleled genius had anticipated the theories of twentieth-century biologists and histologists concerning germ cells, ova, spermatozoa, and the general mechanism of organic life."

At the time Professor Newbold made his first public revelation, Roger Bacon's reputation in intellectual history, which had been immense among nineteenth-century writers, was at a comparatively low ebb. It was no longer believed, for example, that he had been the inventor of gunpowder; and, although the philosophical and scientific insights of his *Opus Majus* had often been strikingly "modern," in many respects Bacon had been as superstitious and unscientific as any of his medieval contemporaries. But Newbold's reading of portions of the Voynich manuscript immediately revived the wonder that once had attended Bacon's name. Not even the most uncritical admirer of the man had dreamed that he had accomplished the feats Newbold found reflected.

For five years Newbold worked feverishly to complete his deciphering of the document. He died before he was able to embody his full findings in a book; but he had constantly discussed his work with a devoted colleague, Professor Roland Kent, who in 1928 published the chapters he had written before his death, along with many of the work sheets and notes he had left. The sensation among historians of science, both in America and abroad, was immense.

Now the authenticity of all that Newbold had found written in the Voynich manuscript depended, of course, upon his system of decipherment. Manly, back at the University of Chicago after release from the Army, had watched his progress with great interest. But as time went on Manly's "cipher brain" rebelled. "The more I studied the nature and operation of the cipher system attributed to Bacon," he wrote later, "the more clearly did I see that it was incapable of being used as a medium of communication, and was indeed not Bacon's work but the subconscious creation of Professor Newbold's own enthusiasm and ingenuity."

When the work sheets and notes were published in 1928, Manly was able to check Newbold's work at every point. What he discovered was profoundly dismaying. The alleged Bacon cipher was ambiguous and flexible—that is, it was capable of being read in various ways. To be sure of this, Manly wrote to Captain W. F. Friedman, a distinguished cryptographer of the Army Signal Corps. Friedman took a passage of the cipher reproduced on a page of the Newbold-Kent volume and applied Newbold's own system to it. Only fifteen minutes were necessary for him to discover what *he* wanted to find in the passage: the interesting sentence, "Paris is lured into loving Vestals."

"Continuation will be furnished upon request," he commented. Manly, checking Newbold's work, found not only that the Bacon cipher failed to fulfil one of the first requirements of any practical code—any message written in it must be capable of only one unmistakable reading—but that in some places Newbold incorrectly transcribed the cipher, and yet emerged with a translation that fitted into all the rest. However painful it was, the conclusion was inevitable: Newbold, whose absolute integrity has never been questioned, was so carried away by the excitement of the chase that he subconsciously allowed his knowledge of medical and other scientific matters to sway his judgment. The amazing anticipations of twentieth-century thought which he found in the manuscript were, in fact, placed there by himself!

To crown all, Manly, upon examining the manuscript itself, was shocked to discover that the basic assumption which had governed the work of Newbold and of everyone else who had inspected the document was wrong. The "microscopic shorthand signs" of which the cipher was composed had never been written there as such. Instead, the use of a powerful magnifying glass and a microscope revealed that these queer symbols were the result of the drying of the vellum, with the consequent cracking of the pigment in the ink. Hence the cipher was not composed of the tiny elements, but of larger symbols, some portions of which had disappeared as the vellum dried.

With profound regret, in 1931 Manly found it necessary to publish in *Speculum* a long article which demolished all that Newbold had achieved by five years of tremendous labor. By technical demonstrations of the cipher's inconsistency and inadequacy and other means, he showed that the secret of the Voynich manuscript, far from being surprised, was as dark as it had ever been. "We do not, in fact, know," he concluded, "when the manuscript was written, or where, or what language lies at the basis of the encipherment." And there the matter rests today.

By applying his specialized knowledge of cryptography to the decipherment, Manly rescued some eminent historians of science from the blunder into which they had fallen simply because they were not equipped to challenge Newbold's methods. Thus, as I have remarked, literary scholarship is sometimes able to pay back the scientists for assistance rendered.*

At this point it would be natural to turn to a consideration of a far more famous Bacon cipher—the one which, according to numbers of enthusiasts, "proves" that Francis Bacon wrote the plays of Shakespeare. When, during a series of radio talks embodying some of the material now included in this book, I ventured to mention the Bacon-Shakespeare controversy, one or two listeners made strenuous efforts to convert me to their heresy. One lady sent me photostats from a certain copy of the 1623 Shakespeare Folio of an initial letter B, enlarged to heroic dimensions, in which she had discovered multifarious cabalistic signs of Bacon's authorship. Then and there I made a solemn vow that, whatever else might be included in my projected book, the Baconian controversy should not. I have never been tempted to renounce that vow!

So let us skirt the quicksands and perch on safer ground. Probably the most notable debt which our present knowledge of English literature owes to cryptographers involves the incomparable diary of Samuel Pepys. In 1724, in accordance with Pepys's will, his fine library and his personal papers were given to his alma mater, Magdalene College,

* Far less momentous, but interesting in its own way, was Manly's solution of a rebus found in a Chaucer manuscript he and Miss Rickert studied in the Royal Library at Naples. An inscription on the first page said, in effect, that this manuscript was the property of Diomede di Leonardis (a member of a distinguished seventeenth-century Italian family) and was formerly in the hands of . . . There the inscription ended. Having satisfied themselves, by the use of the ultraviolet light, that no erasure was involved, Manly and Rickert wondered why the sentence trailed off in such a fashion. Then they noticed that a series of dots following the last word led the eye to a drawing of a bell in the margin. Remembering the renaissance fondness for concealing names in rebuses, they conceived the idea that the bell (*campanello* in Italian) might have some connection with Tommaso Campanella, the Italian renaissance philosopher. It was a wild idea, but it was better than nothing. So, with the aid of interested colleagues in Italy, they conducted some research—and ended by discovering that a Campanella had married into the Di Leonardis family; that J. B. di Leonardis had been Tommaso Campanella's advocate when he was tried for plotting to free Naples from the Spanish tyranny; and that Tommaso frequently referred to himself as Squilla (little bell) and even signed his name with the drawing of a bell! In the light of Tommaso's reputation as atheist and political conspirator, it seems plain that the person who wrote the inscription preferred to conceal as best he could the fact that Tommaso once had owned the Chaucer manuscript.

Cambridge. Among the papers were six leather-bound volumes written in shorthand. One or two visitors to the college library noticed the volumes during the course of the next century, but no one was curious enough to try to find out what they contained.

In 1818 was published the diary of John Evelyn, a contemporary and acquaintance of Pepys, which a fortunate antiquary had discovered in an old clothes-basket at Evelyn's home at Wotton, Surrey. This diary, with its intimate picture of life in the late seventeenth century, was much discussed in English literary circles. Among those who read it was the master of Magdalene, the Honorable and Reverend George Neville, who suddenly remembered that what appeared to be a diary written by Evelyn's friend Pepys was at that moment in his college library. He got it out, was mystified by it, and showed it to his relative Lord Grenville, who had been Secretary of State for Foreign Affairs and thus had a little knowledge of secret codes. Grenville was able to decipher a few pages of the diary, and what he found so much interested him that he urged that the whole be transcribed.

The task was allotted to an undergraduate of St. John's College with the unremarkable name of John Smith. Using the elementary key that Lord Grenville gave him, Smith got to work. He spent three years on the deciphering, often devoting as many as twelve or fourteen hours a day to it. Apart from Grenville's key, which was merely suggestive, he had no guide to the system of shorthand Pepys had used; he had to work out the cipher for himself.

When he finished, Smith turned over his 9,325-page transcript of the diary, aggregating more than 1,300,000 words, to the hereditary visitor of Magdalene College, Lord Braybrooke, who selected what he considered the most interesting portions and published them in 1825. Public interest exceeded that which had greeted the appearance of Evelyn's diary seven years earlier. Pepys's total lack of reticence, his habit of confiding to his secret pages every impulse and act, no matter how disreputable, his unvaryingly colorful account of London life in the first years of the Restoration, his detailed information on political events and on the administration of the Navy—all served to make the diary a classic upon its first publication.

Braybrooke, as editor of the first edition, failed to make clear that he printed only about a quarter of the total. As interest in Pepys grew during the next decades, further portions of the diary were printed, but with no indication of how much was still being suppressed. Finally, in the 1870's, another member of Magdalene College, the Reverend Mynors Bright, decided that it was time that a much fuller edition be published. Taking the original diary, he compared it with one of Braybrooke's editions, in whose margins and interleaves he noted alterations or additions. (The statement, often encountered, that Bright redeciphered the whole of the diary is incorrect.) The result was an edition which presented seven-tenths of the total that Pepys had written. It was just as well that John Smith, who had disappeared into the decent obscurity of a rectory in Hertford, died before Bright's edition came out. It would have depressed him to learn that the full key to the shorthand system which he had laboriously deciphered, with only Grenville's scant notes to guide him, had been available to him all the time! At his very elbow in the Pepysian library at Magdalene College had rested a copy of Thomas Shelton's *Tachygraphy*, a well known system of shorthand which Pepys had faithfully used. Bright, it appears, was the first to recognize Shelton's system as the one Pepys adopted.

Bright's edition was superseded in 1893–99 by that of Henry B. Wheatley. At long last almost the whole of the fascinating diary was made available to the reader; the only omissions were passages totaling a few thousand words which, Wheatley said, "cannot possibly be printed." In 1933, announcement was made of a completely new edition of Pepys, which when it finally appears will, despite Wheatley's pronouncement, print every word that the diarist wrote.

That prospective edition will surprise many who, having read and reread Pepys late into the night, think that they have enjoyed a faithful report of the diary's text. As a matter of fact, those who have examined the original manuscript report that every edition up to the present time has been riddled with errors. The fault was not John Smith's; his full transcript is a model of scholarly accuracy. But Lord Braybrooke was a high-handed editor, and the text he printed in his successive editions abounds in careless omissions, unwarranted insertions, and miscellaneous alterations. Mynors Bright, though he had the opportunity to do so, failed to catch many of these errors when he collated the Braybrooke text with the manuscript. Wheatley in turn based his edition upon Bright's interleaved copy of Braybrooke, thus perpetuating the editorial sins of both Braybrooke and Bright. The forthcoming edition, which will be based upon John Smith's careful transcript and checked at every point with the original cipher manuscript, will, therefore, present for the first time the true text of Pepys's great diary.

So much for the trouble which a man writing in shorthand can create for the scholars of later generations! But to the story of the Pepys diary there is a curious sequel—the discovery of "the American Pepys."

Some ten years ago the officials of the Henry E. Huntington Library at San Marino, California, were examining their collection for materials on the intellectual history of colonial Virginia. One of them took from the shelf a small octavo volume of about one hundred and fifty leaves written in shorthand and a few pages in the longhand of William Byrd of Westover, a man of substance and learning who had been a friend of Wycherley and Congreve in London and was a corresponding member of the Royal Society. The shorthand portion was clearly a journal. So a member of the Huntington staff, Mrs. Marion Tinling, who had made a special study of archaic shorthand, settled down to the job of transcribing it. She began by using as her guide some shorthand entries which Byrd had transcribed from Coke's legal reports. Only after she had transcribed a considerable part of the diary by this roundabout method did she find that Byrd had been using a recognized seventeeth-century system of shorthand, that of William Mason. The shade of John Smith must have smiled compassionately upon her when she made that discovery.

The portion of the Byrd diary which was found in the Huntington Library covers the years 1709–12. Before word of its existence got out, the authorities of the University of North Carolina Library reported that another portion, covering the years 1739–41, was in their collection. Mrs. Tinling transcribed this as well, and it has been printed. A third portion, for 1717–21, is in the Virginia Historical Society at Richmond; but the society firmly refuses to permit it to be published. Those who have seen it say that in it Byrd "describes with Pepysian frankness his amorous adventures in London, where he pursued without discrimination whores, chambermaids, and great ladies." Remembering how the expanding moral tolerance of our time has permitted modern Pepys scholars to reverse Wheatley's judgment on what "cannot possibly be printed," we may hope that eventually the suppressed portion of Byrd's diary will receive the Virginia Historical Society's *Nihil obstat.*

If and when it is printed, this section will probably make the application of the title "The American Pepys" to William Byrd more appropriate than it now is. The two published portions of the diary are invaluable as social history; Byrd reveals himself as a man of classical learning in the grand tradition, a conscientious manager of his plantations, and a sober bearer of civic responsibilities in colonial Virginia. Occasionally, too, there are passages in the Pepysian confessional mood. But in general his diaries never plumb the depths of human consciousness, nor offer a broad panorama of everyday existence, as Pepys's do. For Pepys, after all, is unique—and he is likely to remain so.

THE DESTRUCTIVE ELEMENTS

I

IN the British Museum Library today can be seen an ancient manuscript, the edges of whose pages are charred and flaked so that the endings of many lines are virtually indecipherable, if, indeed, they survive at all. Obviously it not only is of extreme age but has been through harrowing vicissitudes. If it could speak, its narrative of adventures would equal in excitement those melodramatic episodes which were set down, ten centuries ago, on its own vellum leaves.

For this is the *Beowulf* manuscript, one of the most precious of all literary documents—the only known version of the oldest major poem in the English language. The origin of the *Beowulf* story, as well as of this manuscript, is entirely unknown. All we are sure of is that both go back into Anglo-Saxon times, when England was still semi-barbarous, its inhabitants engaged in constant warfare both among themselves and against the common enemy from the north of Europe —an era when the sparks of Christian civilization were kept precariously alive by the few monasteries which dotted the British Isles. Perhaps late in the tenth century after Christ, a monk copied out from an older manuscript this heroic tale, which had been a part of the repertory of some bard as he wandered from kingdom to kingdom, furnishing after-dinner entertainment for the mead-drinking warriors. The recorded history of the present manuscript begins in the middle of the sixteenth century, when it was the property of Laurence Nowell, dean of Lichfield and a pioneer collector of antiquities. It disappeared from view, to turn up later in the collection of Sir Robert Cotton. Cotton was an enthusiastic (and, some say, none too scrupulous) antiquarian. His library, which was augmented after his death in 1631 by his son and grandson, was the richest collection in existence of Anglo-Saxon literary and historical documents. At Cotton House the precious old manuscripts, stoutly bound in leather, were arranged in fourteen tall presses, and Sir Robert designated the manuscripts which belonged in each press by reference to the bust that surmounted it. He used the busts of the twelve Caesars for the purpose; but there were two more presses than there were Caesars, and he drafted Cleopatra and Faustina to preside over numbers thirteen and fourteen. I have always felt that the malign presence of the Empress Faustina in the Cottonian Library (see Swinburne's poem to her) brought about the catastrophe that befell it. In any event, under Cotton's arrangement, the *Beowulf* manuscript was known, as it is still known today, as "Vitellius A. xv"—"A" designating the first shelf under the bust of Vitellius Caesar, and "xv" the fifteenth position on that shelf.

In 1700 the Cottonian Library was deeded to the nation; and after it was decided that Cotton House was too damp and ruinous for the preservation of the manuscripts the collection was transferred to Ashburnham House, which, besides being drier and more spacious, was thought to be "much more safe from fire." Two years passed; then, early in the morning of October 23, 1731, the city of Westminster was aroused by the alarm of fire at Ashburnham House. The first men on the scene saw the flames burning brightly inside the room where Cotton's fourteen book presses stood. Among the crowd which gathered were trustees of the collection, who broke into the burning house, ran to the presses, and feverishly threw hundreds of volumes from the windows. Among these rescuers was Richard Bentley, the Cottonian librarian and the greatest classical scholar of his time, who is reported to have raced from the flaming house "in his dressing-gown, a flowing wig on his head, and a huge volume under his arm." He had chosen for salvation by his own hands the precious Alexandrine manuscript of the Bible. Meanwhile other citizens were laboring at the hand pumps brought by the primitive fire brigade.

A few hours later the portion of Ashburnham House that contained the Cottonian collection lay gutted. Of the 958 manuscript volumes in the library, about a hundred, virtually all irreplaceable, were utterly destroyed; and hundreds more which survived were dreadfully charred and water-soaked. Some of these were restored with as much skill as was then possible, but there remained sixty-one bundles of damaged leaves, the sorting and repairing of which was to be delayed until the middle of the next century. Among the volumes which had escaped with relatively minor damage was the unique manuscript of *Beowulf*, only the edges of which had felt the flames.

What was left of Sir Robert Cotton's proud collection eventually was housed in the British Museum. Like the other salvaged volumes, the *Beowulf* manuscript required immediate care. The heat of the flames had made its vellum, naturally dried by the action of time, extremely brittle; but nothing was done to arrest its disintegration, and, as the decades went by, the margins of the pages, including portions of the text itself, quietly flaked off onto the shelves.

More than fifty years after the fire, a new hero entered the lists. Grímur Jónsson Thorkelin, an Icelander who had become passionately devoted to the study of ancient Danish history, knowing that the library of the British Museum contained documents from the remote time when England and Denmark had been virtually one nation, came to London in 1786 and examined the *Beowulf* manuscript. So interested did he become in its contents that he made a complete transcript of the poem—the first that anyone had made—and hired an assistant to make a second. He then returned to Copenhagen to study them at his leisure.

But then Napoleon occupied Denmark, like Hitler in another century, and England, striking back at Napoleon, bombarded Copenhagen in 1807. At that moment Thorkelin had just completed the task of preparing for the press an edition of *Beowulf*. In the fire that followed the English attack Thorkelin's house was burned, and the manuscript of his edition was lost; but the two transcripts escaped without harm. With a sigh, Thorkelin began his work all over again when the rubble was cleared away. This time the gods, and the British Navy, were kinder, and in 1815 the first printed text of *Beowulf* appeared.

The work attracted much attention among Danish and German

scholars, and finally Englishmen, who had so long been indifferent to the study of their early history and literature, got busy. In 1833 John Mitchell Kemble, brother of the actress Fanny, brought out the first English edition of *Beowulf.* When the original manuscript of the poem was reexamined, it became clear what a great service Thorkelin had performed for scholarship—a service almost undone by the diligence of the British gunners—by transcribing the manuscript. In the five decades which had elapsed since 1786, the neglected volume had deteriorated still more, so that many of the words he had been able to decipher had disappeared entirely. At long last the British Museum took steps to preserve what remained, and each leaf was meticulously repaired, the crumbling edges being mounted on gauze. Today it may be examined by properly qualified scholars. But they must select the right day, because even atmospheric conditions affect the legibility of the charred margins, which have become almost transparent.

Thus we owe our present possession of *Beowulf,* the earliest great monument of English literature, to a series of narrow escapes.* But we know only a part, and very probably the less exciting part, of the full story; for the very fact that the manuscript survived from the tenth century down to the time when it came into the possession of Laurence Nowell is itself miraculous. How many more hairbreadth escapes from destruction did it have in those centuries? That it had such escapes, there can be no question, because, of all the manuscripts

---

* The American counterpart of the *Beowulf* manuscript is probably that of Poe's *Murders in the Rue Morgue.* (Why is it that manuscripts whose literary text is full of violence seem to lead more dangerous lives than others?) In 1841 Poe's story was set in type for *Graham's Magazine.* After the proof was read the manuscript itself was thrown into a wastebasket. One of the apprentices in the shop, J. M. Johnston, retrieved it and took it home to his father, who put it into a music book for safekeeping. Young Johnston later moved to Lancaster, Pa., where he opened a daguerreotype gallery. Three times his house was burned, but each time the manuscript, snug inside the music book, escaped. In 1869 he was cleaning out rubbish and in an absent-minded moment added the music book to the heap in the back yard. A neighbor came along, poked through the pile, recognized the music book, and hurried it back to its owner. In 1881 Johnston, perhaps feeling that his luck was about to run out, sold the Poe manuscript to the publisher of the Philadelphia *Public Ledger,* who gave it to the Drexel Institute of Technology. When the Drexel Institute sold it in 1944 it brought $34,000.

of old English poetry which once existed, only three others of major importance have been preserved.

No scholar specializing in Anglo-Saxon or Middle English literature is without moments of dismay when he thinks of the riches that once abounded in monastic libraries. The Anglo-Saxon specialist in particular is confined, in his attempt to explore the beginnings of English literature, to a slender handful of pre-Conquest verse and prose pieces which can easily be printed in a single volume. Yet, everywhere he turns in his researches, he encounters tantalizing evidence of the heroic epics, the historical chronicles, the religious and devotional works, the popular songs and tales which were current in the England of Alfred and Cædmon and Bede. He finds, for example, in books written after the time of William the Conqueror, brief references to heroes whose exploits were then still so well remembered that it was unnecessary for the medieval author to do more than mention their names.

Some materials which we should prize as part of our literary heritage seemingly never were recorded. Narrative poems like *Beowulf* and *The Fight at Finnsburg* (which was among the manuscripts destroyed in the Cottonian fire, but of which a transcript had luckily been made) were carried about in the memories of generations of bards, or scops, and it was only occasionally that one of them was actually written down. Again, the language of the Anglo-Saxons was merely the vernacular of the times. It had no official standing, and the poems and prose current in it were thought of little moment; anything that really deserved to be perpetuated was written in Latin. Yet it is precisely those pieces in Anglo-Saxon, the great majority of which are now lost, that composed the first English literature. All we know of the lost pieces—and it is merely enough to whet our curiosity—is what we can gather from the meager, faintly patronizing allusions in later Latin or Anglo-French books.

Nevertheless, as the centuries passed and more and more scriptoria, or copying offices, were installed in the monasteries, the body of literary and historical records marked for preservation steadily grew; and, although the major portion of the libraries thus accumulated was devoted to serious works of religion, secular works had their place. But all these tangible evidences of the early Englishman's intellectual and emotional history were at the mercy of his fiercer instincts. The tides of war, put in motion by the invasions of tribes from the Continent, swept over Anglo-Saxon England almost continuously for hundreds of years, and the religious houses were not spared. Time after time their libraries were ruthlessly pillaged and burned, and we can only imagine how many hundreds and thousands of manuscripts, epics and chronicles and saints' lives and lyrics alike, perished by the torch. The decade 867–878 alone, which was perhaps the most ferociously destructive of all, must have witnessed the end of innumerable examples of Anglo-Saxon story and song.

Severe though the losses were, a considerable number of Anglo-Saxon manuscripts survived from these earlier centuries. There remain today the catalogues of several monastic libraries, compiled in the fourteenth and fifteenth centuries, which list many manuscripts whose contents, if not the manuscripts themselves, dated from Anglo-Saxon times. As late as 1731, as we have seen, hundreds of such venerable pieces still nestled comfortably under the busts of the Caesars in Ashburnham House—but then their luck too ran out. Any English manuscript, indeed, which escaped destruction in the Danish raids and the intertribal wars had to look forward to centuries of constant danger. Scarcely a monastery in England did not suffer a disastrous accidental fire at one time or another; and even more immediate and prevalent was the threat of the damp climate and of hungry vermin.

The modern scholar whose chief interest is in medieval literature, roughly from the time of the Norman conquest to the end of the fifteenth century, is a little better off than the Anglo-Saxon specialist. It has been estimated that at least thirty thousand separate manuscripts of literary interest survive from medieval England. Yet even this body of medieval literature is but a small proportion of what once existed; and, whereas the Anglo-Saxon scholar works in a darkness broken only by the fitful beacons of a few surviving records, the medieval scholar is in a no less perplexing situation. In viewing the literature of medieval England and trying to reconstruct the life and thought of the time, he must always remember that he looks through a glass which filters out many colors and fantastically distorts the shapes in the medieval panorama. Unless we allow for the fact that certain classes of medieval literature have survived while others have almost entirely perished, we entertain a lamentably false notion of the Middle Ages. As a distinguished scholar said some years ago: "If the lost [vernacular] poetry had been preserved, the whole history of English literature, prior to Chaucer and Langland, would appear to us in a different light. The homilies and lives of saints, which bulk so largely in Medieval English verse and prose, would subside till they occupied a just, and a small, proportion of our attention. . . . [The river of time] has brought down masses of medieval literature which are sad, weighty, and dull, but has drowned so much which might in some senses be called light, but which was certainly cheering, romantic, and sometimes heroic in spirit."

As in older centuries, literary works depended for survival during the Middle Ages largely upon the labor of monastic scribes. It is no wonder, then, that most of the medieval manuscripts still extant are works which the religious authorities singled out for preservation and diffusion. Medieval libraries were filled with theological treatises, devotional and homiletic works, the lives of saints, manuals of Christian conduct, and so on. But the monks also copied and recopied historical documents of all sorts, and increasingly, as time went on, works of non-religious import.

Today some eighty-five texts of portions of Chaucer's *Canterbury Tales* are known to exist; only sixteen were available to the first editors of Chaucer in 1721. How many more manuscripts were written, and how many of them—one perhaps closer to Chaucer's own text than any we now know—may some day be found? The long labors of John M. Manly and Edith Rickert in studying and editing the text of the *Canterbury Tales* turned up a great deal of evidence that centuries ago many Chaucer manuscripts existed which have now disappeared. In the catalogues of private collections in the seventeenth century, in old sale catalogues, in wills as far back as the middle of the fifteenth century, in the inventories of the personal property of Elizabethan noblemen, even in a scrawled notation in the manuscript of a herbal now at Balliol College, Oxford, they found references to such manuscripts, which cannot be identified with any of those now known.

Manly and Rickert's intensive search for new Chaucer fragments had little result. They did learn, however, that during the First World War the owner of a fragment of an unrecorded Chaucer manuscript offered it for sale to the National Library of Wales; but the library, being out of funds, had to decline it. When Manly and Rickert questioned the librarian years later, he managed to supply clues which led them eventually to this "Merthyr" fragment, which turned out to consist of only three leaves pasted in the back of an old Latin-Welsh dictionary. These stray leaves, however, were so fine as to make Manly and Rickert all the more eager to locate the manuscript from which they were torn.

Now many old manuscripts, like some books that have come down to us from the libraries of our own great-grandfathers, were used centuries ago by children as copybooks or by adults, perhaps to practice writing their names before the unwonted exertion of appending them to legal documents. Some Chaucer manuscripts, indeed, are scribbled all over—one, for example, bears scraps of the catechism and primer sentences in a mid-sixteenth-century hand ("franses copper ded play in the chirch"). Although aesthetically such scribblings are most irritating, they give the scholar invaluable clues to the former owners of the manuscript; and when they occur on stray leaves they may conceivably guide him to the rest of the manuscript. Manly and Rickert, therefore, went to immense pains to run down every name they found on the thousands of Chaucerian leaves they examined. In the case of the "Merthyr" fragment, they found that all the scribbled names were traceable to an area within a few miles of St. Donat's castle in Wales. Hence it was most likely that the manuscript had been kept in the castle, and it was conceivable that the rest of it was still there. They communicated with the present owner of the fragment, who told them that at one time, by some migration of the family owning the castle, its library had been moved to Dublin, where it was accidentally destroyed by fire. Although there was no positive evidence that the Chaucer manuscript was in the library when it was moved, or that the library itself actually was burned, the trail grew cold, and the fate of this Chaucer text, like that of so many others, is still a mystery.

II

THE constant ravages of fire, vermin, damp, and neglect, though they did destroy forever many precious pieces of literature, were counteracted, in quantity at least, by the continued activity of the scriptoria. By the beginning of the sixteenth century the English religious houses were richly endowed with libraries. But now the stage was set for one of the most calamitous episodes in the history of English literature. Henry VIII, as everyone knows, broke with the Pope and declaring his own sovereignty over the Church's vast properties in England, proceeded to confiscate them. The lands, the buildings, and the movable properties he acquired for himself or distributed among his favorites. Although as a child he had shown some bookish inclinations, as King he did not lift a finger to save the monastic libraries from the general ruin. Old Thomas Fuller tells in his *Church History of Britain* how venerable books and manuscripts were destroyed for the sake of the precious stones and metals inlaid in their bindings; and "many an ancient manuscript Bible" was "cut in pieces to cover filthy pamphlets." He quotes the complaint of the antiquary John Bale, "a man sufficiently averse from the least shadow of popery, hating all monkery with a perfect hatred":

A great number of them which purchased these superstitious mansions [the abbeys] reserved of those library books some to serve their jakes, some to scour their candlesticks, and some to rub their boots; some they sold to the grocers and soap-sellers, and some they sent over sea to the bookbinders, not in small number, but at times whole ships full, to the wondering of the foreign nations. . . . I know a merchantman (which shall at this time be nameless) that bought the contents of two noble libraries for forty shillings price, a shame it is to be spoken. This stuff hath he occupied instead of grey paper by the space of more than these ten years, and yet he hath store enough for as many years to come. . . . Neither the Britons under the Romans and Saxons, nor yet the English people under the Danes and Normans, had ever such damage of their learned monuments as we have seen in our time. Our posterity may well curse this wicked fact of our age, this unreasonable spoil of England's most noble antiquities.

Recent scholars have been inclined to think that the losses thus indignantly described were not quite as large as Bale said they were. Nevertheless there can be no doubt that in the tragic decades of religious disturbance the literature of England was sadly impoverished. We shall never know what now-forgotten works of Chaucer, or of the obscure poet who wrote the *Pearl;* what glorious works of medieval religious devotion, what chivalric romances, disappeared forever.

Those manuscript books which were not burned for being tinged with popery were, as Bale said, scattered far and wide. Some of the items that escaped the waste-paper merchants found refuge in libraries on the Continent, where some of them may be hiding to this day.* But they still had to endure all the religious wars which rocked western Europe, and many, having escaped one bonfire in their native land, perished in another in Germany or France. Even if they were preserved through these troubled centuries, they still had to face such perils as the Napoleonic wars, the siege of Strasbourg in 1870, and the plundering of the Italian religious libraries after the abolition of the States of the Church. Nor did they fare any better in the twentieth century. An undeterminable number of English literary manuscripts and rare books, lying still undiscovered in the collections of the Continent, were destroyed in the two world wars. It is all too likely that in 1939 there existed, in Europe from the Netherlands to Russia, literary materials which had never been studied, and of which no trace now remains.

The manuscripts that remained in England after their "liberation" from the monastic libraries were no safer. Not long after the dissolution one notable attempt was made to repair some of the dam-

---

* The migration of English manuscripts to the Continent had begun, of course, before the time of Henry VIII. One of the four extant manuscripts of Anglo-Saxon verse, which contains, in addition to a number of religious homilies, such poems as the "Andreas," "The Fates of the Apostles," and "The Dream of the Rood," had found its way much earlier to the Chapter Library of the Cathedral at Vercelli, in northern Italy. Just how it got there is one of the persistently teasing mysteries of scholarship.

age. Matthew Parker, the Archbishop of Canterbury, sent emissaries through the country to gather up what they could find of the contents of the defunct libraries, and much of what they collected eventually found its way by his bequest to Corpus Christi College, Cambridge. But most of the manuscripts had disappeared into the hands of private families, where they remained until they were destroyed by accident or design, or were sold as waste paper, or (a fortunate minority) were absorbed into private or institutional collections. As a result, for centuries thereafter medieval manuscripts were constantly turning up in out-of-the-way places in England; a whole anthology indeed could be made of the curious anecdotes involving them. Many of these stories are best when not examined too critically. There is, for example, the hoary one about Sir Robert Cotton dropping into his tailor's shop and finding that worthy cutting a measuring-strip from what turned out to be one of the original copies of the Magna Carta. Another legend tells of a man who found a fishmonger in Hungerford Market selling soles wrapped in a leaf from an old folio book, and who, upon inquiring where the fishmonger had found the waste paper, was directed to a warehouse containing seven tons of fifteenth- and early sixteenth-century manuscripts.

A better authenticated story was set down by William Macray in his diverting history of the Bodleian Library, of which he was for many years the librarian:

On the death of the owner of a certain old estate, it was thought wise by heirs or executors to destroy *en masse* certain old writings, books, and papers, which they could not read or understand, and which they were unwilling should pass into other hands, as they themselves did not know what their contents might be. So these wise men of Gotham made a fire, and condemned the books to be burned. But the soul of the village cobbler was moved, for he saw that vellum might be more useful as material for cutting out patterns of shapely shoes and as padding than as fuel; and so he hurried to the place of execution, and prayed that he might have a cart-full from the heap; and his prayer was granted. Some time after, Royce * heard of what had occurred, and by his means the cobbler was "interviewed" and all that was left of the precious load was obtained from him.

* Vicar of a country parish in Gloucestershire.

Among the vellum fragments Royce retrieved, and subsequently gave to Macray, were "some fragments of a fine early thirteenth-century manuscript of one of St. Augustine's treatises, cut and marked for the measure of some rustic foot. That a remnant of an old monastic library perished on this occasion," Macray laments, "there is only too much reason to fear."

Henry VIII's agents, it is true, did not do a complete job of ruining the religious libraries. Those in the cathedrals, for instance, generally were spared, as part of his endeavor to enlist the high prelates and noblemen in his program of church reform. The plundering of the cathedral libraries had to wait for the next century, when the Puritans attended to it with fanatical gusto. A few outstanding ones escaped even then, and today those at Durham and Worcester, relatively unharmed through the centuries, offer a melancholy indication of the size and richness of scores of collections before Henry VIII fell out with the Pope. Many small and remote church establishments, too, missed the general purge, and their old books were spared. But because these collections *were* small and remote—though many of them contained documents of inestimable value for modern scholars—they were neglected throughout the ensuing centuries, and lay at the mercy of fire, the English damp, the rats—and men. There are many depressing stories of housecleaning during which medieval manuscripts were thrown out of cobwebby old muniment rooms. At the church of St. Thomas the Martyr at Bristol, in the eighteenth century, an ignorant churchwarden could have been found cheerfully tearing beautifully illuminated pages from a book of hours to cover an account book. No deep blame attaches to these peaceful pillagers. Except among a handful of antiquarians, during the seventeenth and eighteenth centuries there was no interest whatsoever in papers and books related to the nation's remote past, which few people could even read. Today, whenever the humblest householder stumbles upon some written or printed material that seems to be old, he treasures it, or tries to sell it for the fortune he is sure it must be worth. But until fairly recent times his reaction would have been just the opposite: whatever was old was virtually worthless. No one could have foreseen the day when a rare old book sometimes sells for a king's ransom. It is dismaying none the less to reflect how many thousands of men have been responsible, even if innocently, for the destruction of literary material more valuable in sum, perhaps, than all we now possess.

With the spread of printing in the sixteenth century, the danger of the total loss of literary works decreased. Yet books were published in extremely small editions, and all the hazards that we have so far watched in operation were visited upon them as well as manuscripts. Thus today we read references to thousands of books of which no copies are known to exist. Even worse, perhaps, we have stray leaves from thousands more—many of them having been discovered in the bindings of later books, for the destination of the sheets of unsold books, then as now, was often the binder's shop.

The greatest concentration of these pathetic reminders of books which have themselves perished is found in the British Museum, in the collection of John Bagford. Bagford (1650–1716) was an antiquarian who spent much of his life making a vast collection of samples in preparation for a history of typography which he never wrote. In all, he left to posterity thirty-six big scrapbooks containing detached leaves of manuscripts (selected for their handwriting) and no fewer than ninety-three volumes of single leaves from printed books. Tradition has it that he used to tramp through the countryside, ferreting out old books and manuscripts wherever they existed, and removing pages that struck his fancy from the oldest Bibles, service books, lives of the saints—even Caxtons. Since the great majority of the books he presumably mutilated are unknown apart from these pages, it is no wonder that he has been execrated as "the wicked old biblioclast." However, he has not lacked defenders. One of them points out that he may not have mutilated books at all, but, rather, simply treasured up odd pages wherever he came across them—in chandlers' or fishmongers' or tailors' shops, for example. It is possible that many of his items were salvaged from the ruins of the bookshops around St. Paul's after the London fire of 1666, when uncounted thousands of books were burned in a holocaust the like of which was not seen again until the publishers' warehouses in Paternoster Row were destroyed in the Blitz. And even if he did rip those pages out of intact books, how was he to know that later generations would place so high a valuation on them? Still, had he chosen to collect whole books rather than single pages, what a library of unique copies he would have left to us!

III

THE realm of postmedieval English literature which has suffered most cruelly from the destructive elements is that of the Tudor and Stuart drama. At first glance this may seem a curious statement. It is true, of course, that we possess hundreds of the plays which were composed and performed in that splendid burst of dramatic creation between 1590 and the closing of the theaters in 1642. In addition to some forty of Shakespeare's plays, we have works by Ben Jonson, Marlowe, Dekker, Beaumont and Fletcher, Greene, Marston, Massinger, Shirley, Webster, Middleton, Ford, and another score of Shakespeare's contemporaries and successors. But what is usually forgotten is that, numerous though the plays from this period are which we may still hold in our hands, they represent only a fragment of the dramatic literature that once existed. In all probability, we have lost as many fine plays as we still possess.

The malicious Fate which has destroyed these plays has taken care to preserve for us some small record of them. For instance, we may still study the Stationers' Register, the sixteenth- and seventeenth-century equivalent of modern copyright lists, in which every play had to be entered if its prospective publisher wished to have his legal interest in it protected. We have, as well, the valuable account books of Philip Henslowe, the theatrical magnate of Shakespeare's age, with their wealth of information on the practical aspects of Elizabethan staging. They are rich in mention of plays performed on such-and-such date at the Rose or the Fortune; and many of these plays have subsequently dropped from sight. Other contemporary sources as well tease the scholar with matter-of-fact allusions to plays then very much alive: the chronicles of the two universities (where drama was not merely an entertainment but a device for teaching classical languages); the records of the court, which had command performances at frequent intervals; the many pamphlets of abuse which the

Puritans published in their bitter campaign against the godless stage; and the records of the official licenser of the drama, the Lord Chamberlain.

But while these various kinds of records have survived in good shape the plays whose titles abound in them have had generally bad luck. For one thing, many, if not most, of them were not printed at all, and these are irretrievably lost unless by some miracle the author's manuscript or a playhouse copy has been preserved. Those that were printed had the odds heavily stacked against their survival. They were published in cheap little unbound quartos designed not for a permanent place in a gentleman's library but simply to satisfy a passing interest in a show that was drawing crowds to the playhouses across the river. Their relatively frail format meant that most copies died a natural death long ago. But even if they had been built of stronger stuff, the very character of their contents made them ephemeral; plays were not generally regarded as belonging to polite literature, and shelf space in seventeenth-century libraries was reserved for books of graver cast, such as works on theology and politics. At library-culling time, plays were the first to be discarded. Again, the Puritans had a warrant out for play-books, and whenever, during their supremacy in the middle of the seventeenth century, they had a book-burning, they liked to kindle the fire with a few inflammable relics of the heathen playhouse.

Many collections of old plays owe their existence today to the fact that their owners' indifference was so overwhelming that they could not get around to selling the musty old books to a junkman. Every few years a long-forgotten volume of old printed plays, including perhaps a copy of one of the precious Shakespeare quartos, turns up at the sale of the effects of some last-surviving member of an old family. One of the most remarkable finds of this sort occurred in 1906, when a worn black-letter volume was discovered in a bricked-up chimney during the razing of an old farmhouse in Ireland. The owner, idly thinking it might possibly have some value, tore out a page and sent it to Sotheby's, the great London auction house. Sotheby's took one look at the specimen page and assured their inquirer that they would be happy to sell the volume for him on commission. He thereupon mailed them the book, tied up with grocery string and not even protected by a wrapper. Sotheby's experts discovered that the volume thus confidently entrusted to His Majesty's Post Office contained seventeen pre-Elizabethan plays, several of which had been not only lost but entirely unrecorded. When the contents of the volume were sold off, play by play, they brought over £2,000, which in those days was a remarkable price.*

The most famous story of wholesale destruction of old plays, however, remains to be mentioned. In the Lansdowne Collection in the British Museum rests a folio volume which once was in the possession of John Warburton, an eighteenth-century antiquarian. The book contains the manuscripts of three old plays, *The Queen of Corinth, The Second Maiden's Tragedy,* and *Bugbears,* and a fragment of a fourth. Preceding them is a memorandum by Warburton listing some fifty-six other plays, including three which he attributes to Shakespeare (*Duke Humphrey, Henry I,* and a third, unnamed), and others by Marlowe, Ford, Dekker, Massinger, Middleton, and Chapman. At the end of this list appears, in Warburton's hand, one of the saddest sentences ever penned: "After I had been many years Collecting these MSS Playes, through my own carelesness and the Ignorace of my S[ervant] in whose hands I had lodgd them they was unluckely burnd or put under Pye bottoms, excepting yᵉ three which follows. J.W."

This simple statement, so tragically eloquent even in its misspelling and indifferent grammar, is the only known record of an event which has long been notorious in the annals of English dramatic literature. Probably no other maidservant has been the object of more heartfelt scholarly curses than the unlettered girl who, since her real name is unknown to history, is referred to by nineteenth-century chroniclers with a pleasant sense of fitness as Betsy Baker. But Betsy's shade is in excellent, indeed exalted company; for it was no less a man than the philosopher John Stuart Mill who, having borrowed from his friend Carlyle the manuscript of the first, as yet unpublished volume of *The French Revolution,* inadvertently mixed it with "old papers for kitchen use" at his father's house, thereby sending it to its destruction.

---

* Another important "lost" play which has come to light in our time is Henry Medwall's *Fulgens and Lucres,* some account of which is given on pp. 300–302.

IV

ALTHOUGH the public archives of a nation are primarily of interest to the historian, we have seen how they often prove to contain documents of the first value to the student of literature, such as the coroner's inquest on the body of the murdered Marlowe and the long series of records of the felonious activities of Sir Thomas Malory. If there were space, I could tell how the vast collection of English records now housed in the Public Record Office has been found to include (among many other nuggets of prime biographical data) Shelley's lost letters to Harriet Westbrook, documents relating to Shakespeare's life in London, and the answer to the long vexed riddle of William Congreve's will. It was in the Public Record Office, too, that Leslie Hotson found evidence to controvert the long-standing belief that dramatic activity was wholly absent from the London of the Puritan Commonwealth. Instead, as the newly found legal documents showed, there was a continuing tradition of private, almost "underground" performances during the era when the public theaters were locked.

No one knows how many more such discoveries, some of them perhaps eclipsing in significance any yet made, will be the fortunate lot of patient workers in the Public Record Office.* But when we review the history of the English public records, it is impossible not to wonder what important literary documents, once preserved there— life records, say, of Chaucer and Shakespeare and Milton and a hundred lesser poets—have perished. In the seventeenth century, most of the old records were kept in the Tower of London. When William Prynne became Keeper of the Records in 1661, he found that vast numbers of the documents, "through negligence, nescience, and sloath-

* The size of the collection is indicated by this fact: In 1939 a minor portion of the papers, chiefly those dating from medieval times, was removed to a place of safety, and what remained was concentrated in the basement. After the war, it was first necessary to move *three hundred tons* of records to the upper floors. Into the space thus vacated, the evacuated documents were returned. It took six hundred truckloads to bring these papers back; and, as I say, they represented only a small portion of the total.

fullness had for many years then past layen buried together in one confused chaos under corroding putrifying cobwebbs, dust, and filth in the darkest corners of Caesar's chapel in the White Tower." Resolutely he tried to clean up the mess; he enlisted soldiers and women for the task, but they soon gave up in despair, and his own clerks were "unwilling to touch them for fear of endangering their eyesights and healths by the cankerous dust and evil scent." And so untold numbers of papers continued to fall away into dust; a generation after Prynne made his futile effort to correct the situation, a diarist reported that " 'twas a great trouble to me to see so many Waggon Loads of Records as are here in the most Dirty and perishing Condition imaginable; many peeping out of Heaps of Dust and Rubbish a yard or two in Depth."

A century and a half passed, and still nothing had been done. In 1847 *The Times* remarked with rather heavy editorial irony:

In England we have a very singular way of taking care of our national archives. If the records, like human beings, were open to infectious disease, they would be summarily despatched, for security's sake, to Burying-ground-passage, Johnson's-place, Gee's-court, or some of those favoured localities in which Government are determined to receive the cholera, if it shall unfortunately visit the metropolis, with suitable honours. As this cannot be, we have selected the two next most suitable agents of destruction in order to get rid of our records with as little delay as possible—gunpowder and mildew. In the Tower, one portion of these luckless documents is submitted to the former, in the Queen's Mews to the latter, agency. We may regret that the second chemical process is so slow, but it has this superiority over the means of destruction employed at the Tower—that it is sure. On the other hand, although we may often have occasion to reflect with pain on the immunity from damp enjoyed by the Rolls in the Tower, there is the counterbalancing consideration that at any given hour of the day or night the whole collection may be launched into eternity by the explosion of a magazine.

By some wholly undeserved chance, the looked-for catastrophe did not occur, and a few years later, after long discussion, the present Public Record Office was built. To it were moved all the documents stored for so long in the Tower, as well as the accumulations of more recent times, which had been distributed in over sixty different depositories throughout London. At last the great majority of the public papers were suitably housed, and provision made for their care. But for many—nobody will ever know how many—it was too late.

There is some consolation in the thought that, at least in modern times, the English public records have not been decimated by fire or pillage. The records of Ireland, though, were not so lucky. And thereby hangs a tale.

In 1935 Professor Walter Graham of the University of Illinois was in England collecting manuscript materials for an edition of the letters of Joseph Addison. Among the many leads he was following was one he found in a prospectus for the third volume of A. C. Guthkelch's edition of Addison's writings, the first two volumes of which had been published in 1914. The prospectus alluded to new Addison materials which Guthkelch had collected and planned to include in the third volume; but the outbreak of war had prevented the completion of his work, and he himself had died in 1916. Graham naturally was eager to trace the fresh Addison writings which, twenty years later, still had not been printed. Mrs. Guthkelch, to whom he appealed, told him that her husband's Addison material was then in the possession of Gwendolen Murphy, who happened to be working at the British Museum. Learning of Graham's interest in the Guthkelch papers, Miss Murphy agreed to meet him and his wife at tea in an A.B.C. shop around the corner from the museum. On the appointed day, she appeared with a large net basket of the kind British housewives take to market. It was stuffed with papers. She turned it over to Graham, who took it back to his lodgings and began to explore its contents. Some of the items which Guthkelch's published remarks had led him to believe were in the collection, were missing. On the other hand, the market basket did contain modern transcripts of over a hundred letters from Addison to one Joshua Dawson.

The importance of these letters was immediately clear. They had been written in the years 1708–14—the very years in which Addison was conducting the *Spectator*, the *Tatler*, and the *Guardian*, and thus the years of greatest interest to the literary biographer. Notations on the transcripts indicated that they had been made in 1914, at the

Irish Record Office, by a clergyman Guthkelch had hired for the purpose.

The next step, of course, was to locate the originals of this important series of letters. But here Graham's luck ran out. For in 1922, when the bitter struggle for Irish independence had broken out once again, the Addison-Dawson papers had been sent for safekeeping to the Four Courts in Dublin. The building was seized by the Irish Republican Army and converted into a munitions factory and fortress. Eventually the Free State forces attacked the insurgent stronghold, shelling it with artillery from a near-by park. One shell struck a mine, and the explosion shattered the whole east wall of the building; a fire started, and no effort was made to put it out. Within an hour or two the whole building was gutted, and the contents of the vaults were reduced to ashes. And that was the end of the letters Joseph Addison had written to Joshua Dawson.

Graham, however, when he went to Dublin to verify, so far as possible, the authority of his transcripts, found that the manuscript catalogue of the Irish archives contained abstracts of the lost letters, made many years before. By comparing these with the transcripts he had received from Miss Murphy, he satisfied himself that the copies made in 1914 were faithful reports of what the original letters had contained. And so the scholarly zeal of A. C. Guthkelch, like that of Thorkelin more than a century before, proved to be the means by which later researchers were able to rescue literary material, so to speak, from its own ashes.

V

THIS incident, and others like it, offers a straw for scholars to clutch when they discover that the original papers which they yearn to see have been lost beyond possibility of recovery. If anyone at all was interested in those papers before they were destroyed, there is always the chance that he went to the trouble of copying them. For example, many of the personal papers of Samuel Taylor Coleridge descended to his grandson, E. H. Coleridge, who spent years preparing to use them in a projected biography of the poet. But near the end of the last century virtually the whole collection was lost: it was shipped from London to Torquay, and somewhere en route it disappeared forever. The shock to E. H. Coleridge was so enormous that it prevented his finishing his biography. But, luckily for all future students of the poet, his grandson had made transcripts of most of the papers before they were lost.

It is to a similar accident that we owe much of our knowledge of the life and works of Thomas Lovell Beddoes, an early Victorian physician and poet whose *Death's Jest Book,* a tragedy in the Elizabethan style, is still remembered, and who, modern critics feel, could have been a great poet had he had a more fortunate life. After his death in 1849 Beddoes's manuscripts went to a devoted friend, who published a small selection from them. He in turn bequeathed them, packed in a large chest, to Robert Browning, who was a great admirer of Beddoes's work. Ten years later Browning lent the manuscripts to his friend Edmund Gosse, who published further selections from the poems and utilized the personal papers in a memoir prefixed to his edition. But Gosse did not use more than a fraction of the contents of the box, and the rest remained unprinted.

After Browning's death, the box went to his son Pen, who kept it at his villa near Asolo, Italy. Pen died in 1912, and the next year his library, which included the thousands of books collected by his father and his grandfather, was sold in London. Rich though the collection was, many items which should have been there were missing, and among them was the Beddoes box. What happened to these items, which Pen Browning was known positively to have possessed, is a mystery to this day. Edmund Gosse used to tell his friends that Pen had had differences with his household servants in his last years, and that immediately after his death they had taken their revenge by destroying or appropriating many of his prized books. If the books were carried off, rather than destroyed outright, they may still exist somewhere in Italy. So far as I know, no one has yet tried to trace the families of the servants.

Thanks to Gosse's edition, published in 1890, interest in Beddoes's poetry had steadily grown. Since it was understood that Gosse had by no means exhausted the contents of the box Browning possessed, the news of its disappearance was a shock. Who could tell how much the unprinted papers might have added to the poet's stature, and to our understanding of his eccentric, tortured character? As events proved, such laments were premature.

Although the fact was unknown for many years, Gosse had not been the only man to examine the contents of the Beddoes box. In 1886 Browning had lent it to James Dykes Campbell, a businessman who was an enthusiastic and hard-working literary student in his spare time. During the months that he possessed the box, he had faithfully transcribed everything of importance it contained, even down to every variant reading and correction in the manuscripts of the poems, and to the postmarks and seals on Beddoes's letters. These transcripts were found among his effects after his death in 1895, and nine years later they were sold at Sotheby's; but the fact of their existence attracted no attention, because it was known that the originals were in Pen Browning's possession, and it would be only a matter of years before they could themselves be studied. Thus it happened that when the news came of the loss of the Beddoes box, the Campbell transcripts were entirely forgotten.

Only about 1930 were the transcripts recovered. H. W. Donner happened upon the old Sotheby catalogue which listed them, and traced the collector who had bought them in 1904. He received free access to them, and the result was the publication in 1935 of three volumes in which Bonner printed for the first time the mass of material rejected by Gosse but religiously copied by Campbell. And so the loss of the originals was made good, and students of Beddoes—"the last Elizabethan," as Lytton Strachey called him—had at their disposal a rich store of his poetry, including several successive drafts of *Death's Jest Book,* and of his personal papers.

The full roster of literary works and biographical material preserved through transcripts is a long one. If loyal friends or admirers, or members of the writer's own family, had not gone to the trouble of copying out page after page in longhand, how much should we have lost that is important in English literature! And what poems or personal documents, now assumed to be lost forever, still exist in as yet undiscovered transcripts?

That question is especially teasing when we recall one of the most famous of all the true stories relating to the destruction of literary documents. In the years 1819–21 Lord Byron composed an autobiography of seventy-eight pages which he gave to his friend Thomas Moore, with the instruction that it was not to be printed while he lived, although Moore was at liberty to show it to "the elect." Moore did allow a handful of intimate friends to examine this curious document. Their reactions differed. Some protested that it was so infamous and obscene that it must never be made public; others asserted that they found nothing offensive in it.

When news of Byron's death arrived in London the question immediately arose as to what should be done with these memoirs. There was an extraordinary squabble involving Moore, John Murray (to whom Moore had sold the manuscript), John Cam Hobhouse, Douglas Kinnaird (Byron's legal representative), and the representatives of Byron's half-sister and his estranged wife. The majority insisted that, for the future dignity of the Byron family as well as of the dead poet's name, there was no other possible course than to burn the manuscript. Moore protested, but in vain. On May 17, 1824, in the presence of six witnesses, the manuscript, along with a copy which Moore had made, was ceremoniously thrown into the fire at Murray's house in Albemarle Street.

While the ashes of Byron's memoirs were still smoldering Moore signed a statement that, to the best of his knowledge, no copy had been made of the manuscript except the one that had just been burned; and Murray made another affidavit stating that no copy had been taken after he had bought it from Moore. That seemed to dispose of the matter. But not all scholars have been satisfied. In 1854 Dr. Shelton Mackenzie, who had been in a position to hear the gossip at the time, asserted that Lady Blessington, one of Byron's close friends, had copied every word, but when Moore remonstrated with her she burned her copy—not telling him that her sister also had a transcript. He felt fairly certain that at least five different copies had been made by persons to whom Moore had lent the original. Furthermore, exactly a month after the burning, Washington Irving, then staying at Moore's house at Sloperton, wrote in his diary that he sat up late reading Byron's memoirs! It may be, of course, that this was a slip of the pen, and that what Irving really meant to say was that he was reading Byron's journal, which Moore later published in his life of the poet. But it is strange, to say the least, that we should have two independent reports suggesting that copies of the manuscript were in existence after the episode of Murray's fireplace.

Byron scholars feel that the discovery of one of these copies, although itself enough to create a sensation, would not be as important from the point of view of literary biography as some might expect. Presumably the information the memoir contained is known to us through other sources, such as Byron's inimitable letters. But there is still the remote chance—despite Moore's specific denial—that it might help clarify the most controversial passage in Byron biography, that of the precise circumstances surrounding his separation from his wife.

If the scholar's hope of finding a transcript of a destroyed document is frail, how much more so is his hope of finding the original! Destruction by fire is irrevocable; unlike the phoenix, paper when it has been reduced to ashes remains ashes. But scholars, in whose breasts hope springs eternal, face evidence that the material they seek has been destroyed and examine it with a critical eye. Who says it has been destroyed? Is he in a position to know? From whom did he learn of the destruction? May he have had some ulterior motive for his statement—for example, the desire to put investigators off the scent? By no means all first-rank scholars have consistently asked such questions in the past. That is one reason why the fabulous Boswell papers lay hidden for so long; the stories, repeated through the nineteenth century, that they had perished were never really questioned. Actually, the stories stemmed only from hearsay, or represented a careless generalization from the fact that a certain few of the Boswell papers had been burned. The dramatic discoveries at Malahide and Fettercairn have made modern scholars skeptical of all stories relating to the destructive elements. Yet they have not learned their lesson completely. For many years, students of the late eighteenth century wished to see the original diary of Fanny Burney, the vivacious novelist and pet of the later Johnsonian circle, only portions of which have been printed. Virtually all the present-day experts were sure it was lost, and when one more skeptical than the rest wrote to the wife of the last known owner, she replied that it was lost when her husband's house burned in 1919. Yet in the past few years a large part of that diary has turned up in the Owen D. Young Collection in the New York Public Library!

But I do not mean to end this chapter on so hopeful a note. For every "lost" manuscript that is miraculously recovered, ten thousand are gone forever. In the dark watches of the night, the insomniac scholar who has nothing better to occupy his mind can review the countless episodes which have deprived the world of literary knowledge. He can think of all the fires in libraries rich in literary treasure; not merely the Cottonian, but, for instance, the *three* (in 1813, 1825, and 1851) that gutted the Library of Congress—the last one ruining most of the fine personal library of Thomas Jefferson. He can think of the pillaging by British soldiers of the pioneer library of Thomas Prince at Old South Church, Boston (twenty-five years later a tiny memento of that event, a fragment of Governor Bradford's letter book, turned up in a grocer's shop in Nova Scotia). He can think of the Second World War and the havoc it wrought to Britain's libraries: fifty-nine totally destroyed and twice as many badly damaged, including the Guildhall Library, the Inner Temple, Lambeth Palace, Goldsmiths' College, Gray's Inn; and the British Museum losing a quarter-million volumes alone. He can think of the British Museum's newspaper warehouse in a suburb of London, crammed with irreplaceable files of eighteenth- and nineteenth-century journals. On October 20, 1940, it was bombed out, and for three days thereafter the exposed ruins were drenched with rain, with the result that some 30,000 volumes of newspapers were destroyed.*

* There were compensations. Five nights before the newspaper warehouse was bombed out, a bomb fell on the headquarters of the London Stationers' Company. Apart from destroying a portrait of the wife of Samuel Richardson, the blast did little damage. But it shook loose from a place of hiding a mass of valuable documents on the history of English printing and publishing from the seventeenth to the nineteenth century—material whose very existence nobody had ever suspected.

Or our wakeful scholar can think of the many millions of books and private papers which were given to the salvage drives during the war, and wonder how many rare or unique items were passed on to the hungry pulp mills without their value being recognized. In 1943 it was reported that from the salvage piles of Britain had been culled many first editions of Dickens, Thackeray, and other authors prized by collectors. There will never be an accounting of the equally rare items that were overlooked and, above all, of the collections of family papers, full of possible biographical significance, that went unheeded to the mills.

Or he can fancy himself present on the countless occasions upon which the owner of literary manuscripts in the nineteenth century was waited upon by an autograph collector. The gracious owner riffles through a sheaf of letters from, say, Tennyson or Scott. "Here's a fine-looking signature," he exclaims. "Would this do?" And he takes his library shears and cuts an oblong piece from the sheet, and crumples the rest of the letter into a ball and thrusts it into the waste-basket. . . . Charles Cowden Clarke cut the manuscript of Keats's "I Stood Tiptoe upon a Little Hill" into thirteen separate fragments to gratify souvenir hunters.

Or our scholar, tossing feverishly in his bed, can think of the times that the descendants of great writers moved from one house to another, and, after a glorious housecleaning, consigned all their unwanted books and old papers to a fire in the yard, or called in the waste-paper dealer. A hundred years ago George Brinley, a collector of rare Americana, had a standing arrangement with paper mills near his home that he might go through their incoming shipments before they were pulped. His granddaughter vividly remembered the rainy day when the family came home and found that one of the mills had dumped a wagonload of old books in the front yard. They were furious, but he plunged into the soggy pile and emerged with a rare Indian Bible.

Or he can think of the winter day in Washington, after the first Battle of Bull Run, when the space under the front square of the Capitol, which had been used for storing the government archives, was cleared out in preparation for the billeting of soldiers. A long line of sleighs, laden with the archives of seventy years, wound down through the streets to the Potomac. A gust of wind tore a few sheets loose from one bundle, and a curious bystander, catching them, found they were letters signed by Washington, Hancock, and Jefferson. How many documents written by the statesmen who were also the founders of our national literature perished on that cold day?

Or he can think of the experiences of men of his own generation and profession. For example, of that of Professor James R. Sutherland of Queen Mary College, London, who during the Second World War was called in by a London bookseller to examine a file of *Queen Anne's Weekly Journal* (1735–38)—a periodical completely unrecorded in the bibliographies and unknown to the specialists. The bookseller told him that he had already sold the file to an American university library, to which he was posting it that very week. Sutherland protested, for the German U-boats were then at the height of their power, but the bookseller was undisturbed; nothing he had sent across the Atlantic had yet been lost, he said, and anyway the shipment was insured. Sutherland spent the afternoon making notes on the newspaper's contents. Then the file was sent to the Post Office, and, as things turned out, to its doom—for the ship which carried it was torpedoed. Thus perished, almost on the day of its discovery, the only known file of *Queen Anne's Weekly Journal;* and the only information about it which is preserved is that which the prescient Sutherland noted down during a few hours' study.

But at least, our scholar can reflect, Sutherland was better off than Howard Lowry, the specialist in Victorian literature who is now president of the College of Wooster. Lowry, visiting London before the war, became acquainted with a banker who lived in the same hotel in which he was staying. The banker was in the habit of speaking about George Meredith, though never as Meredith the novelist and poet. When Lowry had got to know him sufficiently well, he asked the banker why he was so fascinated by Meredith. "Meredith," the Londoner replied, "after his first unsuccessful marriage wanted to wed the woman who later became my mother-in-law. Her family thought his talents were more literary than domestic and discouraged the match. But Meredith always remained her devoted friend and the friend of my wife; he wrote my wife a long letter on our wedding day. I'm sorry that we didn't talk of this before. Just three weeks ago in that very fireplace I burned some seventy-five of Meredith's letters—they took up room, you know. Anyhow, they would not have interested you very much, for they were just personal letters!"

SHADES OF MRS. GRUNDY

IN Thomas Morton's popular play first performed in 1798, *Speed the Plough*, appears a character whose name has passed into the common tongue. "Appears" is not quite accurate, because, like Harvey the rabbit, she never is visible. But if she is not present in the flesh, her existence is never forgotten. "What will Mrs. Grundy say?" is the constant anxious query of the on-stage characters. The phrase caught on, so that a century and a half later, Mrs. Grundy's name is still invoked as the symbol of conventional propriety.

The fact that Mrs. Grundy made her debut as early as 1798 reminds us of the error in the common assumption that prudery—bourgeois morality carried to absurdity—was a creation of the Victorian era. As Professor Maurice J. Quinlan has shown in his interesting book, *Victorian Prelude*, a strong movement toward the reformation of manners, morals, and speech was on foot long before the close of the eighteenth century, which we commonly account to have been, morally speaking, a most easy-going age. Now that we can read for ourselves the great sheaves of notes which Boswell made of Dr. Johnson's conversations, we realize that the biographer was himself an expurgator of no mean order. Time after time Boswell, preparing his copy for the printer, softened or totally excised Johnson's most embarrassingly forthright expressions. Thus, particularly under the influence of the Evangelical movement in the Church of England, people were beginning to make an art of turning away from the facts of life—and the language associated with such subject matter—long before the eighteen-year-old Victoria said, "I will be good," and received the crown of Britain.

Mrs. Grundy's name had scarcely begun to be current in common speech before a flesh-and-blood Mr. Grundy appeared on the English scene. His real name, Bowdler, has also become part of our everyday language in the form of the verb "Bowdlerize." It was Thomas Bowdler, you remember, who applied his peculiar talents to a thorough cleansing of the text of Shakespeare, and later of Gibbon's *Decline and Fall of the Roman Empire*, so that no one among the increasing reading public of the early nineteenth century had to fear being corrupted in his cozy armchair by an accidental encounter with a coarse word or an even faintly seductive idea. Bowdler's exertions in behalf of public morality were so well received that he had a host of imitators all through the century, who took it upon themselves (at a nice profit) to strain out the indelicacies from all the standard authors who required such a service. These expurgated versions of the classics were intended mainly for schoolrooms and for that sacred Victorian institution, the family reading circle; but even editions intended for the use of serious students often were purged of offensive matter. What is still the standard edition of Pepys's diary, that of Henry B. Wheatley, is somewhat purified, as every. reader knows who has execrated the recurrent three-dot sign of editorial omission.

If there had been no prudery in the nineteenth century, the task of the modern literary scholar would be easier—but far less entertaining. I have spoken elsewhere of the way in which the Victorian descendants and biographers of men of letters energetically suppressed facts about them which did not fit into the prevalent finicky framework of morality or "good taste." The two most notorious cases, those of Burns and Hawthorne, deserve our particular attention. Neither man—the one living at a time when the cloak was only beginning to be drawn about the inconvenient circumstance that human beings have bodies and bodily urges, the other the citizen of an age when that obscurantism was full-blown—was himself a prude. But the manuscripts they left fell within a few years into the hands of the most strait-laced of editors. What Burns and Hawthorne would have said had they been able to read the first printings of their letters and papers, is matter for amusing speculation. Because they were full-blooded men, they would doubtless bestow a heartfelt blessing upon the recent scholars who, exploding the myth that they were as proper as their descendants, have at last restored them to the world of human beings.

The first editor of Burns's letters, Dr. James Currie, was a bowdlerizer even before Bowdler. In his book, published in 1800 for the benefit of the poet's widow and children, Currie frankly stated that his printed pages often did not report exactly what Burns had written: "It has been found necessary to mutilate many of the individual letters, and sometimes to exscind parts of great delicacy—the unbridled effusions of panegyric and regard." But those were not the only unbridled effusions which Currie "exscinded." Burns was capable on occasion of vigorous Anglo-Saxon prose, but Currie was a squeamish and pedantic soul; so throughout the letters, whenever the poet's phraseology was too vivid for the doctor, it was toned down to a neutral, blameless gray. Burns had been uninhibited in his expression of liberal political and religious views; Currie was a conservative of conservatives. Hence whenever Burns uttered a sentiment abhorrent to the doctor, it was silently suppressed. The result, of course, was a thoroughly emasculated Burns.*

Currie's successors among Burns editors and biographers shared his sins and cultivated a few of their own. They had no compunction about taking passages from several letters, written many months apart and to different correspondents, and printing them as a single letter. If, in their admiration for Burns the poet, they found it necessary for the peace of their consciences to regard the man as a pillar of respectable society, they omitted all the evidence in his letters of healthy animal appetites which he indulged as fully as he was able. If, on the other hand, they were convinced that he was a disreputable rake, they embellished their accounts of him with largely unsupported legends and innuendoes. Which procedure was the more reprehensible—the erection of a factitious plaster saint or the prudery-in-reverse by which the unco guid magnified the scandal in Burns's life in order piously to deplore it—is an open question.

Robert Chambers, a member of the former school of editors, in printing many hitherto unpublished letters of Burns, cut out everything which even faintly suggested blasphemy or impropriety. When-

* For further details on Currie, see pp. 257–258.

ever he found Burns writing "damn" he quickly softened the word to "curse"; and he must have had a bout with his sensibilities before he allowed even "curse" to stand. A later editor in 1877, taking posthumous control of the poet's pen where he wrote to his friend Robert Cleghorn that if bawdry "be the sin against the Haly Ghaist, I am the most offending soul alive," substituted a remark about "the special sin never-to-be-forgiven in this world nor in that which is to come," the preciousness of which would have made Burns shudder.

Only gradually did the high-handed behavior of these nineteenth-century editors come to the attention of critical scholars. That event had to await the flow of the original manuscripts from private owners (who held more than four-fifths of them no more than a generation ago) to public collections, where scholars could at last compare them with the printed versions. The havoc the scholars discovered in the manuscripts appalled them as much as Burns's blunt outspokenness had appalled the early editors. Probably the most notable culprit was none of the men who had ushered new material into print but Mrs. M'Lehose ("Clarinda"), to whom the poet had addressed a series of high-flown love letters. She treasured his letters long after Burns's death, and showed them to friends so often that she wore them literally into tatters; but she also took pains to ink over most of the proper names, snip out addresses (thus mutilating the text on the other side), and apply eradicating chemicals to the passages which seemed to reflect more passion than, in her mature years, she could bear to contemplate.

Not only Mrs. M'Lehose, however, was guilty. A number of other persons who possessed original letters of Burns applied the scissors to them, so that many now look like lacework valentines. The passages which were cut out are, presumably, lost forever. But most of those which were merely inked over can be restored. They turn out to be snatches of bawdy song, or even such remarks, innocent enough to a later generation, as the frank avowal that "I am . . . nettled with the fumes of wine" and the observation that "Urbani has told a damned falsehood." In a letter now in the Library of Congress Burns reports that life in Edinburgh has followed its usual course, "houses building, bucks strutting, ladies flaring, blackguards sculking, whores leering." But hiding the last two words of the passage is the slip of paper an earlier owner of the letter pasted over them in just the manner in which Christina Rossetti hid from her sight, as she read Swinburne's *Atalanta in Calydon,* the horrifying allusion to "the supreme evil, God."

Only one edition of Burns's letters, that by Professor DeLancey Ferguson, prints their texts from the original manuscripts wherever these are available; every other edition—and there are many—is blighted by the work of the purifiers. That is why we are only now beginning to arrive at a true conception of the poet's character. On the one hand, as Professor Ferguson has remarked, we have the denatured Burns of the mutilated, expurgated letters which have been current in print for so long; on the other, the Burns whose fairly heroic propensities for drinking and wenching, though authentic enough, were further magnified by the salacious tongues of the righteous. Neither is the true Burns, who "was neither a Galahad nor the raffish scamp of the oral tradition, but, in his own phrase, 'a frail, backsliding mortal merely.' "

In 1853 Nathaniel Hawthorne, the newly appointed American consul at Liverpool, dined with two of Burns's sons, both of whom had been officers in the Indian Army. It was a memorable occasion for Hawthorne, a great admirer of Burns; four years later, indeed, he made a pilgrimage through the Burns country he was to describe in a chapter of *Our Old Home.* His diary records that after dinner, over the assorted wines and cigars, one of the sons "spoke with vast indignation of a recent edition of his father's works by Robert Chambers; in which the latter appears to have wronged the poet by some misstatements." It is one of the ironies of literary history that the very diary containing this entry was itself destined to undergo expurgation more drastic even than that which Burns's papers suffered at the hands of Chambers and his fellows. One wonders if Hawthorne, hearing the younger Burns fulminate over his father's betrayal at the hands of his editors, uttered a silent prayer that his own private papers—the chief key to posterity's understanding of his character—would meet a kinder fate. If he did, the prayer was not to be heeded for eighty years.

The diary of 1853 was one of a long series of notebooks in which Hawthorne kept a full account of what he did through the many years, the people he saw, the sights that interested him. A few years after his death in 1864, his widow published "passages" from these notebooks, first serially in the *Atlantic Monthly* and later in six volumes. Since it was soon recognized that much of the material in the notebooks had been drawn upon by Hawthorne in his novels, stories, and essays, the published volumes became of first importance to those interested in tracing the way in which he had transformed the raw stuff of daily observation into finished works of literature. While one or two critics thought they detected some difference between the style of the printed notebooks and that of the books which Hawthorne himself had seen through the press, everyone else seems to have accepted Mrs. Hawthorne's statement that she had "transcribed the manuscripts just as they were left, without making any new arrangement or altering any sequence—merely omitting some passages, and being especially careful to preserve whatever could throw any light upon his character."

Nothing could be further from the truth, as Professor Randall Stewart, now of Brown University, discovered when he began to compare the manuscript volumes of the English and American notebooks, in the Pierpont Morgan Library, with Mrs. Hawthorne's editions. Everywhere in the manuscripts he found words and whole passages which she had inked out, and many more which, though not obliterated, were silently omitted when she prepared the printer's copy. The number of separate excisions runs far into the thousands.

A first hasty comparison of the manuscripts with the printed texts of the notebooks convinced Stewart that he had uncovered proof that the prevailing estimate of Hawthorne the man, necessarily based upon the printed volumes alone, was gravely distorted. Simple justice to Hawthorne's memory required that the full text of the manuscripts be given to the world. He therefore copied out the whole of the English and American notebooks as Hawthorne had written them, trying to restore every eradicated passage by seizing upon clues provided by the context or by the beginnings or ends of words which Mrs. Hawthorne had imperfectly inked out. She had, he soon discovered, anticipated the eventual attempt to decipher what she preferred later generations never to know; for in addition to making a solid blot through the body of the word, she had supplied dots, crosses, and projections above and below the line in order to mislead the prying investigator into reading words which were never there. But Stewart obstinately refused to be misled; so far as his sharp eyes and his ingenious reconstructing mind could do so, he repaired her damage and, in 1932 and 1941, printed for the first time the true text of the notebooks.

What had Mrs. Hawthorne sought to conceal about her husband? Despite her statement that she had been at pains to preserve "whatever could throw any light upon his character," she had sedulously eliminated everything which would suggest to the world of the late 1860's that Nathaniel Hawthorne had been a man with normal appetites and a candid eye for all aspects of the human scene about him. The full roster of her excisions—accomplished, it should be added, under the constant advice of James T. Fields, the editor of the *Atlantic Monthly*—is possibly the most comprehensive index we have of the incredible prudery and false elegance of American Victorianism.

In addition to following the eighteenth-century habit of substituting the colorless general, or literary, term for the "vulgar" specific one (*puddle* was turned into *pool, smelt* into *perceived, sprawled* into *sat, scabby* into *defaced*) and amending Hawthorne's honest American idioms to suit New England parlor tastes (*soft soap* became *praise, boozy* became *intoxicated, a little shrimp of a man* became *a little man, eatable* became *edible*), she had expunged every "indelicate" word her husband ever wrote down in his notebooks. *Bosom* was uncompromisingly deleted every time it appeared, even though on one occasion the bosom was that of an Egyptian mummy. So, of course, was the unthinkable, unspeakable *strumpet.* The *bottoms* of chairs, by an extraordinarily nice verbal distinction, were transformed into *seats.* The word *bed* had an evil connotation, and so Hawthorne's matter-of-fact record that he *got into bed* was copied by his widow as *composed myself to sleep.* Other emendations, selected from the hundreds of the kind which Stewart found, include:

Venus, naked and asleep, in a most lascivious posture, altered to *Venus*

bellies, to *bodies* or *rotundity*

baggage, to *luggage*

mess, to *dish*

of that kidney, to *of that class*

wet his trowsers, to *was wetted*

itch, to *fancy*

caught an idea by the tail, to *caught an idea by the skirts*

being once on my legs, to *being once started* (to make an after-dinner speech)

plague, to *tease* or *annoy*

In the English notebooks especially, the novelist, with his ceaseless concern for storing up potentially useful detail, had written down many frank observations on the people, some of them celebrated, whom he met. Mrs. Hawthorne entirely cut out many of these revealing vignettes. Not until Stewart's editions were published did the world know that when Hawthorne saw them, neither Stephen A. Douglas nor Alfred Tennyson was conspicuous for cleanliness of linen; or that a lady beside whom he sat at dinner "had a great pimple on one side of her nose"; or that Harriet Lane, James Buchanan's niece, wore a gown that was "terribly low across the shoulders." The bald head of the Duke of Cambridge, the cockney speech of a minor poet, Bulwer-Lytton's fervent wish that "somebody would invent a new Sin, that I might go in for it"—all were excised by the vigilant Mrs. Hawthorne.

She was no less systematic when it came to direct self-revelations of her husband's personal tastes and temperament. His detailed descriptions of sordid or macabre events, or of scenes in the slums of Liverpool, were either omitted entirely or watered down to innocuousness—an interest in such things obviously did not become a great artist. His confessions that he suffered from "natural indolence" were not allowed to stand. When he recorded that he enjoyed mutton chops or beefsteak for dinner, Mrs. Hawthorne allowed him only tea. His frequent outspoken opinions on this matter and that, such as points of religious doctrine or the inferiority of British ways to American, were sacrificed in order that his notebooks might reveal him as perched on an Olympus too lofty to be concerned with the affairs of mortal men. Although he had a healthy taste for fermented and distilled beverages, his appreciative references to them (as well as his allusion to an occasion on which he was "pot-valiant with champagne") were not tolerated. Nor, even, were his cigars. Nor was his reference to "Tom Taylor, who had a very pretty wife with him"—Mrs. Hawthorne, refusing to preserve for posterity the image of a distinguished novelist with a genially appreciative eye for feminine charms, reduced the passage to the bleak "Mr. Taylor." All in all, she did a magnificently thorough job of divesting her late husband of his earthly garments and presenting him to the world as the archetype of the artist-dreamer, all spirit and no flesh to speak of.

Numerous though Stewart's restorations in his editions are, they are not complete. Try as he would, often he could not pierce beneath Mrs. Hawthorne's heavy ink, and he had to admit that fact in notes. Subsequently, the use of infrared light on pages that defied him has enabled technicians at the Pierpont Morgan Library to solve more than half of the remaining riddles. One of the most interesting passages thus revealed is dated August 1, 1851, when Hawthorne records that he has entertained Herman Melville at his home at Lenox, Massachusetts: "Melville and I had a talk about time and eternity, things of this world and of the next, and books, and publishers, and all possible and impossible matters, that lasted pretty deep into the night . . ." Mrs. Hawthorne, bridling at the rest of the sentence, sternly inked it out; but the infrared lamp has brought it back: "and if truth must be told, we smoked cigars even within the sacred precincts of the sitting room"! A trivial point, perhaps, but a revealing one; for biographers have always assumed that the relations between the two great artists were rather stiff. Melville and Hawthorne might have talked loftily and long of time and eternity, but the evidence hitherto available has not suggested that they were on easy personal terms. The fact that they dared to smoke their cigars in Mrs. Hawthorne's holy of holies, however, throws a new light on their relationship. They may have been philosophical conversationalists, but it is a closer bond that unites partners in domestic crime.

Mrs. Hawthorne's editorial exertions were not confined to the notebooks by any means. In the Huntington Library rest 164 letters which Hawthorne wrote to her, most of them before their marriage. Some time after his death, like Burns's Clarinda, she went through them not only with an ever-ready pen but also with a pair of scissors. It is estimated that about five thousand words of Hawthorne's intimate confidences to his bride-to-be were snipped out and thus lost forever. If one reads as much as can be read of the letters with the unaided eye, Hawthorne appears as an adoring lover and husband—on an exclusively ethereal plane. But when the obliterated passages, some 150 of them, are placed under the microscope and the infrared lamp, another side of Hawthorne as a lover is revealed. In the passages which Mrs. Hawthorne inked out, time after time he speaks frankly and naturally of his love for her as a flesh-and-blood woman. There are numerous avowals of the physical desire which underlay his spiritual devotion. Presumably Mrs. Hawthorne, while her husband lived, delighted in playing the double role of angel and earthly wife; but after his death she chose, understandably enough perhaps, to be remembered only in the first capacity. In deleting all of her husband's candid references to their fleshly love, however, she bequeathed to later generations an unfairly one-sided conception of him.

The total effect of the examination of Hawthorne's original manuscripts, then, has been a radically revised impression of the man. He was far more "human," in the widest and best sense of the word, than we once were allowed to think. Supposedly everyone would have welcomed this restoration to literary history of Hawthorne the human being. But one man at least, the Hawthornes' own son Julian, was incensed. When the publishers of Stewart's edition of the *American Notebooks* gave the press a somewhat sensationalized account of his discoveries, Julian Hawthorne, then an old man living in California, was sought out by the reporters. He was only too glad to give them an interview, and they were only too glad to print it; for he assured them that if he were a young man he would like nothing more than to horsewhip Randall Stewart. "I was fairly safe," Stewart says, "by virtue of his age and three thousand miles, so I made no rejoinder. One would have thought, though, that he might have thanked me for taking the petticoats off his father."

POST-MORTEMS

I

POETS and prose writers alike have been a notoriously sickly lot. Pope was a hunchback and a lifelong semi-invalid. The vigorous George Meredith, who once loved to lead his panting friends on a thirty-mile hike of a Sunday, was reduced to pitiful helplessness by locomotor ataxia. Matthew Arnold had angina pectoris which killed him one day as he was running to catch a tram in Liverpool, ironically the victim of the "sick hurry" of modern life which he so bitterly denounced in his most famous poems. Algernon Swinburne, the orange-haired, green-eyed *enfant terrible* of Victorian poetry, fell in epileptiform seizures in public places like the British Museum. He, indeed, has the distinction of being one of the few English poets ever to take the cure. In 1879, when it was painfully obvious that alcoholism was going to kill him if nothing else did, his lawyer, Theodore Watts (Watts-Dunton) carried him off to a suburban retreat. By firm rationing, and by tactful though not necessarily scholarly references to the drinking habits of men whom he admired, Swinburne was weaned from the brandy bottle and brought eventually to the point where he was quite content with a single bottle of Bass's ale for lunch.*

* "As far as Algernon was concerned," wrote Watts-Dunton's young wife, "he simply gave up brandy because Tennyson drank port, and changed from port to burgundy because that was the tipple of Dumas's immortal Musketeers. Then for an equally good reason he proceeded to claret, and, finally, as it was Shakespeare's drink, to beer." Sir Edmund Gosse, an intimate of Swinburne for many years, branded the tale "preposterous"; but it is well known that there was more than a little friction between him and Watts-Dunton, and in any event, it is the sort of story that disarms skepticism.

But though the seizures disappeared, and along with them, many said, Swinburne's poetic gifts, Watts-Dunton was never able to do anything about the uncontrollable fluttering of his charge's hands and the dancing of his tiny feet when excited—a form of St. Vitus' dance.

As we come to understand more and more of the intricate relationship of body and brain, the pathology so often involved in literary biography grows increasingly important in our efforts to understand the mental states, the obscure psychological motivations, which underlie the creative process. It has long been a commonplace of criticism that the memorable gruffness of Thomas Carlyle's personal manner and the unceasing vehemence of his literary style had at least a part of their origin in his sick body. His famous "dyspepsia" (which today we should probably diagnose as ulcers), his insomnia, his abnormal sensitivity to disturbing sounds, must be taken into account in any attempt to explain him. His wife's case—for Jane cannot be omitted from any consideration of Thomas—is no less interesting. She was as neurasthenic as he, but why? Had her miseries a basis in sexual maladjustment, or in her bitter childlessness? Or did they result from her having had to sacrifice her own proud intellectual ambitions to those of her husband? For over sixty years the biographers have argued such questions.

And any gallery of neurasthenic Victorian ladies must include Elizabeth Barrett, who during her years on that celebrated couch in Wimpole Street became by common agreement the finest female poet ever to write in English. (Christina Rossetti was still unknown.) She had an old back injury, sustained in a fall from a horse when she was a young girl, and she suffered from tuberculosis and the incredibly misguided treatment of her doctors, which consisted principally in dosing her with laudanum and forbidding her the least breath of fresh air. A modern psychiatrist would guess that in addition she was suffering from a sort of hysteria, induced by the ruthless tyranny of her father. She had the most marvelous recovery in literary annals: within a year after Robert Browning took her to Italy, she was climbing mountains with him. All this has its literary relevance. If she had not been the woman she was, illnesses and all, she would not have written the sort of poetry she did—nor would her husband's work have been the same. There can be little doubt that the joy of his wife's miraculously regained health communicated itself to Browning's own art; it was hardly a coincidence that he wrote many of his very finest poems during their fifteen years of marriage.

In recent years many scholars and critics have tried to solve long-standing riddles of literary biography with the aid of medical knowledge. Sometimes they have not even had to call in expert diagnosticians; the record is written plain in the letters and other personalia of the poet. For example, one of the most lamentable chapters in literary history is Wordsworth's so-called "anticlimax," the forty long years of dull versifying which followed the miraculous decade in which most of his lasting poetry was written. What caused this miserable decline of his genius? A British scholar, Professor Edith C. Batho, has argued that one clue may be found in Wordsworth's failing eyesight—a particularly heavy handicap in the case of a poet whose best work owes so much of its effect to the loving felicity of its visual descriptions. Evidently the inward eye which he said was the bliss of solitude was not enough. But whether we accept Miss Batho's theory or not, we can find in the six large volumes of the family letters abundant evidence that physical and mental ailments must have played their part in drying up the springs of Wordsworth's inspiration. He suffered from hemorrhoids in addition to eye trouble; five times in seven years his wife underwent the unpleasant complications of pregnancy; his sister Dorothy lapsed into permanent insanity; his daughter Catharine was partially paralyzed. Although it is true that genius sometimes has triumphed over such a dismal array of circumstances, the fair-minded will admit that they do offer their problems when one is dedicated to writing poetry that praises the benevolence of nature.

Any mention of eye trouble among poets inevitably raises the problem of Milton's blindness. Many readers of Milton feel that the extraordinary splendor of the descriptions in *Paradise Lost*, and the frequency of images of light and dark, can be traced in part at least to the fact that the poem was composed by a man who had become blind. Why did Milton lose his sight? His enemies ascribed his tragedy to God's heavy hand laid on a sinner. In modern times Milton study has spawned a fair number of the fantastic theories which are the inevitable accompaniment of fame. A quarter of a century ago, one Heinrich Mutschmann announced the view that the greatest English epic poet was both a degenerate and an albino, the albinism serving, of course, to account for his eye trouble. Needless to say, this unattractive hypothesis did not gain many adherents. But at the same time an eminent French Miltonist, Denis Saurat, in a detailed study of "Milton devant la médicine," contributed the theory that Milton's blindness was caused by congenital syphilis.

Milton's case is unusual in medico-literary annals because of the fairly large amount of relevant contemporary evidence which has come down to us. He himself left a number of statements describing the symptoms attending the progressive degeneration of his eyesight, and several of his friends set down their own observations of his difficulties and of the appearance of his eyes. Therefore the modern medical man interested in making a post-mortem diagnosis has a good supply of data to work with. In 1933 W. H. Wilmer, of the Ophthalmological Institute at Johns Hopkins University, published a fascinating article written in the form of a clinical case record, complete with details of the patient's family history, his own past history, the stages of his disease, and so on. He even constructed "hypothetical charts of Milton's visual fields from 1643 to 1652." He carefully considered all the earlier explanations of Milton's blindness—albinism, detachment of the retina, congenital syphilis, myopia and its complications, cataract, and chronic glaucoma. Only the last explanation seemed to him to be valid. In the course of his own wide professional experience in treating diseases of the eye, he had encountered many patients complaining of the same subjective and objective symptoms he found in Milton's case record, and nearly all of these patients had proved to have chronic glaucoma ("with," he cautiously added, "perhaps a few patches of choroidoretinitis"). As for the underlying cause of this condition, Dr. Wilmer suggested that it might have been the recurrent emotional disturbances of Milton's active life, which had affected his vasomotor system. This cause-and-effect connection between emotional disturbance and glaucoma he had frequently observed in his own patients.

Plausible though Dr. Wilmer's diagnosis was, it was not universally accepted. At the very time he was conducting his own examination of Milton's case, Eleanor Gertrude Brown, a candidate for the doctorate in English literature at Columbia University, was making an independent attempt to solve the mystery. Miss Brown, who was herself blind, referred Saurat's theory of congenital syphilis to a number of eminent American dermatologists, who were almost unanimous in rejecting it. She then consulted leading ophthalmologists associated with medical schools and hospitals. After considering the evidence she presented—essentially the body of data with which Wilmer worked—they disagreed. Although the majority joined Wilmer in favoring glaucoma as the most likely disease, some good authorities preferred to diagnose Milton's disease as myopia and detachment of the retina. Miss Brown, perhaps remembering Pope's line, "Who shall decide when doctors disagree?" concluded that unless new information is discovered, the cause of Milton's blindness must remain an unsettled question.

During the very years when the blind Milton was dictating the last books of *Paradise Lost* to his amanuensis, a very different sort of man only a mile or two away, in the "closet" of his home hard by the Navy Office, was writing away at a very different sort of work—a work, however, which he never anticipated would one day be looked upon as literature. Two years after *Paradise Lost* was published, Samuel Pepys wrote these moving last words in his diary:

And thus ends all that I doubt I shall ever be able to do with my own eyes in the keeping of my Journal, I being not able to do it any longer, having done now so long as to undo my eyes almost every time that I take a pen in my hand. . . . And so I betake myself to that course, which is almost as much as to see myself go into my grave; for which, and all the discomforts that will accompany my being blind, the good God prepare me!

Although Pepys's alarm proved groundless, and he was to live for many years in full possession of his eyesight, it was the end of the incomparable diary. The nature of his trouble in 1669 therefore is of some interest to literary history. A half-century or more ago, Sir D'Arcy Power, a distinguished medical man and a passionate Pepysian, looked into Pepys's case just as Dr. Wilmer was to look into Milton's. Thanks to Pepys's many detailed descriptions of his symptoms, he was able not only to diagnose the trouble as farsightedness—"hypermetropia with some degree of astigmatism," resulting in severe eyestrain—but even to prescribe the lenses which would have corrected the condition. "For Samuel Pepys, Esq.," he wrote: "Spectacles: + 2 D.c. + 0.50 D. cyl. axis 90°." He even had such a pair of glasses made up by a Birmingham optician! But, though they would have saved the day for a nineteenth-century Pepys, spectacles made to this prescription would not have been available in Pepys's own time, simply because the doctors were unable to diagnose his disease for what it was. Astigmatism was not described as such until the beginning of the nineteenth century. Lacking the knowledge that would have enabled them to fit him with the proper glasses, his doctors recommended instead that he look through a pair of long leather or paper tubes when he was reading or writing. Though they helped a little at first, the tubes were of little use in the long run. But, as Sir D'Arcy observed regretfully, if Pepys had accidentally sat upon them, or squeezed them flat in his hands, he might have gone on writing his diary indefinitely; for if their apertures had been oblong rather than round they would have had roughly the same effect as modern corrective spectacles.

Eyestrain was, of couse, only one of the many physical discomforts Pepys endured. No reader of the diary can fail to be impressed by the transcendent importance of health to Pepys himself. Day after day he recorded his current symptoms and the effects of the often drastic remedies his medical advisers prescribed. (How completely different in their effect upon the reader, by the way, are Pepys's and Wordsworth's frequent recitals of their physical woes! Pepys would not be Pepys without them—they add the last necessary touch to his wonderful self-portrait—but in Wordsworth they are downright embarrassing.) The most valuable portion of Sir D'Arcy Power's essay on Pepys's general health, contributed to the *Lancet* in 1895, was that which offered a medical man's explanation for the abnormally strong sexual cravings of the diarist. Much of Pepys's celebrated incontinence, he suggested, was traceable to the equally celebrated operation which he underwent in his youth for the removal of a stone; the probability was that although the operation rendered temporary relief, it did some permanent injury to his genito-urinary system, which would account for both his incontinence and his childlessness. Translating the diarist's colloquial seventeenth-century English into the crisp parlance of the modern physician, Sir D'Arcy went on to reconstruct, on the basis of Pepys's own records, an actual case history of his lifelong trouble with "the stone," for which the operation in his youth had been only a palliative. In passing, he recalled the fact that Pepys always treasured the stone removed from his bladder in the famous operation—a stone which, according to his fellow diarist John Evelyn, was as large as a tennis ball. In 1664 Pepys recorded having spent twenty-four shillings for a suitable case in which to display it to his friends, sometimes in order to encourage them to undergo a similar operation. That stone, one of the most curious relics in English literary history, is now lost; apparently he failed to bequeath it, along with his manuscripts and his fine collection of rare books, to his old college at Cambridge. Perhaps, on the day when the long-lost play from which *Hamlet* was fashioned turns up, Pepys's admired bladder stone too will be found. Its discoverer will enjoy a unique reputation in the annals of literary scholarship.

We do, however, possess several relics of another literary man's disability. That Byron was crippled was a point upon which he was exquisitely sensitive. But his friends never agreed on the nature of his injury, and it has been one of the moot topics of Byron biography ever since. Contemporary witnesses were divided about evenly on the question of which foot was affected: Byron's own mother (who admittedly did not know him very well), and his friend Stendhal, the French novelist, recorded that it was his right foot; but Mrs. Leigh Hunt, the Countess Guiccioli, Byron's mistress, and Gentleman Jackson, his boxing teacher, maintained it was his left. Others, including his friends Tom Moore, John Galt, and Lady Blessington, were frankly undecided. Nor was there any more unanimity on just what was the matter with whichever foot it was; usually the deformity was spoken of as a club foot, but nobody seems to have been certain. To pile confusion on confusion, Edward Trelawny, the fabulous adventurer who accompanied the poet during his last years, wrote in 1858 that after Byron died in the swamps of Missolonghi he had duped his valet into letting him see the body. Pulling up the shroud, he had discovered that "both his feet were clubbed and his legs withered to the knee—the form and features of an Apollo with the feet and legs of a sylvan Satyr." But twenty years later Trelawny, then a man of eighty-six, republished his recollections of Byron; and in the new edition he changed his account, saying that the malformation was caused by the contraction of the Achilles tendon, which had forced the poet to walk on the forepart of his feet. "Except for this defect," he wrote, "the feet were perfect." No one knows why Trelawny, a notorious liar, altered his story, but a reasonable guess is that the first version was designed to please the popular taste of the time: "the form and features of an Apollo with the feet and legs of a sylvan Satyr" admirably epitomizes the Victorian conception of Byron. But the second seemed to come closer to the actual truth.

To the documentary evidence, furthermore, is added the conflicting testimony of actual relics. Among all the other memorabilia of the poet treasured by the publishing house of John Murray are two surgical boots made for Byron as a child. Both of them are for the right foot. But in the Nottingham Museum rests a pair of lasts upon which shoes were made for the mature Byron. These show no signs of malformation; on the contrary, the shoes made on these lasts would have fitted perfectly normal, well formed feet!

Confronted with this mass of contradictory evidence, the British surgeon H. Charles Cameron, some twenty-five years ago, tried to solve the mystery of Byron's alleged club foot. Instead of attempting to decide, at a distance of a century, which foot had been affected, he reviewed the testimony of eyewitnesses concerning Byron's manner of walking and found that at least there was a substantial agreement that he had a peculiar running or sliding gait, which suggests faulty co-ordination of the muscles. Again, Byron had often said that his injury had been caused at birth. Putting the clues together, Dr. Cameron announced his own diagnosis: Little's disease (first described forty years after Byron's death), which is a spastic paraplegia caused by the injury of the cortex at birth. Its distinguishing symptom is a clumsy habit of walking, characterized by rigidity of the foot and leg muscles and lack of coordination—the very phenomena that Byron's friends remarked upon. No outward deformation is involved, and the varying stories that Byron had such can reasonably be attributed to the all too well known fallibility of witnesses. Everyone knew there was something the matter with the way Byron walked, and attributed it to a deformity without making any close observation. The surgical boots at John Murray's can be accounted for on the hypothesis that they were designed to correct not a malformation but a malfunction of the feet.

But such a case is at best a side issue of literary biography. Medicine has rendered a far more important service in setting the record straight in the case of Robert Burns. As we see in another chapter, with the possible exception of Shakespeare, no famous figure in English literature has been the victim of so much irresponsible myth-making. Until the last twenty or thirty years, Burns biography has been a mass of unfounded gossip, mostly malicious, and half-truths; and what is still worse, it is the most reckless stories about his life that have become permanently fixed in the popular mind. According to the common notion, he was principally distinguished for his sexual exploits and his hard drinking, and the two together ushered him into an early grave.

As Franklyn Snyder remarks in his biography of the poet, there is some documentary support for the popular conception: "Though Burns's bacchanalian verse does not bulk large in quantity, it was obviously written with no mere feigned enthusiasm." The same, certainly, may be said of his amorous verse. But when we closely examine the history of Burns biography, we discover that there is no reason to believe that he was a confirmed debauchee. On the contrary, the people who knew him best during his so-called "evil days" agreed that he lived a sober, orderly life. The mischief actually began only a few years after Burns's death, when his first influential biographer, Dr. James Currie, wrote that he was "perpetually stimulated by alcohol." Every subsequent biographer seized upon the statement (there were many more to the same effect) and embroidered it in his own fashion. And why not? the later memoirists reasoned. Was not Currie, the earliest important biographer, in the best position to know the facts? But modern scholarship puts only the most cautious trust in the first biographer of a man of letters. Perhaps he did have a valuable advantage, in the access to surviving friends of the poet and to papers which later disappeared. On the other hand, what ax had he to grind? What were the pet prejudices, if any, which he allowed to color his account? Whose reputations did he feel obliged to defend, or to denigrate? Under the critical eye of scholarship, Currie turns out to be one of the least dependable and most profoundly opinionated of "source biographers." His sins as biographer are many and diverse, but only two concern us here. One is the deliberate use of biography as a vehicle for a temperance lecture. Dr. James Currie's opposition to the use of alcohol was flavored with a vehemence of which only a Scots teetotaler is capable; and it must have seemed to him foolish not to use the golden material God had given him to impress his readers with the evils of indulgence. Burns did drink—so much was known; he died young and impoverished—again undisputed; *ergo,* he was one more sad victim of the whisky habit. And that is how the whole story started.

The other sin that Currie has to answer for, so far as the myth of the poet's death is concerned, is that he set on foot the story that Burns had venereal disease. Actually the latest biographers have been unable to discover any evidence to support that allegation. On the contrary, we have it on good authority that, except for a recurrent ailment which I am about to mention, he was in generally good health during most of his life; and his wife, Jean Armour, displayed no sign of such infection.

With Currie discredited, the question remains, What *did* cause Burns's death? Within the past twenty-five years two physicians, eager to atone for the scholarly shortcomings of their long-dead colleague, independently have constructed case histories on the basis of all known evidence. The doctors, Sir James Crichton-Browne of Dumfries and Harry B. Anderson of Toronto, reached the same general conclusions. In the whole clinical record of Burns's life they found no symptoms of either alcoholism or venereal disease. Instead they detected, early in his life, symptoms which to their practiced medical minds pointed unmistakably to endocarditis induced by rheumatism. In retrospect they watched the disease reappear from time to time with increasing virulence; and on the basis of the record they could have predicted what actually happened in 1796—namely, the endocarditis became acute, and caused the patient's death in July of that year. Thus a careful scientific post-mortem has finally exploded the vicious old canard that Burns's death was the aftermath of a chill sustained in a drunken coma.

II

EVEN without a Dr. Currie to falsify the record for his own narrow ends, many a standard biography of a literary figure preserves errors relating to the illnesses of its subject, simply because it depends upon evidence set down and gathered at a time when medicine was still as much a matter of superstition as of science. Nowadays it is becoming almost standard practice for a conscientious biographer to go to medical men for a fresh interpretation of the old facts. When, for example, Professor Gordon Ray was preparing his four-volume edition of Thackeray's correspondence, he consulted Chester M. Jones, a member of the staff of the Massachusetts General Hospital and Clinical Professor of Medicine at Harvard, for an authoritative estimate of the novelist's recurrent ill health. Dr. Jones found the evidence in the letters sufficient to "render a fairly adequate analysis quite within the realm of possibility." His diagnosis was that Thackeray suffered from an imposing variety of disorders: bad teeth, headaches, stomach and intestinal disturbances, urethral stricture (possibly caused by an earlier venereal infection), tertian malarial infection, and rheumatoid or infectious arthritis. He even accounted for Thackeray's lifelong devotion to the fleshpots on the grounds of a haunting sense of insecurity, which he never really overcame, and a domestic tragedy, the insanity of his young wife.

Since Thackeray's whole mature life was clouded by his wife's hopeless illness, Professor Ray sought out Dr. Stanley Cobb, the chief psychiatrist at the Massachusetts General Hospital, and asked him what he could make of the known facts surrounding the case. Dr. Cobb, like his colleague, found the evidence abundant enough to allow what he cautiously termed "a tentative diagnosis." He blamed heredity first of all, finding significance in the fact that Mrs. Thackeray's mother had had periods of depression following the birth of her children. Furthermore, he was impressed by the evidence of severe mental stress upon the patient at the time when she was engaged to be married to Thackeray; her mother evidently used every conceivable device to force her daughter to break off the match. But the immediate cause of Mrs. Thackeray's psychosis, in which she lived for fifty-three years, was the fact that she had had three pregnancies in quick succession. "The diagnosis," concluded Dr. Cobb, "is schizophrenia, of a type that often begins with depression and ideas of unworthiness a few weeks after childbirth."

A few celebrated works of English literature have long been supposed to owe their existence directly to a pathological condition of the mind. Perhaps the most famous of all is the fragmentary poem "Kubla Khan," which, according to Coleridge himself, was the result of an opium dream. Until very recently, his account was generally accepted; but Professor Elisabeth Schneider of Temple University has questioned whether we can thank opium at all for the unearthly splendors of Coleridge's poem. After a thorough survey of the recent medical literature on opium and its effects, she finds that there is little or no clinical evidence to support the familiar notion. Until the last twenty years, indeed, medical information depended heavily upon the classic descriptions of opium addiction found in literature, notably those of Coleridge and DeQuincey. Only now is science beginning to abandon such imaginative accounts for more reliable clinical evidence. A few things, Miss Schneider says, are already clear. One is that drug addiction is not inevitably followed by the dire moral, mental and physical consequences that are traditionally ascribed to it. Rather, the opium addict is likely to have been a highly unstable, neurotic person in the first place, and the abnormalities he exhibits are just as likely to stem from his original neuroticism as from his addiction.

Furthermore, Miss Schneider finds that the old idea that opium is remarkably productive of dreams, and that those dreams have a unique quality, has no modern substantiation. If a man is not normally a dreamer, addiction to opium will not make him one. And the special qualities that, thanks to DeQuincey's wonderful reports, are popularly associated with opium visions—the sense of floating, the endless extension of time and space, the horrible sense of fear and guilt—are frequently characteristic of non-opium dreams, especially those of neurotics. Indeed, "opium dreams" no longer appear in scientific literature. Of several hundred recent studies of dreams she has read in medical and psychological journals, not one was connected with opium; and conversely, of several hundred more studies of the effects of opium, not one alluded to "opium" dreams!

Although it is too bad that we have to set aside the romantic story of the origin of "Kubla Khan," the sober facts seem to require us to believe that, far from being the absolute cause of the poet's vision, opium simply helped put his mind in a state which made such thoughts possible. "Coleridge," Miss Schneider concludes, "was in a sort of 'Reverie,' . . . and no doubt he had been taking opium. Perhaps too the euphoric effect of opium rendered his process of composition more nearly effortless than usual. But he was wide enough awake, we must suppose, to write down his poem more or less as he composed it; and we cannot assume that the opium was the cause of the particular character of the poem."

Such a conclusion also tends to destroy the similar notion regarding the origin of the *Confessions of an Opium-Eater*. Disillusioning though it may be, the fact remains that DeQuincey had waking dreams, of the same quality as his more famous ones, long before he began to take opium. It seems likely, indeed, that we owe his magnificent flights of prose not to the effects of opium, but to the impact on his sensitive imagination of his wide reading in the Gothic novel, the tales of the German romantics, and the oriental travel books that were so popular in his formative years.

In the cases of Coleridge and DeQuincey, therefore, modern clinical knowledge has helped scholars correct the long-standing misconception of the way in which their particular kind of dream poetry and prose originated. One effect of this growth of clinical data, as I have remarked, is to release present-day medical men from the former reliance on Coleridge's and DeQuincey's accounts of opium-induced experiences. The case of another famous literary drug addict is quite different.

Dante Gabriel Rossetti, who was seldom a conformist, chose to seek relief in a drug which has few addicts, and the effects of which therefore can seldom be studied clinically. The drug was chloral hydrate, a common ingredient of mid-twentieth-century criminal "knockout drops." Happily for modern pharmacological knowledge, Rossetti was the subject of a great deal of biographical writing. Being unashamed of his addiction, he discussed it and its results freely and fully with his intimates. Some of them recorded not only his accounts, but their own observations of the effects chloral had on him. Hence, as the director of the research laboratory of a Baltimore pharmaceutical firm wrote some years ago, the records of Rossetti's experience with chloral are "the most famous and scientifically the most detailed illustration" which medical annals possess of the effects of this unusual addiction. The Rossetti data not only substantiate the information found on the subject in toxicological literature but at some points significantly supplement it.

The essential facts about Rossetti's addiction are known to every reader of his biography. He began taking chloral about 1869, as a result of his suffering from insomnia, nervous excitability, and delusions of persecution—none of which, it need hardly be remarked, was eased by the doses. (It was not until he was well advanced in his addiction, for instance, that he got to the stage at which he was able to detect outrageous personal abuse hidden in Lewis Carroll's "The Hunting of the Snark" and the latest poems of Robert Browning.) The evil taste of the chloral led him to follow each dose with a chaser of neat whisky. The result of this practice, pharmacologists tell us, was what is technically known as "synergism": the chloral and the alcohol, taken in combination, intensified each other's effects, so that the result to Rossetti's mental and physical health was far more insidious than it would have been if he had taken them separately.

Rossetti's friends differed on the exact amount of chloral he took every day, but they all agreed that it was immense. One alleged that it was twice as much as anyone else known to medical history had taken without killing himself; and it is a fact that shortly before the poet died the chemists who had been supplying the drug refused to continue sending it in the same quantities. Some years after the habit was fully established, one of Rossetti's well-meaning physicians tried to cure him by substitution therapy, diverting him from chloral to morphine. The experiment merely complicated his ills; his depression deepened, and he began to have hallucinations, such as the fancy that the soul of his dead wife, Elizabeth Siddal, had transmigrated into the body of a chaffinch he picked up one day in the garden. Nor was he unacquainted with other drugs. On one occasion he attempted suicide by swallowing a whole bottle of laudanum, the drug which had caused his wife's tragic death; on another he tried a mixture of nux vomica and strychnine. But none of these alternatives had the dire effect upon him which a steady devotion to chloral achieved.

It is no wonder, then, that present-day students of toxicology turn to the abundant Rossetti biographical materials. Rossetti himself no doubt would be pleased to know that out of the wreckage of his life a later generation had managed to salvage something of value—in addition, of course, to his poetry.

III

PROBABLY no English man of letters has been the subject of more protracted post-mortem medical study than the author of *Gulliver's Travels*. His recurrent attacks of vertigo and stomach troubles, his pathological hatred of the human race, his frequent preoccupation with animal filth, his insane last years, and perhaps above all the still unsolved mystery of his relations with "Stella" have enlisted the attention of would-be diagnosticians for a century and a half.

Like Burns and indeed almost every other literary figure whose case history was examined by early nineteenth-century medical men, Swift in the beginning of his long career as a clinical puzzle was the victim of moralizing. One of the first physicians to examine his case, Dr. Thomas Beddoes (whose book *Hygeia* had the significant subtitle *Essays Moral and Medical*), laid it down that his lifelong sickness was caused by such habits and indulgences as were once lumped together under the euphemistic but still sinister head of "early excesses." Although Sir Walter Scott indignantly denied Beddoes's theory, it died the most lingering of deaths. A generation later, in 1835, Swift earned the loving attention of the phrenologists. By a strange coincidence, at the very time that a conference of phrenologists was being held in Dublin, it was discovered that water was seeping into the crypt where he and Stella were buried. Their graves were forthwith opened, and the assembled phrenologists were able to run exploratory fingers over Swift's skull and theorize to their hearts' content. Their conclusions, however, do not detain twentieth-century scholars.

It was not until 1881 that medical scholarship got on what appears now to be the right track. The fact that Swift suffered terrible attacks of vertigo, it had long been felt, probably would provide a major key to the mystery. In 1881 the suggestion was made that the vertigo, together with some of the other recorded symptoms, pointed to Menière's disease, which was said to center around lesions of the inner ear and produce many of the symptoms that tortured Swift. This diagnosis, which was supported by reputable medical authority, held the field for the next four decades, although it was not unchallenged. One writer, for example, included Swift in a large company of literary geniuses whose aberrations could be explained· in terms of manic-depressive psychosis, while another (the indefatigable Dr. George Gould, who will reappear in a little while) found the answer in migraine headaches, caused by eyestrain. With the progress of medical knowledge in the twentieth century, Menière's disease has been recognized to be not a single disease, but a whole series, springing from varied origins. Accordingly, Rossi and Hone, who are among the most recent biographers of Swift, concluded after an exhaustive study that while his malady was essentially what had earlier been described as Menière's disease, it had its eventual seat in the stomach. From the stomach it spread, through that incredibly complicated sympathetic process which modern medicine is only beginning to understand, to the ears, and later manifested itself in such symptoms as vertigo, aphasia, slight paralysis, and lack of coordination. In any event, the old idea that Swift suffered a degeneration of the brain, such as would have been caused by syphilis, has now been rejected by doctors and scholars.

Medical authority has been used also in an attempt to throw light on Swift's curious relations with Esther Johnson, the "Stella" to whom he addressed the famous journal in baby talk. Whether or not Swift and Stella were married has plagued scholars for two full centuries. There is no sound evidence, beyond contemporary gossip, that they were; but Maxwell Gold has recently argued at length that there was a secret marriage which was not consummated, invoking the august authority of Krafft-Ebing to demonstrate that cohabitation was impossible because of Swift's (hypothetical) "sexual anesthesia"—a condition which precludes sexual feeling though it does not necessarily involve impotence. More conservative Swift students have attacked Gold's position as being precariously balanced on a hypothesis perched in turn on a conjecture; but, so long as the school of thought represented by Krafft-Ebing influences modern approaches to problems of human conduct, such explanations are likely to retain their fascination for scholars—and for general readers.

Another eighteenth-century literary figure of more than ordinary interest to the medical man is Dr. Johnson, who wrote when he was sixty-nine, "My health has been from my twentieth year, such as has seldom afforded me a single day of ease." Every reader of Boswell can recall offhand a few of the ailments that prompted Johnson's remark: the King's Evil, in the hope of curing which his parents took him as a child to receive the "royal touch"; his clumsy, rolling gait; his blindness in one eye; the convulsive (and compulsive) gestures and inarticulate exclamations and whistlings which startled so many persons on their first acquaintance with him. Some twenty years ago Sir Humphry Rolleston made a comprehensive study of Johnson's case, beginning with the record of the autopsy performed on his body in 1784. The autopsy report is studded with superlatives—as befits one of the superlative men of English literature. The medical man who wrote it seems to have been in a state of bemused wonder: one organ was "very much enlarged," another "exceedingly fat," a third "adhered very strongly" to its neighbor, a fourth was "exceedingly large and strong," a fifth was "remarkably enlarged." Johnson's gallstone was "about the size of a pigeon's egg." (Compare the size of Pepys's!)

Interpreting the details of the autopsy in terms of modern medicine, Sir Humphry concluded that basically Johnson's complaint had been "longstanding high blood pressure with subsequent renal disease (chronic interstitial nephritis), the kidneys showing an excessive degree of cystic change." Which sounds formidable enough. Sir Humphry went on to compile a full medical report. The roll of diseases from which Johnson suffered is a long one. In addition to those mentioned above (the "King's Evil" being the enlargement and tuberculous condition of the lymphatic glands in the neck), he had asthma, which probably was complicated by his diseased kidneys; dropsy; serious myopia in his one good eye; paracusia Willisii, a peculiar form of deafness characterized by the ability to hear better in the presence of noise; gastrointestinal symptoms; gout; and hemiplegia and aphasia (that is, a slight stroke which he suffered in the year before his death). In the face of such an array of diseases, it is easy to understand why Boswell stressed Johnson's "horrible hypochondria, with perpetual irritation, fretfulness, and impatience; and with a dejection, gloom, and despair, which made existence misery. . . . All his labours, and all his enjoyments, were but temporary interruptions of its baleful influence."

One of the great perplexities of the literary scholar, when he sets out to find medical evidence to illuminate his subject, is how to evaluate the authorities he consults. How much simpler things would be for him had his poet been under the care of an expert physician who left a detailed history of the case! But not every literary man has been so fortunate as Walt Whitman, whose personal physician, after he suffered three mild strokes in 1888, was none other than Dr. William Osler.* In ninety-nine cases out of a hundred, lacking any really dependable account of the case by a contemporary medical authority, the scholar must rely upon the interpretations of more recent physicians. The problem is not so serious when he personally takes his accumulated evidence to a specialist; he can, in such instances, find out what reputation the specialist has in his profession, and whether the opinion he renders is likely to agree with the latest and soundest medical

* The fact that Whitman was attended by Osler, then Professor of Clinical Medicine at the University of Pennsylvania, seems not to be widely known. Whitman himself had no inkling of his doctor's deep literary interests, but his respect for Osler as physician was immense: "He is a great man—one of the rare men. I should be much surprised if he didn't soar way up—get very famous at his trade—some day: he has the air of the thing about him—of achievement."

knowledge. But his bibliographical cards may take him to a discussion printed in a medical journal thirty or forty years ago, and then, in his ignorance of medical matters, he is in danger of being misled by an enthusiast whose opinions may be fatally colored by a professional *idée fixe*. Possibly the post-mortem diagnostician most frequently encountered by literary scholars is Dr. George Gould, whose *Biographic Clinics* in six volumes purported to discover the clue to the illnesses of scores of English and American writers.

Gould (1848–1922), an Ohioan, took a degree in theology from Harvard, after which he returned to his home state as a Unitarian minister in Chillicothe for a year and then became the proprietor of a local bookstore. Presumably the bookish leisure afforded by this occupation laid the foundations of his wide knowledge of literary biography. When he was thirty-seven he decided to study medicine, partly, it is said, to discover what caused his own ill health. He took his M.D. at Jefferson Medical College in 1888, and for many years thereafter was a leading ophthalmologist in Philadelphia.

In the errors of refraction to which the human eye is susceptible, Gould found the answer to many, if not most, of the problems of illness. So passionate was his conviction that he began a crusade at the meetings of medical societies, in the journals, and finally in his collected *Biographic Clinics*, to prove that countless writers and nonliterary geniuses were condemned to lives of physical illness for the sole reason that—they lacked the proper glasses. In a single paper, read before the Canadian Medical Association in 1903, he adduced the symptomatic evidence provided in the writings of fourteen nineteenth-century figures—DeQuincey, the Carlyles, Darwin, Huxley, Browning, Wagner, Parkman, Whittier, Herbert Spencer, George Eliot, G. H. Lewes, Margaret Fuller, and Nietzsche—to show that all of them suffered primarily from eyestrain.

His colleagues were cool to the idea, to say the least. But their coolness only irritated him to further efforts in behalf of his pet theory. He combed through the biographies and letters of more and more eminent men and women, finding always what was to him the telltale syndrome of "headache, insomnia, 'biliousness,' sick-headache, 'nervousness,' dejection, indescribable suffering, inability to do literary work without producing these symptoms, and relief of the symptoms whenever, even for a day or a few hours, literary work was stopped.' To his fellow physicians, these symptoms suggested any of a number of illnesses; and they ventured to say so. With a gift for sustained and bitter polemic rarely equaled among mere literary scholars, Gould assailed their stupidity and bigotry. The battle went on for years and left its memorial in the *Biographic Clinics,* which today remain good reading, whether one is looking for a handy collection of source material relating to the malaises of a poet or simply for a rousing medical dog-fight.

Although the writer of Gould's sketch in the authoritative *Dictionary of American Biography* says that his theories regarding eyestrain are "today widely accepted," the literary scholar accepts at his own peril the interpretation of the evidence in any given case. Gould's whole structure of argument rests on a wealth of indirect suggestions— reports of symptoms set down by men and women who by their very nature were impressionists rather than scientific observers. An analyst less obsessed by the conviction that eyestrain is the ubiquitous villain in the history of genius no doubt could read the same evidence in a variety of other ways—as pointing to stomach disorders, for example, or even plain neurosis. No one who has done much reading in literary biography can fail to be convinced that, though it may not yet be recorded in the psychiatric journals, there is such a disease as the hypochondria of authorship. The necessity of sitting down at a table, taking up the pen, and attempting to reduce one's teeming thoughts to order and intelligibility—or perhaps merely to think!—seems to induce various unpleasant physical disorders. They may be "psychosomatic," perhaps, to the modern physician, but they are indubitably vivid to the unfortunate author. Carlyle, it is well remembered, suffered the tortures of the damned when he was in the throes of composition; and possibly it is a subconscious fear of having his symptoms visited upon us that makes us postpone answering letters. At least, nobody is in a better position to sympathize with the pain-racked man of letters than the literary scholar. He may not have the genius of a great poet, but, as he reflects when he swallows another aspirin and grimly addresses himself to the typewriter to worry out his newest article, he can feel all the concomitant symptoms—and they are *not* due to simple eyestrain! If (to adopt the slightly inaccurate version of what Carlyle really said) genius is an infinite capacity for taking pains, it is also an infinite capacity for enduring them.

ON THE TRAIL OF BYRON

AND now, having sampled the experiences of a number of scholars, let us examine the case history of a single piece of research, for the sake of seeing the variety of adventures which may befall one man in the course of a year. We shall discover that the fascination of literary research is not confined to detached incidents of dramatic splendor, but can be found just as easily in the sum of the scholar's experiences. Even though he may never achieve a Malahide discovery, he cannot bewail the dullness of his life.

For what follows—the only comprehensive narrative of the kind that is in print, so far as I am aware—I am indebted to Professor Leslie A. Marchand of Rutgers University, who, with even more than the usual generosity of modern scholars, has supplied me with a detailed account of what he aptly calls his "Byron pilgrimage." I cannot, of course, tell here, except in general terms, what his voluminous files of newly found data contained when he returned to America after his peregrinations. Eventually he will publish all this new material himself, and those many readers who find a perennial fascination in the life and personality of Lord Byron may count upon a treat. For the purposes of this book, a simple recounting of Marchand's wanderings, the people he met, the new clues he followed, and the surprises they held for him, will be enough.

One would imagine that the great amount of material already in print about Byron—his own letters and journals, which occupy eight fat volumes, and the almost innumerable reminiscences of him by his friends—would be practically exhaustive. But as a matter of fact a large body of Byroniana still is unpublished, and much of it is even unstudied. The contents of the Byron manuscripts owned by the University of Texas, for example, are only now beginning to be revealed to the public. Many more manuscripts of first importance to Byron research lie in the Pierpont Morgan Library and in the Berg Collection at the New York Public Library.

It is not hard to understand, therefore, why Professor Marchand decided a few years ago that it would be worth while to make a systematic search for new Byroniana. In American collections he had already uncovered many letters which had not been printed. If so much material could be found in a country in which Byron had never set foot, how much more might be discovered in the places where he actually had been? He was one of the most footloose poets in literary history, his travels having taken him to Spain and Switzerland and Italy and Albania and the Near East; and wherever he had been, stray letters or manuscripts of his might still exist. Furthermore, in his own time Byron was a European celebrity of the first order; "the pageant of his bleeding heart," in Matthew Arnold's too-famous phrase, was a major spectacle wherever books were read, and every movement of the living body which encased that highly publicized heart was watched with fascination. Hence he made an ineradicable impression upon local memories throughout southern Europe, and, Professor Marchand reasoned, it was not at all impossible that anecdotes of the man had been passed from generation to generation by word of mouth and were ripe for the scholar's harvest—if he could find the people who knew them. Finally, the search for such material, in manuscript or local tradition, would take him through all the regions that Byron had known and written about, and enable him to acquire what could be had by no other means—a first-hand knowledge of the whole wide Byronic background, with all the color and detail that the poet assimilated for his own purposes. Byron's writings were vivid enough when read in a New Jersey armchair; but how much more vivid they would be for a prospective biographer if he followed the poet's footsteps through Europe!

That, then, was Marchand's ambition. In July of 1947, when Rutgers supplemented its grant of a year's leave of absence from his classroom with financial assistance, he sailed from New York on the *Queen Elizabeth*, taking a camera with color film, a supply of woolen underwear for use in the British Museum and elsewhere, and a trunk of assorted groceries for his austerity-weary English friends.

His first port of call in London, logically enough, was the office of John Murray at 50 Albemarle Street. The second in the still unbroken line of John Murrays had been Byron's publisher; in fact, it was he who had practically initiated the pleasant tradition whereby an author's publisher may also serve as his business agent, father confessor, and confidential adviser on all matters professional and private. And the office of the present Sir John Murray, the very room in which Byron used to chat with his publisher and his friends, and in the fireplace of which the ever lamented manuscript of his memoirs was burned, preserves the world's richest collection of Byroniana. Virtually every serious Byron scholar has drawn upon it, but Marchand felt positive that there were still plenty of important papers which had never been examined as closely as they deserved. Events proved that he was right.

Although a stranger he was welcomed by the members of the firm and installed in an office of his own on the top floor of the building, where, day after day, he worked through the dozens of crammed boxes he carried upstairs from Sir John's office. "I soon discovered," he writes, "that the most valuable part of the collection consisted of the letters to Byron from various correspondents—apparently Byron never threw anything away. Here were letters from his earliest school friends, from Lady Caroline Lamb, from Lady Melbourne, from Hodgson and Hobhouse and Kinnaird, all the closest friends of his later years. Most of these had never been printed and never carefully examined by any biographer. It is strange how often biographers neglect letters *to* their subject, which are quite as important biographical evidence as his own epistles. How many obscure passages may be clarified when one has both sides of a correspondence!" Even at night and over week ends he worked on the Murray treasures; he and John Grey Murray, Sir John's nephew, systematically checked great stacks of manuscript letters against the contents of the published volumes, discovering many omissions and errors; and "one pleasant spring day we piled half a dozen boxes of the precious manuscripts into his little car and spent the week end with them at his home near Hampstead Heath, with only time out to fly a kite for the children from Parliament Hill on Sunday morning."

His second step was to communicate with all the leading students of Byron and the Byron circle. Harold Nicolson, the diplomat and essayist whose *Byron: The Last Journey* is the best account of the poet's last years, invited him to his home in Kent. There Marchand copied out unpublished marginalia which John Cam Hobhouse had written in his own copy of Moore's *Letters and Journals of Lord Byron*. But even more important Hobhouse material was to come. At Murray's, Marchand met Michael Joyce, who had just finished his biography of Hobhouse, *My Friend H*. Hobhouse had kept a full diary, some of the volumes of which Marchand had already examined at the New York Public Library and the British Museum. Joyce remarked that the rest of the series, for the years of Hobhouse's intimacy with Byron, was owned by Lady Brenda Hobhouse, widow of a direct descendant, who lived in the old family house near Bath; and that, through the kind offices of a niece, Mrs. John Hobhouse, he had used these volumes the preceding winter—nearly freezing to death in the cold mansion. Because he had been interested primarily in Hobhouse he had not made full notes on the references to the poet. No biographer of Byron had ever seen them. Obviously, therefore, Marchand had to examine the diary for himself.

"A few letters from Joyce and me to Mrs. Hobhouse," he recalls, "were sufficient to arrange for my visit to Farleigh Hungerford. I arrived one fine November day at the Swan Hotel in Bradford-on-Avon, an ancient Saxon town near Bath, and called Mrs. Hobhouse, who came in to get me in her little low-slung English roadster, using some of her precious rationed petrol. When we arrived at Farleigh Court I saw spread out on the floor of the living room the intriguing volumes, some twenty of them, of all sizes and shapes, of the diary that Hobhouse had begun a few days before he and Byron started on their memorable trip to the Near East in 1809. Mrs. Hobhouse had borrowed the diaries from Lady Brenda and brought them over to her house for me to see. Every day for a week I came out and spent the day among the diaries, marking all the pages referring to Byron. Only once in a while did I allow myself to stop and read. On one such occasion I was thrilled by the discovery of the original story upon which Byron based 'Beppo.' Only a small portion of the diary had been published (and that imperfectly) by Lady Hobhouse's daughter; a few comparisons with the manuscript diaries showed how much that was important had not been printed. For instance, Lady Dorchester had omitted the whole detailed story of how Hobhouse had prevented an elopement of Byron and Lady Caroline Lamb when the latter invaded his chambers in St. James's Street in 1813.

"Although 'Aunt Brenda' was a little uneasy about the volumes of the diary, Mrs. Hobhouse held them for me until I could send a photographer out from London to make 1,100 microfilms: the whole of the diary of 1809–10 (covering the period of the first pilgrimage), the whole of that recording Hobhouse's trip with Byron across the Alps, their stay in Milan, Venice, and Mira, and all other pages referring to Byron. In many ways this was the most important 'scoop' that I made during my whole year abroad."

Back in London, through a friend Marchand was invited to a party at the Westminster flat of Lady Mander (Rosalie Grylls), who had published a life of Mary Shelley and another of Jane Clairmont, the mother of Byron's daughter Allegra. Among the guests was Lord Abinger, a young man who had not long before succeeded to his title upon the death of his father. Many years ago the elder Lord Abinger had inherited one of the three portions into which the papers of the Shelley family had been divided after the death of Shelley's daughter-in-law. Although these are of the utmost value for the study of Shelley and his circle, only Lady Mander, among the host of Shelley scholars, had been allowed to examine them. But when the present Lord Abinger learned of Marchand's mission, he volunteered to let him see his treasure and make what use he could of it. For almost a week, after the party in Westminster, Marchand went daily to the Abinger town house near Sloane Square and buried himself in the letters of Mary Shelley, Jane Clairmont, Trelawny, and the other members of the circle in Pisa during the years when the biographies of Byron and Shelley virtually merge into a single story. From these days of work he emerged with some sixty long letters, many of them throwing wholly new light on Byron at Pisa and Genoa, which Lord Abinger allowed him to have microfilmed.

Sometimes nothing, not even manuscripts, can bring a prospective biographer closer in spirit to his hero than meetings with the descendants of the poet and his friends. When Marchand went to Nottingham with the primary purpose of visiting Newstead Abbey, the ancient Byron estate with its memories of the youthful poet and his friends holding midnight revels in the manner of Gothic romance, dressed in monks' robes and drinking from a skull cup, he was entertained at lunch by the then holder of the Byron title, an eighty-six-year-old retired Anglican clergyman. Except for his lively wit and his ability to write a personal signature that had an uncanny similarity to that of the poet, the living Lord Byron was not perceptibly akin to his unchurchly predecessor; but he was proud of him just the same. Although he possessed no manuscripts of the poet, he did all he could to help the visitor gain a further sense of intimacy with Byron even at the distance of a century and a half. Through him, Marchand was invited to visit Annesley Hall, where Byron's early flame, Mary Chaworth, had lived:

"There in the spring, when the daffodils were glorious in the Park, I spent a week end and took a picture of one of the direct descendants of Mary Chaworth, standing by the garden wall near a wooden door which Byron had riddled with holes in his pistol practicing, and wearing a dress and shawl of Mary which had been preserved in the family chest.

"Another journey that yielded no manuscripts or letters but was full of Byron associations was a visit to a descendant of one of Byron's earliest loyal friends, Elizabeth Pigot. Cuthbert Becher Pigot, greatnephew of Byron's friend at Southwell during his Harrow days, lived the life of a country squire in a lovely thatched cottage, built in 1560, near Lavenham, Suffolk. Mr. Pigot is as much of a Byron enthusiast as was his great-aunt. Before I left he had presented me with some authentic hairs of the poet from a lock which Elizabeth Pigot had clipped when Byron's curls were a light auburn."

But perhaps the most dramatic episode during Marchand's months

in England occurred when friends took him for a drive through the
lovely hills of Surrey. Since every scholar's holiday is modeled after
that of the fabled busman, they stopped at the provincial bookstores
along the way on the off chance that they might find some Byroniana.
One proprietor answered Marchand's query by saying: "Yes, we have
a few books on Byron. In fact, we bought recently a number of books
from the library at Ockham Park."

Mention of Ockham Park is enough to make any Byron scholar's
heart skip several beats. On this estate had lived the Earl of Lovelace,
the poet's grandson, among whose family papers rested what are
probably the most crucial of all documents for Byron biography—
certain papers that strongly support the old allegations of incest between Byron and his half-sister. Lord Lovelace had caused a furor in
1905 by publishing some of these in a volume called *Astarte;* he was
old and crotchety, and a year later, seeing poachers in the distance as
he walked out upon his flagged terrace, he followed them into the park,
returned heated and angry, and died shortly thereafter. His widow
had lived on in the mansion until the 1930's. Although she had permitted one or two Byron biographers to have a glimpse at the family
archives, they were unable to make public all that they found. After
her death, as Marchand knew, the papers had passed to a relative, and
had become inaccessible to all inquirers. The estate itself had been
allowed to fall into melancholy, weed-grown decay, and its only residents in the past fifteen years had been soldiers billeted there during
the war. But evidently the family agents were selling off stray books
and minor items that had been left behind in the house. What, then,
might this country bookseller possess?

Marchand looked through the lot, but it was just the ordinary
miscellany that would be cleared out of any old house. He bought for
a few shillings a presentation copy of Lady Lovelace's life of her
husband, and was about to leave. Then the bookseller remembered
something. He rummaged around and brought forth three little notebooks with worn leather covers. "Here are some notebooks that came
from Ockham Park," he said. "They have writing in them. I don't
know what they are, but if you want them you can have them."
Marchand took one look and recognized the handwriting, small, even,

and neat. He thanked the bookseller in as calm a voice as he could command, and he and his friends returned to their car. Then he proclaimed his prize. They were the private notebooks of Byron's own wife!

On the remainder of that day's motor trip, Marchand confesses, he saw little of the Surrey countryside. In the back seat he was busy with the notebooks. Two were commonplace books: one written by Annabella Milbanke, the future Lady Byron, when she was only seventeen; the other, four years later. Their store of moralized comments on her reading of Bacon, Pliny, Massinger, Horace, Cowper, Rochefoucauld, and Madame de Staël threw revealing light on the mind of the young girl, so unsuspecting of the tragedy that was soon to befall her.

In the second notebook Marchand found an entry written only three days after her first letter to Byron. In it she recorded the types of characters most interesting to her, among whom she counted "Characters determined by Disappointment. . . . Hence arise, in most instances, either Misanthropy or Despondency." "It is evident," he comments, "that when she spoke of 'natural benevolence changed to suspicious coldness' and 'every kind impulse' being 'repelled by the consideration of Man's unworthiness,' she had already formed a partially true but tragically inadequate conception of Byron's character; if only she could marry him she could bring out his benevolence!"

Elsewhere in this book I speak of the improvements in scholarly procedure which have been made possible by contemporary science. One other experience Marchand had before he struck out for the Continent illustrates still another way in which the researcher can put modern inventions to his own uses; unhappily, in America at least, it is not often available to the humble pursuer of literary truth. In October, 1947, Marchand was invited to give a fifteen-minute talk on the "Third Programme"—the nightly array of fine music and serious talks on literature, philosophy, art, and history by which the British Broadcasting Corporation caters to the tastes of a class of listeners almost totally neglected in the calculations of the American radio industry. In his talk he outlined his plans for scouring all the localities covered by the Byronic pilgrimage for stray biographical materials.

The mail evoked by the broadcast and by the subsequent publication of his talk in the BBC's weekly magazine included a letter from a businessman whose firm supplied all the electric power for Athens and who later as a gesture of good will toward Byron scholarship was able to obtain hotel reservations there for Marchand—no small favor at a time when the American Mission to Greece had taken over most of the hotel space. In that talk, also, Marchand had mentioned that he hoped somehow to have access to the great store of letters exchanged by Byron and his last love, Countess Guiccioli; they had not been seen by any biographer, though they were known still to exist. Just before he left England, a young man came up and introduced himself as a friend of the Marchesa Iris Origo, author of a volume on Allegra, Byron's daughter by Jane Clairmont. The Marchesa had read Marchand's talk. and she sent word that at that moment she had in her hands all the Byron-Guiccioli correspondence, lent to her by the Countess' descendant, Count Gamba, with authority to edit it for publication (the resultant book, an important one, was published as *The Last Attachment* in 1949); but Marchand was welcome to come and see the treasures for himself.

Fortified by such rich expectations, Marchand left for the Continent. First he went to Switzerland, where a former British consul and a professor at the University of Geneva escorted him to all the locales associated with the exiled Byron—the Villa Diodati, overlooking Lake Geneva and the distant Jura Mountains, where the third canto of *Childe Harold* had been composed; the château at Coppet where Byron had often visited Madame de Staël; the site of the Hôtel Secheron where Byron had first met Shelley. Then to Montreux, where in Byronic solitude (British austerity having cut off the usual flood of tourists) Marchand explored the Castle of Chillon, and listened in Bonnivard's dungeon, as Shelley and Byron had done together a hundred and thirty years earlier, to the monotonous lapping of the water against the stone walls. But there is a limit to the extent to which even the most devoted scholar wishes to follow in the footsteps of his subject, and instead of crossing the Alps into Italy in a lumbering Napoleonic carriage, as Byron had done with Hobhouse, Marchand settled for a compartment on the Simplon-Orient Express to Milan, and completed his journey to Venice aboard a streamlined bus roaring down an express highway.

In Venice, though, he once again was back in the Byronic setting. He walked through the Frezzaria, the narrow street just off the Piazza San Marco, in which had lived the "merchant of Venice" in whose house Byron first stayed. He remembered that the poet promptly fell in love with the merchant's black-eyed wife, Marianna Segati, "pretty as an antelope." But he was more eager to see the Palazzo Mocenigo on the Grand Canal, which Byron had occupied during most of his Venetian sojourn. It took some doing to get inside this; but again luck was with him, for the director of the British Information Service in Venice, to whom he applied for aid, turned out to be an enthusiastic Byronian himself, and the librarian in his office happened to know a young artist couple who occupied a flat in the very house. She arranged for Marchand to be invited there for tea; and his hosts showed him the carriage quarters on the first floor where Byron had kept his famous menagerie, the balcony overlooking the Grand Canal from which he had watched the Carnival procession, and all the spacious chambers through which he had limped—and where, after his return from the Fenice Theatre or a Carnival ball, he had sat by his gin and water, writing poetry until after dawn.

One other Venetian scene associated with Byron was the monastery on the island of San Lazzaro, near the Lido, where he "took lessons in Armenian, glad to find in the study something craggy to break his mind upon." In the craft provided by a somewhat milder latter-day incarnation of Tita, the fierce-whiskered gondolier whom Byron described in his letters, Marchand went out to the island and was taken in hand by a friendly little Armenian monk who proudly displayed the library where Byron had studied, and the printing press where the monks had turned out several works on Byron and his translations from the Armenian.

From Venice to Rome, by plane; and there Marchand kept his appointment with the Marchesa Origo, who showed him the bundles of Byron-Guiccioli correspondence she was editing, as well as the bulky manuscript of the Guiccioli's *Vie de Byron*, full of otherwise unknown details of her life with her English lover. In Rome also

Marchand called at the Keats-Shelley Memorial, the house in the Piazza di Spagna where Keats had died.* One of the founders of the memorial had worked for years collecting original materials for a biography of Byron in his Italian period. At his death just before the Second World War, there came to the memorial several boxes of his notes. Marchand and the Marchesa Origo were the first scholars to examine the boxes carefully; they turned out to contain a voluminous collection of copies of government and police documents from all the principal cities where Byron had attracted the attention of the security officials because of his suspected political intrigues.

Then he took a British European Airways plane to Istanbul, and devoted a week to savoring the sights and smells of a locale half of which the young Byron could never have dreamed of, half of which had not changed since his day: new Chevrolet taxis inching their way through the ceaseless stream of pannier-laden donkeys and horses and human beasts of burden; the forbidding walls of the serail, the Sultan's palace, where certain diverting scenes of *Don Juan* are laid; the ancient covered bazaar, which was pure Near East in Byron's time but nowadays rubs an uneasy elbow with Brooklyn. But, valuable though this first-hand immersion in the Turkish atmosphere was for the devoted reader of Byron's poems, Marchand knew that there was little chance that Byron lore could be found here, and he flew to Greece.

"As I rode into the city from the airport," he writes, "passing white or pastel pink or blue tavernas by the sea, and rounding the base of the Acropolis came into Syntagma Square, I fell in love with Greece

* The story of what happened to the Keats relics contained in this house during the Second World War is not without its romance. In 1943, when it was anticipated that Rome would become a battleground, the relics, including a lock of the poet's hair, his deathbed portrait by Severn, manuscripts, and first editions of his poems, were sent to the Abbey at Monte Cassino. At that time, it was unthinkable that the abbey itself would be destroyed. After the Germans turned the abbey into a fortress, a Maltese archivist, Don Mauro Inguanez, asked and received permission to pack and move his personal belongings. The next morning, on the outskirts of bomb-shattered Cassino, the priest in his dusty habit managed to thumb a ride to Rome on a German truck. In the dilapidated suitcase and box that rode with him were the Keats relics, which he took to sanctuary in a Roman monastery. After the fighting ended in Italy they were restored to the Keats-Shelley Memorial.

at first sight, and I began to feel, what I was to feel even more when I got out of Athens, the appeal that the country must have had for the young Byron on his first pilgrimage." But Byron had had all the leisure in the world, and Marchand had to work on a strict schedule, so that he might get back to his classes at Rutgers in the fall. The easy-going tempo of life in Athens was exasperating. "Here everyone belonged to the 'four-hours-for-lunch club' and all libraries and offices closed at one o'clock and didn't open again until four-thirty or five. It was very pleasant to drive out to a taverna by the sea at Phaleron or Munychia (where Byron used to make frequent excursions on horseback from the Capuchin monastery at the foot of the Acropolis in 1810 and 1811), to have a leisurely lunch at a table by the beach, eating delicious barbunya and drinking retsina, but if one had two appointments in the morning, how could he find any time to dig into the manuscripts at the National Library or the British School?"

Furthermore, in the winter of 1947–48 Greece was still very much at war, and even though Athens itself was as brutally "normal" as American cities were in 1941–45, and the night clubs were packed, travel outside the city was almost impossible for a civilian on a mission involving merely a long-dead poet. But Marchand was determined to follow Byron's footsteps no matter where they led, and he had to visit Missolonghi, where, in 1824, they had ended. In January he left Athens on the crack train of what was then the one more-or-less-regularly operating railroad in Greece—a two-car Diesel-electric train which was optimistically expected to cover the 137 miles from Athens to Patras between nine A.M. and five P.M. It was understood in Athens that the train would arrive at Patras on time only if it was not derailed or held up by the bandits who swarmed in the mountains of the Peloponnesus; one event or the other occurred every two weeks or so. Until the last twenty miles the trip was uneventful; Marchand enjoyed, like Byron, the lovely glimpses through the olive groves of the Gulf of Corinth and Mount Parnassus in the distance. But then there was a clattering and bumping, and the passengers knew that the usual had happened—the train was off the tracks. They sat, resignedly waiting for the bandits to arrive and do their worst. But before the good news penetrated to the near-by hideouts, the crew herded the travelers into a single car brought up by an ancient engine from a near-by siding, and they screeched and puffed triumphantly into Patras.

From Patras, Marchand took a little caïque (familiar to readers of Byron's eastern tales—then a sailboat, but now a motorboat with sail auxiliary) across the Gulf of Patras, and then a toy railroad across the marshes to Missolonghi itself. The large number of soldiers in the vicinity reminded him that the guerrilla war was now uncomfortably close; in fact, there had been a battle a few miles away only a week or two earlier. But what better background for one's view of the last home of Byron than a desultory, indeterminate war in the hinterland? *
The whirligig of time, Marchand reflected with satisfaction, had managed to reproduce, as if for his personal benefit, some of the conditions that had prevailed when Byron lay dying of swamp fever and three doctors at the end of his somewhat quixotic attempt to bring aid to the Greek rebels. Nevertheless it took an effort of imagination to conceive of Missolonghi as it had been in those dismal April days of

* Marchand was not the first modern literary scholar to pursue his researches against a background of war in Greece. During the First World War, farther north in Macedonia, a distinguished British scholar managed to do a great deal of work on his edition of Dr. Johnson's *Journey to the Western Islands of Scotland* and of Boswell's complementary account of the famous tour. Dr. R. W. Chapman's description of his pursuit of knowledge under difficulties is so entertaining that it deserves to be quoted: "I had a camp beyond Smol Hill, on the left bank of the Vardar, and a six-inch gun (Mark XI, a naval piece, on an improvised carriage; 'very rare in this state'), with which I made a demonstration in aid of the French and Greek armies, when they stormed the heights beyond the river; I think in June. This was in the early hours of the morning, and a very pretty display of fireworks. Twelve hours later, I remember, Mark XI was still too hot to touch. But long weeks of inactivity followed. I had a hut made of sandbags, with a roof constructed of corrugated iron in layers, with large stones between, to allow perflation; and here, in the long hot afternoons, when 'courage was useless, and enterprise impracticable,' a temporary gunner, in a khaki shirt and shorts, might have been found collating the three editions of the *Tour to the Hebrides*, or re-reading *A Journey to the Western Islands* in the hope of finding a corruption in the text. Ever and again, tiring of collation and emendation, of tepid tea and endless cigarettes, I would go outside to look at the stricken landscape—the parched yellow hills and ravines, the brown coils of the big snaky river at my feet, the mountains in the blue distance; until the scorching wind, which always blew down that valley, sent me to the Hebrides. These particulars are doubtless irrelevant; but I like to think that the scene would have pleased James Boswell." (By permission of the Oxford University Press, from Johnson and Boswell: *A Tour to the Hebrides*, edited in the Oxford Standard Authors series by Dr. R. W. Chapman.)

1824. "The warm sun," he writes, "gave a kind of glamour to the pastel buildings and even to the fishermen's huts built on stilts in the water and the sailboats on the lagoon with a full brilliant rainbow over them. This was not the gray and monotonous view that struck Byron's eyes as he looked out on the marsh-bound town and the storm-beaten waters during his last discouraging days." But Byron was unforgotten in the town; the main street bore his name, and a monument with a bas-relief of his head stood on the bare spot of ground where his house once had been.

This, then, was Missolonghi. Now back to Patras—the caïque on the return trip bringing additional unexpected suggestions of Byron in the fact that among its passengers were fourteen captured bandits, handcuffed with heavy chains and guarded by stern-faced Greek soldiers in mufti and carrying rifles and tommy guns. Were these unhappy creatures, Marchand wondered, descendants of Byron's Suliote warriors? They might well have been, for the mountain warfare to which they were accustomed has continued without interruption from Byron's day to our own.

As Marchand continued his odyssey through the Greek hinterland, he met hospitality and friendliness equaled only by that which he had already enjoyed in England. When he turned up at the mayor's office at Argostoli, deep in the Cephalonian mountains, with letters from friends in Athens, the whole business of the town was disrupted in order to show the American gentleman where Byron had been. An expedition was organized to Metaxata to see the house where the poet had lived for several months before proceeding to Missolonghi, and another to the place still known in local tradition as "Byron's rock," where the poet used to sit and dream into the distance as he had done in his youth on the flat gravestone in Harrow churchyard. Then, lured by stories that an old man still lived whose father had known Byron, Marchand crossed the bay and went into the hills, with a French-speaking Greek as guide. In a modest little house he found the man and his wife, who immediately brought out cakes and little glasses of ouzo, the pale liqueur which is the usual offering of hospitality in Greece. The old gentleman supplied some reminiscences of his father, in whom Byron had seen promise when he was a boy at Argostoli.

Unfortunately he knew of no letters from Byron to his father; but to Marchand it was enough thus to have reached within two handshakes of Byron.

In the island of Ithaca was the same open-handed hospitality: the name of Byron, a century and a quarter after the poet's death, was an open sesame even for a perfect stranger. The schoolmaster, the mayor, and their friends entertained him. In a grimy taverna, Marchand met a young man whose cousin was the abbot of the monastery, Mone Katharon, atop the highest mountain of the island, where, according to an untrustworthy account, Byron once spent a night in wild misery with some unnamed pains and cramps. The upshot of the meeting was that Marchand, his new friend, and the abbot drove up the mountain in a 1930 Ford taxi, stopping en route to pick up large sacks of groceries and the abbot's special cook. When they arrived at Mone Katharon, wind-beaten on its lofty summit but bathed in the mild January sunlight, the abbot superintended the activities at the open hearth in the kitchen; and after Marchand had looked his fill at Byron's Isles of Greece dotting the blue Ionian Sea, he was called to a magnificent dinner of roast chicken, rice, spaghetti, salad, and white wine.

"It was with reluctance," he writes, "that I left Ithaca before sunrise the next morning on a tiny caïque bound for Patras. After being buffeted about for nearly twelve hours in an open boat on the Gulf, I was glad to board the train again for Athens. But as the cars jogged along over uneven rails along the Gulf of Corinth, I felt that I had gained a picture of the background of Byron in Greece that no amount of reading could have given me."

But he had still not been everywhere that Byron had been in Greece. In particular, he wanted to visit Jannina, on the Albanian frontier, where Byron and Hobhouse had gone to visit Ali Pasha. The great trouble was that Jannina, like Missolonghi, was in highly dangerous territory; not long before, a bloody battle had been fought only a few miles away. But since he had gone to Missolonghi and the Ionian Islands and returned unscathed, why not Jannina? A Greek commercial air line made several scheduled flights to Jannina every week, weather permitting—the weather being very important, because there was no airport at Jannina, but only a level sheep pasture which was a morass for three days after every rain. If Marchand managed to get to Jannina, there was no telling when he could expect to return: a good drenching rain could end air travel, and therefore, under the circumstances, *all* travel for ten days or two weeks. Still, he decided to risk it: "The Greek pilots probably knew the route very well; nevertheless I must confess to some nervousness when, passing low over the hills skirting the northern shore of the Gulf of Corinth, and cutting inland just above Missolonghi, they followed the stream beds and mountain valleys, thus getting under the low ceiling but seeming to scrape the wings on the sides of the crags that towered above us on both sides. It was a relief when we finally circled over the lake and the town and came down to a safe landing on the sheep pasture." Despite his un-Byronic mode of travel to Jannina, once on the ground he found much to authenticate Hobhouse's description of the locality; the shepherds' huts, the laden burros, and the capote-clad peasants had not changed at all.

But he was faced with a problem which was by now familiar to him. In Italy he had got along all right with his knowledge of Italian, where English would not do; but in Greece, knowing no Greek, he had had to rely upon finding someone who spoke French or English. In Jannina he found only a waiter whose French was barely sufficient to understand Marchand's order for lunch. But as he sat at his meal, Marchand thought he heard a word or two of English, apparently spoken by two men in officers' uniforms who were lunching at a table in the corner; so he went over to them, introduced himself, and found that they were members of the United Nations' special Balkan Commission, assigned to observing the fighting on the frontier—one an American colonel, and the other a French captain. Immediately the United Nations came to the rescue of Byron scholarship by assigning to Marchand, for the afternoon, a Greek liaison officer who spoke French. In the company of this man, who knew the locality well, he made his pilgrimage to the house where Byron and Hobhouse had lived, to the mosque on a high cliff above the lake, and to the ruins of Ali Pasha's castle.

So his luck was still holding; and it held the next day, when the skies were clear and the plane for Athens could take off without any trouble from the Jannina sheep pasture. His diligent exploration of the Byron country was almost at an end, but in the busy days that followed he managed two side trips to other places that inspired the poet, one of them in a jeep belonging to Greek War Relief. There was still much to do in Athens. The director of the National Archives had sorted out long-buried Byron documents for his inspection; the British School of Archaeology proved to have some letters to Byron, left to it by a British historian who had known the poet in Greece; and a Greek collector put at his disposal some important manuscripts, including letters from Count Gamba, the brother of Teresa Guiccioli, to which Byron had added postscripts. Escorted about Athens by a young Greek lawyer who neglected his practice for the purpose, Marchand located a photographer who had just received a microfilm machine from America, the only one in all Greece, and had his new treasure-trove photographed. By this time his quest had achieved so much local fame that the editor of a daily newspaper asked him to write an article on his impressions of Greece from the point of view of a Byron enthusiast. It appeared as a front-page feature, translated into Greek by the editor and accompanied by a passport photograph of the visitor, the day before he left Greece.

And now time was growing short. Marchand flew back to Rome, where he attended to the microfilming of four hundred pages of manuscript he had found in the Keats-Shelley Memorial. Then to Florence, to see the house where Teresa Guiccioli had spent her last days and written her *Vie de Byron;* to Pisa, Leghorn, Bologna, and Ravenna, to see houses in which Byron had lived and written poetry in the midst of love-making and revolution; and back to Venice. Then to England, where he resumed work in his attic room at John Murray's. When his labors at Murray's ended, he made up a list of the documents in the "Byron Room" which he wanted microfilmed. "Sir John," he recalls, "must have been appalled by my list, for I am sure that no one else had ever made such a staggering request for reproductions of his precious documents and letters. But his generosity did not waver, and my request was granted. For a whole day the Murray outer office was converted into a photographic shop while I stood over the young man who did the job—sixteen hundred microfilms!"

Marchand sailed back to New York a few days later with, all told, nearly four thousand frames of microfilm of prime source material, most of it never before utilized in Byron biography, in addition to transcripts of other documents. And in his memory, aided by a fine collection of Kodachrome pictures of every Byronic spot he had visited, he carried more first-hand knowledge of the Byronic background than any other scholar had ever acquired.

There had been disappointments, of course. He had tried his best to locate the letters from Augusta Leigh, Byron's half-sister, to her friend Mrs. Villiers, which could be expected to throw much light on the circumstances surrounding Byron's separation from his wife; but the present descendants of Mrs. Villiers were unable to help him. Likewise, he had written to the granddaughter of the attorney who had represented Lady Byron in the separation business, one of the two or three people who knew the real reasons for the separation. "But he," the granddaughter, Miss Lushington, wrote, "held that papers in connection with divorce and matrimonial troubles belonged to the two people concerned and to them only, and before his death he burnt them all." And that was that.

But Marchand's success clearly outweighed his failures. Aided by publishers, fellow scholars, descendants of members of the Byron circle, librarians from Texas to Athens, mayors of obscure Greek towns, Italian gentlefolk, Greek War Relief, and the United Nations, he had achieved his ambition—or at least the first phase of it. Now for the second part: to write a new life of Byron, utilizing all this new material. What will his slant be? "I shall scarcely know myself," he says, "until I have fitted together all the pieces of the jig-saw puzzle. But following the Byron trail has illuminated for me many obscure facets of a life that was not only one of the most picturesque and sensational but also one of the most meaningful both for his own times and for ours. The satiric, realistic Byron, cutting through shams with a clear sharp intellect, is still very much alive and is a fascinating and stimulating personality, one that will certainly do more good than harm in our modern world. It is not necessary to hide his foibles and weaknesses—none knew them better than himself or was freer in divulging them. I think that what will come out in the end (for I have only begun to write the biography) will be a Byron more interesting, more to be admired than the half-knowledge or suppressions of the past have shown him to be."

THIRTEEN

THE SEARCH FOR SAMBIR

TO tell the truth, men and women incurably afflicted with wanderlust could hardly choose a more agreeable profession than literary scholarship. Given a suitable research project, and the necessary time and money, they would have a perfect rationalization for their itching feet. The history of modern scholarship has plenty of distinguished precedents. In gathering the materials for her exhaustive study of the antecedents of the Barrett and Browning families, Jeannette Marks lived for months in the West Indies. One summer during the 1930's, Howard F. Lowry and Chauncey Brewster Tinker devoted their holiday to traveling to Switzerland in the hope of finding a clue to the mysterious girl who, eighty years earlier, charmed the youthful Matthew Arnold and became the "Marguerite" of some of his best known lyrics. They went to the Alpine resort of Thun, where Arnold is thought to have met her, hoping somehow to trace her through the hotel register or through some wispy local tradition of a summer romance between a girl and a dandified young Englishman. The hotel register for that far-away period, however, had been destroyed, and no one in the town remembered having heard his parents or grandparents speak of such a love affair. So they came back to America empty-handed, but with memories of a pleasant outing.

Although I do not have the statistics handy, I imagine that the all-time record for scholarly mileage, at least for mileage expended in the pursuit of a single little cluster of facts, must be held by the man who searched for Sambir. It is a story that deserves to be better known.

Somewhere in Borneo, in 1887–88, there occurred a fortuitous and fateful meeting between a Polish mariner, sailing out of Singapore as first mate of the Arab-owned steamer *Vidar*, and a morose Dutch trader. The sailor was to become famous as Joseph Conrad; the trader was to contribute to the beginnings of Conrad's fame as the inspiration for the protagonist in his first novel, *Almayer's Folly.* Conrad himself always felt that his encounter with "Kaspar Almayer" had been of crucial importance in his career. "If I had not got to know Almayer pretty well," he wrote in *A Personal Record,* "it is almost certain there would never have been a line of mine in print." For, having once met the man, he could not forget him; and even though at that time his literary interests were avowedly those of the amateur— after all, he was a professional seaman, who had just won his master's papers—he got to work on a short novel built about the man he called Almayer. For five years (1889–94) he amused himself with his manuscript, in his leisure hours as second mate aboard a Congo River steamer, later as an unemployed, fever-weakened seaman in Glasgow and London, and finally as first mate of a steamer on the England-Australia run. He had no thought of turning to writing as a career; all his ambition was concentrated upon winning a command of his own. But while he searched for that command his first novel, *Almayer's Folly,* appeared—shortly followed by *An Outcast of the Islands* and *The Nigger of the "Narcissus"*—and Conrad, dogged by ill health and faced with the necessity of supporting a wife and son, reluctantly realized that his future livelihood was not on the bridge but at the writing desk. And so Almayer—whoever he might have been—gave the first impetus to Conrad's career as novelist.

That is one reason why students wanted to know more about the original of Almayer. Another reason is that it has always been known that for his earliest important novels Conrad, like Melville, drew his raw materials directly from his own observations and experiences during his seafaring years. Many of his characters were modeled after men whom he had known in Africa or the Dutch East Indies; many of his basic situations had their real-life counterparts. Therefore, to understand the precise manner in which Conrad's art of fiction developed, it is important to learn, so far as possible, with what sort of raw materials he began, and how he selected and modified them as he worked them into his novels. For instance, was Almayer, in the novel, a fairly faithful representation of the man Conrad had known, and was the story of the novel based on actual events? Or did Conrad merely take certain memorable traits of the man for his portrait of Almayer, and build up about the fictional figure a narrative which had no source in fact?

Conrad, in his autobiographical volume, wrote at some length of the meeting with Almayer (as he also called the real-life figure) in Borneo, but he supplied no clues, geographical or other, which would lead to an identification of the man. In 1924 his biographer, Jean-Aubry, sought out Captain Craig, the master of the *Vidar*, aboard which Conrad had shipped from Singapore to Borneo. Craig, then over seventy, for the first time supplied the historical Almayer with a definite habitation. The village of "Sambir," in Conrad's novel the scene of the struggle between Almayer and the Rajah Lakamba, in reality, said Craig, was the Borneo village of Bulungan forty miles up the Bulungan River; and it was the Bulungan River that Conrad named the "Pantai"—the secret of whose navigable cha.:nel only Almayer's father-in-law, Captain Tom Lingard, knew until the day the Arabs discovered it and thus destroyed his trading monopoly.

To Dr. John D. Gordan, now curator of the Berg collection at the New York Public Library, such a clue was too inviting to be resisted. Twelve years after Jean-Aubry's *Joseph Conrad: Life and Letters* appeared, Gordan, working on his exhaustive study of Conrad's early career as a novelist, decided to follow Conrad to Borneo: indeed, to visit "Sambir" itself, and to find out what he could about the man whom Conrad called Almayer, and about prototypes of the other leading characters in *Almayer's Folly*.

Across the United States he went in the summer of 1939, his wife and sister with him; then by ship to Australia, and finally north by plane to Soerabaja in Java, where he begged the aid of the Bataafsche Petroleum Maatschappij, the great Dutch company some of whose oil fields lay near Bulungan. The officials were polite, helpful, and incredulous. "Obviously," Gordan recalls, "they couldn't imagine what we wanted, and certainly we must have seemed suspicious characters in those days of international competition for oil." But they gave him directions for reaching Bulungan if he really insisted on visiting such a God-forsaken spot in the wilds of Borneo.

Following the directions, Gordan left Soerabaja one Saturday morning by plane, crossing the Java Sea which Conrad had plied in the *Vidar* and halting for passengers at the very ports which he had known. High over Borneo he flew, over the great delta of the Berouw River, at which he gazed with the impersonal interest of the traveler, never dreaming that that area would turn out to have a very direct connection with his search. Then the plane reached the delta of the Bulungan River, in the forested upper reaches of which the village of Bulungan lay hidden, and glided down toward the oil tanks on the island of Tarakan lying offshore.

The Dutch oil officials at Tarakan welcomed Gordan and his companions at the company's *passanggrahan* (rest house); but they also could not conceal their amazement over the purpose of the visit. "We were following the trail of a Polish seaman who had written novels in English about run-to-seed Dutchmen who lived among Malays in Borneo? Obviously we were harmless, and obviously we were crazy." But crazy people must be humored, and so the oil men supplied a motor launch and two native seamen and sent Gordan on his fifty-mile trip across the bay and up the Bulungan River. At last, he exulted, he was on his way to "Sambir"!

The launch sped past the fishing weirs strung like fences in the mouth of the river, and into the maze of channels into which the delta was divided. The palms crowded down to the edge of the water; only occasionally did a native village appear where, as the sun went down, men and children were seen bathing and the smell of wood smoke and cooking food came over the river. It was a strange and not a little unnerving situation for the young Harvard literary scholar: the Malayan seamen could speak no English, and he knew neither Dutch nor Malay; and here he was, in the midst of the tangled Borneo jungle, on his way to a village not even marked on most maps, with the tropical night closing in! But as the stars came out he took comfort in the appearance of the Southern Cross and the Big Dipper; "Sambir" at least was in the same world.

After the launch had pushed up the dark jungle river a few more miles the seamen pointed ahead and began to chatter in their native tongue. There was a glare in the sky—the reflection of the street lights of the Dutch settlement of Bulungan. Arc lights in the remote interior of Borneo! Had Gordan come all these thousands of miles to steep himself in the atmosphere Conrad had known, only to find himself back in twentieth-century western civilization?

But the launch headed for the opposite shore, where the Malay portion of Bulungan, lighted only by feeble oil lamps, straggled along the river. At the landing he was met by Mrs. Fisk, an American missionary to whom the officials of the Bataafsche Petroleum Maatschappij had given him a letter of introduction. Although it was true that her husband was absent in Java assembling a hospital plant with which he planned to extend his mission to the Dyaks still farther inland, she assured Gordan that only in this respect, and that of the arc lights across the river, had Bulungan moved forward since Conrad's time. The arc lights, she explained, had been installed by the reigning sultan, who had become infatuated with such illumination during a visit to the Netherlands—but they were the only modern touch to be found in the vicinity. The next morning he discovered for himself how right she was: "On the Sultan's side of the river was a low line of native houses broken by the cupola of the mosque and the two-story palace, like a small, old-fashioned beach cottage, comfortably surrounded by verandas. Our side of the river also had a two-story building, the combined general store and hotel run by a Chinaman. At the landing stage was a huge banyan tree firmly anchored by its aerial roots, and shading a dark brown godown. The river bank was decorated with crude statues of lions and Malays erected in honor of Queen Wilhelmina by Her Majesty's Dutch, Chinese, and Malay subjects."

So here was Bulungan, a primitive settlement peopled by mixed breeds, almost swallowed up by the Bornean jungle—a settlement right out of the pages of Conrad. Now, what about Almayer and his relatives? In reply to questions, Mrs. Fisk said that although she had lived in the village for many years she could not recall having heard either of Almayer or of his father-in-law, Captain Tom Lingard. However, Lieutenant Boelhouwer of the Dutch garrison might be able to help. So to the lieutenant they went. He too failed to recognize either name, and at this point the quest for Almayer might have ended forever, in a total blank; but in the garrison office was a record clerk, named

Pangemanan, who came to the rescue. Yes; he had heard of Captain Tom Lingard. In fact he had himself known Jim, Lingard's swaggering nephew, whom everyone called Tuan (Lord) Jim. Uncle and nephew had traded together until, after a quarrel, the former had returned to England, while Tuan Jim, remaining in Borneo, lived off the profits of money lent to a prominent Chinese merchant. He had died about 1925, leaving several children born to him by his native wife. (In *Almayer's Folly*, too, the elder Lingard had gone back to Europe, after the collapse of his trading monopoly. As for Tuan Jim, in Pangemanan's recollections of him Gordan recognized several characteristics of Conrad's hero in *Lord Jim*.)

Even more exciting, Pangemanan knew who Almayer had been! The name of the man Conrad had met was Olmeijer—he had simply Anglicized the Dutch spelling. Without knowing Conrad's model, Pangemanan had known his family. Olmeijer, he told Gordan, had had several children—not one, as Captain Craig had reported to Jean-Aubry—and one of the daughters had married Andrew Gray of Samarinda, farther down the coast of East Borneo. She was living there now.

The search for Sambir was having its initial fruits. *But*—and here was the shock and surprise of the whole long trip—Bulungan turned out not to be Sambir at all! Pangemanan had known Lingard and the Olmeijers not in Bulungan, but in Berouw—an equally remote settlement on the Berouw River, over which Gordan had flown so carelessly the day before. Because of a slip of Captain Craig's memory in Jean-Aubry's interview with him Gordan had been following the wrong scent all this time; but, by one of those coincidences which sometimes come to the rescue of scholars in their darkest moments, his mistake had turned into good fortune. For in revealing that Bulungan was *not* Sambir, Pangemanan was able to give him fresh clues which he otherwise might never have obtained.

Berouw, the true Sambir, deep in the Bornean jungle, was inaccessible to Gordan; but the fact that one of Olmeijer's daughters was living in Samarinda raised his hopes, for before setting out in the motor launch from Tarakan he had arranged to return to Soerabaja by trading steamer, and the steamer was scheduled to call at Samarinda. Back down the swift Bulungan he went, and thence to the hospitable quarters of the oil men on Tarakan.

The *Van Swoll*, the very sort of steamer upon which Conrad had shipped in these Celebes waters, made a leisurely voyage down the east coast of Borneo. Under a full moon it put into the Kotei River, eventually reaching Samarinda. The captain himself took Gordan to visit Mr. and Mrs. Gray, son-in-law and daughter of Olmeijer. At last, Gordan thought, he was about to meet persons who had actually known the man Conrad knew! But now came a fresh shock. At the family's combination lumber mill, lemonade works and ice factory, he was told that the Grays no longer lived in Samarinda; they had moved to Malang, in Java. However, their son, who operated these industries, was on his way back from a visit to them, and his ship, the *Pahud*, was to touch at Balikpapan tomorrow, when the *Van Swoll* too would be there.

The next day Gordan, aboard the *Van Swoll*, reached Balikpapan only to find that the *Pahud* had already been in port for several hours and young Mr. Gray had gone off to visit friends in the town; the steward on the *Pahud* did not know who they were. Gordan tried to reach him at the club and the rest house, with no success. Finally, in desperation, he walked the streets looking for a man whom he would not recognize even if he saw him. The *Van Swoll* was getting ready to depart. Gordan dashed back to the *Pahud*—and there Gray was. He records:

Olmeijer's grandson, short, thick-set, with a clear tan skin and an agreeable smile, said, Yes, he had heard that a certain Conrad had written a story about his grandfather. Had I written it? That was good, because it was not a nice story, it did not tell the truth. He had tried to get the book—wasn't it called "Conrad's Folly"?—sending even to Singapore for it. He confessed that he really knew little about his mother's family. But his parents would certainly see me at Malang to answer all my questions; they too wanted to clear up the falsehoods that this writer had circulated. He would telegraph them that I was coming. We shook hands—I shook hands with a grandson of Almayer's!—and I rushed off to the *Van Swoll*, which was impatiently blasting her whistle.

The round trip from Soerabaja to Tarakan had been a matter of sixteen hundred miles; its net result, in addition, of course, to the collection of a great deal of Conradian local color, was the discovery that Olmeijer's daughter lived in Malang, which was just fifty miles from Soerabaja! If Gordan had had the right clue when he set out he could have saved himself a week of travel through Dutch East Borneo. But now, at last, he was on the right track. An hour's train ride took him to the pleasant Javan town of Malang, where the Grays were expecting him. First Mr. Gray, a hearty eighty-year-old Scotsman, had to tell his own story. He had come out to Java in 1879 and, prospering in several businesses, had married Olmeijer's daughter. He had known Captain Craig well, but had never met Conrad.

Then his wife, Johanna Elizabeth, third child in a family of eleven, had her turn. Her father's name, she told Gordan, had been William Charles, not Kaspar (though there was a Kaspar in the family, from whom Conrad had perhaps derived the suggestion). Like Conrad's character, he had left his birthplace in Java for Berouw (Sambir), and he too had been a trader in gutta, rattan, and rubber, highly respected by everyone. In some respects, such as incurring the suspicion of the Dutch authorities because of his friendship with the native Dyaks, and shipping his goods to the outside world through Tom Lingard, Olmeijer's life seems to have directly suggested passages in Conrad's novel. But the more the Grays told of Olmeijer, the clearer it became that in no sense had Conrad used the man as a formal model. Rather, he had taken certain characteristics—his moroseness, his liking for pretentious display, his perpetual sense of frustration—and altered others as he saw fit. It was in this respect, rather than in any attempt to transfer Olmeijer's life literally to his pages, that Conrad may be said to have used the Bornean trader as a model. "Clearly," Gordan says, "*Almayer's Folly* was not a record of the life of William Charles Olmeijer but an expansion of the impression made upon the novelist by the man's personality."

Back in Soerabaja, Gordan had one more call to make—to the grave of Olmeijer, who had died, according to Mrs. Gray, not of opium addiction (as the fictional Almayer did) or of a wound sustained in a python hunt (as Captain Craig had alleged), but after an operation for cancer. In the Peneleh Cemetery near the city, a grassless, treeless desert of whitewashed vaults and graves, Gordan found B821, "a single low vault like a solid table of whitewashed brick. In the center of the sloping top was inserted a white marble plaque almost covered by a wreath of silvered palm leaves." On the plaque was recorded simply the fact that here lay Carel Olmeijer, who was born at Grissee (a town northwest of Soerabaja) in 1799 and died in 1877, "deeply regretted by his children." According to the cemetery records, five of his children were buried in the same vault, including William Charles. Of the younger Olmeijer's influence on the life of a great English novelist, no word was anywhere recorded. Gordan at that moment was the only man in the world, apart from Olmeijer's family, who knew that here in Peneleh Cemetery was the grave of the man who had inspired Conrad to become a novelist. But the discovery had been worth a trip halfway around the world.

DISCOVERIES

ALTHOUGH it has been my chief intention in this book to show how modern literary scholarship has its elements of romance, it has also become clear, I hope, that the adventurous scholars have notably increased our store of literary materials. In addition to the immense wealth of biographical data unearthed in the past half-century, enabling us to understand as never before the characters and personalities of the great English and American men of letters, we now may read a substantial number of works of literary art whose very existence was unknown two or three or four decades ago. Some of these newly found literary works I have already alluded to. Now, to round off our conception of the fruitfulness of scholarly research, let me treat of a handful of other such works whose very titles are missing from the histories of literature familiar to readers of a generation ago. Some of them have indisputable intrinsic value; others are primarily important for the light they throw upon historical tendencies or upon the development of a major literary figure; but all serve, in one way or another, to enrich our store of literary knowledge.

The Book of Margery Kempe

About the year 1501 there came from the press of Wynkyn de Worde, one of the first English printers, a leaflet of only eight pages called *A Shorte Treatyse of Contemplacyon . . . Taken Out of the Boke of Margerie Kempe of Lynn.* Those who read Margery's thoughts on God and His relation to men and women presumably were improved; but no one knew who she was, and although Wynkyn's tiny pamphlet was reprinted in a collection of religious treatises in 1521, she was almost entirely forgotten in the centuries that followed. Where the book was from which Wynkyn had taken his small selection, no one knew.

During the past fifty years or so, however, there has been a notable revival of interest in the history of English mysticism and in the woman's side of medieval religion. Most of the books of theological speculation and devotion were, of course, written by men, such as Richard Rolle, the hermit of Hampole; but in the Middle Ages an occasional woman, more gifted and articulate than her many sisters who spent their lives in the contemplative and austere atmosphere of the nunnery, was moved to record, for the edification of others, her personal religious experiences. Often these experiences had a genuine quality of ecstatic mysticism.

Under such circumstances it was almost inevitable that Margery Kempe should be rediscovered. In 1910 Professor Edmund Gardner produced a new edition of the 1521 anthology, to which he gave the title *The Cell of Self-Knowledge*, and students of mysticism immediately recognized Margery's reflections, brief though they were, as source material of prime importance.

In 1934, an American scholar, Hope Emily Allen, was in London. Under a grant from the American Council of Learned Societies she was continuing her long researches into this very subject of medieval feminine piety. At that time there had been deposited in the Victoria and Albert Museum, in South Kensington, an anonymous medieval manuscript which was the autobiography of a religious woman. The manuscript itself was the property of Colonel William Erdeswick Ignatius Butler-Bowdon, in whose family it had been from time immemorial. Nobody had ever examined it before he took it to the museum and asked that it be identified. The librarian consulted three of the best English authorities on medieval devotional literature, none of whom could throw any light on the manuscript. One of them, however, Evelyn Underhill, who was the author of an excellent book on religious mysticism, suggested that Miss Allen might be able to do so, because she had turned over so many manuscripts of the same sort in the course of her work. Miss Allen, who had long been familiar with Margery through Gardner's reprint, made the identification without any trouble when she was called in. Here was the long-lost "book of Margery

Kempe" from which Wynkyn de Worde had printed brief extracts. The subsequent publication of the manuscript, first in a modernized edition and then in one with full scholarly apparatus, under the editorship of Miss Allen and Professor Sanford B. Meech, immediately won Margery Kempe a new place in the gallery of English medieval authors. Though she was herself illiterate, she had dictated a fascinating self-portrait of what must today be frankly called a religious fanatic. The wife of a burgess of the town of Lynn, and the mother of fourteen children before she and her husband agreed to a life of continence, Margery began to see visions and to converse with Christ, the Virgin Mary, and various saints. When advanced in years, by medieval standards, she made many pilgrimages, to Jerusalem and Rome and elsewhere on the continent. Her religious mania led her to make hysterical public demonstrations; when her eyes fell upon a crucifix, or when she was taking communion, she gave vent to loud screams which, she records with satisfaction, were audible even outside the church. Her peculiarities of dress and her constant manifestations of devotional ecstasy drew crowds wherever she went. On one occasion, in a church at Leicester, the people "stood upon stools for to behold her." She must, it may be observed without malice, have been quite a spectacle.

Few readers maintain that Margery's guileless account of her easy colloquies with Christ and the saints, and of her awareness of the commotion she caused among her beholders, has any great artistic merit. But the discovery of her book has provided rich material for psychoanalytic study of extravagances of religious feeling. And even if one is not concerned to find frustrations and complexes at the root of her innocent exhibitionism, the story she dictated is a human document of substantial importance. Through the publication of Colonel Butler-Bowdon's old manuscript, we have received valuable new information that helps us to understand the atmosphere of an age when faith was still strong, and the signs of divine grace were so unmistakable that to proclaim one's possession of them to the whole world was a duty.

Medwall's "Fulgens and Lucres"

The period of transition between the religious morality play, as typified by *Everyman,* and the regular secular drama which culminated in

Shakespeare, is an obscure passage in the history of English dramatic literature. It has long been recognized that there was a continuous dramatic tradition from the Middle Ages to the time of Queen Elizabeth, but most of the plays that provided the links in the chain during the early sixteenth century have vanished. The few that have survived, most of them scarcely more than dialogues with a rudimentary dramatic interest, have been intensively studied by those seeking to understand the way in which the drama of Shakespeare's day evolved.

The type of play which succeeded the morality in the early Tudor period was called the interlude. In contrast to the earlier type of English play, it laid increasing emphasis on worldly subject matter; the characters were not merely walking personifications of abstractions, but became somewhat individualized; there was a stronger element of realism. One writer of interludes at the end of the fifteenth century long recorded in the histories was Henry Medwall, chaplain to Cardinal Morton. Only one complete play of his, however, was known to exist, an interlude on a moral theme called *Nature*.

But it was known that Medwall had also written *Fulgens and Lucres*,* for in the Bagford Collection at the British Museum were two stray leaves from a printed copy of it. In the 1890's an examination of typographical evidence proved that the play had been printed by John Rastell, an early sixteenth-century printer whose wife was the sister of Sir Thomas More. Scholars drew from the two leaves such meager information as they could concerning the nature of the whole play; and one of them seemed actually to have seen a complete copy. In 1885 the noted student of the early English drama James Orchard Halliwell-Phillipps, in writing of *Fulgens and Lucres*, had made remarks about the play which could not possibly have been based merely upon an examination of the two leaves in the British Museum. Unless he had spun those remarks out of his own fancy (a hobby in which Halliwell-Phillipps did not often indulge) he had had access to evidence unknown to other scholars. But he had died without recording the source of his information.

Thus matters stood until March, 1919, when the collection of plays owned by Lord Mostyn of Mostyn Hall, county Flint, Wales, came up for sale at Sotheby's. In it was found the long-desiderated complete

* That is, *Fulgentius and Lucrece*.

copy of *Fulgens and Lucres*—a copy of the edition printed by Rastell between 1513 and 1519 and, as was subsequently learned, the very copy which Halliwell-Phillipps himself had examined! It was immediately purchased by the agent of Henry E. Huntington, and today it is treasured in the Huntington Library in California. Two editions have made the text of this unique copy available to scholars everywhere.

Fulgens and Lucres turned out to be an interlude in two parts, apparently composed for performance at Lambeth Palace in 1497, when Cardinal Morton was entertaining Flemish and Spanish ambassadors. It dealt with the romantic dilemma of the Roman heiress Lucres, who had to choose between two suitors, one of high birth and one of low, and who in the end chose the latter. As counterpoint to this serious theme Medwall added low-comedy characters in the manner already established by the older plays. It need scarcely be added that the interest of *Fulgens and Lucres* is almost entirely historical. But as "the earliest English secular drama" it is now discussed in every narrative of English dramatic development.

The Poems of Thomas Traherne

In the year 1895 one William T. Brooke, a London book collector, was indulging in his favorite recreation by rummaging through the contents of a secondhand book barrow in one of the city streets. He rapidly turned over and discarded the usual trash, and then suddenly lighted upon two well preserved manuscript volumes that were decidedly out of the ordinary: one an octavo filled with prose, the other a folio composed of mixed verse and prose, both written in the same seventeenth-century hand. These deserved looking into! The sidewalk dealer was only too glad to accept a few pence for them, and Brooke carried them home.

As he studied the verse contained in the first half of the folio, his excitement grew. It was good poetry, deeply religious, with a treatment of childhood and nature that suggested the work of the mystic-physician Henry Vaughan. But a search of the published poetry of Vaughan revealed none of these pieces. Brooke became convinced that what he had found in the book barrow was a totally unknown collection of Vaughan.

So he took his prize to his friend Alexander Grosart, who during his long career as editor of the texts of Elizabethan and Jacobean literary works had learned a great deal about the characteristics of the poets of the age. Dr. Grosart caught his enthusiasm and bought both of the manuscript volumes: plainly, this *was* Vaughan's work; and his next task would be to bring out a new edition of the poet, incorporating the material Brooke had unearthed.

But Grosart died two or three years later while his edition of Vaughan still awaited a publisher, and his library was sold to a dealer. Meanwhile Brooke had spread the news of the discovery among his friends, including Bertram Dobell, one of the most attractive figures in the late Victorian book world. Dobell, originally an errand boy, had become a collector and rare book dealer, and a charming occasional writer on literary subjects in addition. When he heard that the two manuscript volumes were for sale, he went to the dealer who was offering them—a friend of his—and inspected them. They caught his fancy, too; and he bought them, along with a third volume in the same handwriting which Grosart had acquired at some other time.

Although he had high respect for the opinions of Brooke and Grosart, Dobell could not bring himself to believe that the prose and poetry in the volumes were the work of Vaughan. The resemblances between them and his known work were striking; and yet—the differences were equally arresting. Vaughan's characteristic mood was quiet, austere. The mood of the newly found poems, though they too had religious themes, was usually joyous, fervent. And many of the sentiments in these new-found poems were completely at variance with those familiar to readers of Vaughan.

Dobell confided his doubts to Brooke, who began to share them and then suddenly remembered something. Some years before, while he was ransacking obscure volumes of seventeenth-century verse for an anthology he was compiling, he had found, in a little book called *A Serious and Patheticall Contemplation of the Mercies of God, in Several Most Devout and Sublime Thanksgivings for the Same* (1699), a poem that had the same undefinable feeling which was found in the pieces in the mysterious folio volume. Perhaps it would pay to have another look at the 1699 volume, a copy of which was in the British Museum. When Brooke and Dobell did so, they were convinced; there was an unmistakable similarity between the poems there and in the folio. A single author had written them all, and it was not Vaughan. But who was he? The *Contemplation of the Mercies of God* was as tantalizingly anonymous as the manuscript folio.

But in the preface there was a clue. The author of these ecstatic religious poems, it was said, had been a chaplain to Sir Orlando Bridgman, and he had died young. Bridgman was easily identified as a statesman under Charles II; and he had had a chaplain named Thomas Traherne.

So far, so good; now to find out more about Traherne. That was not hard, for Dobell went at once to Anthony a Wood's *Athenae Oxonienses,* a biographical dictionary published in 1691, which gives sketches of all the old worthies associated with Oxford. There he found what he was looking for: Thomas Traherne, son of a Hereford shoemaker, had entered Brasenose College in 1652, taken his M.A. in 1661, and become rector of a parish near his boyhood home; furthermore, he had published two works: *Roman Forgeries* (1673) and *Christian Ethicks* (1675).

The chase was getting warm. Dobell feverishly searched through the two acknowledged Traherne volumes for conclusive proof that the man who had written them had also written the poetry in the manuscript folio. And finally, in the *Christian Ethicks,* he discovered the vital link; for there, in black print, was one of the very poems which were contained in the folio! The proof was complete.

"Will the reader," Dobell modestly wondered when he introduced Thomas Traherne to the twentieth century, "accuse me of undue vanity if I say that it was with a good deal of self-satisfaction, and no little rejoicing, that I welcomed this confirmation of the opinion which I had formed solely upon critical grounds?"

By such an excellent piece of detective work was the name of Thomas Traherne restored to the annals of English poetry. In 1903 Dobell pridefully published the poems, following them in 1908 with the prose passages, to which he gave the title *Centuries of Meditations.* "In so doing," writes a recent student of Traherne, "he gave back to the modern world something rare and beautiful which had been hidden from men's eyes since the seventeenth century." Immediately an interest sprang up in Traherne; more facts about his life were unearthed; in time two or three other printed volumes were identified as being from his pen; and his poetry shared in the general revival of enthusiasm for seventeenth-century verse that was a fruitful literary phenomenon of the first part of our century.

But the story of Traherne's rediscovery was not quite ended. Ten years after Dobell announced his identification, another scholar, searching in the British Museum for something else, encountered a manuscript volume in the Burney Collection called *Poems of Felicity,* "by Tho. Traheron B.D." Strangely enough, although it was fully and correctly entered in the catalogue of the collection, Dobell and Brooke had overlooked it during their quest for material relating to Traherne, as had all the students who had been attracted to the poet following the publication of Dobell's volumes. Upon examination, the manuscript, copied by Traherne's brother from a now lost original, proved to contain some of the poems in the Dobell folio—as well as a number of others which were not there. Thus, by a fortunate chance, our store of the poetry of Thomas Traherne was increased.

Though Traherne's worth as a devotional poet has been exaggerated by some students who allowed their excitement over the romantic circumstances I have just narrated to overrule their judgment, at his best he charms by his childlike innocence and ingenuousness. Lacking the frequently high artistry of his fellow religious poets, Crashaw, Vaughan, Quarles, and George Herbert, his lines too often are flat and crude. But sometimes the radiant freshness and sincerity of his feeling forces the reader to suppress his dissatisfaction with the technical ineptness. No one has ever regretted the accident which cast those two manuscript volumes before the eyes of the curious William Brooke, or deplored Dobell's detectivelike persistence in identifying their author. After two and a quarter centuries of total obscurity, Thomas Traherne now enjoys a secure, though modest, niche in English poetical history.

The Poems of Edward Taylor

Edward Taylor was, in a sense, the American Traherne. Although his poetry has few resemblances to Traherne's, he was a younger contemporary of the long neglected English poet, and his dramatic rediscovery came about through another curious accident of literary scholarship.

In 1936, Thomas H. Johnson, a member of the faculty at the Lawrenceville School in New Jersey, was pursuing research in his specialized field of colonial American literature. In the course of his work he consulted John L. Sibley's voluminous *Biographical Sketches of Graduates of Harvard University,* published in 1881—a much more scholarly but on the whole less fascinating compilation than Wood's *Athenae Oxonienses;* and there he happened upon a sketch of the life of Edward Taylor, a Harvard graduate in the class of 1671. Taylor, Sibley recorded, had spent his long life as a pastor and physician, exactly as Traherne's greater contemporary, Henry Vaughan, had done. Whereas Vaughan had ministered to the spiritual and bodily needs of the villagers in a remote part of Wales, Taylor had done so in Westfield, Massachusetts. At the end of the sketch was appended a list of his writings, all of which, Sibley said, remained in manuscript; and two items in the list immediately enlisted Johnson's attention: "God's Determinations Touching his Elect" and "Sacramental Meditations," which was described as "a series of 150 poems, containing from three to twenty-five stanzas each, continued through a period of 38 years."

Here, Johnson thought, was treasure-trove indeed—the extensive works of a totally unknown early American poet! But where were the manuscripts so temptingly described? Sibley was vague, writing that Taylor's library "descended to his grandson, President Stiles [of Yale], and it is thought that many of the manuscripts which he gave to his grandson before the death of the grandson's father, Isaac Stiles, are in the library of Yale College." The first thing Johnson did therefore was to write to the Yale University Library, inquiring if the manuscripts Sibley mentioned were where he said he "thought" they were.

Back came the answer: They were indeed! But, curiously enough, Sibley had been wrong. At the time he published his biographical dictionary the five volumes of manuscript mentioned were not at Yale at all, but in the hands of Taylor's direct descendant, an eighty-five-year-old gentleman residing in Canandaigua, New York. By the purest chance he decided two years later, in 1883, to deposit them in the very library where Sibley had hazarded they already were. If he had had an affection for some other institution than Yale, Johnson's search might well have been as long drawn out as most such scholarly chases are.

But why had no one ever bothered to examine the manuscripts during the half-century since they came into Yale's possession? Simply because, at the time they were acquired, no one was interested in colonial American literature. They were correctly catalogued and put away on the proper shelf. Subsequently, when early American writings began increasingly to enlist the study of specialists, no one happened to observe the entry in the Yale Library's catalogue of manuscript holdings.

Johnson immediately began to study the manuscript volumes so fortuitously revealed, and the result was exciting. Taylor proved to have been a poet of no mean gifts, although they were not of the kind of which his fellow Puritans could have approved. He had an intense religious emotion which carried him over into mysticism, as it had carried some of the great Anglican religious poets of his century. But what sets him conspicuously apart from other colonial American poets is his use of richly sensuous imagery, almost in the manner of the Roman Catholic poet Richard Crashaw, and of homely, realistic metaphors suggestive sometimes of John Donne and sometimes of George Herbert. Taylor had to express his devotional feeling in terms of the delights of earthly life. It was no doubt because he feared his contemporaries would be outraged by his frank sense of the physical that he refused to publish what he had written. At all events, the rediscovery has been one of the most discussed events of the last decade among students of American literature, and a substantial critical and appreciative literature is growing up about him. In the frequently heard statement that he was "the greatest poet of New England before the nineteenth century" may be the same incautious enthusiasm which for a time inflated the reputation of Traherne. But it has been a happy development, this unlooked-for finding of poetry full of color and vivid imaginativeness in an era which was thought to have produced nothing better than the dull verses of Anne Bradstreet and Michael Wigglesworth.

The Conway Letters

Horace Walpole's manuscripts and *objets d'art* have been the quarry of one of our most diligent modern scholars—Wilmarth S. Lewis, who has scoured the four corners of the earth in behalf of his great collection at Farmington, Connecticut; but he was himself no mean chaser of other men's letters. In August, 1758, he arrived at Ragley Hall, Warwickshire, the seat of the old family of Conway. No sooner had he entered its gates than he realized his instincts had not betrayed him: the place was a treasure-house. Here were priceless portraits, including an "incomparable" picture by Sir Peter Lely; here were literally heaps of old documents. He wrote to his friend George Montagu:

> Think what I have in part recovered! Only the state papers, private letters, etc., etc., of the two lords Conway, Secretaries of State. How you will rejoice and how you will grieve!—They seem to have laid up every scrap of paper they ever had, from the middle of Queen Elizabeth's reign to the middle of Charles the Second's. By the accounts of the family there were whole rooms full, all which, during the absence of the last and the minority of the present lord, were by the ignorance of a steward consigned to the oven and to the uses of the house. What remained, except one box that was kept till almost rotten in a cupboard, were thrown loose into the lumber-room, where, spread on the pavements, they supported old marbles and screens and boxes. From thence I have dragged all I could, and have literally, taking all together, brought away a chest near five feet long, three wide and two deep, brim full. Half are bills, another part rotten, another gnawed by rats, yet I have already found enough to repay my trouble and curiosity, not enough to satisfy it.

Walpole borrowed all these papers, intending to publish at least the more important of them at his Strawberry Hill Press. But for some reason the project fell through, and they were returned to Ragley, where the family, at last awakened to their value by his enthusiasm, took precautions against rats and stewards. Upon the death of their descendant the third Marquis of Hertford, the manuscripts went to John Wilson Croker, the waspish reviewer, who eventually gave them to the nation. They are now divided between the British Museum and the Public Record Office.

Despite Walpole's excitement, the Conway papers still had not been examined by scholars when Professor Marjorie H. Nicolson, now of Columbia University, came upon them in the 1920's. Her immediate interest was in Henry More, the seventeenth-century Cambridge Platonist, who had written many letters to Lady Anne Conway. As a specialist in the philosophical backgrounds of English literature, Miss Nicolson expected to draw from the letters only the data she needed on More's ideas; but no sooner had she looked through a few of them than her original plan faded into the background. More, of course, was a seminal figure in the thought of his age; Lady Anne, for her part, was a woman of great classical and philosophical learning, some of whose ideas indeed were adopted by her friend Leibniz, and whose personal charm, despite lifelong ill health, captivated many of the most eminent men of the day. But it was not primarily the intellectual brilliance of these two correspondents that impressed Miss Nicolson as she scanned their letters; rather, it was the remarkable character of the relationship between the two. For here, she realized, "was a tale of Platonic love between a man and a woman, who were perhaps the last people in history who really understood what those words meant."

Having become fascinated by the More-Conway correspondence, Miss Nicolson determined to fill in the gaps in the collection before her, for the British Museum held only More's letters to Lady Anne. Where were her letters to him—as well as the many letters written by the Conways to other correspondents? She took up the trail.

From one library to another [she writes] the chase led. . . . Collections of manuscripts mentioned in early journals or notes were traced from owner to owner, through wills and catalogues of sale, only to prove that within the present century the collections had been broken up, and the parts dispersed over two continents. The possibility of

finding a series of papers mentioned by only one bibliophile led to a
journey, to whose end [I] arrived too late, to find that within a year
the old librarian had died, leaving no written record of his knowledge.
Long days of search often proved barren, short days sometimes full
of wealth. Luck and coincidence led to the discovery of facts which
had remained obstinately hidden from zeal. Gradually fragment after
fragment fell into place. . . . From a chaos of torn and faded letters,
petitions, bills, and order books, from crumbling journals and diaries,
from wills, from commonplace books and college records, scattered
throughout England, one character after another appeared, in firm,
clear outline against a background of stirring events. And what a story
it was! *

Although she was unable to discover all Lady Anne Conway's letters,
her diligent research brought many to light, including those to her
husband and to her father-in-law, and some at least of those she wrote
in reply to Henry More. In all, Miss Nicolson transcribed more than
five hundred letters and documents concerning the Conways and their
friends. Those which were most intimately related to Lady Anne and
Henry More she published in a large volume called *Conway Letters*
(1930). In it the main focus is, naturally, the exchange of philosophical speculation between the two. But in addition there are intimate
glimpses of all sorts of men and women celebrated in history, from
William Harvey, Sir Isaac Newton, Thomas Hobbes, and Robert
Boyle, to the outcast Quakers William Penn and George Fox; and
constant small vignettes of life in the turbulent seventeenth century,
when the English beheaded their king, London was ravaged by pesti-
lence and fire, and men's minds reeled from the impact of the new
scientific discoveries. The Conway letters are indispensable for a knowledge of the intellectual searchings that went on in an age of philosophical revolution; but, for the general reader at least, they are chiefly fascinating because of their revelation of human personalities and the
environment in which they lived out their lives. Henry More and Lady
Anne Conway and their wide circle of friends were speculative thinkers,
but they were also human beings living in space and time. No wonder
Walpole was beguiled by what he found at Ragley, and no wonder

* From *Conway Letters,* edited by Marjorie H. Nicolson. New Haven: Yale
University Press, 1930. Quoted by permission of the publishers.

Miss Nicolson shared his excitement when she repeated his experience, at a distance of more than a century and a half, in the British Museum.

Browning's "Essay on Chatterton"

Every book on Robert Browning asserts that his only piece of extended prose is the introduction to the volume of forged Shelley letters which Edward Moxon published, and then promptly suppressed, in 1852. Future books on Browning, if their authors have kept abreast of the latest scholarship, will not repeat the statement. This is why.

A few years ago Professor Donald Smalley, now of Indiana University, was reading a book called *Works and Days*, published in 1933. The volume was a collection of excerpts from the joint journal of two Victorian poets, Katherine Bradley and her niece Edith Cooper, who wrote together under the pen-name of Michael Field. These ladies had been correspondents of Browning, and in his last four years they had had some personal association with him and his sister. Six years after his death, they spent a fortnight with the sister, Sarianna, in his son Pen's home at Asolo. There, they recorded, they saw "heaps and heaps of letters," proof sheets, and other Browning memorabilia which were destined to be lost after the death of Pen in 1912. And, one rainy day during that visit, Edith Cooper confided to the diary: "Now I am going to read 'the Old's' article on Tasso and Chatterton in the *Foreign Quarterly Review* for July, 1842."

"The Old," it was explained in *Works and Days*, was the ladies' familiar name for Browning. Evidently, then, they had been told by the poet's sister or his son that he had written and published an article on Tasso and Chatterton, a copy of which remained among the Browning papers. No one, before Edith Cooper, seems ever to have recorded that fact. Although by 1895 the much-mocked Browning Society had accomplished most of its solemn self-appointed task of snapping up and considering its idol's every trifle, not even its tireless leader and Browning's first bibliographer, F. J. Furnivall, had heard of his essay. And, although presumably *Works and Days* found a certain number of readers when it appeared, Smalley alone recognized Miss Cooper's little sentence as a clue to an unknown literary work. His job was simple. All he had to do was look up the volume of the *Foreign Quarterly Review* for 1842—and there the essay was!

In 1948 he reprinted it, with an elaborate commentary, in a 200-page volume. The unsigned essay on Chatterton (Tasso is disposed of in a few pages—Victorian reviewers were never bound by the titles of their articles) offers valuable insight into the earliest phase of Browning's lifelong habit of "case-making"—of special pleading in behalf of maligned figures in history. Chatterton, he felt, was misunderstood; Victorians thought of him primarily as a child of unpleasant precocity, and a fraud to boot. Browning therefore hastened to correct the current opinion. From his wide background of reading he deliberately selected and slanted the facts in Chatterton's biography which would serve his purpose, evolving "from Chatterton's pathetic story of moody pride, frustration, and suicide the plan and the protagonist of an edifying moral drama," as Smalley remarks. He then wrote the "moral drama" in the form of a lengthy review, with all of the casuistical ingenuity which he was later to exercise in "Mr. Sludge, the Medium" and *The Ring and the Book*. Serious readers have always been aware that Browning's handling of data was easy-going in the extreme, and his logic frequently slippery; but Smalley's rediscovery of the forgotten essay on Chatterton dramatically underscores the fact.

The Brontës' Childhood Fantasies

When Charlotte Brontë died in 1855, at the age of thirty-nine, she left a mass of personal papers which her husband, the Reverend Arthur Bell Nicholls, lent to Elizabeth Gaskell while she was writing her *Life of Charlotte Brontë*. Among them Mrs. Gaskell found a package "containing an immense amount of manuscript in an inconceivably small space; tales, dramas, poems, romances, written principally by Charlotte, in a hand almost impossible to decipher without the aid of a magnifying glass." Having enough to do as it was, Mrs. Gaskell did not try to find out in detail what these thousands of tiny pages contained. Instead, she contented herself with making a note of their existence, and when she had finished her book she returned them to Mr. Nicholls.

No one heard anything more about them until forty years later, when Clement Shorter, a London bookman, wishing to clear the copyright of some of Charlotte's letters he had acquired, visited the aged Nicholls on his farm in Ireland. Before he returned to England he succeeded in purchasing most of her papers, which he then resold to his friend Thomas J. Wise. The letters and literary fragments, Shorter and Wise eventually published; but neither man considered the scores of manuscript booklets worth deciphering. Wise therefore, after setting aside a few items for his own library, had the remaining pieces sumptuously bound, and fed them onto the market. As curious souvenirs of a romantic life, they were snapped up by collectors and scattered all over Great Britain and the United States.

Among the purchasers was John Henry Wrenn, whose collection went to the University of Texas. There, in the early 1920's, Fannie Ratchford picked up one of the booklets, written when Charlotte was twenty-one, and immediately was intrigued by it. What had impelled the young woman to write these thirty-five pages in a hand so tiny that a powerful magnifying glass was required to read it? She transcribed the text, which covered over a hundred pages in typescript—and, far from being explained, the mystery deepened. The miniature book proved to contain a group of character vignettes, held together by a vague shadow of a plot and dealing with personages named Wellesley, Castlereagh, and Townshend. But only the names linked Charlotte's characters with actual historical figures; otherwise they seemed wholly fictitious. The setting suggested England at some points, Ireland at others, and the Continent at still others. To Miss Ratchford, everything was confusion; yet to Charlotte Brontë everything must have been plain as day, for she wrote of her characters, her settings, and her situations with a familiarity obviously born of long acquaintance with them.

The answer then, Miss Ratchford thought, must be that this booklet was not intended to stand alone, but was an installment in a long serial story; she had simply had the misfortune to arrive in the middle. But now that her curiosity was aroused, she had to find out the rest of the story, before and after. And so she began to trace the scores of booklets which Wise, concerned only with their monetary value as Brontë association items, and totally indifferent to their possible literary significance, had dispersed over Britain and America. For twenty years her search went on. She located a large collection of the booklets in the possession of Henry H. Bonnell of Philadelphia, a devoted Brontë student; others she tracked down, a single item here, a dozen of them there, in public and private libraries from Leeds to Cincinnati. In all, she was able to locate and study over a hundred separate manuscripts, most of them by Charlotte but some by her brother Branwell. (Many more, I might add, are still unrecovered.) Ranging in size from small octavo to scarcely more than an inch square, nearly all of them were written in a tiny hand imitative of printing type. Most of them bore elaborate title-pages with signatures and dates, and were carefully sewn into covers made of household wrapping paper.

During the long period of Miss Ratchford's search, other scholars printed the text of some of the miniature manuscripts she had examined, and in 1933 she herself issued a volume called *Legends of Angria*, containing a further selection of hitherto unprinted Brontë pieces. But not until 1941, when she published her fascinating book, *The Brontës' Web of Childhood*, did the reading public learn the full, amazing story that lay in, and behind, those curious booklets.

In 1826, when Branwell Brontë was nine, his father had brought him a new set of wooden soldiers. Each of his three sisters, Charlotte, Anne, and Emily, had selected one for her special pet. Charlotte's was immediately named the Duke of Wellington. With their soldiers as *dramatis personae*, and Wellington as the hero, the children began a long series of plays laid in Africa, filled with wars, international intrigues, and similar excitements. Unlike other children, the Brontës, left to their own devices in the isolated village of Haworth, their young imaginations constantly replenished by their reading, did not tire of their make-believe. Month after month they added further details to their imaginary land and invented new and complicated situations to keep their constantly expanding cast of characters busy.

Then, three years after the gift of the wooden soldiers, they turned journalists and historians. Branwell began to produce a magazine, modeled upon *Blackwood's* but small enough for the wooden soldiers to hold in their hands. This new periodical contained articles and departments of timely interest to the inhabitants of Glass Town, the capital of the imaginary kingdom. From the first, the Brontë girls contributed to the magazine, and eventually Charlotte took it over. From writing the monthly issues of a serious magazine it was only a step to writing whole books; for after all, if the magazine contained the customary advertisements and reviews of new books, the books themselves had to be made to exist.

All through the years of their adolescence, the four Brontës continued their make-believe, which steadily became more sophisticated as they matured and their reading widened. While the others branched out into new territory, Charlotte remained faithful for a long time to the Glass Town area at the mouth of the Niger and the set of characters, now so intensely real to her, with which it had been peopled. Turning from the writing of magazines, travel accounts, and histories, she devoted herself to Glass Town miscellanies and fiction. In 1833, when she was seventeen, she wrote no fewer than twelve novels in her minute hand; one, running to 34,000 words, required a booklet of only twenty-five pages!

And then, by an amicable arrangement with Branwell, Charlotte moved her operations from Glass Town to a newly organized kingdom to the east named Angria, where Arthur Augustus Adrian Wellesley, the Byronic son of her earlier hero, the Duke of Wellington, was enthroned. With Wellesley to his magnificent new capital went most of the "young and rising generation of the city," who had been created in Charlotte's earlier novels and histories. In the five years 1834–39, during which she passed her twentieth birthday, the part of Charlotte's life which really mattered was passed not where her physical body happened to be, at Haworth or the school at Roe Head, but where her imagination constantly dwelt, in her beloved Angria. The Angrian romances, essays, and miscellanies she composed in these years amount to hundreds of thousands of words. Most of them were written in the person of Arthur Wellesley's younger brother, an indefatigable observer and chronicler of all that happened in Angria, from a complicated affair of amorous passion among the high-born to the newest political entanglement. Only in 1839, when she was twenty-three, did Charlotte formally take leave of the dream world which had filled her imagination for so many years.

Although the fact was entirely unsuspected until Miss Ratchford made her patient survey, the hundred or more booklets now known to be extant contain a quantity of Charlotte Brontë's writing exceeding that of her published works. But it is not their remarkable bulk (much in little!) that makes these newly studied manuscripts so important; nor is their significance of the same order as that of the juvenilia which have come down to us from other authors. Although Miss Ratchford was perhaps overenthusiastic when she wrote that "these little books hold in their tiny script the most remarkable romance in literature and the most accurate record of the evolution of genius extant in any language," they are nevertheless, in the strict sense of the word, unique. Nothing like them exists in the case of any other author. They show that, in ten of the most impressionable years of her life, Charlotte Brontë lived in a dream world infinitely more real to her than that in which she had her physical being; and it was while she directed the destinies of her many characters in Glass Town and Angria that she was unconsciously preparing herself to be a novelist. As Miss Ratchford shows in a long chapter called "Fruits of the Almond Tree," time after time, in the creation of *Jane Eyre* and the less known novels, she drew her characters and situations from memories of what she had written as an adolescent in the chronicles of Glass Town and Angria. That she modified and refined this daydream material in the light of her subsequent experience of the real world does not detract at all from the vital place the fantasy-stories have as the raw stuff of her mature fiction.

Emily Brontë meanwhile was collaborating with her sister Anne in a cycle of stories, laid on the imaginary North Pacific island of Gondal. Except for a few stray fragments, her manuscripts were entirely destroyed, but they may well have been as extensive as Charlotte's. Until fairly recent years it was not known that the poems which would insure Emily's place in literature, even had she not written *Wuthering Heights*, were originally embedded in her stories of Gondal. When she copied them into the manuscript which Charlotte discovered on a momentous day in 1845, she took care to erase all evidence of their origin; and after her death, when Charlotte was about to publish more of her sister's poems, she too deleted all references to Gondal. The result is that many of the poems have been interpreted as being subjective and autobiographical, whereas they actually were written for specific characters and situations in her Gondal cycle. Only by reading them in terms of their narrative context, so far as the story can be reconstructed from the meager hints which remain, can their original, intended significance be understood. The many biographers who have based their portraits of Emily on the assumption that her poems are consistently expressive of her inner self have presented a romantic figure; but it is not the Emily Brontë who lived.

The literature which has grown up about the Brontës is immense; few other figures in English literary history have attracted so many devoted students. Only one or two other writers have been the occasion of as much fantastic speculation and myth-making. In the lack of positive evidence, there has arisen a host of theories about their alleged secret love affairs, their relations with one another, and the sources of the materials in their books. But now that, at long last, we have learned of the paramount part which the long-continued fantasy of Glass Town, Angria, and Gondal had in their lives, we are on our way to a far sounder understanding of those remarkable young women. The myths that have been spun about their years of development seem contrived and feeble indeed, now that we have learned at least a part of the truth.

But now I must bring my recital of recent literary discoveries to a close; for this book, after all, has been designed to be only illustrative, not encyclopedic. In it my theme, as Chaucer's Pardoner confided to his fellow pilgrims, "is alwey oon, and evere was"; and to expostulate further, as another ingratiatingly garrulous character in literature put it, "were nothing but to waste night, day, and time"—and the tolerance of my readers.

The literary scholar, looked at from the viewpoint adopted in this book, is a man whose professional life happily retains the charms of a number of hobbies. He is a puzzle solver on a grand scale—and his puzzles have the great additional fascination of being found in a natural state, totally uncontrived. He is an explorer as surely as is a mountain climber or a wanderer in uncharted caves, even though his adventures may take place in the stacks of a California library or in a somnolent English village. And as for being a collector! But whereas the common run of men indulge their magpie instincts in accumulating stamps or stones or beetles, the scholar indulges his by the ceaseless gathering of facts, which take the physical form of bulging files of note cards, transcripts, photostats, and microfilms. Like most passionate devotees of a hobby, scholars are an enigma to their uninitiate friends. The pursuit of the out-of-the-way literary fact is a slightly esoteric kind of sport; to the outsider it seems almost a vice, harmless to be sure, but still a vice.

Yet what rewards even the outsider, if he is at all interested in literature, may reap in time from his friend's hobby! From those bushels of notes, representing data tracked down during many an adventurous quest, may come a radically revised interpretation of the life and character of a great poet, or of the meaning of his most important poems. Only when you carefully compare a history of English or American literature written half a century ago with one which has just come from the press—or two biographies of the same man of letters, written fifty years apart—can you begin to understand the difference that scholarly research has made in our knowledge of literature. Too often there is a long lag between the publication of research and its utilization by popular biographers and critics, and a great deal of the new material unearthed in recent decades has not yet become general knowledge. But, even though the process sometimes is lamentably slow, the results of research gradually are absorbed into books designed for the general reader. Eventually old familiar "facts" which have been disproved by patient research are found no more, and new discoveries, and new interpretations based on those discoveries, take their place.

"Private Vices, Publick Benefits": that was the subtitle old Bernard de Mandeville used for his once famous satire, *The Fable of the Bees*. It sums up rather neatly, I think, the worth of the literary researcher. From the delightful vices of the adventurous scholar, the book-loving public does indeed—however incompletely and belatedly—receive its reward.

BIBLIOGRAPHICAL NOTES

IN the notes that follow, I list, chapter by chapter, the chief printed sources of my information (but by no means all of them—such a list would run to more hundreds of items), and in addition name occasionally books and articles to which the reader may turn for other narratives on the same general subjects.

I should like also to mention, for the convenience of readers whose curiosity about the adventurous side of literary scholarship is not sated by the contents of the present book, a few other titles: all of them guaranteed to be entertaining, and at times downright exciting, reading. Probably the all-time classic of literary detective work is *The Road to Xanadu* (enlarged edition, Boston, 1930), in which John Livingston Lowes traces the workings of Coleridge's imagination as it drew upon unconscious reminiscences of his reading for the creation of "The Rime of the Ancient Mariner" and "Kubla Khan." Besides being a thrilling narrative of scholarly research, and stylistically the very definition of learning worn lightly, it is a monumental contribution to our understanding of how the poetic mind operates. John Matthews Manly's *Some New Light on Chaucer* (New York, 1926) is a readable account of his attempts to identify historical figures as the models for some of Chaucer's characters. Not all of his proposed identifications, it should be added, have been accepted by other scholars. Frederick A. Pottle's *Shelley and Browning* (Chicago, 1923) is a demonstration of how traditional notions of one poet's influence upon another must be revised after one has gone to the trouble of tracing down the actual copy of the book from which the later poet got his knowledge of the earlier. In a delightful article called "The Romance of Scholarship," *Colophon*, new series, III (1938), 259–79, Charles R.

Anderson recounts the adventures he had in the course of his research for his volume on *Melville in the South Seas*. And in *The Quest for Corvo* (London and New York, 1934), A. J. A. Symons has written an absorbing biography in the unusual form of a research narrative— "Corvo" being, of course, the eccentric and mysterious Frederick William Rolfe, author of *Chronicles of the House of Borgia* and *Hadrian the Seventh*.

Two other books, though one is not concerned with specifically English literary research and the other not with literature at all, may be recommended: *Sleuthing in the Stacks* (Cambridge, Mass., 1944), a collection by Professor Rudolph Altrocchi of his adventures in the tracing of specific themes through several literatures, and Frank Maloy Anderson's *The Mystery of "A Public Man"* (Minneapolis, 1948), an admirable detective narrative showing how the techniques of research described in the present book, when used by a professional historian, at long last provided what seems to be a solution to one of the most tantalizing riddles in American history.

And finally, for the sake of those readers of *The Scholar Adventurers* who are too young to remember when they first appeared, I should make categorical mention of the books and articles written in the 1920's and 1930's by A. Edward Newton, A. S. W. Rosenbach, Vincent Starrett, and Edmund Lester Pearson—all full of bookish anecdotes of the general sort I have recounted, but told from the point of view of the bibliophile rather than that of the professional scholar.

CHAPTER I: *The Secret of the Ebony Cabinet*

Most of the information relating to the successive Boswell discoveries has been taken from the introductions to the following volumes: Thomas Seccombe's edition of the *Letters of James Boswell to the Rev. W. J. Temple* (London, 1908); *Private Papers of James Boswell from Malahide Castle*, Vol. I (Mt. Vernon, N.Y., 1928); Frederick A. and Marion S. Pottle, *The Private Papers of James Boswell from Malahide Castle: A Catalogue* (London and New York, 1931); and Claude Colleer Abbott, *A Catalogue of Papers Relating to Boswell, Johnson, and Sir William Forbes Found at Fettercairn House, 1930–31* (Oxford, 1936). I have also drawn details from many articles on the successive discoveries published in periodicals, such as the London *Times Literary Supplement* and the *Saturday Review of Literature*, from 1928 onward. The *New York Times*, Nov. 8, 1948, pp. 1 and 18, printed several valuable articles on the occasion of the Grolier Club display of Col. Isham's completed collection. For a preliminary portrait of the Boswell newly revealed in the Malahide papers, see Frederick A. Pottle, "The Life of Boswell," *Yale Review*, XXXV (1946), 445–60.

CHAPTER II: *The Case of the Curious Bibliographers*

The classic work on Wise's forgeries is, of course, that by John Carter and Graham Pollard: *An Enquiry into the Nature of Certain Nineteenth Century Pamphlets* (London and New York, 1934). Since the Carter-Pollard exposé, a large literature has grown up on the subject of the forgeries, most of it in literary and scholarly periodicals; although I have made full use of it, it is too extensive to list here. For additional details of Carter and Pollard's work, previously unrevealed, see Carter's article, "Thomas J. Wise and His Forgeries," *Atlantic Monthly*, CLXXV, 93–100 (Feb., 1945). A good account of Wise's whole career, including much material on his activities as under-cover speculator in literary rarities (notably the sack of Swinburne's manuscripts and books) is Wilfred Partington's *Forging Ahead* (New York, 1939). This book was expanded and rewritten for its London edition, under the title *Thomas J. Wise in the Original Cloth* (1947). The latter volume prints the reminiscences of Wise which G. B. Shaw wrote in a copy of *Forging Ahead*. Fannie E. Ratchford edited *Letters of Thomas J. Wise to John Henry Wrenn* (New York, 1944). A "footnote" to the Carter and Pollard *Enquiry* is a brochure by the same authors, *The Firm of Charles Ottley, Landon & Co.* (London and New York, 1948), in which they add four Swinburne items to the still growing roll of the forgeries.

CHAPTER III: *The Quest of the Knight-Prisoner*

Edward Hicks published his discoveries in *Sir Thomas Malory: His Turbulent Career* (Cambridge, Mass., 1928); for a critical account of this volume, with some factual corrections, see A. C. Baugh's review in the *Journal of English and Germanic Philology*, XXIX (1930),

452-57. Baugh announced his own finds in an article, "Documenting Sir Thomas Malory," *Speculum*, VIII (1933), 3-29. A summary of our present knowledge of Malory's life is given by Eugène Vinaver in his edition of *The Works of Sir Thomas Malory* (Oxford, 1947)— i.e., the separate stories from which Caxton made the *Morte Darthur*— I, xiii-xxviii. Vinaver's discussion of the significance of the newly discovered Winchester manuscript is contained in the same volume. Hicks and Vinaver summarize the essential information unearthed earlier by Kittredge and Chambers. For the last few pages of this chapter I am heavily indebted to my friend and colleague, Prof. Robert M. Estrich.

CHAPTER IV: *Hunting for Manuscripts*

An interesting general discussion of the technique of hunting for manuscripts, from which I have lifted one or two anecdotes, is James M. Osborn's paper, "The Search for English Literary Documents," *English Institute Annual: 1939* (New York, 1940), pp. 31-55. The story of Mason Wade's discovery is from the Introduction to his edition of *The Journals of Francis Parkman* (New York, 1947). That of the Garrick version of *Hamlet* is told by George Winchester Stone, Jr., in *Publications of the Modern Language Association*, XLIX (1934), 890-921. On Mary Rogers, see Samuel Copp Worthen, "Poe and the Beautiful Cigar Girl," *American Literature*, XX (1948), 305-12. The material on Shelley's Neapolitan daughter is from Newman I. White's *Shelley* (New York, 1940), II, 546-50, 570.

Among the most delightful reminiscences yet published of scholars' dealings with the owners of manuscripts are those by Logan Pearsall Smith, in the chapter on "Hunting for Manuscripts" in his *Unforgotten Years* (Boston, 1939), which contains a number of amusing stories in addition to the one I repeat. Wilmarth S. Lewis, the owner of the great collection of Walpoliana and editor of the Yale edition of Walpole's letters, described some of his adventures in "Searching for Manuscripts," *Atlantic Monthly*, CLXXVI, 67-72 (Sept., 1945), and in other papers contributed to the same periodical. Geoffrey Hellman's excellent profile of Lewis and his "Walpole factory" appeared in the *New Yorker*, Aug. 6 and 13, 1949. On the feud in Emily Dickinson's family and its effects upon public knowledge of her life and work, see Millicent Todd Bingham, *Ancestors' Brocades* (New York, 1945), and John Erskine's article, "The Dickinson Saga," *Yale Review*, XXXV

(1945), 74–83. The anecdote about the diaries of William Cullen Bryant's mother is taken from Tremaine McDowell, "Hunting Without Gun or Camera," *Colophon*, new graphic series, I (1940), 87–92, which contains several other anecdotes relevant to our purposes.

The stories involving James L. Clifford, Thomas W. Copeland, John C. French, Gordon S. Haight, Thomas O. Mabbott, and Gordon N. Ray, I owe to the courtesy of these gentlemen. Nearly all of them are published here for the first time.

CHAPTER V: *Exit a Lady, Enter Another*

Leslie Hotson narrated his discovery of the Marlowe inquest records in *The Death of Christopher Marlowe* (London and Cambridge, Mass., 1925). For a survey of all that has subsequently been learned about the circumstances of Marlowe's death, including his activities as a secret agent, see John Bakeless, *The Tragicall History of Christopher Marlowe* (Cambridge, Mass., 1942), I, 141–89.

In the twenty-five years since the Marlowe discovery Hotson has made a number of other spectacular finds; and he is one of the few scholars who have thought it worth while to share the excitement of his adventures with the general public. A number of his narratives appeared during the 1930's, among them "The Adventure of the Single Rapier" (on the murder of Henry Porter, a minor dramatist contemporary with Shakespeare) and "Shakespeare and Mine Host of the Mermaid," *Atlantic Monthly*, CXLVIII (1931), 26–31, and CLI (1933), 708–14. In *Shakespeare Versus Shallow* (Boston, 1931), and *I, William Shakespeare* (London, 1937) he reported his discovery of new documents pertaining to Shakespeare's life. Another period of research in the Public Record Office netted him "Shelley's lost letters to Harriet," which he published under that title (London, 1930). His essay on "Literary Serendipity," published in *ELH: A Journal of English Literary History*, IX (1942), 79–94, is an entertaining account of the atmosphere of the Public Record Office and of the trials and delights he has experienced there.

Two little books contain the stories of the pursuit of Annette Vallon as told by the scholars involved in it: *Wordsworth's French Daughter,* by George McLean Harper (Princeton, 1921), and the somewhat more substantial *William Wordsworth and Annette Vallon*, by Émile Legouis (London and New York, 1922). Among the later studies of Wordsworth which have been powerfully influenced by these revelations may be named Herbert Read's (London, 1930) and Hugh I'Anson Fausset's (*The Lost Leader:* London, 1933).

CHAPTER VI: *A Gallery of Inventors*

An up-to-date account of literary forgeries in general remains to be written—and what a book it could be! Meanwhile, J. A. Farrer's *Literary Forgeries* (London, 1907) contains fairly good narratives of the principal forgers. Mark Holstein's "A Five-Foot Shelf of Literary Forgeries," *Colophon*, new series, 11 (1937), 550–67, and Vincent Starrett's essay, "The Fine Art of Forgery," reprinted in William Targ's *Carrousel for Bibliophiles* (New York, 1947), pp. 313–29, cover the ground more briefly. E. H. W. Meyerstein has written the standard life of Chatterton (London and New York, 1930). There is no recent general study of Macpherson. An entertaining account of the Ireland forgeries is John Mair's *The Fourth Forger* (London and New York, 1938). Gerald D. McDonald gave brief descriptions of the forgeries at the New York Public Library in its *Bulletin*, XXXVII (1933), 200–204, and XLI (1937), 623–28.

Amazingly enough, there is no formal life of John Payne Collier. The best contemporary account of Collier's exposure is C. M. Ingleby, *A Complete View of the Shakspere Controversy* (London, 1861). Ingleby was strongly biased against Collier, but time has proved that he chose the side of the angels. He included a number of fine facsimiles of the annotations in the Perkins Folio. For a general survey of the Collier forgeries as they affect Shakespearean scholarship, see E. K. Chambers, *William Shakespeare* (Oxford, 1930), II, 384–93. On the forgeries at Dulwich College, see W. W. Greg's Introduction to *Henslowe's Diary* (London, 1904), I, xxxvi–xlv. S. A. Tannenbaum's suspicions of Forman's "Book of Plaies," as well as of other documents he believed Collier forged, are aired in his *Shaksperian Scraps* (New York, 1933). What seems to be the final verdict on his pleading *in re* Forman was delivered by J. Dover Wilson and R. W. Hunt in "The Authenticity of Simon Forman's 'Booke of Plaies,' " *Review of English Studies*, XXIII (1947), 193–200. In another volume, *Shakspere Forgeries in the Revels Accounts* (New York, 1928), Tannenbaum revived the old charge that Collier had forged certain official documents relating to early seventeenth-century dramatic performances. I have not gone into that tangled business here; but the curious may find a summary of the earlier discussion, plus a brilliant use of the evidence provided by wormholes, in A. E. Stamp, *The Disputed Revels Accounts* (London, 1930). It will be obvious from my pages on Tannenbaum that he was intent on finding Collier in every dark hole and dusty corner; his books and articles should be read only in the light of the reviews they received from Elizabethan specialists. Other material on Collier presented here has been levied from Hazelton Spencer's "The Forger at Work: A New Case Against Collier," *Philological Quarterly*, VI (1927), 32–38; William Ringler, "Another Collier Forgery," London *Times Literary Supplement*, Oct. 29, 1938, pp. 693–94; and a passage in Giles Dawson's paper, "The Authenticity and Attribution of Written Matter," *English Institute Annual: 1942* (New York, 1943), pp. 90–95. On the little matter of the flyspeck on the First Folio, see Robert M. Smith in the *Colophon*, new series, I (1935), 25–32.

For my account of the career of Major Byron I have depended largely on the scholarly study of this subject by Theodore G. Ehrsam in *The Shelley Legend*, by Robert M. Smith *et al.* (New York, 1945), pp. 50–83. Much of the remainder of *The Shelley Legend* is taken up with an elaborate discussion of the Shelley letters which Smith and his coauthors believe Byron to have forged. No one should read *The Shelley Legend* without immediately referring to three crushing review-articles by leading American Shelley authorities: Frederick L. Jones in *Publications of the Modern Language Association*, LXI (1946), 848–90, Newman I. White in *Studies in Philology*, XLIII (1946), 522–44, and Kenneth Neill Cameron in the *Journal of English and Germanic Philology*, XLV (1946), 369–79.

The best study of "Antique" Smith is found in William Roughead's *The Riddle of the Ruthvens and Other Studies* (Edinburgh, 1919), pp. 147–70. (Roughead, I cannot resist confiding to those who have not made his acquaintance, is always fascinating reading. His numerous volumes on famous crimes, written with an inimitable dry wit, are unsurpassed in their field.) J. DeLancey Ferguson contributed a shorter essay on Smith, from the standpoint of the professional Burns scholar, to the *Colophon*, Part XIII (1930).

CHAPTER VII: *The Scholar and the Scientist*

The story of Root and Russell is told in their article, "A Planetary Date for Chaucer's *Troilus*," *Publications of the Modern Language Association*, XXXIX (1924), 48–63; for additional details I am indebted to Prof. Root. The Shelley narrative is from Newman I. White, *Shelley* (New York, 1940), I, 280–83, 650. Two informative articles by Eugene B. Power on the scope of recent and current microfilming programs for scholarly purposes are "The Manuscript Copying Program in England," *American Archivist*, VII (1944), 28–32, and "University Microfilms: A Microfilming Service for Scholars," *Journal of Documentation*, II (1946), 23–31. Charlton Hinman described his first collating machine in "Mechanized Collation: A Preliminary Report," *Papers of the Bibliographical Society of America*, XLI (1947), 99–106. Information on his second machine I owe to a private communication from Prof. Hinman. William J. Neidig published the results of his examination of the misdated Shakespearean quartos in *Modern Philology*, VIII (1910–11), 145–63, giving a brief résumé of earlier discussion on the subject as well as thirteen full-page plates that show his method of work. A more popular account by the same author appeared in the *Century Magazine*, LXXX (1910), 912–19. Greg's essay "The First Folio and Its Publishers," printed in a collection by various hands, *Studies in the First Folio* (London, 1924), contains his theory as to what lay behind the misdating. The best account of modern scientific methods for examining manuscripts is that of Capt. R. B. Haselden, *Scientific Aids for the Study of Manuscripts* (Oxford, 1935). The story of the discovery of a possible new Shakespeare signature is told by Joseph Q. Adams in the *John Rylands Library Bulletin*, XXVII (1943), 256–59.

CHAPTER VIII: *Secrets in Cipher*

On the Voynich manuscript, see John M. Manly, "The Most Mysterious Manuscript in the World," *Harper's Magazine*, CXLIII (1921), 186–97; William Romaine Newbold, *The Cipher of Roger Bacon* (Philadelphia, 1928); Manly's later article, "Roger Bacon and the Voynich Manuscript," *Speculum*, VI (1931), 345–91; and Fletcher Pratt, *Secret and Urgent: The Story of Codes and Ciphers* (New York, 1939), pp. 30–39. The anecdote concerning the rebus in the Chaucer manuscript is taken from Manly and Rickert's *The Text of the Canterbury Tales* (Chicago, 1940), I, 379–80.

The material on Pepys and his decipherers has been gathered from a number of sources, including Arthur Bryant, *Pepys: The Man in the Making* (London, 1947), pp. 392–93; J. E. Bailey, "On the Cipher of Pepys' 'Diary,' " in *Pepysiana* (supplementary volume of Wheatley's ed., London, 1899), pp. 270–80; and William Matthews, "Pepys' Transcribers," *Journal of English and Germanic Philology*, XXXIV (1935), 213–24. Announcement of the discovery and deciphering of William Byrd's diary was made by Louis B. Wright in the *Huntington Library Quarterly*, II (1938–39), 489–96. Those interested in another relation between cryptography and literary studies should see William F. Friedman, "Edgar Allan Poe, Cryptographer," *American Literature*, VIII (1936), 266–80, and William K. Wimsatt, Jr., "What Poe Knew About Cryptography," *Publications of the Modern Language Association*, LVIII (1943), 754–79.

CHAPTER IX: *The Destructive Elements*

Much material of the sort sampled in this chapter can be found in the voluminous writings of Isaac D'Israeli, such as *Calamities of Authors* (1812) and *Curiosities of Literature* (1791–1823), both of which were several times reprinted during the nineteenth century. An entertaining little book on the subject is William Blades's *The Enemies of Books* (London, 1888). Holbrook Jackson tells some other anecdotes relating to the destruction of books in his *Anatomy of Bibliomania* (London and New York, 1932), pp. 515–62. In an article in the *Colophon*, Part VII (1933—unpaged), David A. Randall offers a brisk survey of specific literary items that have been lost, from Skelton's *Garlande of Laurell* down to T. J. Hogg's *Leonora*.

For my account of the *Beowulf* manuscript I have levied upon Friedrich Klaeber's Introduction to his edition of *Beowulf, and The Fight at Finnsburg* (3rd ed., New York, 1936) and Kemp Malone, "Thorkelin's Transcripts of *Beowulf*," *Studia Neophilologica*, XIV (1942), 25–30. On the Cottonian Library, see Arundell Esdaile, *The British Museum Library* (London, 1946), pp. 226–31. For the story of the vicissitudes of the *Murders in the Rue Morgue* manuscript, see Ernest Boll in *Modern Philology*, XL (1943), 302–15.

On the lost literature of Anglo-Saxon and medieval England, these fairly recent articles are especially recommended: R. W. Chambers, "The Lost Literature of Medieval England," *Library*, 4th series, V (1925), 293–321; F. C. Jones, "Spoil from the English Monastic Libraries," *Contemporary Review*, CXXXVI (1929), 91–97; R. M. Wilson, "Lost Literature in Old and Middle English," *Leeds Studies in*

English, No. 2 (1933), 14–37, No. 5 (1936), 1–49, and No. 6 (1937), 30–49; the chapter "The Wanderings of Manuscripts" in James West-fall Thompson, *The Medieval Library* (Chicago, 1939); Robin Flower, "Lost Manuscripts," *Essays by Divers Hands: Transactions of the Royal Society of Literature*, XVIII (1939), 107–36; and Neil R. Ker, "The Migration of Manuscripts from the English Medieval Libraries," *Library*, 4th series, XXIII (1942), 1–11.

The story of the search for the "Merthyr fragment" of the *Canterbury Tales* is found in J. M. Manly and Edith Rickert, *The Text of the Canterbury Tales* (Chicago, 1940), I, 8, 363–64; and on pp. 606–45 they give a formidable catalogue of the lost manuscripts of the *Tales*. On John Bagford, see the account by W. Y. Fletcher in *Transactions of the Bibliographical Society*, IV (1898), 185–201, and the Introduction to *The Bagford Ballads*, ed. by J. W. Ebsworth (London, 1878).

The most comprehensive catalogue of the lost plays is found in Gertrude M. Sibley, *The Lost Plays and Masques, 1500–1642* (Ithaca, N.Y., 1933). On Warburton and his pie cook, see "The Bakings of Betsy," *Library*, 3rd series, II (1911), 225–59—an important article in which W. W. Greg, on the basis of discrepancies in Warburton's list, seems to uncover evidence of chicanery in the publishing business during the Commonwealth. Another recently found list of plays now lost is described by Joseph Q. Adams in "Hill's List of Early Plays in Manuscript," *Library*, 4th series, XX (1940), 72–99. In connection with my brief mention of the burning of the manuscript first volume of Carlyle's *French Revolution*, it is worth while to note that the somewhat heretical suggestion has been made that Mrs. Taylor may have burned it herself; see W. A. Hirst, "The Manuscript of Carlyle's *French Revolution*," *Nineteenth Century and After*, CXXIII (1938), 93–98.

Material on the state of the public records in the seventeenth century is from David C. Douglas, *English Scholars* (London, 1939), an informative and entertaining book which offers a vivid picture of the conditions under which the pioneer English antiquarians (1660–1730) worked. A sketch of the history of the public records from the earliest times is found in V. H. Galbraith, *An Introduction to the Use of the Public Records* (Oxford, 1934). On the Addison-Dawson letters, see Walter Graham in *Philological Quarterly*, XVI (1937), 97–104; for additional details I am indebted to Mrs. Graham.

The story of the Campbell transcripts of Beddoes's papers is told by H. W. Donner in his Introductions to *The Browning Box* (Oxford, 1935) and *The Works of T. L. Beddoes* (Oxford, 1935). On the Byron memoirs, see Ethel C. Mayne, *Byron* (New York, 1924), pp. 448–52, Howard Mumford Jones, *The Harp That Once*— (New York, 1937), pp. 237–44 and 349, and the correspondence in the London *Times Literary Supplement* touched off by a leading article on Jan. 22, 1938. The anecdotes concerning Thomas Prince's library and George Brinley are from Carl Cannon, *American Book Collectors* (New York, 1941), pp. 9–10, 80: Cannon's volume, a mine of information on the activities of American bibliophiles, has other excellent anecdotes. The story of the dumping of parts of the national archives into the Potomac is found in Mary A. Benjamin, *Autographs* (New York, 1946), pp. 222–23—another good source of anecdotal material. The loss of *Queen Anne's Weekly Journal* was reported by James R. Sutherland in the *Periodical Post Boy*, Mar. 1950.

CHAPTER X: *Shades of Mrs. Grundy*

The material on Burns is taken from J. DeLancey Ferguson, "Some Aspects of the Burns Legend," *Philological Quarterly*, XI (1932), 263–73, and from the Introduction to his edition of Burns's letters (Oxford, 1931). Randall Stewart's introductions to Hawthorne's *American Notebooks* (New Haven and London, 1932) and *English Notebooks* (New York and London, 1941) make detailed analysis of the various categories of Mrs. Hawthorne's expurgations. Stewart's article in the *Huntington Library Quarterly*, VII (1944), 387–95, gives the results of his examination of the so-called "love letters."

CHAPTER XI: *Post-Mortems*

A detailed study of Elizabeth Barrett's experiences with laudanum is found in Jeannette Marks, *The Family of the Barrett* (New York, 1938). On Wordsworth's illnesses, see Edith C. Batho, *The Later Wordsworth* (Cambridge, 1933). The paper by Dr. Wilmer on Milton's blindness was published in the *Bulletin of the Institute of the History of Medicine*, I (1933), 85–106; Miss Brown's study, *Milton's Blindness*, appeared in New York, 1934. On Pepys's ailments see Sir D'Arcy Power, "Why Samuel Pepys Discontinued His Diary" and "The Medical History of Mr. and Mrs. Samuel Pepys," in *Occasional*

Papers of the Samuel Pepys Club, Vol. I (London, 1917), 64–93. Dr. Cameron's article, "The Mystery of Byron's 'Club Foot,'" appeared in *Notes and Queries*, CXLVI (1924), 281–85; and a more recent summary of the case by him was published in the *Listener*, Apr. 28, 1949, pp. 703–4. On Burns, see Franklyn Bliss Snyder's *Life* (New York, 1932), pp. 431–36. The material on Thackeray is from Gordon N. Ray, *Letters and Private Papers of William M. Thackeray* (Cambridge, Mass., 1945–46), I, 518–20 and IV, 453–59. Miss Schneider's important article on "The 'Dream' of *Kubla Khan*" appeared in *Publications of the Modern Language Association*, LX (1945), 784–801.

A full study of Rossetti from the point of view of pharmacology is David I. Macht and Nellie L. Gessford, "The Unfortunate Drug Experiences of Dante Gabriel Rossetti," *Bulletin of the Institute of the History of Medicine*, VI (1938), 34–61. The history of medical opinion on Swift's disease is handily summarized in Maxwell B. Gold, *Swift's Marriage to Stella* (Cambridge, Mass., 1937), pp. 130–31 n., and fully discussed in Mario M. Rossi and Joseph M. Hone, *Swift; or, The Egoist* (London, 1934), Chap. V. On Dr. Johnson's ailments, see Sir Humphry Rolleston, "Samuel Johnson's Medical Experiences," *Annals of the History of Medicine*, new series, I (1929), 540–52. Dr. George M. Gould's *Biographic Clinics* appeared in six volumes (Philadelphia, 1903–1909). The relations between Whitman and Osler are studied in two articles by William White in *American Literature*, XI (1939), 73–77, and the *Bulletin of the Institute of the History of Medicine*, XV (1944), 79–92.

Charles MacLaurin's *Post Mortems of Mere Mortals* (Garden City, N.Y., 1930), which has not been drawn upon for this chapter, is a good collection of diagnostic essays including such literary figures as the Pepyses, Gibbon, Dr. Johnson, and Henry Fielding. MacLaurin was a well known Australian surgeon. Lewis J. Moorman in *Tuberculosis and Genius* (Chicago, 1940) treats of such figures as Stevenson, Keats, Shelley, and Katherine Mansfield.

CHAPTER XII: *On the Trail of Byron*

This entire chapter is based upon a narrative written especially for me by Professor Marchand. The anecdote about the rescue of the Keats relics from the abbey at Monte Cassino is from a communication by Flight-Lieut. S. J. Webb to the London *Times Literary Supplement*, Sept. 30, 1944, p. 480.

CHAPTER XIII: *The Search for Sambir*

Here I am indebted to Dr. John D. Gordan, who generously supplied me with a copy of his unpublished article on his adventures in Borneo. I have supplemented it from his book, *Joseph Conrad: The Making of a Novelist* (Cambridge, Mass., 1940), pp. 15–20, 35–54.

CHAPTER XIV: *Discoveries*

The circumstances surrounding the identification of the *Book of Margery Kempe*, I have taken from the introduction to the first volume of the Early English Text Society's edition (London, 1940), and from information kindly supplied by Miss Allen herself. On the discovery of the unique copy of *Fulgens and Lucres*, see the preface to the edition by F. S. Boas and A. W. Reed (Oxford, 1926).

Bertram Dobell's own account of his identification of Traherne, first printed in his edition of the poems (London, 1903), may also be read in Gladys I. Wade's *Poetical Works of Thomas Traherne* (London, 1932), especially pp. lxxvi–xci. Some additional details are in Miss Wade's biography of Traherne (Princeton, 1944), Chap. I. In the *Colophon*, new graphic series, I (1939), 101–4, Thomas H. Johnson told how he discovered Edward Taylor's poetry. The preface and "Prologue" to Marjorie H. Nicolson's *Conway Letters* (London, 1930) contain some of the most eloquent writing I know on the subject of scholarly detective work. Professor Smalley's edition of Browning's essay on Chatterton was published at Cambridge, Mass., in 1948. On the story of the Brontë juvenilia, the best sources are Madeleine Hope Dodds, "Gondaliand," *Modern Language Review*, XVIII (1923), 9–21, the introduction to *Legends of Angria*, edited by Fannie E. Ratchford and William Clyde DeVane (New Haven, 1933), and the whole of Miss Ratchford's book, *The Brontës' Web of Childhood* (New York, 1941).

INDEX